Teaching
Early Modern
English Prose

Presented to Purchase College
by
Gary Waller, PhD Cambridge

State University of New York
Distinguished Professor

Professor
of Literature & Cultural
Studies, and Theatre &
Performance, 1995-2019
Provost 1995-2004

Modern Language Association of America
Options for Teaching

For a complete listing of titles,
see the last pages of this book.

Teaching
Early Modern
English Prose

Edited by

**Susannah Brietz Monta and
Margaret W. Ferguson**

The Modern Language Association of America

New York   2010

Part III: Teaching Selected Authors

Part IV: Crossings and Pairings

Part V: Resources

Acknowledgments

This book originated in conversations, by e-mail, about our shared interests in and perplexities about teaching early modern prose in various kinds of undergraduate courses. We thank Heather Dubrow for initially suggesting this editorial collaboration. We also thank our editors at the Modern Language Association: Joe Gibaldi—who was immensely intelligent and encouraging over the years of the book's gestation—and James Hatch, Sonia Kane, and Angela Gibson, who have helped us through the book's endgame. We are grateful for the smart and detailed advice we received from members of the MLA Publications Committee and from two anonymous readers.

We thank our contributors for their patience, their willingness to revise their essays, and their many bibliographic and editorial suggestions as drafts of the book appeared on its special Web site. Deborah Harkness deserves special mention for her willingness (and ability) to write an essay on Bacon at a fairly late stage in the book's development. Claire Preston and Stephen M. Fallon also wrote essays, on Browne and Milton respectively, in response to belated requests. We thank colleagues at our home institutions and elsewhere who have made suggestions for improving the book and for sharpening the teaching questions it poses; Margaret Ferguson acknowledges special debts to Frances Dolan for ideas about teaching noncanonical prose and to Jean Carr for ideas about American teachers of prose. Our debts to many other scholars who have written on early modern prose are signaled, though incompletely, in the introduction, in the various essays' notes, and in the suggestions for further reading. At the moment when this collaborative project is on the verge of becoming a printed object, a version of what Rabelais envisioned as "frozen words" (*parolles gelées*), the editors wish to acknowledge that what follows is part of a polylogue that extends far beyond the borders of this book.

We've benefited immensely from our graduate assistants' help both intellectual and material. At Louisiana State University, Jennifer Keegan worked tirelessly on many important tasks before the book's submission, and James Ayers and Greg Molchan assisted with later stages in the book's development. At the University of California, Davis, Genevieve Pearson and Vanessa Rapatz helped us create a list of electronic and print teaching resources, and at the University of Notre Dame, Magdalena Nerio collaborated with Genevieve Pearson and saw the volume through its final stages. We are grateful to Natalie Grand for help with the index and final copyediting queries.

Our children, all six of them (two arrived in the years since this book began), deserve acknowledgment for having given us immense pleasure; they have also contributed significantly to the pace of the book's making, which can best be described with the Erasmian adage *festina lente* (make haste slowly). Our spouses, David Simpson and Anthony Monta, have helped with this book in innumerable ways. Margaret Ferguson is especially grateful for David's astute critique of an early version of the introduction, and we are both grateful to Anthony for creating and maintaining the book's Web site at Louisiana State University.

Finally, we thank each other; though we have met in person only a handful of times, we have learned a great deal—about early modern prose and also about teaching, writing, reading, parenting, and rereading—from the process of shepherding this project from concept (and wish) to what you have in your hands.

**Margaret W. Ferguson and
Susannah Brietz Monta**

Introduction

For Virginia Woolf, the experience of reading a work of early modern English prose led to "drousy languor" (qtd. in Relihan 21). Few readers today,
among them college teachers of literature, have much time, it seems, for
drowsing over a page or even a long sentence of Renaissance prose. While
most English teachers would agree that Renaissance prose makes crucial
contributions to cultural and literary history—to the history of the novel,
for instance, as well as to the histories of scientific, religious, philosophical, political, and literary-critical veins of thought—there is considerably
less agreement about how (or indeed whether) to teach early modern
prose in undergraduate English courses. This book is designed to make a
case for the possibilities, and attendant pleasures, of teaching more Renaissance prose, more often, in postsecondary literature courses.

Renaissance prose is less often taught in the United States undergraduate curriculum than poetry and drama are for a complex mixture of
practical and historical reasons. Some of the latter have to do with the development of English as an academic discipline in North American colleges
during a century—the nineteenth—when neither United States nor Cana-
dian scholars could subscribe wholeheartedly to the distinctly nationalist,
or more precisely imperialist, rationales for the value of Renaissance prose

articulated by those English Romantic writers who, according to Neil Rhodes, first constructed sixteenth- and seventeenth-century prose "as a distinct entity and granted [it] a literary status comparable with the achievements of Renaissance poetry and drama" (1).[1] William Hazlitt found such writers as Francis Bacon, Thomas Browne, and Jeremy Taylor to be the exemplars of "the genius of Great Britain" (qtd. in Rhodes 3); such writers, who had been enthusiastically embraced by Samuel Taylor Coleridge as "the great patterns or integers of English style," had "something in them," Hazlitt proclaimed, "that savoured of the soil from which they grew: they were not French, they were not Dutch, or German, or Greek, or Latin; they were truly English. . . . The mind of their country was great in them, and it prevailed" (qtd. in Rhodes 2). But the British Empire had not prevailed in its former colony of the United States of America, and the history of the reception of Renaissance prose, in both educational and publishing spheres, is marked by an emergent American nationalism that tends (then and now) to scorn, as decadent and time wasting, certain highly elaborate modes of discourse. Although classic writers of the American Renaissance such as Herman Melville and Nathaniel Hawthorne were significantly influenced by the ornate styles and "curious" subject matters of writers such as Thomas Browne and Robert Burton, Noah Webster offers a more typically American view of Browne as "pedantic" and unfit to be included in dictionaries aiming (as Webster's own did) to "give the world a standard of the English Language" (qtd. in Rhodes 5).[2]

If an American critic named Fitz-James O'Brien could suggest, in an 1853 article for *Putnam's Monthly Magazine*, that Melville could "make a notch on the American Pine" if only he would "avoid Sir Thomas Browne" and his "gorgeous and metaphorical manner" while "diet[ing] himself for a year or two on Addison," we should not be surprised to find the broad and heterogeneous field of Renaissance prose represented not by Browne but by Francis Bacon, the exemplar of a "plain" style, in one of the first undergraduate literature courses to be taught after the subject of "English" achieved departmental status at Harvard College in 1872 (qtd. in Rhodes 6). In 1876, the Harvard philologist Francis James Child introduced a college course on Shakespeare's plays and "a literature course emphasizing Chaucer, Bacon, Milton, and Dryden" (McMurtry qtd. in Graff 66). For college teachers in the second half of the nineteenth century who were attempting to counter widespread views that English literature was somehow an effeminate subject mainly pursued by "the desultory reader in his leisure hours . . . an accomplishment only," a "soft snap" in contrast to "hard" subjects like Greek or philosophy, it made sense to promote a pedagogical canon in which recognizably great poets from the past reigned along with a prose writer whose very name conjured up the rigors and benefits of science. Bacon might be useful in the struggle to establish modern language and literature study as an enterprise requiring specialized knowledge from teachers and providing real benefits to American students.[3] Thus seeking distance from unprofessional "men of letters" and from the notion that "any body can teach English" (or German or French), H. C. G. Brandt argued at the first meeting of the MLA, in 1883, that "a scientific basis dignifies our profession" (Graff 68).

At the same time, English departments needed to be able to develop a special territory as their own, one that was not just an addendum to or ornament of scientific discourse. Poetry and drama (especially the Shakespearean drama) proved more valuable than prose did as a subject matter for college English teachers who were trying to legitimate their new discipline by showing that it had a distinctive kind of knowledge to impart. Poetry (and for the so-called New Critics in both England and North America, that meant mainly lyric poetry) could be taught as an autonomous, rewarding, and manageable object of a specifically literary kind of attention, whereas prose, especially the kinds valued by English Romantics like Coleridge and Hazlitt, was enormously promiscuous in its "hydropdique immoderate desire" for knowledge, as John Donne described his own thirst for learning in a letter of 1608 (qtd. in Harvey 72). Not only did many famous prose texts belong to other academic disciplines—Thomas Hobbes's *Leviathan* and Richard Hooker's *Of the Lawes of Ecclesiastical Polity* to the history of political theory, for instance—but even those works whose metaphorical "gorgeousness" might be thought to make them distinctively literary tended to confound the boundaries between literature and other disciplines as these were being defined and defended in the years before and after World War II.

In truth, then, early modern prose—even the prose of canonical authors like John Milton and John Donne—was never a canonical object of study in the American undergraduate curriculum. Our book argues, however, that at the present time, when canonicity is under scrutiny for all sorts of reasons, and also when many college teachers of English are both affected by and skeptical of the economically driven institutional division of labor that tends to separate "literature" instruction (in our period, usually conceived as instruction on drama and poetry) from "composition" (which in fact we all teach with every writing assignment), it is appropriate to reconsider the pedagogical uses of prose for the teaching of critical reading and writing. The essays collected here suggest that study of Renaissance prose can initiate serious discussions about prose styles in the classroom. Because Renaissance prose is often quite self-conscious both about its literary ambitions and about its rhetoric, style, audience, voice, and genre, it allows us to raise questions about modern divisions between the teaching of "literature" and the teaching of "composition." There may, indeed, be a connection worth exploring between taking prose as an object of study in the literature classroom and fulfilling our mission to teach writing whether or not we are in an institution that formally separates composition and rhetoric instruction from the literature curriculum.

Although Renaissance prose may not strike most teachers as a viable source for models for imitation by modern students, teaching short passages by writers such as Mary Wroth or Francis Bacon or Thomas Nashe can help students acquire a metalanguage for describing and revising their own practices in syntax, diction, and even punctuation. In his valuable study *The Evolution of English Prose, 1700–1800,* Carey McIntosh offers a succinct and engaging discussion of how the punctuation marks we call the comma, the colon, and the period derived from the Greek names for metrical units of different lengths in sentence types that came to be known (amusingly, for some modern students) as "loose" or "periodic" (McIntosh 79; Clark 254).

A rough estimate of material included in the English Short-Title Catalogue indicates that at least eighty percent of works printed in English between 1500 and 1700 were works of prose.[4] Yet in many modern English courses representing Renaissance culture, poetry predominates. Syllabi for such courses not only show the ideological imprint of some of the historical processes sketched above but also implicitly accept a hierarchy of cultural value articulated by some canonical Renaissance writers themselves. If Philip Sidney regarded epic or "heroicall" poetry as "the best and most accomplished kind" (49) and Milton, eager to write his own epic, deprecated his political prose as work of his "left hand" (808), why should we try to include prose by Sidney or Milton in courses already rushed in their efforts to survey the riches of early modern literature? And if Nashe wrote his *Unfortunate Traveller* in what modern critics agree is a "low" rhetorical style, why try to include other of his works, most with less engaging plots than the *Unfortunate Traveller*'s, in one's Renaissance literature course? The contributors to this volume do not claim that teaching prose texts is either easy or necessarily more valuable than teaching poetic texts, but we do attempt to answer the questions posed above, and we do suggest that teaching the Renaissance to undergraduates without some sustained attention to prose—including the prose "in" works usually classified as poetry or drama—gives an impoverished picture of the past and arguably of our present culture as well.

But there are signs of change, and our book reflects and responds to them. Since the 1970s, critical movements such as feminism, postmodernism, new historicism, and cultural studies have interrogated the boundaries between disciplines and types of discourse in ways that encourage new pedagogical approaches to prose produced in an era when divisions in secular and religious knowledge were at once multiplying and becoming objects of reflection and dispute. Moreover, recent critical developments have had material effects that make it easier to teach early modern prose today than it was even a decade ago. The most recent editions of the Norton and Longman anthologies of English literature, for instance, include many more selections from prose writings by women than earlier editions did; the Norton has a section entitled "Women in Power" containing prose letters by Mary, Queen of Scots, and Lady Jane Grey as well as a significantly expanded selection of Queen Elizabeth I's speeches. The big anthologies often draw on editing labors done for new paperback editions of specific prose writers such as Arbella Stuart and Anne Askew—figures heretofore studied, if at all, mainly in specialist journals and in graduate courses.

Feminist critics interested in recovering little-known women writers from the past often share, with new historicists and others influenced by postmodernist theory, a desire to challenge distinctions between "high" and "low" cultural productions as well as the distinction between (literary) text and (historical) context. Here too, major anthologies of English literature are reflecting critical and scholarly initiatives in ways that enrich the field of prose available for teaching. The Longman anthology has a new section called "Tracts on Women and Gender," for instance, that includes materials from popular pamphlets as well as from the pens of humanists such as Desiderius Erasmus. Interrogating the text-context distinction, the most recent edition of the *Norton Anthology of English Literature* has a new section entitled "Faith in Conflict" containing selections from different English translations of the Bible, from William Tyndale's *Obedience of a Christian Man*, and from Askew's *First Examination*, among other sixteenth-century prose works. This section clearly points to (and allows further exploration of) an emergent field of early modern English cultural studies that has many affinities with the old (interdisciplinary) field of rhetoric. Early modern religious debate is seldom separate from political debate and often includes opinions on topics that continue to be contested in our own society: marriage, for example; divorce; censorship; the ability of women to rule; what constitutes a "truthful" kind of language and when certain kinds of lies are permissible. Protestant writers scorned Catholics as "equivocators" while using various types of equivocation; moreover, as Debora Shuger observes in her fascinating study of "sacred rhetoric," "Puritans accused High Churchmen of using rhetoric, a charge which the latter denied; after the Civil War, Anglicans directed the same accusation against Dissenters, a charge again rejected" (3). Divisions within Protestant culture as well as between Protestants and Catholics were thus frequently explored in prose claiming not to be tainted by rhetoric: this is a rhetorical and ideological position that dramatically anticipates the antirhetorical stance limned by many nineteenth- and twentieth-century Americans, epitomized (as we have seen) in Webster's attacks on Browne and brilliantly questioned by Richard Lanham in his book about the teaching of college writing, *Style: An Anti-textbook*.[5]

Recent criticism has enriched the prose available through anthologies and paperback editions while also calling attention to prose texts that once would have been considered "un" or even "sub" literary; as Naomi Conn Liebler observes in her introduction to a new collection of essays on early modern prose fiction, the growing book trade in sixteenth-century London saw an "increased production of such genres as romance, travel narrative, trickster and cony catching tales" (5). Cony-catching tales, usually produced as cheap pamphlets ostensibly aimed at exposing the nefarious tricks of rogues, were part of a new genre of urban writing that, like travel tales, crossed and recrossed the boundaries between fiction, nonfiction, and advertising. Despite increased critical attention to the diverse and often hybrid genres of early modern prose, however, there have been relatively few attempts to translate new—or indeed older—critical approaches to early modern prose for the undergraduate college classroom.[6] Translation, as a "carrying across" that inevitably transforms that which it transports, is a fitting name for one of our book's major aims. Designed for the Modern Language Association's Options for Teaching series, the present collection seeks to translate ideas—and debates—about the medium of Renaissance prose and its many genres into forms usable in a variety of undergraduate courses serving students from different backgrounds, at different stages of their education, who nonetheless have in common the task of increasing their mastery of written English. By considering how one might teach a number of different prose writers and genres, some long known to literary scholars, some recently recovered, but all, it's fair to say, unfamiliar to most American undergraduates, our volume attempts to make current remappings of the early modern literary landscape pedagogically legible.

The book does so in part by drawing on our contributors' experiences of teaching early modern prose in a wide range of courses. These include the first half of the traditional survey of British literature; survey courses on English Renaissance literature (designed for both English majors and nonmajors); courses on early modern women's writing and on canonical authors such as Milton and Edmund Spenser; courses on English Reformation literature, on early modern religion and literature, and on early modern English Catholicism and literature; courses on Shakespeare, among them courses focusing on Shakespeare and gender and on Shakespeare and religion; courses on seventeenth-century literature, early modern autobiography, early modern cultural studies, and on poetry, style, and poetics. Our contributors have also taught early modern prose in introductory composition courses, writing-intensive literature courses, and courses offered under the rubric of writing across the curriculum. Versions of many of these courses have been taught at the graduate level, with assignments including instruction in how to read texts downloaded from electronic databases such as *EEBO* (*Early English Books Online*). Such assignments, stressing the history of the book and pamphlet as material objects, have been successfully attempted in some of our contributors' undergraduate courses.

Given this range of courses, the essays collected here explore ways in which teachers might present early modern prose writings in relation to more familiar dramatic and poetic texts without relegating prose to the status of contextual or background reading. Some of our contributors offer new perspectives on how one might teach prose both within and alongside texts usually classified as poetry or drama. Conversely, some contributors consider the work that imaginative genres and a fundamentally rhetorical poetics do when refracted through prose works written during the Renaissance—a time when, as Constance Relihan has remarked, prose was often "artistically marginalized"—considered frivolous or "common"—even as print technology was making it ubiquitous (17).[7] The volume as a whole aims to make prose more visible for undergraduate teachers, thus countering the widespread critical perception of early modern prose as a peculiarly transparent medium that does not require decoding. In a collection designed mainly for undergraduates in the United Kingdom, Roger Pooley writes that "from the perspective of our own time, the history of prose could be written as a history of deliberate hiddenness" (1). Making a similar point, Elizabeth Fowler and Roland Greene argue in *The Project of Prose* that while early modern poetry has the cultural status of a "visible" object, prose from the same period is deemed "invisible . . . coterminous with its contents . . . a disposable vehicle" (3). Note that these critics do not attribute an "intrinsic" hiddenness to prose, as Wlad Godzich and Jeffrey Kittay seem to do in their provocative study of "the" emergence of prose (in thirteenth-century France) as a written "signifying practice" yoked to an emergent political state and constitutively marked by a "game of self-concealment" (209). While in some historical moments prose may be characterized by self-concealment or what some English Protestant writers and modern businesspersons value as plainness or clarity, much prose, in contrast, calls conspicuous attention to itself (think of Browne and Burton, not to mention Joyce and Nabokov). Our essays call attention not only to the range of early modern prose writing but also to the variety of competing definitions of prose from intellectuals discussing (and using) the medium both in the Renaissance and today.

In a project that in some ways resembles translation, our contributors attempt to build bridges between different critical traditions of prose study while they also attempt to negotiate the gap that always exists between what one does in one's own classroom and what one says—in more general terms—to one's fellow teachers, among them readers who do not necessarily share the writer's knowledge base. Translation work of this kind requires greater attention to defining terms and explaining allusions than one tends to find in critical works on prose, whether these belong to the older line of criticism focused on issues of "prose style" or to the newer line of historicizing commentary that focuses on the "ideological charge" carried by different prose forms, including ones that lack classical models and that confound modern disciplinary boundaries.

It is perhaps no accident that the older school of scholarly criticism on English prose began in essays by Morris Croll based on graduate seminars that he taught at Princeton in the 1920s.[8] Hardly a familiar name even among specialists in Renaissance literature, Croll is the father (as it were) of a tradition of debates about Renaissance English prose style that often categorizes different texts by means of adjectives that require specialized knowledge of classical literature (Ciceronian, anti-Ciceronian, Attic) or of linguistics. The one critic in this tradition whose claims would be readily understood by most modern American undergraduates is R. F. Jones, who locates the modernity of English prose in the advent of a (Baconian) "scientific" style in the seventeenth century.

Chiefly concerned to establish the beginnings of a modern English prose style, the critics who participate in the scholarly debates about prose style have much to teach anyone interested in the history of the English language and its enormous efflorescence, in the Renaissance, through imitation of classical and Continental texts. Work in this critical tradition, which continues in such recent collections as *Style: Essays on Renaissance and Restoration Literature and Culture in Memory of Harriett Hawkins* (Michie and Buckley), may be used by college teachers both to enrich the ways in which students analyze individual sentences and to prompt reflection on the general cultural significance of an ongoing debate about what English is and isn't in relation to other languages and to various notions of racial, ethnic, religious, and linguistic identity. A North American college teacher might well introduce undergraduates to the long history of debates about English prose styles by noting continuities between sixteenth-century and modern debates about "proper" English: in both periods, one can find versions of an antijargon position passionately held in contrast to versions of a position that advocates borrowing terms from foreign sources to enrich the native tongue (for examples of early modern invectives against neologisms—what Thomas Wilson calls "straunge ynkehorne terms" or "outlandishe Englishe"—imported from Latin and other languages, see Blank 40–41).

Other recent scholarship has turned away from the study of style in an effort to bring the study of prose into closer dialogue with recent theoretical and methodological innovations. Introducing their wide-ranging collection of essays about Renaissance prose, Fowler and Greene call for a new approach to prose as a site of exciting intellectual and cultural exchange that helped shape modern concepts both of prose genres and of prose as a medium (5). Arguing that early modern prose has not been "accounted for by theories of genre, and perhaps cannot be," Fowler and Greene ask us to look again—or anew—at the large body of prose texts "not easily described by the analytical tools appropriate to poetry, drama, or the novel." How, they ask, do new prose forms arise and mingle in the early modern era, across national borders and across the Atlantic as well, "to invent and effect the aspirations of newly restless social groups such as middle-class business men, educated women, colonists, and *mestizos*"? (7).

Our volume is greatly indebted to Fowler and Greene's effort to take the study of Renaissance prose beyond the domain of what usually counts as literature. And yet our contributors are less willing to bid farewell to the old traditions of stylistic inquiry than Fowler and Greene seem to be. Fowler and Greene dismiss the older debates focused on "prose style" in one paragraph, contending that "such a use of 'style' effectively turns 'prose' into an adjective and attenuates many of the relevant aesthetic and cultural issues" (2). Agreeing that such issues deserve sustained attention, we suggest that an interest in style need not be incompatible with an expanded understanding of the terrain of early modern prose, especially if questions about the English language, in all its historical and modern hybridity, serve as a bridge between studies of prose style and studies of the ideologies carried by many prose forms. The work of such critics as Colin MacCabe and Paula Blank illustrates the value of yoking style and ideology as objects of study: in *The Eloquence of the Vulgar*, MacCabe discusses William Caxton's quest for an English style that is similar to Dante's paradoxical ideal of an illustrious vernacular—a language not spoken by the common people; and in *Broken English*, Blank analyzes the social significance of competing conceptions of English and of the changing meanings of the word *dialect* (MacCabe 67; Blank 7). The phrase *prose style* need not, in any case, signal that the first term is conceptually or grammatically subordinate to the second; as the *Oxford English Dictionary* notes, *prose style* may be read as a compound noun phrase ("Prose" [substantive noun]). And if one does choose to use or construe *prose* as an adjective, one is participating in a long and often complex tradition of description and inquiry: the word *prose* has been used not only as a noun but also as an adjective—and as a verb meaning "to translate or turn into prose"—since the late middle ages, ever since the term entered English from Latin ("Prose" [verb]). The English word *prose* indeed carries many complexities attached to the history and figurative range of the Latin *prosa*, a noun derived from the adjective *prorsus*, meaning "straightforward, . . . direct" ("Prose" [substantive noun]). But the term in either its English or Latin forms, as Godzich and Kittay remind us, is far from straightforward and direct. On the contrary, the history of the word itself deconstructs the common assumption that *prose* can be defined as that which is not poetry. Fowler and Greene question that binary opposition too; they do so, we suggest, in ways that can be supplemented rather than countered by a concern with issues of style.

Our contributors seek a middle way between the approaches of those who, like Croll, attend primarily to questions of style and language and those who, like Fowler and Greene, fear the limitations such approaches may impose on the study of prose. The study of the formal and linguistic properties of prose can open up wider forms of cultural analysis. Richard Strier proposes the phrase *indexical formalism* to describe the premise that "formal features of a text, matters of style, can be indices to large intellectual and cultural matters" (211). Illustrating the relevance of Strier's concept for the study of prose, our essays both retain the analysis of prose style and engage broader questions of cultural study. Versions of indexical formalism, which are illustrated in many essays in the current volume, may help students think in new ways about the cultural meanings of their own stylistic choices.

Fowler and Greene point to some of the paradoxes informing many calls for new approaches to prose, including the present one, when they compare the allegedly "untheorized" field of prose to a huge and unexplored continent, Antarctica; they suggest that the essays in their volume will not be bound by adherence to previous critics' ideas of what would be "indispensable to a survey of the period's canonical prose." The geographic analogy is striking and creatively polemical but also (arguably) misleading; many early modern writers themselves offered theoretical reflections on prose, often under the rubric of "rhetoric" and sometimes as part of debates about "reforming" a mother tongue deemed faulty by bi- or trilingual intellectuals. Moreover, the series these editors offer to illustrate an idea of canonicity has an almost Borghesian flavor: "Castiglione, Elyot, Machiavelli, Euphuism, prose drama, the character, the penséc, Padre Vierira, the captivity narrative, and so on" (1). As this list unfolds, it seems ironically to support the argument made here that Renaissance prose never was a "canonical" subject in American college English departments or even in graduate departments of comparative literature.[9] We suggest that whether an undergraduate class is devoted to Richard Hooker's *Laws* or Richard Hakluyt's *Voyages* or Mary Wroth's *Urania* or John Milton's *Areopagitica*—or even to a few passages from such works—most students will be encountering material that is new to them, written in a language whose diction, syntax, and practices of allusion may be difficult and strange. And yet the essays in this volume posit that individual teachers can do much to help students engage with the prose they encounter from a distant culture. If our arguments prove even partially true for the readers of our book, the territory of early modern prose might be likened not only to Antarctica but also to Edgar Allan Poe's purloined letter: it is something that is at once missing and right before our eyes, but not to be found without labor. Brought into pedagogical view, early modern prose writing won't become a territory any of us can confidently own, but it may show us a great deal about what earlier writers did— and hence about what we and our students might also do—with the large and always changing resources of the language that is and isn't our own.

Since our book seeks to encourage college and university faculty members to teach a selection of prose genres and styles much broader than most of us explored in our own survey courses in college and graduate school, these essays range widely over sixteenth- and seventeenth-century prose. The renewed study of early modern prose has challenged the usual periodizations that divided sixteenth- from seventeenth-century courses and pre-1660 materials from those produced after the Stuart Restoration; thus we include essays on late-seventeenth-century figures (Aphra Behn, John Bunyan, Mary Astell) alongside considerations of sixteenth-century writers. Our contributors highlight editions and textbooks useful for particular authors, genres, and emphases; we have also included at the end of our book a section entitled "Selected Resources for Teachers," which lists multiauthor print editions of early modern prose and a selection of helpful electronic resources.

Our essays address both practical concerns in the teaching of prose writing (what approaches help undergraduates engage with early modern prose writing?) and theoretical ones (in what ways may prose writing enhance courses stressing multicultural and/or feminist perspectives? what sorts of reading practices do particular prose genres demand of students?). These essays are not, however, how-to manuals; our contributors do not presume to know what teaching methods will work in every situation, with every group of students. Instead, our contributors make strategic suggestions as starting points that may be adapted for particular courses, students, and pedagogies.

Aiming not at full coverage (a chimera) but rather at provocative and useful forays into our topic, we have organized our essays into four sections. Connections may, of course, be made across these inevitably rather arbitrary boundaries. The first section, "Perspectives on Prose," contains essays on broad issues pertaining to the study of early modern prose. One essay engages with and updates scholarship on style—the subject, as noted above, of much work on early modern prose through most of the twentieth century. Others discuss the prevalence of rhetoric and rhetorical training in prose writings ranging from the most formal literary works to popular broadsheets and address the slippery problem of defining non-fiction prose in the period.

The second section, entitled "Kinds of Prose" (with a nod to Rosalie Colie), features essays on particular bodies of prose work united by genre, formal features, discursive similarities, or particular purposes. These essays consider relatively familiar prose genres, such as the sermon and the essay, as well as lesser-known bodies of prose work that have nevertheless proved central to much recent scholarship, such as writings on marriage and familiar letters. Essays in this section focus on how prose writings are shaped by, and shape, different types of discourse that entail different kinds of implicit contracts between writer and reader. Our contributors' attention to questions of genre and "family" of discourse provides a way for teachers to help students who are relatively unprepared for the reading of unfamiliar prose forms and to counter modern students' tendency to see prose texts as simply instrumental communication (or, alternatively, as frustrating stretches of words on a page). Essays included here are necessarily selective in the particular examples that they discuss, but this selectivity is balanced by their works-cited lists and, in some cases, by lists of additional bibliographic resources that represent the genre or discourse under discussion. These essays provide information and debating points for teachers focusing on entire or provocative parts of prose works.

Our third section, "Teaching Selected Authors," aims to help teachers easily refer to sustained discussions of major figures and their works. There are fresh discussions of familiar authors here (John Donne, John Milton, Philip Sidney, John Bunyan) as well as of some writers who, though well known in literary-critical circles, are relatively unknown to most undergraduate students (Mary Wroth, Queen Elizabeth I, Richard Hooker, Thomas Hobbes, Thomas Nashe, Francis Bacon, Thomas Browne).

In our fourth section, entitled "Crossings and Pairings," contributors consider how the study of prose may be pursued across boundaries between different languages, authors, and genres of discourse. One essay takes a feminist approach to the study of educational tracts; another considers the translation of euphuism, that most precious of prose styles, to surprising venues; and another examines the challenges of teaching a prose-fiction writer alongside a more famous dramatic contemporary. Our volume closes with two meditations on translation itself: an essay on translation and early nationalist and colonialist discourses, and another on biblical translation. To end with these considerations of translation seems fitting for a book that seeks above all to make the worlds of scholarship and pedagogy speak to each other, richly and reciprocally, in prose.

Notes

1. Rhodes remarks that there is "no general account of the critical reception of the subject" of Renaissance prose, but his own excellent introduction helps remedy this defect.

2. Webster is specifically regretting Browne's presence in Johnson's *Dictionary:* "the style of Sir Thomas is not English; and it is astonishing that a man attempting to give the world a standard of the English Language should have ever have mentioned his name, but with a reprobation of his style and use of words" (qtd. in Rhodes 5).

3. As Kathryn T. Flannery observes, the establishment of the Royal Society in England soon after the restoration of the monarchy was a major factor in creating Bacon "as the father of a secular English science" (134) and the model of a "Manly, Elegant, Pertinent" style of discourse (Tenison 62, qtd. in Vickers 233–34; qtd. also in Flannery 134). See also Thomas Sprat on the virtue of "plainnesse" (qtd. in Carey's useful survey of Renaissance prose 405). Nineteenth-century American textbooks aimed at postsecondary students, including those preparing for college entrance exams, provide further evidence of a pedagogical taste for a "plain" prose style. As Jean Carr has pointed out to us, a series called English Prose Classics that was republished in America in the 1870s includes a volume of Bacon's essays annotated, according to the author of the introduction, "with a view . . . to make . . . [prose classics such as Bacon's essays] useful in schools for philological purposes, for acquiring a better knowledge and command of English literature" (Boyd 5).

4. Our estimate is based on samplings of the two catalogs edited by Pollard and Redgrave (for books printed from 1475 to 1640) and by Wing (for books printed from 1641 to 1700). We excluded material that would push that estimate considerably higher, including, for instance, printings of the Bible in English (not considered entirely prose, of course), the Book of Common Prayer, popular catechisms, and official government proclamations.

5. Lanham's "anti-textbook" argues against the American tendency to fetishize a clear, or plain, style. For a critique of this book and more recent work by Lanham, see Flannery 189–96.

6. Notable exceptions to this generalization include the collection of essays by Rhodes; several essays in the MLA volume *Teaching Tudor and Stuart Women* (Woods and Hannay); and *English Prose of the Seventeenth Century, 1590–1700,* edited by Pooley.

7. It is worth noting in this connection that there is no index entry for *prose* in the new *Cambridge Companion to Shakespeare*; although Margreta de Grazia's study "Shakespeare and the Craft of Language" in that volume includes fascinating discussions of diction and syntax, none of her examples is from a prose passage. Teachers often rely on the old generalization that Shakespeare's noble characters speak in blank verse, while his lower-class (or mad) characters tend to use prose or doggerel rhymes. For a cogent critique of this generalization, see Burris.

8. See also Rhodes's discussion of Croll (8); the Croll "line" of scholarly debate is nicely summarized and capped by Fish, one of the few critics in this tradition concerned with undergraduate as well as graduate teaching, in *Self-Consuming Artifacts*, a book much less familiar to the general academic community than Fish's work on Milton's poetry is. For a detailed discussion of and bibliography for the Croll line of criticism, see Mueller, ch. 1.

9. On the term *canonical* as a replacement for the older term *classic*, and for a cogent critique of the common analogy between the "closed" biblical canon and the "process by which literary texts come to be preserved, reproduced, and taught in the schools," see Guillory 6.

Works Cited

Blank, Paula. *Broken English: Dialects and the Politics of Language in Renaissance Writing*. London: Routledge, 1996. Print.

Boyd, James Robert. Introductory. *Lord Bacon's Essays*. By Francis Bacon. New York: Barnes, 1872. 5–15. Print.

Burris, Quincy Guy. " 'Soft! Here Follows Prose'—*Twelfth Night* II. v. 154." *Shakespeare Quarterly* 2.3 (1951): 233–39. Print.

Carey, John. *English Poetry and Prose, 1540–1674*. Ed. Christopher Ricks. London: Sphere, 1970. Print.

Clark, Sandra. *The Elizabethan Pamphleteers: Popular Moralistic Pamphets, 1580–1640*. Rutherford: Fairleigh Dickinson UP, 1983. Print.

Colie, Rosalie. *The Resources of Kind; Genre-Theory in the Renaissance*. Ed. Barbara K. Lewalski. Berkeley: U of California P, 1973. Print.

Croll, Morris. *Style, Rhetoric, and Rhythm: Essays by Morris W. Croll*. Ed. J. Max Patrick and Robert O. Evans. Princeton: Princeton UP, 1966. Print.

De Grazia, Margreta. "Shakespeare and the Craft of Language." *The Cambridge Companion to Shakespeare*. Ed. De Grazia and Stanley Wells. Cambridge: Cambridge UP, 2001. 49–64. Print.

Fish, Stanley. *Self-Consuming Artifacts*. Berkeley: U of California P, 1972. Print.

Flannery, Kathryn T. *The Emperor's New Clothes: Literature, Literacy, and the Ideology of Style*. Pittsburgh: U of Pittsburgh P, 1995. Print.

Fowler, Elizabeth, and Roland Greene. Introduction. *The Project of Prose in Early Modern Europe and the New World*. Ed. Fowler and Greene. Cambridge: Cambridge UP, 1997. 1–14. Print.

Godzich, Wlad, and Jeffrey Kittay. *The Emergence of Prose: An Essay in Prosaics*. Minneapolis: U of Minnesota P, 1987. Print.

Graff, Gerald. *Professing Literature: An Institutional History*. Chicago: U of Chicago P, 1987. Print.

Guillory, John. *Cultural Capital: The Problem of Literary Canon Formation*. Chicago: U of Chicago P, 1993. Print.

Harvey, Elizabeth D. "'Mutuall Elements': Irigaray's Donne." *Luce Irigaray and Premodern Culture: Thresholds of History*. Ed. Harvey and T. Krier. London: Routledge, 2004. 66–87. Print.

Lanham, Richard. *Style: An Anti-textbook*. New Haven: Yale UP, 1974. Print.

Liebler, Naomi Conn. Introduction. *Early Modern Prose Fiction: The Cultural Politics of Reading*. Ed. Liebler. New York: Routledge, 2007. 1–17. Print.

MacCabe, Colin. *The Eloquence of the Vulgar: Language, Cinema and the Politics of Culture*. London: British Film Inst., 1999. Print.

McIntosh, Carey. *The Evolution of English Prose 1700–1800: Style, Politeness, and Print Culture*. Cambridge. Cambridge UP, 1998. Print.

Michie, Allen, and Eric Buckley, eds. *Style: Essays on Renaissance and Restoration Literature and Culture in Memory of Harriett Hawkins*. Wilmington: U of Delaware P, 2005. Print.

Milton, John. *The Reason of Church Government Urg'd against Prelaty*. 1641. *The Complete Prose Works of John Milton*. Ed. Don M. Wolfe. Vol. 1. New Haven: Yale UP, 1953. 745–866. Print.

Mueller, Janel. *The Native Tongue and the Word: Developments in English Prose Style, 1380–1580*. Chicago: U of Chicago P, 1984. Print.

Pooley, Roger, ed. *English Prose of the Seventeenth Century, 1590–1700*. London: Longman, 1993. Print.

"Prose." Substantive noun. Def. 6. *Oxford English Dictionary*. 2nd ed. 1989. Print.

"Prose." Verb. *Oxford English Dictionary*. 2nd ed. 1989. Print.

Relihan, Constance. *Fashioning Authority: The Development of Elizabethan Novelistic Discourse*. Kent: Kent State UP, 1994. Print.

Rhodes, Neil. Introduction. *English Renaissance Prose: History, Language, and Politics*. Tempe: Medieval and Renaissance Texts and Studies, 1997. 1–18. Print.

Shuger, Debora. *Sacred Rhetoric*. Princeton: Princeton UP, 1988. Print.

Sidney, Philip. *An Apology for Poetry*. Ed. Forrest G. Robinson. Indianapolis: Bobbs, 1970. Print.

Sprat, Thomas. *History of the Royal Society*. London, 1667. Print.

Strier, Richard. "How Formalism Became a Dirty Word, and Why We Can't Do Without It." *Renaissance Literature and Its Formal Engagements*. Ed. Mark David Rasmussen. New York: Palgrave, 2002. 207–15. Print.

Tenison, Thomas, ed. *Baconiana; or, Certaine Genuine Remains of Sir Frances Bacon*. London, 1679. Print.

Vickers, Brian. *Francis Bacon and Renaissance Prose*. Cambridge: Cambridge UP, 1968. Print.

Wilson, Thomas. *The Arte of Rhetorique*. 1553. Ed. Thomas J. Derrick. New York: Garland, 1982. Print.

Woods, Susanne, and Margaret Hannay, eds. *Teaching Tudor and Stuart Women Writers*. New York: MLA, 2000. Print.

Part I

Perspectives
on Prose

Ronald Corthell

What Is Early Modern
Nonfictional Prose?

In an introductory section of his influential essay "The Logical Status of Fictional Discourse," John Searle briskly attempts to dispose of any possible confounding of literature and fiction; literature cannot be limited to works of fiction, nor are all works of fiction necessarily literary. Sounding like Terry Eagleton a few years later in *An Introduction to Literary Theory*, he goes on to insist that "there is no trait or set of traits which all works of literature have in common"; "that 'literature' is the name of a set of attitudes we take toward a stretch of discourse, not a name of an internal property of the stretch of discourse"; and that "the literary is contiguous with the nonliterary" (320).[1] While theorists as diverse as Searle and Eagleton can agree on this broader understanding of literature, the linkage between literariness and fictionality endures. For example, a recent National Endowment for the Arts (NEA) report on declining consumption of literature by American readers defined literature as fiction, poetry, and drama.[2] This essay on early modern prose nonfiction ruminates on problems of definition raised by Searle's essay: the persistence of definitions of literature as fiction, the contiguity of the literary and the nonliterary, the binary opposition of fiction and nonfiction. In teaching early modern prose, one is inevitably faced with what we think of as postmodern quandaries: What, or when, is nonfictional prose literature? Is Walter Raleigh's *Discovery of Guiana* properly thought of as fiction or nonfiction? How should we understand the facticity of texts like *Hydriotaphia* or *The Anatomy of Melancholy*? Who is the author of *The Examinations of Anne Askew*? As Elizabeth Fowler and Roland Greene note in *The Project of Prose in Early Modern Europe and the New World,* early modern prose is distinguished by a "mobility" and "pressure for . . . experimentation" that generate new critical questions about new kinds of texts (Introduction 6–7). The study and teaching of early modern prose nonfiction is, at its best, an interrogative activity that explores relations among literacies, literariness, representation, gender, class, and canonicity.

Prose nonfiction presents special challenges to definition. The phrase is very nearly a double negative. Nonfiction is the other to fiction, while prose has occupied a similar position relative to verse, an "achievement of the left hand," or, as Wlad Godzich and Jeffrey Kittay put it, "everything else" (xi).[3] Teaching nonfiction prose (or verse, for that matter) runs up against the history of our discipline, for by the turn of the twentieth century literature had come to be identified as fictional discourse (Guillory 35). Indeed, the question of the relation between fictionality and literature has been debated for centuries. Philip Sidney equivocates on the issue of prose and poetry, literary and nonliterary discourse in *The Defence of Poesy*. Early in the text he blurs the line between fiction, poetry, and history: "even historiographers, although their lips sound of things done and verity be written in their foreheads, have been glad to borrow both fashion and perchance weight of the poets" in "their passionate describing of passions, the many particularities of battles which no man could affirm, or . . . long orations put in the mouths of great kings and captains, which it is certain they never pronounced" (5–6). Similarly, on the question of prose, Sidney notes that

> indeed the greatest part of poets have appareled their poetical inventions in that numbrous kind of writing which is called verse—indeed but appareled, verse being but an ornament and no cause to poetry, since there have been many most excellent poets that never versified. (12)

George Puttenham is less nuanced in his definition of poetry, all but equating it with verse (62–63).[4] It is also worth noting that Puttenham agrees with Godzich and Kittay in regarding verse as more ancient than prose: "The profession and use of poetry is most ancient from the beginning—and not, as many erroneously suppose, after but before any civil society was among men" (Puttenham 60).

Thus a constant in writing about and anthologizing nonfictional prose has been what might be called a rhetorical "defence of proesy." In the introduction to his 1967 anthology of seventeenth-century prose, David Novarr denies that "any cultivated seventeenth-century author" such as Milton would have recognized even the most fundamental binarism of literary and nonliterary (11). The confusion of the literary with fiction is, he suggests, an aftereffect of the growth and importance of the novel: "We have the novel in mind when we separate prose into fiction and nonfiction" (19). But, as Novarr argues, drawing on the then-fresh structuralism of Northrop Frye, the novel is only one form of fiction; "the prose masterpieces of the seventeenth century are fictive works" in the sense of "a work made for its own sake in the image of its maker" (18). There are two self-canceling moves here that tend to characterize most rhetorical defenses of prose nonfiction: a claim that our modern understandings of literature were not those of premodern authors and a definition of literary discourse according to modern protocols—in Frye's terms, it is self-directed. It is worth reflecting further on this phenomenon, since it seems to take us to the heart of the matter of prose nonfiction.

Since 1977 the journal *Prose Studies: History, Theory, Criticism,* for which I serve as an editor, has mounted a kind of rhetorical defense of nonfictional prose. In the tenth-anniversary issue, the founding editor Philip Dodd rededicated the journal to one of its inaugural aims: interrogating the ideology of literature from the marginal vantage point of prose nonfiction. Noting that this purpose remained as yet unrealized, Dodd admitted that "those of us involved in nonfiction studies simply underestimated the power (in Foucault's sense) of dominant definitions of Literature to contain nonfiction studies within their own terms" (5). Two excellent attempts to theorize early modern nonfictional prose, published contemporaneously with Dodd's essay, illustrate his point. In "Defining Nonfiction Genres," Ann E. Imbrie critiques "the tendency of modern genre theory to neglect nonfiction prose" (45); drawing on Renaissance literary theory, Imbrie recovers "the moral basis of literary form," an approach to literary form, she argues, that underlay a Renaissance understanding of genre capacious enough to admit prose nonfiction into the canon (55). Taking a different path, Walter R. Davis looks to twentieth-century theorists as diverse as the Russian formalists, Michel Foucault, and Jacques Derrida "to explore the sort of claim we make for literary theory when we teach writings that were not originally intended to be received as 'belles lettres' like poetry and fiction, as if in fact they are poetry and fiction" (85). I shall have more to say about Davis's provocative essay, but at this point I want to emphasize the degree to which his approach to prose nonfiction is framed, as Davis puts it, by "a similar set of presuppositions as those we use for poetry . . . [including] structure, style, persona, tone, subtext, and the like" (85). In both critics, Imbrie and Davis, one again senses contrary motives—a wish to redraw the boundaries of the province of literature, on the one hand, and an attempt to locate nonfictional prose within a formalist province of literature as we know it, on the other.

Novarr's anthology for the seventeenth century is organized around an overlapping selection of major authors (Bacon, Burton, Walton, Browne, Bunyan, and Pepys) and genres (essays, characters, short lives, and letters). One woman writer, Dorothy Osborne, is represented by three letters she wrote to William Temple. Twenty years later, Davis opens his essay with an overview of works likely to be assigned in a course on seventeenth-century nonfictional prose: Francis Bacon's *Essays* and philosophical works; characters; sermons by John Donne and Lancelot Andrewes; Donne's *Devotions*; Robert Burton's *Anatomy of Melancholy*; Thomas Browne's *Religio Medici*, *Urne-Burial*, and *Garden of Cyrus*; Jeremy Taylor's *Holy Living* and *Holy Dying*. The interesting additions of religious writing in the forms of sermons and devotional literature no doubt testify to the influence of scholars such as Louis Martz, Barbara Lewalski, and Joan Webber. Davis remarks on the diversity of kinds in his list, though it will strike readers today as still narrowly focused on writing by men of high-church proclivities. I shall suggest that Davis points a way toward an opening of the canon, but his approach is still controlled by an idea of literature as a self-directed discourse, in the sense both of writing about writing and writing about the self. A review of the early modern scholarship published in *Prose Studies* over the past ten years indicates that the grip of formalism and belletristic criticism of prose nonfiction is loosening. In general, the expanding canon of nonfictional prose participates in the disciplinary movement away from formalist approaches and Arnoldian ideas of culture. All of which is to say that it has probably become even more difficult than it was twenty years ago to determine "what counts" as nonfictional prose in early modern England.

Thus one piece of the interrogative approach to teaching early modern nonfictional prose would be a review of the contents of some representative anthologies of early modern literature over the past half century. The aim here is the creation of some provisional taxonomies of prose texts selected for professors and their students in early modern literature courses based on such criteria as gender, genre, topicality, purpose, style, and audience. This survey can provoke fruitful debates on topics more typically discussed in courses on literary theory, but here informed by an engagement with literary history in two senses—the change through early modernity of what was written and read (and who wrote and read these texts) and the shifting criteria for inclusion in the canon over the more recent past. The extent of this interrogation will be determined, of course, by the level and scope of the course. In any case, such an investigation will also reveal that a significant body of early modern, and especially seventeenth-century, nonfictional prose continues to "count" because it is very beautiful. The glorious periods of the King James Bible, of Donne, Browne, and Taylor challenge the prose-poetry binarism, arching like a rainbow over the tumultuous decades that separate Christopher Marlowe's "mighty line" and John Milton's rolling thunder. There are beauties of other kinds to be enjoyed in the isometrics of Andrewes, the lapidary precision of Bacon, the high jinks of Thomas Nashe or Martin Marprelate, and the scripturalist "realism" of John Bunyan. In prose works by these writers one finds a fusing of medium and message typically ascribed to poetic discourse, as well as a new sense of the power of the medium to represent worlds seen and unseen.

The exploratory work on the canon suggested above can offer a new purchase on these works by situating them within a more complex and diverse field of "prosification." Why did prose become so artful and powerful in the seventeenth century? This question is, I think, the real issue Davis wanted to address in his essay. Noting that "roughly beginning in the 1630s and running through the 1650s" prose moves from the margins of culture to the center, where it "becomes a way of living in print," he provocatively suggests, again echoing Foucault, that "writing prose becomes something you do when you cannot do something else or do otherwise, a substitute, a creation of counter-memory" (92). While Davis tends to describe this change as a series of transgressions by individual authors, his sense of a broad cultural context for these individual productions provides a bridge to the approach taken by Godzich and Kittay, who treat verse and prose not as the creations of individual writers but as signifying practices. What interests them is the gradual shift in medieval France from verse to prose as the dominant signifying practice. They explain that this shift occurred in medieval France because the jongleur culture needed to be replaced by a new signifying practice, a practice they ultimately connect to the emergence of new forms of authority embedded in the early modern state. A comparable placement of English prose in the context of literary and cultural history is needed to account for the proliferation of prose nonfiction in early modern England.

Our definitions of *prose nonfiction* would do well, then, to emphasize both terms in the phrase in order to engage it as a signifying practice at the center of both large and small cultural movements of early modernity. A list of the topics of essays in *Prose Studies* over the past ten years can highlight a few of these: historicism, political radicalism, religious dissent and sectarianism, political absolutism and centralization, courtiership, colonialism, republicanism, *querelles des femmes*, domesticity, marriage, news, privacy. Writing and reading vernacular prose nonfiction on these topics created new relations among writers, readers, and reality. We need to supplement formalist analysis with an understanding of the ways in which nonfictional prose changes the subject position of writers and readers in relation to the topics enumerated above—from location in a "poetic" into a "prosaic" world.[5]

That said, I do not mean to minimize the value of stylistic analysis in teaching early modern literature. The rich variety of styles in early modern prose offers an unparalleled opportunity for students to discover and reflect on aspects of prose often neglected in both literature and composition courses, even at the advanced level. It is important for advanced students to learn, for example, that a work like William Strunk Jr. and E. B. White's *Elements of Style* is a historically situated canon of style, to discern its roots in the "plain style" of the seventeenth century, and maybe even to explore some of the pleasures of difficulty and obscurity in writing that fails the test of clarity but satisfies other literary appetites.

Because of the dominance of stylistic approaches, nonfictional prose has been defined largely from the perspective of the *writer's* self-fashioning. Morris Croll's work on the anti-Ciceronian movement in prose brilliantly linked stylistics to questions of self-representation in nonfiction, in addition to placing English prose writers in a broad European context (a direction not followed by scholars after Croll). In the introduction to his 1971 collection of criticism of seventeenth-century prose, Stanley Fish asserts that "in a very real way, Morris Croll is the only begetter of this anthology" (vii). Croll is also an influence behind Joan Webber's *The Eloquent "I,"* an important work that took some first steps toward new ways of conceptualizing the notion of Renaissance self-fashioning as a nexus of literary style and ideology. By the same token, Croll's strength as a scholarly progenitor had the effect of limiting the discussion of prose to questions of style. One feels this sense of constriction in Fish's *Self-Consuming Artifacts*, where he struggles to free his thinking from long-standing controversies yet returns in an epilogue to the erstwhile debate on style with another explanation for the polarization of prose styles through much of the seventeenth century and the dominance of the plain style at the end of the century. In a sense, his notion of "affective stylistics" was an attempt to deconstruct the opposition between "ordinary language" and poetic language in order to get at prose without focusing on style.[6] His practice, however, favors texts by canonical authors, where, by his own admission, "evidence of control is overwhelming" (*Self-Consuming Artifacts* 409). Predictably, Fish's affective stylistics did not have the intended effect of moving criticism away from stylistics; the canon of nonfictional prose continued to be defined as prose with style, whether self-satisfying or self-consuming.

Historicism, old and new, and feminism finally broke ground for the study of nonfictional prose. By destabilizing traditional distinctions between text and context, background and foreground, in literary studies, new historicists provided the means for rescuing nonfiction from its supporting role to literature defined as fiction. Theories of circulation, textuality, and intertextuality seemed to offer a new way to do what Fish had envisioned and more: they provided a method of reading prose that would open a window into reading practices and afford a purchase on what texts did to early modern readers—in new historicist terminology, on the processes of subjectification in early modern England. However, as numerous critiques have pointed out, new historicist practice continued to privilege the fictional, canonical text.[7] Ironically, perhaps, the more important critical work on noncanonical, nonfictional prose has come from British critics working in parallel with new historicists but influenced by more traditional historicisms, including Marxism. In his groundbreaking *Perfection Proclaimed: Language and Literature in English Radical Religion, 1640–1660,* Nigel Smith, acknowledging the new historicism, argues that "there is no division between fields of evidence and critical approaches which we often define as literary and those which we call historical" (vii). Analyzing leading characteristics of nonconformist discourse, Smith goes on to present an account of what might be called "radical religious self-fashioning and cultural poetics" in the later seventeenth century. Two

prominent aspects of his study point the way toward opening the canon—
a move into the later century and the revolution, a notable lacuna in
monarch-centered new historicist work, and a turn to radical religious
writing, a surprisingly unexamined topic in new historicism. Books such
as Thomas Corns's *Uncloistered Virtue* have worked in similar ways to
open the doors of literary criticism to radical political pamphlets and tracts
of the period.

Smith's discussion of the female prophets Sarah Wright and Anna
Trapnel points to the single most powerful force redefining nonfictional
prose studies over the past two decades, namely, the recovery of women's
writing and reading. The Brown University Women Writers Project, now
the Women Writers Project (WWP) and Women Writers Online, led the
way in challenging assumptions about the early modern literary system.
Anthologies of women's writing and full-length texts such as those published in the series Women Writers in English 1350–1850 derived from
the WWP have created new categories for nonfiction that elude traditional
genre theory. This is a welcome development for, as Novarr notes in the
introduction to his 1967 anthology and as Fowler and Greene suggest in
their recent collection, "early modern prose has not been accounted for
by theories of genre, and perhaps cannot be" (Fowler and Greene, Introduction 5; see Novarr 15). Anthologists of women's writing are mapping
new territories for early modern English studies by editing nonfictional
writings not yet granted statehood in the republic of letters and thus
contributing to the "more-than-literary investigation" encouraged by
Fowler and Greene (Introduction 6).[8] Of the 136 items in the new docu-
mentary anthology *Reading Early Modern Women*, edited by Helen Ostovich and Elizabeth Sauer, 83 (61%) are nonfictional texts. These include
legal documents and depositions, controversial pamphlets, essays, letters
(both "familiar" and philosophical), mothers' legacies, medical manuals,
devotional texts, prophecies, translations of learned treatises, and life
writing of enormous variety, including biography, autobiography, travel
writing, memoir, and diary. Although Ostovich and Sauer describe their
book as organized by genre, their collection, like the groundbreaking
anthologies of Betty Travitsky and Charlotte Otten before them, actually
overwhelms a generic system of classification with sections titled "The
Status of Women" and "Religion, Prophecy, and Persecution." For example, a selection from Katherine Evans and Sarah Cheevers's account of
their sufferings at the hands of the Inquisition is placed in the section
"Religion, Prophecy, and Persecution," though it could easily be assigned

to "Life-Writing." Indeed, much of the religious prose of the period commands the interest of scholars today because of its grounding in particular experiences of awakening, abuse, and imprisonment recorded in the multifarious forms of life writing in the period.

In addition to challenging the genre system, nonfictional prose by early modern women questions one of the most basic assumptions of literary study, raised in Foucault's famous query, "What is an author?" What, exactly, do we mean when we identify someone as a writer? Take the case of the now canonical nonfiction text *The Examinations of Anne Askew*. Is it correct to refer to Anne Askew as the writer of this text? This is the core question of the brilliant scholarship of Thomas Freeman and Sarah Elizabeth Wall in their study of John Foxe's edition of the *Examinations* in *Acts and Monuments*. Freeman and Wall demonstrate how Foxe, usually portrayed by scholars as an unobtrusive editor who allows Askew's voice to ring loud and clear, shaped and augmented the text he likely used as copy-text for his *Acts and Monuments;* how he, like John Bale, worked to minimize her subversive potential; and how the editions of *Acts and Monuments* created slightly different portraits of Askew in order to address particular religious and political issues of the day. The search for the real Askew uncannily resembles the attempt by church authorities to get at her inwardness in their "examinations." In place of traditional notions of authorship, Freeman and Wall refer to "what can only be termed syndicates of writers" who produced a significant body of early modern writing/prose; such a system of literary production enlarges our understanding of the early modern idea of authorship to include editors, a tendency "perhaps especially noticeable in the study of early modern women writers" (1193). Relationships between editors and women writers were not always consensual, sometimes resulting in "a distortion or a subversion of the original texts" (Freeman and Wall 1193).

Finally, at the risk of sounding paradoxical, I want to suggest that the fiction-nonfiction binarism itself is challenged by what we call prose nonfiction of the period. Arthur Kinney has noted that in many early modern texts "what is 'fact' is often fabrication and propaganda" and that "the Tudors were supplying a printed culture where our cleaner, neater divisions of fiction and fact were unknown and remain largely inappropriate" (426). In Stephen Greenblatt's often-cited formulation, one of the signs of power in the Renaissance "is the ability to impose one's fictions on the world" (13); those fictions were typically inscribed in what we today would call nonfictional texts. Controversial writing, which comprises a substantial portion of the printed books of the period and of the literature examined by Smith and Corns, discussed above, seriously compromises a hard-and-fast distinction between fiction and nonfiction. In *An Humble Supplication to Her Maiestie* (published in 1600 with a *fictional* imprint of 1595, the year of the author's execution), the Jesuit Robert Southwell critiques the Elizabethan government's charge of Catholic sedition laid out in the proclamation of 1591. Southwell's response to the proclamation is two-pronged: he presents his own text as a statement of the facts, while characterizing the proclamation as a fiction; and, he argues, the government's text demonstrates "little acquaintance with the Prince's [Elizabeth's] stile," which has been "abused to the authorizing of Fictions" (2). Prophecies and visionary texts of the period interrogate our ready distinction between fiction and nonfiction as well as our complacencies about genre. Seventeenth-century readers were free to approach Anna Trapnel's visions as symbolic texts like Revelation, as autobiography, and as devotional literature. As scholars and teachers we need to be cognizant of the range of interpretations available to early modern consumers of these texts. In early modern writing, the question of fictionality cannot be fully answered, as Searle maintains, by the writer's intention; we must also consider the reader's use of the text—which is to say that our study of the reading of prose nonfiction, no less than its writing, must avoid the fallacy of transparency.[9]

Early modern production and consumption of prose nonfiction offered new kinds and combinations of pleasure and instruction as writers and readers became increasingly comfortable and creative with a medium that proved remarkably flexible in its power to delineate private and public experience, both to describe and challenge "what is." The "popularity" of prose constitutes its greatest strength. In addition to searching for traditional markers of literariness in nonfiction, we need to extend our scholarship and teaching about prose nonfiction through study of the various markets and literacies of nonfiction that emerged, especially in the seventeenth century, in discourses of government, dissent, gender, domesticity, health, and science.[10] Godzich and Kittay argue that, beginning in the early modern period, prose gradually replaced poetry (verse) as the dominant signifying practice of Europe. One could make a parallel case for the rising value of nonfiction and hybrid forms of fiction and nonfiction in the literary marketplace from early modernity to postmodernity. If the NEA survey is accurate, most of our students will be more familiar with such works from our own time than with contemporary fiction and poetry.

Teaching early modern prose nonfiction has perhaps never been more timely.

Notes

1. It should be noted that Searle does insist that "why we take the attitudes we do will of course be at least in part a function of the properties of the discourse and not entirely arbitrary" (320).

2. See McLemee. The article reports on a study conducted in August 2002 by the NEA as part of its *Survey on Public Participation in the Arts.* As Charles McGrath suggests in a critique of the NEA report, the NEA's definition of literature as fiction is a notion "that used to flourish in certain English departments, especially those in thrall to the so-called New Criticism" (3).

3. In Godzich and Kittay's account of the "emergence of prose" in thirteenth-century France, prose seems to be coupled with nonfiction in an early request for a translation into unrhymed French of the Latin verse *Chronicle of Turpin,* in their view a foundational moment for prose: "it is nothing but lies that they tell and sing, these singers and jongleurs. No rhymed tale is true; everything they say is a lie" (xiv).

4. For a discussion of the theories of fiction in Sidney's *Defence* and Puttenham's *Arte of English Poesie,* see Greene. For "poetry" and "poesie" in Sidney and Puttenham, Greene "generally" reads "the modern term 'fiction,'" though in a note he acknowledges "the interesting question of where Sidney's and Puttenham's phenomenological term, 'poetry'—that is, fiction—intersects with formal poetry or verse" (200n5).

5. Foucault's often-cited chapter "The Prose of the World" in *The Order of Things* deals with this shift from another angle.

6. "[W]e have for too long, and without notable results, been trying to determine what distinguishes literature from ordinary language" (Fish, *Self-Consuming Artifacts* 408).

7. See, for example, Holstun: "This is not to say that new historicists do not turn to nonliterary texts, but these works typically appear in the traditional role of contexts for the central literary works . . ." (192).

8. Although the essays collected in Fowler and Greene "attempt to witness generic issues in the context of a more-than-literary investigation, and to widen the boundaries around the concept of genre as well" (Introduction 6), only one (by Jones) focuses on women writers, or, rather, "women-voiced pamphlets" of the Swetnam controversy.

9. "Roughly speaking, whether or not a work is literature is for readers to decide, whether or not it is fiction is for the author to decide" (Searle 320).

10. See also Fowler and Greene: "How do such texts attain audiences, aesthetic and persuasive power, closure? How does the incipient genre of the colonial *relacion* determine what Europeans know and believe of the Americas? How do forms arise to invent and effect the aspirations of newly restless social groups such as middle-class businessmen, educated women, colonists, and *mestizos?*" (Introduction 7).

Works Cited

Corns, Thomas N. *Uncloistered Virtue: English Political Literature, 1640–1660.* Oxford: Clarendon, 1992. Print.

Davis, Walter R. "Genre and Non-fictional Prose." *Prose Studies* 11.2 (1988): 85–98. Print.

Dodd, Philip. "Literature, Fictiveness and the Dilemma of Nonfiction." *Prose Studies* 10.1 (1987): 5–8. Print.

Fish, Stanley E. Introduction. *Seventeenth-Century Prose: Modern Essays in Criticism.* Ed. Fish. New York: Oxford UP, 1971. vii–viii. Print.

———. *Self-Consuming Artifacts: The Experience of Seventeenth-Century Literature.* Berkeley: U of California P, 1972. Print.

Foucault, Michel. "The Prose of the World." *The Order of Things: An Archaeology of the Human Sciences.* New York: Vintage, 1973. 17–45. Print.

Fowler, Elizabeth, and Roland Greene. Introduction. Fowler and Greene, *Project* 1–14.

———, eds. *The Project of Prose in Early Modern Europe and the New World.* Cambridge: Cambridge UP, 1997. Print.

Freeman, Thomas S., and Sarah Elizabeth Wall. "Racking the Body, Shaping the Text: The Account of Anne Askew in Foxe's 'Book of Martyrs.'" *Renaissance Quarterly* 54.4[1] (2001): 1165–96. Print.

Godzich, Wlad, and Jeffrey Kittay. *The Emergence of Prose: An Essay in Prosaics.* Minneapolis: U of Minnesota P, 1987. Print.

Greenblatt, Stephen. *Renaissance Self-Fashioning: From More to Shakespeare.* Chicago: U of Chicago P, 1980. Print.

Greene, Roland. "Fictions of Immanence, Fictions of Embassy." Fowler and Greene 176–202.

Guillory, John. "Literary Study and the Modern System of the Disciplines." *Disciplinarity at the Fin de Siecle.* Ed. Amanda Anderson and Joseph Valenti. Princeton: Princeton UP, 2002. 19–43. Print.

Holstun, James. "Ranting at New Historicism." *English Literary Renaissance* 19.2 (1989): 189–225. Print.

Imbrie, Ann E. "Defining Nonfiction Genres." *Renaissance Genres: Essays on Theory, History, and Interpretation.* Ed. Barbara Kiefer Lewalski. Cambridge: Harvard UP, 1986. 45–69. Print.

Jones, Ann Rosalind. "From Polemical Prose to the Red Bull: The Swetnam Controversy in Women-Voiced Pamphlets and the Public Theater." Fowler and Greene 122–37.

Kinney, Arthur F. *Humanist Poetics: Thought, Rhetoric, and Fiction in Sixteenth-Century England.* Amherst: U of Massachusetts P, 1986. Print.

McGrath, Charles. "What Johnny Won't Read." *New York Times* 11 July 2004, sec. 4: 3. Print.

McLemee, Scott. "Americans Found to Read Less Literature than Ever." *Chronicle of Higher Education* 16 July 2004: A1+. Print.

Novarr, David. Introduction. *Seventeenth-Century English Prose.* Ed. Novarr. New York: Knopf, 1967. 3–35. Print.

Ostovich, Helen, and Elizabeth Sauer, eds. *Reading Early Modern Women: An Anthology of Texts in Manuscript and Print, 1550–1700*. New York: Routledge, 2004. Print.

Otten, Charlotte F., ed. *English Women's Voices, 1540–1700*. Miami: Florida Intl. UP, 1992. Print.

Puttenham, George. *Art of English Poesy. Sidney's* The Defence of Poesy *and Selected Renaissance Literary Criticism*. Ed. Gavin Alexander. London: Penguin, 2004. 55–203. Print.

Searle, John R. "The Logical Status of Fictional Discourse." *New Literary History* 6.2 (1975): 319–32. Print.

Sidney, Philip. *The Defence of Poesy. Sidney's* The Defence of Poesy *and Selected Renaissance Literary Criticism*. Ed. Gavin Alexander. London: Penguin, 2004. 1–54. Print.

Smith, Nigel. *Perfection Proclaimed: Language and Literature in English Radical Religion, 1640–1660*. Oxford: Clarendon, 1989. Print.

Southwell, Robert. *An Humble Supplication to Her Maiestie*. Ed. R. C. Bald. Cambridge: Cambridge UP, 1953. Print.

Travitsky, Betty L., ed. *The Paradise of Women: Writings by Englishwomen of the Renaissance*. 1981. New York: Columbia UP, 1989. Print.

Webber, Joan. *The Eloquent 'I': Style and Self in Seventeenth-Century Prose*. Madison: U of Wisconsin P, 1968. Print.

Lauryn S. Mayer

Cultivating the Commons: Early Modern Rhetoric, Pamphlet Writing, and the Undergraduate Reader

In a 2003 talk at the University of Minnesota's Center for Writing, Patricia Bizzell, then the president of the Rhetorical Society of America, discussed some of the forces shaping the future of rhetoric studies. In particular, she pointed to the increased interest in what she terms "rhetorics of heterogeneity," noting that scholars in this field

> directed our attention to texts and authors practically unknown to traditional historians of rhetoric, sometimes because we didn't have the methodological approaches necessary to construe them as rhetorical, and sometimes because the work itself was hidden from view, fragmented, or lost.

She also remarked that a growing number of scholars interested in rhetoric, dispersed across a wide variety of academic disciplines, have noticed that rhetorical study may support and challenge assumptions about a culture or historical period. I was greatly interested in her ideas, for she was describing the way I have been teaching early modern prose for the past few years: putting the forgotten rhetors of the early modern printed pamphlets and ballads into contact with the more traditional canonical authors and demonstrating how a knowledge and deployment of rhetorical skills form a link between the "popular" and the "literary." In the process, I've found that including the pamphlet material stimulates students to make more thoughtful assessments about the period as a whole and to put these lesser-known texts into fruitful dialogue with their better-known cousins. Moreover, it is becoming increasingly easy to accommodate this inclusion, as the number of resources for pamphlet facsimiles grows.

Early modern pamphlets provide a wealth of material to galvanize the undergraduate reader, and instructors now have increasing access to this trove through recent publications and online resources. The best current source is the mammoth *Early English Books Online* (*EEBO*), which provides everything available in Pollard and Redgrave's *Short-Title Catalogue* (1475–1640), Wing's *Short-Title Catalogue* (1641–1700), the *Thomason Tracts* (1640–61), and the *Early English Tract Supplement*. The *EEBO* site, however, requires institutional subscription and may not be available on many campuses. *Literature Online*, a more widely subscribed-to database, has a large selection of early modern pamphlets, as does the *Renascence Editions* site; the online *Lampeter Corpus of Early Modern English Tracts* (forthcoming at the time of publication), and the Women Writers Project's online database *Women Writers Online*. Anthologies of pamphlets are also becoming more common: Susan Gushee O'Malley's collection of Jacobean pamphlets on women and Randall Martin's facsimile edition *Women and Murder in Early Modern News Pamphlets and Broadside Ballads, 1573–1697* are a welcome addition to the earlier anthology by Joseph Marshburn and Alan Velie. This burgeoning of resources helps instructors such as me to break down the wall dividing the "popular" from the "literary": two categories that have been artificially divided by the mechanisms of pedagogy and publication. The two textbooks most often used for undergraduate surveys—the Norton and Longman anthologies—either ignore the presence of popular literature almost completely or relegate it to the ghetto of "context," important only insofar as it "illuminate[s] underlying issues in a variety of major works" (Damrosch xxxi). Although the Longman editors have made a laudable effort to include pamphlet material, the imposed division of what the general editor David Damrosch views as transcendent "imaginative" literature from historically fixed "popular" (i.e., unimaginative) writing encourages the reader to strip-mine the pamphlets for cultural data, rather than view them as important texts in their own right. However, in a culture where the drama frequently took its cue from pamphlet literature, where social status and mores were in flux, and where print found a ready market in all classes, this distinction begins to look more like naturalized imposition than a natural disposition. Pamphlet writers deliberately made use of rhetorical strategies, authors such as Henry Peacham wrote both rhetorical manuals and pamphlets, and influential or controversial pamphlets such as those written by Martin Marprelate created a rhetorical style of their own. In the following sections, I try to provide a general outline of the way that rhetoric became more accessible to non-Latinate readers, how the pamphlets themselves served as rhetorical models for a wide audience, and how rhetoric developed into a shared preoccupation among both "literary" poets and "popular" pamphleteers.

The unprecedented flood of texts made possible by William Caxton's introduction of the printing press in 1476, the increasing number of readers produced by post-Reformation education, the Tudor strategy of employing "new men" (such as Thomas Cromwell, the son of a Putney cloth worker who rose to the inner circle of Henry VIII's advisers through the study of common law) and endowing them with titles and wealth unfettered by connections to older landed powers, and the adoption of rhetoric as a tool for social advancement—these conditions led to a growing body of rhetoric texts in English. In Leonard Cox's *The Arte or Crafte of Rhetoryke*, the first rhetoric text written in English, we can see how Cox attempts to address both his patron's interests and the needs of an everlarger group of non-Latinate readers. He is at first careful to direct his text at a young audience, who could not be expected to grapple with a similar work in Latin. However, in his opening address to Hugh Farrington (the abbot of Redding and patron of the grammar school where Cox taught), he quickly moves to point out the benefits of his text to readers at large:

> [Rhetoric] is very necessary to all suche as wyll either be Advocates and Proctours in the Law, or els apt to be sent in theyr Prynces Ambassades to be techers of goddes word in suche maner as may be moost sensible & accepte to theyr audience and finally to all them havynge any thyng to purpose or to speke afore any companye (what somever they be). . . ." (Cox A2v)

Although English was not the language of diplomacy or law, it is important to note that Cox intends his book to give a thorough grounding in rhetoric not only to these fledgling advocates and ambassadors but to a much larger audience: "all them havynge any thyng to purpose or to speke afore any companye." To underscore this last point, Cox explains his decision to translate and compile an English text as a response to an imagined community of English-speaking supplicants; he is ". . . wyllynge therfore for [his] part to help suche as are desirouse of this Arte (as all surely ought to be which entende to be regarded in any comynaltie)" (Cox A3r). Moreover, his introduction ends with a decided refusal of linguistic and pedagogical elitism: "Every good thyng (after the sayengis of the Philosopher) the more common it is, more better it is" (Cox A4v–A5r).

The text itself is designed to make "common" both the matter and style of classical authors. Terms are translated into English and explained simply; early examples, such as Cicero's attack on Clodius, appear throughout the work, helping link the structures of rhetoric in the reader's memory. Excerpts from Homer, Sallust, Aristotle, Cicero, Demosthenes, Plato, Terence, and Livy are carefully chosen for their appeal (Cox B5v) and explained in historical context. While learning the craft of rhetoric, Cox's reader can also accrue the cultural currency of "auctors."

In discussing invention, Cox focused mainly on particular aspects of rhetoric; similarly, his contemporary Richard Sherry concentrated on tropes and figures. Thomas Wilson's *The Arte of Rhetorique*, however, compiled these earlier works into the first complete treatise on the subject in the English language. It was eagerly devoured by the reading public, going through eight editions between 1553 and 1585. The text's popularity is no doubt partly a result of its comprehensiveness; Wilson's real skill, however, lay in creating a decidedly "English" rhetoric for his audience and in providing a set of literal "commonplaces" from which his students could gather material.

Throughout the text, Wilson insists on two guiding principles. First, he advocates the use of "plain and simple" English terms as opposed to Latinate "inkhorn" words. In contrast to Cox, Wilson makes this choice not simply because plain words are easier to learn, but because they are the most likely to achieve their end of persuasion.

Like Cox, Wilson translates technical terms into English, but more aggressively, showing how the most intimidating Latin term can be reduced to blunt common sense, as he does when defining *dispositio* as

> the settlying or orderying of things invented for [the argument's purpose] called in Latine, dispositio, the which is nothyng els but an apt bestowing and orderly placing of thynges, declaring where every argument shal be sette, and in what manner every reason shal be applied. (Wilson A3v)

A simple explanation introduces the term, while a reassuring reminder of that simplicity follows afterward: it is "nothyng els" but arrangement, something everyone knows how to do.

This same accessibility marks Wilson's use of examples, which might have been culled from contemporary pamphlets such as the antipapist tracts of John Bale or the defense of married clergy by William Salesbury. In explaining the term *definite question* to the reader, Wilson cites two politically charged topics as examples:

> Whether now it be best here in Englande, for a Prieste to Marie, or to live single. Whether it were mete for the kynges maiestie, that now is, to marie with a straunger, or to mary with one of his own subiectes (Wilson ai[r]–aii[v])

This emphasis on the "here and now" provides a link between the terms and structure of classical rhetorical practice, and the disputes, news, and rumor swirling around the sixteenth-century Londoner.

These strategies—simplicity, repetition, and contemporaneity—serve another purpose. They set the text firmly in the memory of the audience member, thus potentially freeing him or her from a continual dependence on the text and facilitating a broader spread from literate reader to nonliterate listener. Wilson champions this kind of educational dispersal through his second guiding principle: his insistence on knowledge accumulated through models both written and heard, and on the model itself as the most suitable vehicle for instruction:

> Now before we use either to write, or speake eloquently we must dedicate our myndes wholly, to folowe the moste wise and learned menne, and seke to fashion, as well their speache and gesturying as their wit or endityng. The whiche when we earnestly mynde to do, we cannot but in tyme appere somwhat like them. For if thei that walke muche in the sone, and thinke not of it, are yet for the moste part sonne burnt, it cannot be but that thei, which wittyngly and willyngly travail to counterfete other, must nedes take some color of them and be like unto theim. (Wilson A2v)

While Wilson mentions frequently the necessity of imitating the wise and the learned, these qualities in no way suppose a university degree, or in fact anything beyond access to models and a spirit willing to take on hard mental labor. Wilson's view recurs in later works on rhetoric. Knowledge and the consequent benefits of eloquence appear to be most easily achieved through ready access to books, but are nonetheless available, like sunlight, to those willing to seek out appropriate models, whether in scholarly treatises, sermons, or popular pamphlets. Even women, Wilson notes wryly, can provide motivational models for the beginning orator: "he must use muche exercise both in writyng and also in speaking. Yea, what maketh women go so fast with their wordes. Marie practise, I warraunt you" (Wilson A3r).

Although Henry Peacham's *The Garden of Eloquence* opens with a complaint that few books of rhetoric in English have been printed, he is sufficiently confident in his market, and in the rhetorical competence of non-Latinate readers, to focus his entire text on the specialized subject of tropes and figures. Like Cox, Peacham sees the practice of rhetoric as a practice that cuts across class lines. In describing the need to master the tropes, he argues that

> the knowledge of them [is] so necessary, that no man can reade profitably, or understande perfectly, either Poets, Oratours, or the Holy Scriptures, without them, nor any Oratour, able by the weight of his wordes, to perswade his hearers, having no hope of them. (Peacham A3r)

Peacham divorces eloquence from any specific group and links it with what he considers natural and specific to humanity—namely, the ability to speak and reason: "herein it is that we do so farr passe & excell all other creatures, in that we have the gift of speech & reason" (Peacham A4v). Although Peacham is careful to follow Aristotle in making a distinction between inherent gifts and their conscious deployment (Aristotle 33; bk. 2, ch. 1), where gifts become virtues of particular individuals through habitual manifestation in an approved form such as persuasive speech, his argument nevertheless recharacterizes rhetoric not as part of a course of study reserved for those with access to formal education but as the skills of critical thinking and apt speaking that are available to all, an argument furthered by the more democratic nature of cheap print itself. Peacham himself became a model for his readers, as he turned his own skill in rhetoric into a successful career as a pamphleteer, producing highly influential and popular texts such as "The Compleat Gentleman," "Thalia's Banquet," and "Coach and Sedan."

In a print climate where pamphleteers engaged in vitriolic debates on topics ranging from treason to topknots, pleaded with readers to abandon their vices, or attempted to paint crimes in the most lurid light possible, it seems scarcely necessary to point out the writers' vested interest in rhetoric or the value of studying their productions as the informal means of transmitting rhetorical models to a population at large. Readers could learn how to disguise a double-edged satirical attack in petition form from the 1693 "Petition of the Widows . . . for a Redress of Their Grievances." Beginning as the putative widows' simple request for husbands, the text goes on to attack both the widows and their detractors:

> To begin with the loss of a maidenhead, about which they make so horrid a clamour; we could tell them sad stories about several of their betters, that on the wedding-night have fancied they have dug up this same chimerical treasure, though it was stolen many months before; nay we have a hundred and more of our company here, that, if occasion were, could attest this on their own personal knowledge. But, if no women can please them without this imaginary wealth . . . we see no reason why a young widow may not be as capable of obliging them as the best virgin in the world. It is but using a few astringents before, and, at the critical moment, crying out, "Fie sir, will you split me up?" . . . If this is their dear diversion . . . we promise them to howl, and sigh, and roar every night in the year, as heartily as an ox when he is led to the slaughterhouse. ("Petition" C3v)

The pamphleteer and playwright Thomas Dekker taught his readers the value of the extended metaphor in his gruesome depiction of plague-stricken London:

> What an unmatchable torment were it for a man to be bard up every night in a vast silent Charnell-house? . . . the bare ribbes of a father that begat him, lying there, here the Chaplesse hollow scull of a mother that bore him; round about him a thousand Coarses, some standing bolt upright in their knotted winding sheetes, others halfe mouldred in rotten coffins, that should suddenly yawne wide open, filling his nosthrils with noisome stench, and his eyes with the sight of nothing but crawling wormes. . . . And even in such a formidable shape did our diseased Citie appear in. (Dekker C3v)

Gerrard Winstanley, writing for the Levellers, demonstrates how to use allegory to link the political and the eschatalogical in making arguments:

> [E]xperience shows us that in this work of community in the earth . . . is seen plainly a pitched battle between the lamb and the dragon, between the spirit of love, humility, and righteousness . . . and the power of envy, pride, and unrighteousness; the latter power striving to

hold the creation under slavery, and to lock and hide the glory thereof
from man; the former labouring to deliver the creation from slavery,
to unfold the secrets of it to the sons of men, and so to manifest himself to be the great restorer of all things. And these two powers strive
in the heart of every single man, and make single men to strive in opposition, one against the other, and these strivings will be until the
dragon be cast out, and his judgement and downfall hastens apace;
therefore let the righteous hearts wait with patience upon the Lord. . . .
(Winstanley 2)

Elizabeth Caldwell's speech before her execution for the attempted
murder of her husband provides a perfect model of *occupatio*'s and anapho-
ra's devastating potential, as Caldwell pointedly "refuses" to blame her
husband for his neglect and dissolute behavior. At a time when husband
murder was considered petty treason and when the condemned were
expected to shoulder all blame for their actions, Caldwell's accusations
served to recast her as victim rather than villain:

I speake it not to lay anything to your charge, for I doe love you more
deerely, then I doe my selfe, but remember in what a case you have lived,
howe poore you have many times left me, how long you have beene
absent from mee, all which advantage the devull tooke to subvert mee.
(Dugdale C1v)

For the most part, however, scholars studying these pamphlets have
focused primarily on the content of the pamphlets as evidence of an event,
custom, or ideology or as the site to unearth contemporary attitudes
thereabout. One problem lies in the nature of rhetoric itself: an art designed to achieve a particular social end may persuade without being ob-
trusive. Another problem, however, lies in the current perception of
rhetoric as it relates to literature. As I noted earlier, the insistence on
linking "literature" with a rather limited definition of "imagination/
imaginary" has the effect of devaluing the kind of creative re-creation of
events, places, people, or concepts that is the foundation of rhetorical
skill. Rhetoric in this sense appears as meretricious window dressing on
an underlying reality, instead of the imaginative creation of a reality
(Clark 162).

Just as one set of scholars damns the pamphlets for being insufficiently
imaginative, another set of scholars tends to dismiss them for their lack of
specificity and objectivity, seeing them as rather overwrought forerunners

of more responsible historiography. Rhetoric comes off badly here as well, since it is seen as an extraneous stain on what might have been a more accurate report of the circumstances.

The double nature of rhetoric—at once too utilitarian to be "literary" and too imaginative to be objective—is echoed in the uneasy pedagogical attitudes toward pamphlet literature itself. However, it is in this double nature that we can find a way to bring together the "literary" and "popular" texts: in their shared agenda of using language to create images and influence emotions. Recognizing this agenda allows us to take another look at "literary" texts as arguments while also appreciating the pamphlet genres as repaying careful rhetorical analysis. For example, even a casual look at the Short-Title Catalogue of A. W. Pollard and G. R. Redgrave or of Donald Wing will reveal the expansion and development of the penitential pamphlet from about 1630 to 1690. By 1672, the form is so well developed that the convicted matricide Henry Jones is advised by a well-meaning local minister to model his own penitence (in both thought and written expression) on the earlier penitential pamphlets recounting the crimes of Bishop Atherton, Nathaniel Butler, and Thomas Savage (*Bloody Murtherer* B3r). We can also begin looking more closely at the reasons for certain pamphlets' popularity in the light of their rhetorical strategies and power over readers as well as of their possible historical considerations. Philip Stubbes's hagiographic account of his wife's life and death went through an astonishing twenty editions between 1591 and 1688. With an estimate of about 700–800 copies per print run (Voss 1), this is a staggering number of copies sold, with little or no critical attention to the work. We can also move away from the unpromising dyad of "literary" text on the one hand and pamphlet as content on the other to look at the methods that these texts use to present arguments on a particular topic or at the rhetorical strategies used by the different genres of pamphlet and drama.

Finally, the pamphleteers' agenda in providing vivid examples and topics of popular interest proves invaluable to instructors attempting the difficult task of interesting students in early modern prose. While authors such as Philip Sidney and Thomas More can provide abundant examples of the kind of formal rhetorical strategies in which early modern audiences delighted, undergraduates new to early modern prose and its challenges can find more alluring and accessible examples in the witches, wanton women, rogues, and penitents of the popular press. Pamphlets have the added benefit of showing an attention to language in a large cross-section of early modern England; one of the best ways of showing that love of rhetorical fireworks and wordplay was not the sole property of the upper classes is to show its prevalence in decidedly "lowbrow" literature.

In the pamphlets, with their vivid images, verbal gymnastics, and popular topics, the early modern reader and the undergraduate, the historian, the critic, and the rhetorician may mingle happily. The "commons"— the place that became a synonym for the threatened freedoms of the middle and lower classes with the institution of enclosure—is an apt metaphor as well for the flexible movement of rhetorical skills across class and gender lines. To bring the power and richness of early modern prose to twenty-first century students, we need rhetoric as a force that cuts across current pedagogical enclosures: "popular" and "literary," "poetic" and "prosaic."

Works Cited

Aristotle. *Nicomachean Ethics*. Trans. Terrence Irwin. Indianapolis: Hackett, 1985. Print.

Bizzell, Patricia. "Future Directions for Rhetorical Traditions." Center for Writing, U of Minnesota, September 2003. Address.

Bloody Murtherer; or, The Unnatural Son, His Just Condemnation of the Assizes Held at Monmouth, March 8, 1671–72. London, 1672. Print.

Clark, Sandra. *The Elizabethan Pamphleteers: Popular Moralistic Pamphlets, 1580–1640*. Rutherford: Fairleigh Dickinson UP, 1983. Print.

Cox, Leonard. *The Arte or Crafte of Rhetoryke*. London, 1530. Print.

Damrosch, David. Preface. *The Longman Anthology of British Literature*. Ed. Damrosch. New York: Longman, 1999. xxix–xxxiii. Print.

Dekker, Thomas. *The Wonderful Yeare*. London, 1603. Print.

Dugdale, Gilbert. *A True Discourse of the Practises of Elizabeth Caldwell*. London, 1604. Print.

Lampeter Corpus of Early Modern English Tracts. REAL Centre. Chemnitz U. June 1998. Web. 8 Oct. 2008.

Marshburn, Joseph, and Alan Velie, comps. *Blood and Knavery: A Collection of English Renaissance Pamphlets and Ballads of Crime and Sin*. Rutherford: Fairleigh Dickinson UP, 1973. Print.

Martin, Randall, ed. *Women and Murder in Early Modern News Pamphlets and Broadside Ballads, 1573–1697*. Facsim. ed. Aldershot: Ashgate, 2005. Print.

O'Malley, Susan Gushee, ed. *"Custome Is an Idiot": Jacobite Pamphlet Literature on Women*. Urbana: U of Illinois P, 2004. Print.

Peacham, Henry. *The Garden of Eloquence*. 1577. Menston: Scolar, 1971. Print.

"The Petition of the Widows, in and about London and Westminster, for a Redress of Their Grievances." London, 1693. Print.

Renascence Editions. Ed. Risa Stephanie Bear. U of Oregon. Web. 8 Oct. 2008.

Voss, Paul J. *Elizabethan News Pamphlets: Shakespeare, Spenser, Marlowe, and the Birth of Journalism.* Pittsburgh: Duquesne UP, 2001. Print.

Wilson, Thomas. *The Arte of Rhetorique.* London, 1553. Print.

Winstanley, Gerrard. *A Letter to the Lord Fairfax and His Council of War.* . . . London, 1649. Print.

Women Writers Online. Women Writers Project. Brown U. Web. 8 Oct. 2008.

Mary Moore

Desiring Styles: Renaissance Prose Styles and Teaching by Imitation

Taught through imitation and translation as part of grammar and rhetoric,[1] early modern writing style substantiates thought, makes it sensible—audible when spoken, visible and audible when read—through devices of syntax, word order, diction, figuration, rhythm, and sound.[2] *Lexis* in Greek, *locutio* and *elocutio* in Latin (Kennedy 15), *style* in French (the latter relating to pen and to form)—the names of style suggest its relation to reading, speaking, and writing, and thus to the human body as well as to the material world in which we act. Perhaps encouraged by neoplatonic views of "outer appearance" as "an image of inner being," Renaissance writers often take the human body as metaphorical vehicle for style (Plett 369). Thus Ben Jonson asserts in *Discoveries* that "language most shows a man: speak, that I may see thee. It . . . is the image of the parent of it, the mind" (qtd. in Sawday 186), and, not surprisingly, Renaissance scholarship mirrors these metaphors: Claire Preston notes that Philip Sidney creates "a fictional universe of legible pictures in which all artificial and natural phenomena have potential 'countenance'" (97), and Patricia Parker argues that Montaigne expresses an ideal of stylistic "virility," an image as physical as it is rhetorical.

These uses of material and, particularly, bodily metaphor to discuss style, further substantiated below, present engaging possibilities for teaching style in Renaissance texts. For one thing, style's metaphoric physicality suggests that it can represent, even present, images. Syntax in particular may become mimetic and almost performative, enacting events and states of body and mind. Thomas Malory's conjunctive syntax supports imagery of extension that imitates the chivalric processes he represents as desirable (Mueller);[3] John Milton's serpentine syntax can imitate Satan's erring thought, even at times building architecture so physically suggestive as to represent the rising of aspiration and its ironic undercutting; Sidney's balanced parallelisms enriched with figuration sometimes bespeak the desire for balance through aristocratic stability. No wonder writers from Louise Labé to Roland Barthes have linked writing to pleasure; writing style helps give shape and habitation to the imagined.[4]

Early modern terminology and descriptions of style further support approaching style as embodying and substantiating content. *Sentence*, for example, means a grammatical unit but also denotes style and thought, suggesting that thought manifests itself directly in the style of sentences. *Member*, derived from the Latin and used in the grammar school rhetoric *Rhetorica ad Herrenium*, an influential textbook of the period (Kristeller 3; Ward 126), denotes clauses and phrases but also refers to parts of the body and to persons who are parts of a corporate entity such as a guild or a kingdom's body politic. Puns on *member* are rife in both French and English Renaissance texts, evoking the male sexual member, thus representing and reinforcing gendered constraints on secular female writing and publishing. The *Rhetorica ad Herrenium* further relates style to the human body as it discusses vices: thus the "swollen style" is like a swelling that "often resembles a unhealthy condition of the body, so, to those who are inexperienced, turgid and inflated language often seems majestic" (Pseudo-Cicero 265); the same model applies to the "Slack" (265) and the "Meagre" (167). According to Debora Shuger, classical rhetorics often describe styles through the opposition between images of "the athlete and the soldier," a contrast related to distinctions between "the full" and "the thin," between "musical symmetry and tense muscular power"(*Sacred Rhetoric* 21). The English poetic stylist George Puttenham further relates poetic styles to a text's "shewing itself gallant or gorgeous" or being "left naked and bare" (qtd. in Plett 368), a metaphor that may owe its provenance to the pervasive early modern emblem of Rhetorica as a female figure (Plett 368). Style shapes her nobility of form and her dress.

Style's capacity to imitate and embody what prose speaks makes it co-incident with language's origins in Western European thought. From Augustine's narrative of infantile signs in the *Confessions* (5) to Petrarch's *Rime sparse* to Lacan's mirror stage, thinkers and writers have imagined language as originating in desire.[5] It is no wonder, then, that the traits of a desired object seep into and "color" sentences in expressive texts. Imitating the absent and desired object, making present, although in a secondary sense, what is desired, styles help create at least a ghost of the pleasure of presence and possession. Furthermore, style contributes to self-fashioning in Stephen Greenblatt's sense.[6] Describing the self fashions a self that the one presented or designated as author can wear and be, can perform.

I base my teaching of Renaissance prose style on this conception of style as representing desires, and I set up a process of analysis and imita-tion linked to close reading of style as mimetic.[7] I focus on syntax because it structures other elements of style. The practice of reading, analysis, and imitation that I describe in this article refreshes students' knowledge of syntax, enhances their understanding of how various desires—political, erotic, spiritual—penetrate language, improves their reading of all texts, and enriches their own writing styles through analysis and performance of decorous, varied, vivid prose.[8]

I preface this article's discussion of teaching, as I do my actual teach-ing, with a reading of excerpts from Michel de Montaigne's preface to the *Essais,* "Au lecteur." I present Montaigne first because his style (of the type formerly called Senecan or *style coupé* [Williamson 112]), and Flo-rio's translation of him, influenced Renaissance English enormously, as other translations and the process of translation itself did.[9] Furthermore, the text's raw self-display readily engages students. Montaigne expresses his desired self-image quite clearly: "Je veux q'on m'y voie en mon façon simple, naturelle et ordinaire, sans contention et artifice: car c'est moi que je peins" (xxiii). As Florio translates, "I desire therein to be delineated in mine owne, genuine, simple, and ordinarie fashion, without contention, art or study; for it is my selfe I pourtray" (12).[10] Like Ben Jonson's notion of speech as self-portrait, quoted above, Montaigne's verb *peiner* and the verb *m'y voie* ("to be seen here") depict the text as visual self-representation, while the speaker purports to present this image without art or study. Yet figures of speech represent artfulness: *façon* puns on *la face* and evokes surfaces or outward appearances as well as the related verb *facconer* ("to make, sculpt, or model in clay" or "to fashion"), a sense Florio's translation reflects. By claiming artlessness with a word that enacts the wit of punning,

Montaigne ironically shows art as he disclaims it. This gesture empowers in ways that syntactic style implies: the pointed clause "for it is my selfe I pourtray," like others in the passage, enacts a prerogative: without qualification, disclaimer, or trope of modesty, Montaigne's present tense speaks and performs self-display. "It is my selfe" predicates the self as object of vision and language, while "I pourtray" claims the position of author. This doubling of subject-object positions presupposes the agency and authority to present a self through public, secular writing, a power that gender and class permit, even as it demonstrates the style for which Montaigne was famous.[11]

Montaigne's self-representation and its supporting style become more material and hyperbolic, and thus more clearly a display, near the preface's conclusion:

> Que si j'eusse eté entre ces nations qu'on dit vivre encore sous la douce liberté des premieres lois de nature, je t'assure que je m'y fusse tres volontiers peint tout entier, et tout nu. Ainsi, lecteur, je suis moy-mesme la matiere de mon livre. (xxiii)

> For if my fortune had beene to have lived among those nations, which yet are said to live under the sweet liberty of Natures first and uncorrupted laws, I assure thee I would most willingly have pourtrayed myselfe fully and naked. (Florio 12)

The nude male body as an emblem, a fictive frontispiece, genders authorship and readers because it discourages an "honest" woman's gaze, perhaps invites a homoerotic gaze, and suggests that if self-representative authorship is self-display in the nude, a chaste woman cannot undertake it.[12] If allusion to aboriginal innocence contradicts the erotic implications of nudity, the preface's image in print in France, not embodied in the primordial Eden of the New World, still constructs the reader as voyeur, the writer as exhibitionist. This hint of eroticism mirrors other elements of his writing: his essays elsewhere associate the male body with the desire for "virile" style that Parker's important article explores, positing an ideal of male erotic potency and performance.[13] Not surprisingly, Paul Regosin describes this text as "consubstantial" with its author,[14] echoing the self-reflexive grammar of "je suis moy-mesmes la matiere de mon livre." Alliterating his own initials, Montaigne desires a text that would embody him as a virile male, "Montaigne," who will outlive Michel de Montaigne. Claiming to be "la matiere," or content, but, cunningly, also the materiality of his text, Montaigne claims to be his own text.[15]

Presented with this text and set loose with a few questions about Montaigne's expressed desires and related imagery, diction, and syntax, students quickly recognize its transgressive self-display and its implications in terms of attitudes to modesty, textuality, style, and self-representation. I intervene at some point by writing on the board some of the Renaissance grammatical and stylistic terminology discussed previously, asking students to notice implicit imagery and leading them to draw connections among style, embodiment, and desire.

The idea of self-fashioning through prose that emerges from this reading of Montaigne becomes a motivating force in the work that follows. But a historical divagation on styles must preface further discussion of teaching, just as it prefaced my work in the classroom. Like their early modern precursors, contemporary students must learn what style is through categories that enable distinctions. Early modern categories, however, were varied and complex. Shuger most usefully describes them:

> Renaissance terminology for stylistic analysis draws upon four principal categories, all borrowed from classical rhetoric . . . (1) the genera dicendi—the Roman categories of low/plain, middle and grand styles (or their Greek equivalents); (2) its classical prototypes: for example, a style may be labeled as Senecan, Tacitean, or Ciceronian; (3) its characteristic features, especially syntactic: Renaissance rhetorics thus classify styles as periodic, curt, copious, laconic, pointed, loose; and (4) the related distinction between Attic (brief), Asiatic (copious) and Rhodian (intermediate) styles. These categories are not exclusive; . . . Nor are they unambiguous. ("Conceptions" 176)[16]

Shuger's synthesis reveals not only the richness and variety of paradigms about style but also the difficulties that these would offer to American students, most of whom do not know the classical authors and sources that these terms reflect or the related elements of style. But rather than reject the models our authors knew, I build on them by focusing on syntax and adding categories that recent scholarship such as Shuger's and Janel Mueller's have elucidated. Shuger points out, for example, that classical theories of style do not entirely account for all English styles: "Euphuism, scientific prose, and the doctrine-and-use sermon" developed separately from classical prose ("Conceptions" 173). Furthermore, as both Shuger and Mueller argue, stylistic categories acquired hierarchial value based on an unspoken preference for complexity linked to subordination and periodic structure; thus Ciceronean periods engaged more scholarly attention and interpretation than the somewhat pejoratively named "loose" or "plain" styles that rely on conjunctive linkage (Mueller 16). The earlier twentieth-century work of Morris W. Croll and George Williamson exemplifies Shuger's and Mueller's points. Brilliant in defining and analyzing elements of syntax and in modeling ways of reading style, such scholars not only focused on classical models but also limited the texts and styles deemed worthy of attention, and they strongly influenced subsequent scholars to do likewise. To rectify both the emphasis on one kind of complexity and the gaps relevant to vernacular prose, Shuger defines the Christian grand style, based on approaches to sublimity conveyed in Greek, neo-Latin, and European handbooks; Marc Fumaroli redefines Ciceronian styles to include a plainer model derived, perhaps, from Cicero's letters, which became the style of choice in the French nation-state; Mueller explores the previously neglected uses of conjunctive syntax and its potential literary power in Tudor and later Renaissance vernacular styles. Others introduce new stylistic paradigms such as Heinrich Plett's contrast between humanistic and courtly styles intended for poetry but obviously applicable too to prose.[17] In all, then, late-twentieth-century scholarship applies a sophisticated consciousness inflected by social and political history to prose styles and to scholarship about them and expands the canon of styles, so to speak, a movement Renaissance scholars will recognize in all specialties. With these considerations in mind, then, I have attempted to synthesize (and no doubt have oversimplified) prose styles for teaching in appendix 2 and have also identified elements of prose style for students to learn and use in appendix 1.

Having introduced desiring style through Montaigne, I proceed with other texts to teach more about analysis and then to introduce imitation. I choose and closely read texts that, like Montaigne's preface, explicitly express desire. Marginal writings in early modern texts often do this, and meandering through a literature textbook will unearth these and other engaging passages. Thomas Hoby's introduction to *The Courtier*, a character's self-description in Lady Mary Wroth's *Countesse of Mongomery's Urania*, a snippet from Queen Elizabeth's many speeches, a passage from Donne or Robert Burton provoke detailed analysis and engaging discussion.[18] A passage I have read and taught successfully from Queen Elizabeth's last speech to a parliamentary closing session (351–54 [19 Dec. 1601]) reveals much about how a text expresses political desire. Furthermore, the speech's transmission in two versions necessitates my introducing discussion of textual materiality: Elizabeth's speeches may have been performed rather than written and may have been reconstructed by listeners (Marcus, Mueller, and Rose), thus complicating authorship and nuancing how we read desire. In the following discussion, I have used version 1 of the speech to exemplify the role of close reading in teaching style. I make its problematic textual status explicit to students only after our work on style, when we tease out the implications of the speech's provenance. Here is the passage:

> First civilly: yourselves can witness that I never entered into the examination of any cause without advisement, carrying ever a single eye to justice and truth. For though I were content to hear matters argued and debated pro and contra, as all princes must that will understand what is right, yet I look ever (as it were) upon a plain table wherein is written neither partiality nor prejudice. My care was ever by proceeding justly and uprightly to conserve my people's love, which I account a gift of God not to be marshaled in the lowest part of my mind, but written in the deepest of my heart, because without that above all, other favors were of little price with me, though they were infinite. Beside your dutiful supplies for defense of the public—which as the philosophers affirm of rivers coming from the ocean, return to the ocean again—I have diminished my own revenue that I might add to your security, and been content to be a taper of true virgin wax, to waste myself and spend my life that I might give light and comfort to those that live under me. (346)

Subordinating her "I" to parliament's "yourselves" as she opens, Elizabeth establishes notions of balance and even-handedness that her style embodies. This structural motif—duality and balance—imbues image, syntax, and semantics, radiating in metaphors of number, likeness, and contrast; source and origin; and more: "pro and contra," a blank and inscribed writing tablet, people and queen, heart and mind, diminishing and adding, river and sea enact duality and exchange. Harmonically, balanced syntax supports these elements and creates expectations that it also fulfills: thus the people's love is "not to be marshaled . . . but written," and the queen "diminishes" that she "might add." Syntax and imagery thus signify reciprocity and fulfill expectations just as the queen claims that she herself does, creating a stylistic analogue for the queen.

But the queen's desire for her people's love may contradict her desire for power as a ruler, without reciprocity, as a singularity. The analogy of the plain table, a blank tablet or writing surface, exemplifies this subtle motif. Initially, the writing tablet conveys openness, depicting the queen's mind or soul as blank, and in the later extension of the writing metaphor, the people write their love "in the deepest of my heart," filling the blank tablet. Yet the speech, emerging from her mouth and body, her heart, has already been spoken by the queen, and thus authored. Elizabeth thus contains the imagined writing of the people in her own text and body. Likewise, signifiers of singularity weave through the dualistic imagery: the queen's one eye suggests singularity of perspective despite "advisements"; the singular river enters and combines with the sea; the singular "taper of true virgin wax" resembles the letter *I* and the number 1. The concluding sentence reinforces this singularity through syntax: repetition of the taperlike "I," no longer subordinate, syntactically places the queen above the people who now are subordinate, "under" their ruler. While the taper will spend itself endowing her people with light, like Spenser's Una, the queen remains the one whose power inheres in her oneness, her singular virginity. Like her occasional use of the word *prince*, which eschews femininity without claiming the full masculinity of king, this speech is duplicitous, double: it desires both rule and reciprocity, dominance and exchange. Indeed, this analysis, a narrative of my own textual discoveries, reveals both the pleasure and the necessity of close reading as preparation for teaching style: the close reading enriches my sense of the text, but it also enables me to pose questions that help students discover the text.

Reading done, I prepare the students for our exploration of Elizabeth's speech by assigning out-of-class work the night before on what I tactfully call a review of the terms shown on appendix 1. I gain cooperation for this arduous but necessary step through course requirements: substantial credit for informal writing in and out of class, discussions based on this informal writing, grading criteria for formal papers that reward analysis of syntactic styles.[19]

The day's classwork begins, then, with small-group analysis of a single passage of Queen Elizabeth's speech, our initial goal to understand some elements of syntactic style. With the relevant speech in hand, I ask them first, often with a brief written prompt, to read the passage, try to understand its gist, and discuss (in a sense, verbally paraphrase) each sentence's meaning. We share their paraphrases briefly, correcting misapprehensions and probably noting some stylistic elements. Then students return to their group focus to identify sentence elements defined in appendix 1, taking notes as they work. Again, we share findings in the whole group. I expand on student observations, often including the speech's play with balance and parallelism. While students find this analysis difficult, I consider their difficulties as part of the process, a part I will follow up on later. My responses at this point encourage rather than criticize; my classes already know that in discussion they are responsible for sorting wheat from chaff. Once a group has found some stylistic elements, I ask them to name a style that seems to fit that sample from the handout (appendix 2)—a difficult task with Queen Elizabeth, whose public language avoids extremes of stylistic display. Perhaps a style I have called balanced subordinate suits this speech, but correctness is not the goal; rather, the ability to understand and argue for a particular category will be significant.

Before moving on to more analysis and, eventually, imitation, I help students connect style to representation through a set of follow-up questions, either building on their insights or leading them to share my own: What does the image of the plain table add to the speech? How is writing exchanged? What do the phrases "pro and contra" and "neither partiality nor prejudice" add to the speech? How do sounds reinforce meanings? What aspects of syntax mimic balance? What does imagery of deep and low, heart and mind, queen and people, rivers and sea have in common, and how do these pairs differ? What images and diction suggest unity or oneness? What would the taper look like? What does the taper do? Such specific questions and the insights they generate lead into discussion of meaning and its connection with style.[20] I continue this unit by asking the students to suggest what image of self the text seems to desire and how the kind of style might help to achieve those desires. Whatever responses they make will be inscribed on the ephemeral surface of the chalkboard, the better to be embroidered on, enriched, and discussed further.

We conclude this discussion with a turn to the text's provenance, a turn that lays the groundwork for reading style and its possible meanings in texts that represent others as well as selves. I now reveal that the text is a memorial reconstruction and ask what light this fact sheds on the text as "self-representation." Students easily realize that the text may in fact represent its recorder's desired image of Elizabeth and can represent her self-construct only in so far as the recorder has reconstructed her speech accurately. A fruitful follow-up can consider how the second version of this speech represents her and can pursue the kind of oral performance that Leah Marcus's essay in this volume suggests.

Now that the students have seen and performed some prose analysis, beginning to understand how style imitates desired objects, I will engage them in doing more of their own analysis and eventually in imitation. Following the pattern described above, and with other passages of prose I provide, I have them repeat the small-group process described previously. Imitation follows. To begin imitation, I explain my intention and pick from the sample of prose we have analyzed a sentence that I feel is imitable—it clearly follows some stylistic form without being too complex. I then assign a range of possible topics for imitation, which may be amusing but not bawdy: a self-description by the author of the model passage including sleeping or bathing habits, a letter from one to another Renaissance figure on Queen Elizabeth's strengths or weaknesses, a sentence from a speech by Elizabeth on a contemporary state occasion in the United States, and so on. The topics must be open enough to permit imagination and possibility of elaboration, yet specific enough to encourage detail. Then I produce an imitation of a sentence from one of our models on the board, pointing out my own difficulties as I go. I start by analyzing the sentence's structure aloud, then creating the core for a similar sentence and adding to it, modifying as I go to reflect my stylistic aim, modeling a recursive process. The students then are asked to imitate a sentence in the passage they have chosen, starting out by analyzing its structure, core first, then creating a core, and expanding on it.[21] During this process I tour the room, reading, complimenting, suggesting additions or alterations. Next I have the students repeat the process, go into small groups where they all read their imitations, and then select one for reading aloud. The group process here shelters the less-successful imitators, even as the public reading becomes the payoff for students: imitations often are witty and smart, rarely boring, even if the stylistic sense remains imperfect.

I often round off this set of processes with several steps. Noting the difficulties we experience with stylistic analysis and imitation, I ask students to write about and discuss what they have learned about Renaissance writers' skills and what they can deduce about early modern pedagogy. Our difficulties thus teach us as much as our achievements. Students often notice the length and complexity of Renaissance sentences as impediments to their work. However, as they learn through further analysis and practice that complex thought requires complex syntax, they realize how subordination, balance, and parallelism can enhance their own textual self-fashioning. I may ask them to do more imitations at home, picking at least three writers with different styles, and I will share successful or especially witty sentences with the class. The next formal essay assignment requires some stylistic analysis to support a thesis of their own, and subsequent discussions of Renaissance prose writers begins with analysis and imitation of style.

Once students learn sentence imitation, it becomes an inspiring, useful, and, dare I say it, even a joyous method. The range of prompts is limited only by the professor's imagination. Some ambitious prompts an instructor might use after students are at ease writing imitations might include the following: as an animal, describe in one sentence of one hundred words an essay you have written, imitating Burton's bear imagery in "Democritus to His Readers"; preface a formal writing assignment by imitating Montaigne's "Au lecteur"; write a two-hundred-word sermon on a topic of your choice, imitating Donne; write a speech for Queen Elizabeth's acceptance of the 2008 Democratic or Republican presidential nomination. Not only do students engage more deeply with early modern texts and improve grades on formal essays, they also may discover that they too can desire, imagine, and write selves.

Notes

1. Early modern prose style involves disciplines now distinct: grammar, poetics, rhetoric, logic, epistemology and psychology. See Percival (330) and Plett (356). For brief histories of rhetoric and style, see Vickers (15–50); Murphy's *Synoptic History* and "One Thousand Neglected Authors"; Shuger's authoritative opening chapters (14–54); and Mueller's introduction, esp. 1–17. Plett, Kristeller, Ward, and Percival also touch on histories of style. See also Fumaroli and Plett, who define Renaissance styles and ideological nuances.

2. Aristotle's *On the Soul* provides necessary background for studying early modern style because the powers and effects of style connect closely to ways of knowing and thus to the senses.

3. See Corns's opening analysis of Bunyan's style in this volume, which also reveals complexity in so-called plain style.

4. See the prose *épistre* that prefaces Labé's *Œuvres poétiques* (42–43) and Barthes's readerly *Pleasure of the Text* on writerly enjoyments, esp. "Babil/Prattle" (4, 6), "Langue/Tongue" (37).

5. See Moore 36–38.

6. In this volume, other essays also address self-fashioning, prose, and style: see Lamb on life writing as self-fashioning, Fallon on Milton's self-fashioning

in prose, Corthell, especially on the value of stylistic analysis and on seventeenth-century texts written "for [their] own sake in the image of [their] maker" (Novarr, qtd. in Corthell); R. Moore addresses stylistic analsyis of Quaker prose, showing how the new "spirituality demanded expression in a new prose style."

7. Sentence modeling, a process advanced by Frances Christiansen in the 1970s, involves imitation staged through analysis and exercises, a practice that inspired my use of imitation in teaching early modern prose.

8. Also see Reilly, in this volume, on teaching modern students through imitation.

9. In this volume, see Uman's opening on the importance and influence of translation.

10. In the master's and upper-division courses I teach, we do not read the French, though I supply it and point out relevant words and phrases.

11. Need I document that women got in trouble for writing fiction and secular poetry, and succeeded in publishing religious works and translations more readily?

12. See the previous note; early modern women's textual self-display in secular works, as Mary Wroth's and other textual histories show, was discouraged.

13. See Regosin's neat desciption of Montaigne'e style (208). Parker explores the Roman background for the analogy of style to the male body and the preference for a male style.

14. On this term, see Parshall 22 and Regosin, who uses the term throughout his indispensable study, starting on page 3. Relevant to self-portraiture and substantiality in "Au lecteur," see 156, stressing liveliness, and esp. 170–73.

15. Montaigne's essays sometimes belie his desire for virile style explicitly and implicitly (Parker 211).

16. *A Handlist of Rhetorical Terms*, by Lanham, defines many terms. See Kennedy on Greek definitions of style (5–7) and Vickers on early modern rhetorical figures of thought and speech. Among classical sources that influence my discussions of style, see Pseudo-Cicero, *Rhetorica ad Herrenium*, book 4; Aristotle, *Rhetoric*, book 4; Cicero, *On the Orator* (bk. 3, pars. 19–212 [17–169 in Rackham's trans.; 230–90 in May and Wisse's ed.]); and Augustine, *On Christian Doctrine*, book 4, for discussion of right uses of rhetoric and figuration for Christians. For earlier influential scholarly definitions, see Croll 51–102; Williamson 32–60. Discussions and samples of Gorgias's and Isocrates's styles can be found in Bizzell and Herzberg, including Gorgias's "Encomium of Helen" (38–42) and Isocrates's "Against the Sophists" (43–49).

17. Some of the exclusions identified include Tudor prose, whose conjunctive syntax was considered inferior to logical subordination; English Bibles; and European (as opposed to English and classical) rhetorics that reflected Greek as well as Roman stylistic models (Mueller 2–3; Rhodes, "History Language" 8–10; Plett 357; Shuger, *Sacred Rhetoric* 3–6, 126–28).

18. Mueller's book is peppered with fine analyses of style, as is the present volume.

19. I teach writing-intensive literature courses with enrollments of twenty-four or fewer; I manage my workload including the reading of much informal writing through strategies I learned through Marshall University's Writing across the Curriculum Program.

20. Teaching Montaigne's "Au lecteur," I ask questions such as, What does the metaphor of painting mean literally, and what does it imply? Are paintings necessarily true? What aspects of language, image, and sentence structure suggest a desire for simplicity? Are there contrasting elements of style, and, if so, what are they, and what do they suggest? How does the image of the writer "tout nu" strike you as a reader? How do you imagine that this image might have struck Renaissance male and female readers? Finally, how might this preface help orient readers of Montaigne's essays?

21. With less-advanced students, I sometimes provide on the board or in a handout a sentence and a related form with blank spaces for their elaboration. Thus Montaigne's pointed sentence becomes: "I want to be seen as ——, and not as —— ,   : for I ——."

Works Cited

Aristotle. *On the Soul and On Memory and Recollection*. Ed. and trans. Joe Sachs. Santa Fe: Green Lion, 2001. Print.

———. *The Rhetoric*. Trans. W. Rhys Roberts. New York: Modern Lib., 1984. Print.

Augustine. *On Christian Doctrine*. Trans. D. W. Robertson, Jr. New York: Macmillan, 1958. 117–64. Print.

———. *St. Augustine's* Confessions. Trans. E. B. Pusey. London: Dent; New York: Dutton, 1932. Print.

Barthes, Roland. *The Pleasure of the Text*. Trans. Richard Miller. New York: Hill, 1975. Print.

Bizzell, Patricia, and Bruce Herzberg, eds. *The Rhetorical Tradition: Readings from Classical Times to the Present*. Boston: Bedford, 2001. Print.

Cicero. *On the Ideal Orator*. Trans. and ed. James M. May and Jakob Wisse. New York: Oxford UP, 2001. Print.

———. On the Orator, *Book III;* On Fate; Stoic Paradoxes; The Divisions of Oratory. Trans. H. Rackham. Cambridge: Cambridge UP, 1942. Print. Loeb Classical Lib.

Clucas, Stephen. "'A Knowledge Broken': Francis Bacon's Aphoristic Style and the Crisis of Scholastic and Humanist Knowledge-Systems." Rhodes, *English Renaissance Prose* 147–72.

Croll, Morris W. *"Attic" and Baroque Prose Style*. Ed. J. Max Patrick and Robert O. Evans, with John W. Wallace. Princeton: Princeton UP, 1969. Print.

Elizabeth I. *Elizabeth I, Collected Works*. Ed. Leah S. Marcus, Janel Mueller, and Mary Beth Rose. Chicago: U of Chicago P, 2000. Print.

Florio, John. *The Essays of Montaigne. Done into English by John Florior, anno 1603*. New York: AMS, 1967. Print.

Freccero, John. "The Fig Tree and the Laurel: Petrarch's Poetics." *Petrarch*. Ed. Harold Bloom. New York: Chelsea, 1989. 43–55. Print. Modern Critical Views.

Fumaroli, Marc. "Rhetoric, Politics, and Society: From Italian Ciceronianism to French Classicism." Murphy, *Renaissance Eloquence* 253–73.

Kennedy, George A. *A New History of Classical Rhetoric.* Princeton: Princeton UP, 1994. Print.

Kristeller, Paul Oskar. "The Scope of Renaissance Rhetoric: Rhetoric in Medieval and Renaissance Culture." Murphy, *Renaissance Eloquence* 1–19. Print.

Labé, Louise. *Œuvres complètes: Sonnets, élegies, débat de folie et d'amour, poésies.* Ed. François Rigolot. Paris: Flammarion, 1986. Print.

Lanham, Richard A. *Analyzing Prose.* 2nd ed. London: Continuum, 2003. Print.

———. *A Handlist of Rhetorical Terms.* 2nd ed. Berkeley: U of California P, 1991. Print.

Marcus, Leah S., Janel Mueller, and Mary Beth Rose. Preface. Elizabeth I xi–xxiv.

Montaigne, Michel de. *Oeuvres complètes de Michel de Montaigne,* Les essais I, *texte du manuscript de Bordeaux.* Ed. A. Armaingaud. Paris: Conard, 1924. Print.

Moore, Mary. *Desiring Voices: Women Sonneteers and Petrarchism.* Carbondale: Southern Illinois UP, 2000. Print.

Mueller, Janel M. *The Native Tongue and the Word: Developments in English Prose Style, 1380–1580.* Chicago: U of Chicago P, 1984. Print.

Murphy, James J. "One Thousand Neglected Authors: The Scope and Importance of Renaissance Rhetoric." Murphy, *Renaissance Eloquence* 20–36.

———, ed. *Renaissance Eloquence: Studies in the Theory and Practice of Renaissance Rhetoric.* Berkeley: U of California P, 1983. Print.

———, ed. *A Synoptic History of Classical Rhetoric.* Davis: Hermagoras, 1983. Print.

Parker, Patricia. "Virile Style." *Premodern Sexualities.* Ed. Louise Fradenburg and Carla Freccero, with Kathy Lavezzo. New York: Routledge, 1996. 201–22. Print.

Parshall, Peter. "Portrait Prints and Codes of Identity in the Renaissance: Hendrik Goltzius, Justus Lipsius, and Michel de Montaigne." *Word and Image* 19.1-2 (2003): 22–37. Print.

Percival, W. Kenneth. "Grammar and Rhetoric in the Renaissance." Murphy, *Renaissance Eloquence* 303–30.

Plett, Heinrich F. "The Place and Function of Style in Renaissance Poetics." Murphy, *Renaissance Eloquence* 356–75.

Preston, Claire. "Sidney's Arcadian Poetics: A Medicine of Cherries and the Philosophy of Cavaliers." Rhodes, *English Renaissance Prose* 91–108.

Pseudo-Cicero. *Ad C. Herennium de Ratione Dicendi (Rhetorica ad Herennium).* Trans. Harry Caplan. 1954. Cambridge: Harvard UP, 1989. Print.

Regosin, Richard L. *The Matter of My Book: Montaigne's Essais as the Book of the Self.* Berkeley: U of California P, 1977. Print.

Rhodes, Neil, ed. *English Renaissance Prose: History, Language, and Politics.* Tempe: Arizona State U, 1997. Print. Medieval and Renaissance Texts and Studies 164.

———. "History Language and the Politics of English Renaissance Prose." Rhodes, *English Renaissance Prose* 1–18.

Sawday, Jonathan. "Shapeless Elegance: Robert Burton's Anatomy of Knowledge." Rhodes, *English Renaissance Prose* 173–202. Print.

Shuger, Debora K. "Conceptions of Style." *Cambridge History of Literary Criticism.* Ed. Glyn P. Norton. Vol. 3. Cambridge: Cambridge UP, 1999. 176–86. Print.

———. *Sacred Rhetoric: The Christian Grand Style in the English Renaissance.* Princeton: Princeton UP, 1988. Print.

Vickers, Brian. *Classical Rhetoric in English Poetry, with a New Preface and Annotated Bibliography.* Carbondale: Southern Illinois UP, 1989. Print.

Ward, John O. "Renaissance Commentators on Ciceronian Rhetoric." Murphy, *Renaissance Eloquence* 126–73.

Williamson, George. *The Senecan Amble.* London: Faber, 1951. Print.

Appendix 1:
Some Aspects of Syntax, Sound, and Sense Related to Style

> Sentence lengths and placement of sentence cores: Mueller's "canonical sentoid," traditional grammar's independent clause.
>
> Kinds of verbal linkage among sentence parts, or relative absence of them: subordination or coordination, the latter including Mueller's broadened definitions of conjunctive syntax to include some nonrestrictive elements such as participial phrases, appositives, absolutes, and noun phrases.
>
> Types of clauses: restrictive or nonrestrictive, subordinate or coordinate, and so on.
>
> Clauses' balance and parallelism or lack thereof, asymmetry: the way clauses compare in structure and length, including meter if present.
>
> Figuration: presence and kinds of figures of speech and thought including pleonasm; degree of sensory play and emphasis.
>
> Sonority: alliteration, assonance, meter, or rhythm and the relations of these to clause and phrase structure.
>
> Levels of diction: Latinate, elegant words on the "high" end versus rude, vulgar, and common language at the other.

Appendix 2:
A Preliminary Syntactic Key to Some Early Modern Styles

Periodic Balanced

End-positioned core, considerable length, consistent use of subordination and frequent sets of clauses of equal lengths suggest the Ciceronian period; dashes of alliteration may emphasize but not dominate structure.

Balanced Subordinate

An opening core might structure most sentences, but some periodic sentences of moderate length appear too. Frequent clauses and phrases of equal lengths show up with parallelism, antithesis, and analogy used often but not exclusively. Briefer versions are common with figures of speech that support such structures. Philip Sidney's romance prose often follows this model, as do Queen Elizabeth's speeches and Bacon's less aphoristic moments.

Balanced Coordinate

A core often opens this coordinate sentence, which is structured through parallelisms, repetition of linking words, and nonrestrictive clauses. Biblical prose, as Mueller discusses it, fits this model with the addition of the sense parallelism she discovers. Sometimes pleonastic, this prose also appears in Malory and other Tudor writers.

Asymmetrical Running

The core opens the sentence that develops through clauses and phrases of unequal lengths, use of both subordination and coordination to link phrases, some parallelism for emphasis and rhythm. With rich imagery, frequent nonrestrictive clauses, and introspective or spiritual focus, this syntax supports the Christian grand style as Shuger defines it, exemplified by the prose of Donne, Burton, and others.

Balanced Embellished

This syntax emphasizes equal clause lengths, and, whether running or periodic in structure, advances with frequent parallelisms, analogies, and antitheses; in addition, it uses sonority to emphasize structure—alliteration, assonance, even rhyme may appear. This style may sometimes become so tricky as to become opaque. Like the Isocratic or Gorgian classical models, sometimes called sophistic, this style or something like it arises in euphuism.

Running Curt

Often opening with its core, having clauses of unequal length, some very brief, often lacking conjunctions and subordinating pronouns, this syntax revels in dislocation, leap, and break. Such structures support what Williamson calls the Attic style; with the addition of rich metaphor, imagery, and subtle sonorities, this style appears in some of the works of Nashe, Montaigne, Bacon, and others.

Part II

Kinds of Prose

Lori Anne Ferrell

Religious Persuasions: Teaching the Early Modern Sermon

Theological, theatrical, occasional, and (not inconsequentially) entertaining, sermons were perhaps the best suited of all early modern literary and religious forms to capitalize on the doctrinal, political, and rhetorical intricacies of a paradoxical age. Weekly, even daily, sermons played a central role in the early modern parish, court, and parliament, as preachers called for divine guidance, gave religious instruction, and referred subtly (or not so) to the political issues of the day. Their words often went on to longer life in print. Sermons thus consistently provide the most characteristic documentation of the complex, shifting nature of England's post-Reformation culture.

Only recently, however, have early modern English sermons begun to receive sustained attention on their own terms from scholars of literature, history, or religion. They deserve better representation on the reading lists of undergraduate and graduate courses—and not only in those classes offered by Anglophile departments of religion or Anglican schools of theology. Sermons afford important insights into history and literature as well as theology—all three of which are subjects that fall within the larger purview of cultural studies, an interdiscipline that encompasses the literary turn in historical studies as neatly as it does the religious turn in new historicism. The form is tailor-made for teaching concepts basic to an understanding of early modern England's doctrinal beliefs and homiletic practice, political and social theories, and cultural assumptions and commonplaces. Better yet, the archives abound with sermons. And perhaps most important of all, sermons allow students a clear glimpse into a now-obscured world, one that was Bible saturated and God centered.

Any study of the early modern English sermon begins, then, with the recognition that a sermon does not so much represent a genre as it does a cultural collaboration: it is both text and event. As text, it participates in a long Christian tradition of rhetorical, theological, homiletic, and exegetical practice: it has a basic structure, a specialized lexicon, and a well-defined job to do. As event, it satisfies an occasion, inhabits a physical and cultural setting, and follows (or confounds) the expectations of its audience. The writer and preacher of the sermon is the agent who connects text and event; in their responses, the congregation or reading audience (including those of the present-day classroom) brings text and event full circle.[1]

Sermon as Text

While sermons are by no means a Protestant invention (we are only beginning to understand how central preaching was to medieval culture, especially in the territories covered by preachers of mendicant orders such as the Franciscans and Dominicans), the massive ecclesiastical and theological changes associated with the Reformation in Europe signaled, arguably, the profoundest transformation in the form and purpose of the sermon in the history of homiletics. Once regarded as a vehicle for moral instruction, the Protestant sermon became regarded instead as a necessary adjunct, for some the necessary adjunct, to salvation. In England, where faith was reformed by statute, the sermon also became a powerful instrument of statecraft. Sermons were thus always a part of English religion, but in the post-Reformation era they took on new doctrinal and political urgency, in the process reshaping the relation of England's culture to the words of the Bible.

Then as now, the sermon takes as its primary task the exegesis of a particular biblical text, whether chosen by the preacher or as demanded by the church's lectionary. The work of the preacher was to apply the words of the text to the condition of his audience and the circumstances of the

day. To do so, every sermon played its own variation on the standard exegetical schema, which, in the brisk words of the mid-seventeenth-century
theologian John Wilkins, was tripartite: "Explication, Confirmation, Application" (5). The preacher would first "divide" the originating scriptural passage, highlighting verses, phrases, or even single words. From
these excerpts he would derive what William Perkins called "a few and
profitable points of doctrine." These points were then opened up in a process called "explication," and the concepts, moral and spiritual, that they
illustrated would be made relevant, or "applied," to the needs and expectations of his auditory (Perkins 99–130 [chs. 7–8]).

Early modern preachers enlarged on, or "confirmed," the biblical text
by means of topoi, or commonplaces of argument. This did not so much
indicate that preaching was a branch of rhetoric as reflect the early modern English theory of homiletics that stressed that rhetorical techniques
were supposed to serve the overall purpose of the sermon. Preaching was
a "sacred office" rather than a school exercise (Morrissey, "Scripture" 686).
Those commonplaces, therefore, were most often scriptural, but some
preachers were not above employing pagan learning—classical arguments
(if the audience, or the preacher, was self-consciously learned) to clinch an
argument and explain the biblical text. They could also use appeals to
common sense and congregational experience to buttress their points.
Their choices—lofty or homely—signaled their awareness of the important need for *decorum*, the process by which preachers assessed the "persons, the time, and the place" of their sermon and made certain that the
rhetorical style of their sermon and the substance of their words were appropriate to the social and political condition of their congregants.

The structure that held their arguments in place was expected to be
overt, and by the early seventeenth century we often find English preachers using (more or less accurately) the well-known principles set out in
the text-dividing logic of Pierre de La Ramée, or Ramus. The use of such
a bluntly recognizable rhetorical blueprint (one so schematic that it could
be rendered visually by means of elaborately bracketed graphs) served a
twofold purpose: first, the overbearing clarity of the structure acted as a
strong point in favor of the rightness of the argument itself, and, second, it
made sermons memorable—an important asset in an age when people depended on their powers of aural recollection to retain crucial information.
This is why many sermons come to us in the diaries and commonplace
books of people who did not preach them but had instead heard them.

Sermon as Event

Just as students must discover the underlying, permanent structures of a sermon, its contexts in the most literal and literary sense, they must ascertain its early modern location. Establishing the setting of a sermon—whether pulpit, market cross, gallows, or parliament—allows an exploration into its purpose, stated or otherwise. Which is to say, it allows a class to contextualize a sermon in the more general methodological sense: to establish its participation within, and generation of, social meaning.

To do so opens the variegated world of early modern England to full view. Sermons were preached, it sometimes seems, any place early modern English men and women congregated. While we most often think of the sermon as a feature of Sunday worship, sermons were also preached at sessions of parliament; at funerals and weddings; and at the royal courts of monarchs, their consorts, their heirs, and their courtiers. Sermons were preached out of doors at the sites of the great medieval market crosses, like Paul's in London; they were preached to mark the progress of that mighty movable stage of justice known as the assize; and they were preached at executions, under the gallows or by the pyre, within the hearing of the unhappy condemned.

And this is to mention only some of the sermon's official or legal settings. The Church of England monitored preaching in a variety of ways, ensuring that potential firebrands and heretics would not gain a hearing in a religiously volatile time. The episcopal system, with its jurisdictional bishops appointed by the monarch, and the universities of Oxford and Cambridge, wherein churchmen held administrative posts, were well-suited and well-placed for the task of examining and overseeing preachers, while the bishop of London oversaw the press and disallowed the printing of sermons considered seditious or heretical.

Preachers could not preach without license in early modern England, something that students—who often find the operation of state-controlled, involuntary religion so archaic as to be incomprehensible—need to keep foremost in their minds as they consider the cultural impact and political reach of any sermon. Licensing was contingent not on demonstration of homiletic, scriptural, or rhetorical skill or on any particular proof of the preacher's piety but on a cleric's subscription to the articles of the church, submission to the monarch's supremacy over the English church, and acceptance of the Book of Common Prayer.

But sermon censorship, like all forms of government control in England, could be a spotty and mismanaged affair. Outside the watchful—or, sometimes, winking—eye of ordained authority, sermons could be heard aplenty: for example, in the environs of the "liberties" of London, a lawless border zone where bawling corner preachers, sounding for all the world like Zeal-of-the-Land Busy, competed with the theatrical stage for an audience. Still others were delivered clandestinely, to separatist congregations outlawed by church and state.

This almost-tectonic slippage between official control and sermonic dissent is an important underlying context for understanding the politics of the early modern sermon. For the sermon's long-standing spiritual mandates—to instruct and to exhort—were ones that (theoretically at least, and inherently coded in Protestant doctrine) underwrote a freedom of speech that the imperfect mechanisms of early modern governmental repression could not silence entirely. Despite the impressive mechanisms in place to control preaching, many sermons with the power to discomfit the monarch and his leading churchmen thus survive in print or in the (hostile) records of their episcopal or university examination. And one important institutional response, sermons that were preached by clerics handpicked by the monarch (and often subsequently ordered into print) and were aimed against other, offending sermons, allows us to trace a set of challenges and counter-challenges between governments and subjects acting out of equally politic and conscientious motives.

All of this means that students of the sermon confront a rich and diverse archive of manuscript and printed sources when they set to work. Mary Morrissey has estimated that at least fifteen percent of all texts listed in the *English Short-Title Catalogue* are sermons, a carefully conservative but still-extraordinary claim. In addition, manuscript sermons abound in ecclesiastical and public record offices and in the holdings of research libraries in the United States and abroad. And while there are few long runs of sermons by a single preacher—John Donne or Lancelot Andrewes are two premier exceptions that prove this rule—there do exist large caches of sermons preached in particularly identifiable and sharply characteristic settings: funeral sermons for Puritan women, sermons preached on parliamentary fast days, or sermons preached at court in times of national emergency, to name only a few.

In recounting all these essential points to consider in the teaching of the early modern sermon, however, we run the risk of overlooking its primary contribution to classroom discourse: its intrinsic interest and the intellectual and aesthetic pleasures that unpacking it can yield. What follows, then, are some suggestions on how one such sermon, a sly and witty exposition by a seventeenth-century master of the form, can be opened up in the classroom for the purposes of teaching a number of important concepts about early modern religion, monarchical and parliamentary politics, gender relations, and women's fashion.

Robert Wilkinson, *The Merchant Royall*, 1607

On 6 January 1606/07, Robert Wilkinson preached a sermon at the English court of James VI of Scotland and I of England to mark the wedding of Lord James Hay, a Scot, and Honora Denny, an Englishwoman. It was Twelfth Night, a holiday marking the end of Christmas prohibitions on marriage. The audience was composed of members of the court, foreign ambassadors, and the king, whose assumption of the English crown was very recent. These few, bare facts allow historians easily to locate the sermon in its political moment: the last gasp of James's early, overreaching, and unsuccessful attempt single-mindedly to establish full political union between Scotland and England.

The Hay wedding was, then, orchestrated to send a message to the court about the king's desires about union, metaphorically reproduced in this particular Anglo-Scottish union. And if that were all Wilkinson's wedding sermon signified, it would be fairly interesting to historians of high politics—still another piece of evidence (more diverting and imaginative, it must be said, than many of the lackluster defenses of union prepared by the king's aggrieved and bullied statesmen) that James was a tireless advocate of his ill-starred plan right up to the moment it failed, the victim of implacable parliamentary opposition, that same year.[2]

But the Hay wedding sermon can be expanded to cover even larger territory. To do so requires a thorough examination of not only the scriptural passages it draws on but also the generic requirements of epithalamial homiletics and the rhetorical requirements of decorum. In the passage below, Wilkinson divides and unfolds the logic of his sermon's base text, Proverbs 31.14, "She is like the merchants' ships, she bringeth her food from afar," by isolating the first phrase and linking the proverbial text to references to the New Testament book of Revelation and the Old Testament book of Genesis:

> *She is like a ship* (saith Salomon) and it may well be, for the world is
> like the Sea: for so saith S. *John, Before the throne there was a sea
> of glasse*, Revel. 4. and that was the world, transitorie and brittle as
> glasse, tumultuous and troublesome like the sea. . . . The feare, the
> care, the anguish that daily accompanieth the bodie and soule of
> man; the labours & sorowes certaine, the casualties uncertaine, the
> contentions and unquietnes of them that live among us, the sharpe
> assaults and oppositions of them that hate us, but chiefly the unfaith-
> fulness and treacherie of them that seeme to love us: against these
> storms to save men from drowning did God ordaine the woman,
> as a ship upon the sea, that as *Noah* made an Arke, and by that
> Arke escaped the flood . . . as much as to say, a ship to save him. . . .
> (Wilkinson 5–6)

Wilkinson connects the *woman-a-ship* topos to the ark, a symbol of (in
ascending order) conjugal cooperation, the church, and salvation from
sin; furthermore, and more effectively, he produces a sense of danger by
way of the Revelation citation, pinning it down with the image of a de-
ceptively still, ominously glassy ocean. Here is, then, a sequence of inter-
locking metaphors: marriage as safe harbor in an uncertain, possibly hostile environment; marriage, as in the New Testament miracle at the
wedding at Cana, as a symbol of Christ's love for and delivery of his
church; and then, by logical extension, marriage as a symbol of Christ's
sacrifice to save humanity, just as the ark preserved Noah, his family, and
all those animals gathered together in cooperative pairs.

But given its setting and purpose, the passage also has political work
to do. And so Wilkinson attempts to persuade the members of his audience, elicit their assent, by commonsense appeals to their cultural experience of marriage. In the passage cited above, Wilkinson alludes to less
happy, less cooperative unions with his poignant remark about "the un-
faithfulness and treacherie of them that seem to love us." The imagery
becomes almost claustrophobic (befitting, perhaps, the overriding metaphor of an enclosed ship); with its incessant piling up of terrors and assaults, it calls forth the sense of disloyalty at very close quarters. It is here
that Wilkinson introduces a standard wedding-sermon warning about the
fidelity and obedience a wife owes her husband:

> [A] ship is the hugest and the greatest, and yet commanded (as ye see)
> by the helme or sterne, a small peece of wood; so ought the wife
> (though a great commander in the house) yet to be turned and ruled
> by a word of her husband. *Salomon* saith not, she is like a house (as

many women be, as good remove a house as to disswade or weane them for their wils) but like a ship. . . . (Wilkinson 11)

With the pointed remark about the house, however, Wilkinson transforms a standard admonition to wives to know their marital place into a warning to members of Parliament (many undoubtedly present in this auditory and—if members of the House of Lords, well aware of their subterfuged opposition to the king's union scheme) to know their places and to follow the king's desires. Here, then, Wilkinson echoes James VI and I's well-known, well-publicized, frequent use of the language of marriage to describe his ruling relationship to England: the preacher broadcasts the king's political desires, using the king's words, in the presence of the king.

James I enjoyed a good sermon, and he occasionally liked a touch of the earthy in his homiletics. Wedding sermons are celebrative, rather earthy affairs in themselves, and in the next passage we also see Wilkinson expound the ship metaphor at the expense of the bride, but (no doubt) to the amusement of the king and his courtiers:

> But of all qualities a woman must not have one qualitie of a ship, and that is, too much rigging. Oh what a wonder it is to see a ship under saile, with her tacklings, and her masts, and her tops, and top gallants, with her upper deckes, and her nether deckes, and so bedeckt; with her streames, flagges, and ensignes, and I know not what; yea but a world of wonders it is to see a woman created in Gods image so miscreate oft times & deformed, with her French, her Spanish, and her foolish fashions, that he that made her when hee lookes upon her shall hardly know her, with her plumes, her fannes, and a silken vizard, with a ruffe like a saile, yea a ruffe like a rainebow, with a feather in her cap like a flag in her top, to tell (I think) which way the winde will blow. (Wilkinson 13)

And yet even this whimsical sumptuary warning (which even indulges in a bit of rhythmic, mildly smutty nonsense with the line "upper deckes, and . . . nether deckes, and so bedeckt") contains (alongside its criticism of women, another staple of wedding sermons) a not-so-subtle political statement. The references to French and Spanish foolery reproduce one characteristic type of early-seventeenth-century English anti-Catholicism.

These are only a few of the points that can be drawn out of one famous sermon of the period. *The Merchant Royall* is witty and gossamer-light (it was enormously popular and frequently reprinted), but sermons were a serious business in early modern England, a staple of its literary and religious culture. Given the attention and respect paid to the impact of words in a religiously logocentric age, they deserve to be a staple of the classroom today; they certainly are in mine. I have assigned this sermon in a wide variety of interdisciplinary, history, religion, and literature courses, using it to illustrate the essential early modern concepts of domestic conduct, public and private spheres, the relation of parliamentary and monarchical politics, and the powerful languages of sacramental practice in sixteenth- and seventeenth-century England. It is particularly effective when read aloud, capturing all the cadenced punning and clever auditory wordplay an early modern audience would have expected from its elite preachers. In the twenty-first-century classroom, the seventeenth-century *Merchant Royall* performs admirably, entertaining and instructing in equal measure. In this, we might say, it continues to deliver the goods.

Notes

1. Here I draw heavily on the excellent overview provided by Mary Morrissey in her historiographical review, "Interdisciplinarity and the Study of Early Modern Sermons," and in her seminal article "Scripture, Style and Persuasion in Seventeenth-Century English Theories of Preaching." In what follows I am indebted to Morrissey for the crucial definition of sermons as texts and events, as are all scholars of this subject to her recent meticulous and groundbreaking work on the functions and styles of preaching in early modern England.

2. I have written about this particular sermon elsewhere and at length in *Government by Polemic* 38–40; "Sacred."

Works Cited

Ferrell, Lori Anne. *Government by Polemic: James I, the King's Preachers, and the Rhetorics of Conformity.* Stanford: Stanford UP, 1998. Print.
———. "The Sacred, the Profane, and the Union." *Politics, Religion, and Popularity: Essays in Honour of Conrad Russell.* Ed. Thomas Cogswell, Richard Cust, and Peter Lake. Cambridge: Cambridge UP, 2002. 45–64. Print.
Morrissey, Mary. "Interdisciplinarity and the Study of Early Modern Sermons." *Historical Journal* 42.4 (1999): 1111–23. Print.
———. "Scripture, Style and Persuasion in Seventeenth-Century English Theories of Preaching." *Journal of Ecclesiastical History* 53.4 (2003): 686–706. Print.
Perkins, William. *The Arte of Prophecying; or, A Treatise concerning the Sacred and Only True Manner and Methode of Preaching.* London, 1607. Print.
Wilkins, John. *Ecclesiastes; or, A Discourse concerning the Gift of Preaching as It Fals under the Rules of Art.* London, 1646. Print.
Wilkinson, Robert. *The Merchant Royall: A Sermon Preached at White-Hall before the Kings Maiestie, at the Nuptials of the Right Honourable the Lord Hay*

and His Lady, upon the the Twelfe Day Last Being Januar. 6. 1607. London, 1607. Print.

Suggestions for Further Reading

Thanks to the work of two ecclesiastically opposed reprint-publication societies founded in the nineteenth century, many sixteenth- and seventeenth-century English sermons have been featured in the volumes published by the Parker Society and the Anglo-Catholic Library. The select bibliography below includes some representative works.

Andrewes, Lancelot. *Ninety-Six Sermons.* 5 vols. Oxford, 1865–71. Print.

Bradford, John. *The Writings of John Bradford.* Cambridge, 1848. Print.

Church of England. Certain Sermons or Homilies *(1547); and,* A Homily against Disobedience and Wilful Rebellion *(1570): A Critical Edition.* Ed. Ronald B. Bond. Toronto: U of Toronto P, 1987. Print.

Cressy, David, and Lori Anne Ferrell. *Religion and Society in Early Modern England: A Sourcebook.* London: Routledge, 1996. Print.

Donne, John. *The Sermons of John Donne.* Ed. George R. Potter and Evelyn M. Simpson. 10 vols. Berkeley: U of California P, 1953–62. Print.

Ferrell, Lori Anne, and Peter McCullough, eds. *The English Sermon Revised.* Manchester: Manchester UP, 2000. Print.

Jewel, John. *The Works of Bishop Jewel.* Vol. 1. Cambridge, 1845. Print.

King, Henry. *The Sermons of Henry King (1592–1669), Bishop of Chichester.* Ed. Mary Hobbs. Aldershot: Scolar, 1992. Print.

Latimer, Hugh. *Sermons of Hugh Latimer, Sometime Bishop of Worcester, Martyr, 1555.* Cambridge, 1844. Print.

McCullough, Peter. *Sermons at Court.* Cambridge: Cambridge UP, 1999. Print.

Sandys, Edwin. *The Sermons of Edwin Sandys.* Cambridge, 1841. Print.

Shami, Jeanne. *John Donne and Conformity in Crisis in the Late Jacobean Pulpit.* Cambridge: Brewer, 2003. Print.

Wabuda, Susan. *Preaching in the English Reformation.* Cambridge: Cambridge UP, 2002. Print.

Peter C. Herman

Early Modern Prose
and the Uses of
the New World

In my experience, while students are often willing, by and large they are not as prepared as one might like for the rigors of early modern literature. They find prose especially difficult because of the sometimes obscure language, labyrinthine syntax, and sheer length of some pieces of fiction (consider Sidney's *Arcadia* and Mary Wroth's *Urania*). Consequently, in order to introduce these students to the joys of prose, I have devised a thematic unit on travel for my survey courses on sixteenth- and seventeenth-century literature (my institution does not offer a course exclusively on early modern prose fiction) that could also serve as a model for an advanced seminar or graduate course.[1]

Three caveats before I begin: First, the texts discussed in this essay do not represent, and are not meant to represent, a full cross-section of travel writing in early modern England. I have picked them for their pedagogical utility—in particular, for their length (short), their thematic coherence (they often refer to one another), and their availability in inexpensive editions. What follows is not a theoretical discussion but a practicum for incorporating early modern prose fiction into early modern survey courses. Second, following my university's mandate that we strive to "globalize" our course offerings, these texts are not completely restricted to those written in English for English audiences. Rather, they reflect the reception and use of New World themes across time, genres, and national boundaries. Third, I deliberately mix fictional and nonfictional texts in my courses, since part of the point in teaching this section is to demonstrate just how porous the boundary separating fact from fancy can be in early modern travel writing.

There are several advantages to this approach. First, it significantly broadens the scope of the student's understanding of travel literature. For the most part, students think of travel in terms of self-exploration or self-understanding. As T. S. Eliot puts it at the end of "Little Gidding": "We shall not cease from exploration / And the end of all our exploring / Shall be to arrive where we started / And know the place for the first time" (lines 239–42). While there is clearly some (poetic) truth here, the texts I have gathered collectively demonstrate how early modern travel literature could be harnessed for a wide variety of purposes, for example, social criticism, a probe of the distinctions between fact and fiction, exploration of the potential and limits of science and of the origins of political organizations, and so forth. Much more than self-knowledge is at stake. Travel literature, in other words, challenges Eliot's understanding of travel as a vehicle for self-knowledge by illustrating that travel does not necessarily lead to knowing where you started from for the first time but, rather, to realizing that you do not know at all the place you ended up.

I begin with photocopies of Christopher Columbus's famous, widely translated letter to Luis de Santangel describing his first voyage and excerpts from Amerigo Vespucci's letters to Lorenzo de'Medici and Piero Soderini (originally published in *Mundus Novus* [1494] and the *Letters* [1505]). Students realize, of course, that Columbus's narrative is a record of conquest, that he writes to inform Europe that he has "taken possession" of the islands "for their highnesses" (2). Discovery, in other words, is another form of domination, and students are quick to hold Columbus in contempt as the originator of Western imperialism. While there is some merit to this view, I try to move the class away from denunciation to analysis. How does Columbus confront the radical otherness of this new, entirely unknown culture? In particular, we discuss the strategies by which Columbus seeks to underscore the truth of his narrative, how he distinguishes his account from other travelers' tales ("In these islands I have so far found no human monstrosities, as many expected" [14]) through the emphasis on first-person witnessing of events: "although men have talked or have written of these lands, all was conjectural, without suggestion of ocular evidence" (18). Yet at the same time, Columbus engages in exactly what he criticizes. There remain, Columbus writes, "two provinces to which I have not gone. One of these provinces they call 'Avan,' and there the people are born with tails" (12). Right from the start, fact and fiction are deeply intertwined in New World narratives, and one can perhaps see in Columbus's reaching for a familiar legend to describe a place he has not seen an attempt to defuse the incommensurability of the New World.

I then ask students how Vespucci's texts rely on and extend Columbus's letter. Students note how Vespucci uses much the same rhetoric as Columbus (e.g., the emphasis on "wonder" and "marvel"), but we also note how Vespucci more openly interprets the New World in terms of the Old. For example, the islands "are so beautiful and fragrant that we thought perhaps we had entered the Earthly Paradise" (5), and "their life is rather more Epicurean than Stoic or Academic because as I state, they hold no private property" (42). Like Columbus, Vespucci uses various strategies to differentiate his letters from fictional narratives. The proliferation of navigational details (e.g., "from Lisbon, our point of departure, 39 degrees from the equator, we sailed fifty degrees beyond the equator . . ." [54]) increases the verisimilitude and the narrator's credibility, as does his appeal to corroborating accounts ("I can cite witnesses to this" [43]) and firsthand knowledge of what he writes about. Those "philosophers" who claim that "one cannot live within the Torrid Zone because of its great heat are confuted," because Vespucci himself has seen that "so many people live within it that they outnumber those outside it . . . which is most certain proof that practice is of greater worth than theory" (8). Yet like Columbus, Vespucci also mixes fact with fantasy, in particular, sexual fantasy:

> They have another custom that is appalling and passes belief. Their women, being very lustful, make their husbands' members swell to such thickness that they look ugly and misshapen; this they accomplish with a certain device they have and by bites from certain poisonous animals. Because of this, many men lose their members, which rot through neglect, and they are left eunuchs. (49)

As Louis Montrose notes, Vespucci takes a "crude and anxious misogynistic fantasy" and projects it onto the New World (181), the fiction mixing uneasily with the technical details assuring the reader of the narrative's fidelity to truth.

After we have established a list of commonalities, of tropes, concerning the descriptions of the New World, we move to Thomas More's *Utopia* in Robinson's 1556 English translation, "the first piece of travel literature produced in England's Age of Discovery," as Mary Campbell notes (212). I begin by drawing the class's attention to the overt allusion to Vespucci ("[Hythlodaeus] joined himself in company with Amerigo Vespucci, and in the three last voyages of those four that be now in print, and abroad in every man's hands" [12]), and I then direct class discussion toward why More so clearly wants his reader to have Vespucci in mind as he or she reads *Utopia*. How does *Utopia* draw on and possibly offer a critique of the presentation of the New World in Vespucci's letters as well as the Columbus letter? Students are quick to point out that More consciously blurs the distinctions between fact and fiction, whereas Vespucci and Columbus are probably unconscious about what they are doing, and this insight creates the ground for the next question: How do the Utopians differ from the natives in Vespucci? How does the relation between the Old and New World change in More's text? Does More continue the radical assumption of European superiority that Stephen Greenblatt considers a constituent element of early modern travel literature (*Marvelous Possessions* 9)? Or do the "wise and godly ordinances of the Utopians" put into question the assumption that the New World is without civilization (More 44)? that its inhabitants are fit only for conversion and conquest? While Columbus regarded the natives as little more than credulous, timid children who consider him as a celestial visitor (his interpreters "went running from house to house and to the neighbouring towns, with loud cries of, 'Come! Come to see the people from Heaven!'" [10]), More imagines the possibility of a New World civilization that not only equals Europe but in many ways surpasses it (Herman 112).

The pedagogical advantage of moving directly from *Utopia* to *The New Atlantis* is that students can immediately see Francis Bacon actively engaging More's text and, by extension, those by Vespucci and Columbus. Like More, Bacon consistently plays with the line separating fact from fiction. When in *The New Atlantis* Joabin says, "I have read in a book of one of your men, of a Feigned Commonwealth, where the married couple are permitted, before they contract, to see one another naked" (174), the class is presented with a fictional character citing a real book about a fictional place that the character assumes is real. Trying to untangle the real from the unreal can be dizzying, as the boundary between fact and fiction keeps shifting. Or, more accurately, the very concept of a boundary between the two becomes impossible to maintain. Furthermore, the intertextuality invites the class to spend some minutes comparing and contrasting the two fictional islands in the New World. Having just read *Utopia*, students might remember that Hythlodaeus also does not think much of the practice Joabin cites ("in choosing wives and husbands they observe earnestly and straitly a custom which seemed to us very fond and foolish" [*Utopia* 90]), and so Bacon's Bensalem corrects More's fictional island. Yet the correction is only partial, for the Bensalemites adjust rather than reject Utopian customs:

> [T]hey have a more civil way [of discovering bodily defects]; for they
> have near every town a couple of pools . . . where it is permitted to one
> of the friends of the man, and another of the friends of the woman,
> to see them severally bathe naked. (174–75)

Does Bacon invite us to view the Bensalemites skeptically, just as More invites us to view the Utopians skeptically?

We then move to examining how Bacon, like More, uses his fiction to question European assumptions about the New World by inverting Columbus and Vespucci. Whereas the mariners in the earlier texts proclaim their excellent seamanship, Bacon's are hardly masters and commanders of the ocean ("we gave ourselves for lost men, and prepared for death" [152]). Whereas Columbus and Vespucci take charge immediately and happily let the natives consider them divine, in Bacon's short fiction the natives of Bensalem take charge, and the sailors consider the Bensalemites almost divine. Along the same lines, whereas Bacon, Vespucci, and More bring Christianity to the natives, the Bensalemites not only are already Christians but have received the upgraded version of Christianity direct from God (160).

Finally, we see in Bacon's *New Atlantis* an inversion of the most important feature of traditional New World narratives. At this point I introduce, through class handouts, excerpts from Walter Raleigh's *The Discovery of Guiana* to establish how the English conceived of exploration as a vehicle for exploitation.[2] For example, in the dedicatory epistle, Raleigh writes:

> The country hath more quantity of gold, by manifold, than the best
> parts of the Indies or Peru; all or most of the kings of the borders are
> already become her majesty's vassals, and seem to desire nothing more
> than her majesty's protection, and the return of the English nation.
> (381–82)

The point is not to improve the welfare of the Guianians but to increase English "riches and glory" (382). Yet in Bacon's New Atlantis, the natives do the colonizing, and Europe is colonized. Bacon thus reverses the subject positions in Columbus, Vespucci, Raleigh, and others, while continuing More's project of offering a critique of the European incursion into the New World. Whereas Europe uses the New World as a source for gold (something More criticizes in *Utopia*), the Bensalemites send out spies to mine Europe for knowledge:

> [E]very twelve years there should be set forth out of this kingdom two ships . . . whose errand was only to give us knowledge of the affairs and state of those countries to which they were designed, and especially of the sciences, arts, manufactures, and inventions of all the world; and withal to bring unto us book, instruments, and patterns in every kind. (167–68)

Bacon situates his fiction in the context of New World narratives not only to create a forum for his new view of knowledge (whose purpose is not moral improvement but "the effecting of all things possible" [177]) but also to denounce the European obsession with wealth as well as European imperialism.

Next up is Bishop Francis Godwin's fascinating yet rarely taught *The Man in the Moon*, possibly the first piece of science fiction.[3] Like the other authors we have looked at, Godwin consciously situates his book in the tradition of New World travel narratives. When the author of the introductory epistle, for example, declares "thou hast here a new discovery of a new world" and celebrates "our discovering age" (71), he echoes the 1505 translation of Vespucci's letters, which circulated under the title *Novus Mundi*, and he hopes the present text "may find little better entertainment in thy opinion than that of Columbus" (71). Godwin also mimics Columbus's and Vespucci's astonishment at what they find. The narrator, Domingo Gonzales, exclaims at the sight of a lunar building that "for beauty and hugeness as all our world cannot show any near comparable to it" (96), and the homogeneity of lunar language is "a marvelous thing to consider" (102). And just as the two earlier explorers are regularly struck by how everything in the New World is "totally different" (Vespucci 51), so does Gonzalez find a radical dissimilarity between terrestrial and extraterrestrial flora and fauna: "So their herbs, beasts, and birds, although to compare them with ours I know not well how, because I found not anything there, any species either of beast or bird that resembled ours anything at all" (94).

Moreover, just as Bacon writes *The New Atlantis* with More's *Utopia* in mind, so does Godwin write *The Man in the Moon* with Bacon in mind. Like his predecessor, the New World is now a stage for displaying the new knowledge, as it were. Marooned on an island, the narrator forms a hypothesis: that he "might enable a man to fly" (80) through harnessing of birds, and he then employs the scientific method to prove his theory: "In this cogitation having much laboured my wits and made some trial, I found by experience" the precise technique that would work (80). He uses his flight to the moon not only to test the wisdom of the past against reality but also to prove the correctness of the avant-garde work of Galileo:

> I found by this experience that which no philosopher ever dreamed of, to wit, that those things which we call heavy do not sink toward to the centre of the earth as their natural place, but as drawn by a secret property of the globe. (87)

Godwin also picks up on the ironic withholding of information that is so much a part of Bacon's *New Atlantis*. For example, before revealing how the Bensalemites know so much about the world while the world knows nothing of them, the governor makes clear that he will not reveal all: "I shall say to you I must reserve some particulars, which it is not lawful for me to reveal" (162). Godwin's narrator does the same. After promising "notice of a new world, of many most rare and incredible secrets of nature" (74), Gonzalez immediately states that he will tell only those secrets that do not threaten Catholic orthodoxy or the stability of Spain:

> But I must be advised how I be over-liberal in publishing these wonderful mysteries, till the sages of our state have considered how far the use of these things may stand with the policy and good government of our country, as also with the Father of the Church, how the publication of them may not prove prejudicial to the affairs of the Catholic faith and religion. . . ." (75)

This commonality, however, points to the fundamental difference between Godwin and his predecessors, such as Bacon. In *The New Atlantis*, the withholding of information suggests once more the superiority of Bensalem to Europe. But in Godwin, it is tied to his evident distrust of travel, even as he uses travel to demonstrate the superiority of the new philosophy. It is not an accident that his narrator is a Spanish dwarf who subordinates his tale to the interests of Spain and Catholicism and who served with the "Duke of Alva" in the Netherlands, a man, as the text's editor writes, "known for his ruthless and efficient repression of the Protestants" (115n4). Gonzalez, in other words, is someone who would repulse Godwin's English Protestant readership. What does this say, I ask the class, about travel, about science, and about the New World?

I follow Godwin's text with Henry Neville's bizarre yet enjoyable *The Isle of Pines* (1668), in which a servant, George Pines, finds himself shipwrecked on an island with four women; they soon populate the island with their copious offspring (1,789 children proceeded "from his loins" [201]). Like all the other authors, Neville emphasizes the mediated nature of travel narratives: the text of *The Isle of Pines* originates in a letter recounting the past that is introduced to the reader in a letter contained within another letter. Thus the fiction's textual history demonstrates yet again the porous boundaries between fact and fancy in this period. *The Isle of Pines* was immediately popular both in England and on the Continent, where it was translated into Dutch, French, Italian, German, and Danish. These translations were in turn republished in the eighteenth century in anthologies of (ostensibly) true travel and discovery narratives (Maltzahn).

Yet unlike the narratives of Columbus, Vespucci, More, Bacon, and Godwin, *The Isle of Pines* records the meeting not between Europe and a fundamentally alien culture but between a European and an originally European society that must re-create itself, a topic that must have been of considerable interest to Neville, who entered Parliament after the execution of Charles I, fell out with Oliver Cromwell, and whose translation of Niccolò Machiavelli appeared in 1675. In the world *Isle of Pines* depicts, the sexual idyll immediately following the shipwreck yields, in the process of time, to the pressure of an ever-increasing population. Discovering that "in multitudes disorders will grow, the stronger seeking to oppress the weaker" (201), the patriarch George Pines "did set forth . . . laws to be observed" (202) by his descendants, and these laws, interestingly enough, concern religion ("whosoever should blaspheme or talk irrelevantly of the name of God should be put to death" [202]), sexual conduct (rape earns burning to death), the sanctity of private property, and exempting the ruler from criticism (those defaming the governor shall be whipped for the first offense, "exploded from the society" for the second [203]). Given that Neville himself never shied away from criticizing those in power (he was "so obnoxious to Cromwell as to be banished from London in 1654" [qtd. in Maltzahn], and in the Restoration "he maintained his reputation as a republican" [Maltzahn]), it seems unlikely that he could have seriously endorsed this rule. Instead, it seems that Neville is doing here what

Greenblatt suggests Thomas Harriot does in *A Briefe and True Report of the New Found Land of Virginia*: in other words, testing the hypothesis that religion (and civil society in general) "was invented to keep men in awe" (*Shakespearean Negotiations* 26).

I bring this unit to a conclusion with Aphra Behn's *Oroonoko*. By the 1680s, of course, the New World is no longer so new, yet Behn is still very much drawing on the rhetoric first established by Columbus and Vespucci, especially the presence of "wonder" and the deliberate, highly conscious deconstruction of the line separating fact and fiction. But we also see how Behn, like More, uses her New World setting as a vehicle for critcizing the Old World (e.g., Oroonoko's assertion that "there was no Faith in the White Men, or the Gods they Ador'd" [56]) and how Behn adds a new element by using the New World to reflect on the English Revolution, as the book concludes with Caesar's dismemberment being used to terrify the island's slaves "with frightful Spectacles of a mangl'd King" (65), language that in 1685 was sure to summon the image of another mangled king: Charles I.

By this point, two goals have been accomplished (I hope). The first is that students find early modern prose approachable and relatively easy to read. The second is that students come away with a more sophisticated understanding of how the New World functioned in early modern narratives. They should see that from the start, early modern narratives about the New World explored the porous and labile boundary separating fact from fiction, and they should have a keen awareness of how the meaning of the New World is equally far from stable or fixed. But one matter should be clear: no matter who the author, early modern writers thought about the New World in a wide variety of ways, and from the start they were far from uncritical of the meeting between the Old and New Worlds.

Notes

1. I have, however, commandeered the course English Prose Fiction from Its Beginnings by arguing that prose from the early Tudor period constitutes English prose fiction's real beginnings, not Defoe.

2. On the complex relations between narrative and description on Raleigh's text, see Campbell 211–54.

3. I cite Butler's edition. Since I completed this essay, another classroom edition of this text, by William Poole, has been published.

Works Cited

Bacon, Francis. *The New Atlantis*. Bruce 149–86.
Behn, Aphra. *Oroonoko*. Ed. Joanna Lipking. New York: Norton, 1997. Print.

Bruce, Susan, ed. *Three Early Modern Utopias:* Utopia, New Atlantis, The Isle of Pines. Oxford: Oxford UP, 1999. Print. Oxford World's Classics.

Campbell, Mary. *The Witness and the Other World: Exotic European Travel Writing, 400–1600.* Ithaca: Cornell UP, 1988. Print.

Columbus, Christopher. *The Four Voyages of Columbus: A History in Eight Documents, Including Five by Christopher Columbus, in the Original Spanish, with English Translations.* Ed. Cecil Jane. New York: Dover, 1988. Print.

Eliot, T. S. *Four Quartets.* 1959. London: Faber, 1972. Print.

Godwin, Francis. *The Man in the Moon.* Ed. John Anthony Butler. Ottawa: Dovehouse, 1995. Print.

———. *The Man In the Moon.* Ed. William Poole. Peterborough: Broadview, 2009. Print.

Greenblatt, Stephen. *Marvelous Possessions: The Wonder of the New World.* Chicago: U of Chicago P, 1991. Print.

———, ed. *New World Encounters.* Berkeley: U of California P, 1993. Print.

———. *Shakespearean Negotiations: The Circulation of Social Energy in Renaissance England.* Berkeley: U of California P, 1988. Print.

Herman, Peter C. "Who's That in the Mirror?: Thomas More's Utopia and the Problematic of the New World." *Opening the Borders: Inclusivity and Early Modern Studies, Essays in Honor of James V. Mirollo.* Ed. Herman. Newark: U of Delaware P, 1999. 109–32. Print.

Maltzahn, Nicholas von. "Neville, Henry (1620–1694)." *Oxford Dictionary of National Biography.* Oxford UP, 2004–09. Web. 1 Oct. 2004.

Montrose, Louis. "The Work of Gender in the Discourse of Discovery." Greenblatt, *New World Encounters* 177–217.

More, Thomas. *Utopia.* Bruce 1–148.

Neville, Henry. *The Isle of Pines.* Bruce 187–212.

Pagden, Anthony. "Ius et Factum: Text and Experience in the Writings of Bartolomé de Las Casas." Greenblatt, *New World Encounters* 85–100.

Raleigh, Walter. *The Discovery of Guiana.* 1596. *The Works of Sir Walter Ralegh.* 1829. Vol. 8. New York: Franklin, 1964. 391–478. Print.

Vespucci, Amerigo. *Letters from a New World: Amerigo Vespucci's Discovery of America.* Ed. Luciano Formisano. Trans. David Jacobson. New York: Marsilio, 1992. Print.

Susannah Brietz Monta

Teaching with Passions; or, Bringing Martyrologies into the Classroom

I teach martyrologies as a gateway into a culture suffused with religion, a culture that is seemingly very different from ours but that has, as the label "early modern" indicates, concerns that resonate in striking, sometimes jarring ways with our own. While we typically refer to our period of study as "early modern" or perhaps the "English Renaissance," the fact that it is also the "Reformation era" seldom appears in literary-critical nomenclature. The Reformation (I use the term to encompass both the Protestant and Catholic varieties) should play at least as vital a role in early modern literature courses as, say, the French Revolution in courses on Romanticism. But given the Reformation's complexity and ongoing controversies over its cultural impact, teaching the Reformation in sixteenth- and seventeenth-century literature courses is an admittedly daunting task. Martyrologies can make that task manageable. They are short, engaging, and (since their generic family tree includes familiar forms such as biography and autobiography) relatively accessible. They contain in miniature the most important concerns of the Reformation era, presented with excruciating clarity.

In early modern England there were plenty of poor souls on whose life narratives martyrologists could hone their skills. During the sixteenth and seventeenth centuries, England saw the most intense religious persecutions in its history. Under Henry VIII, both reformers and traditionalists suffered; Mary I's heresy proceedings resulted in at least 285 executions (Hansford-Miller; Nuttall); and Catholics in the late sixteenth and seventeenth centuries endured protracted persecution. Many texts were written to commemorate those who died as martyrs for their faith(s). These works proved extremely popular. John Foxe's *Actes and Monuments*, commonly known as the *Book of Martyrs*, went through nine editions between 1563 and 1684, six of those by 1610; over fifty works concerning the persecution of English Catholics were printed between 1566 and 1660.

American students reading these texts must first understand that in early modern England people could be prosecuted for nonconformist religious belief and/or practice and that for the most part church and state collaborated in enforcement efforts. Under Mary Tudor's renewed medieval heresy legislation, ecclesiastical and state authorities worked together to bring Protestant dissenters to trial and execution. In later Protestant regimes, Catholic priests and recusant Catholics were tried by the state; the government insisted that these Catholics were prosecuted for treason, not religion. Yet the identities of recusant Catholic and of traitor became, in popular discourses as well as in law, tightly intertwined; Catholic martyrologists gleefully point this out when they argue that if religion were not at stake, offers of pardon would not be extended to those recusant Catholics who agreed to attend Church of England services.

Why did authorities select persecution as their weapon of choice? Why didn't martyrs simply compromise or capitulate? In martyrologies, the assumptions that both drove early modern religious persecutions and inspired martyrs to persist to the death are on display: religious truth is singular, and it is knowable; dissenters' dangerous opinions contaminate orthodoxy, so dissenters must not be tolerated; believers must be willing to confess to the death; heaven is real, and its rewards well worth earthly torments. Of course, early modern people did not uphold these assumptions unfailingly. The vast literature encouraging English Catholics to embrace suffering rather than the easier alternative of lukewarm conformity or so-called church-papistry suggests the contentiousness of the penultimate assumption within Catholic communities. But martyrologies' popularity and influence also indicate that the clarity martyrs offered through their refusal to compromise was attractive amid the Reformation era's traumatic fragmentation of Western Christianity. Indeed, martyrs' confessions and deaths were thought to indicate that martyrs' beliefs were not only sincerely held but also that those beliefs were true. When challenging representations of people they deemed pseudomartyrs, Reformation controversialists proclaimed, "non poena sed causa"—"the cause, not the death" makes the martyr. But this Augustinian refrain is uttered so often that one begins to suspect that its repetition was necessary because many people believed quite the opposite. The epistemic force of traditional hagiography—that the dying witness, brave, patient, and constant, provides confirmation of truth—was still firmly in place.

Martyrologies are valuable in the classroom in part because the struggles between martyrs and their interrogators lay bare the period's religious faultlines. These include, inter alia, struggles over the proper relation between the material and the supernatural; the number and nature of the sacraments; the proper structure of the church; the relative soteriological value of grace, faith, consent, and works; and the relation between religious speech and structures of gender and class. Martyrologies insist on drawing firm lines between saints and sinners; they function primarily to argue for and demarcate, not merely record, religious difference. Yet those statements of religious difference were shaped by a generic frame that was often cross-confessionally, and somewhat uncomfortably, shared (Monta, *Martyrdom*). Generally speaking, martyrologies owed a great deal to Christian tradition; martyrologists tended to read contemporary history as an extension or echo of earlier persecutions and of biblical narratives about Christ and the protomartyr Saint Stephen. Martyrological narratives may comprise an overview of the martyr's virtuous life; the event provoking the martyr's arrest; the martyr's interrogations and/or trial (during which the martyr is expected to articulate his or her beliefs without revealing an inordinate desire for death); and the drama of the execution scene, at which the martyr often confessed again his or her beliefs, when allowed, and witnessed through a good death to the verity of those beliefs. Divisions or distinctions between Protestant and Catholic martyrologies are not always easy to draw, since polemicists struggled precisely over who was the legitimate inheritor of true Christian tradition. For instance, John Foxe was not averse to using wonders and marvels in his stories of martyrs, while Catholic writers relied heavily on rhetorics of inwardness, personal conviction, and conscience to demonstrate their martyrs' sincerity and integrity. Still, asking students to attend to matters of convention, style, and argumentation—familiar tools in the English major's belt—helps them evoke the complicated religious issues literally at stake.

If the devil is in the details, so too are the riches of the Reformation. In my experience, students eagerly mine Anne Askew's *Examinations* for insights into the period. These texts are a manageable length and accessible through Elaine Beilin's exemplary edition. Askew's story was also edited for inclusion in Foxe's *Actes and Monuments*; the last three books from the four editions of the *Actes and Monuments* that were printed during Foxe's lifetime (in 1563, 1570, 1576, and 1583) are now available online in a variorum edition (*John Foxe's Book*). As Beilin's detailed introduction makes clear, Askew is condemned under the Act of Six Articles, which officially upheld the doctrine of transubstantiation. That is, she was executed by a religio-political regime that had officially broken from the Catholic Church in its ecclesiastical structure but not necessarily in every point of its legally encoded theology. That she died for denying a Catholic doctrine upheld by a king who had rejected papal authority cautions students against overly simplified views of early modern religion.

With a little intertextual unpacking, the subtleties of the debates over transubstantiation are available in Askew's first words and in the remarks on them by John Bale, who was Askew's first publisher and who interwove commentary throughout her text. In response to her interrogators' first question, "yf I ded not beleve that the sacrament hangynge over the aultre was the verye bodye of Christ reallye," Askew answers with another one: "wherfore S. Steven was stoned to death? And he sayd, he coulde not tell. Then I answered, that no more wolde I assoyle [answer] hys vayne questyon" (20).[1] Askew alludes to Acts 7, in which Stephen preaches a sermon against idolatry, condemning those who find God in "temples made with hands" (*New Testament*); consequently, he was stoned and became the church's protomartyr. Later, in Acts 17, the newly converted persecutor Saul/Paul reiterates Stephen's message. Askew implies that those who uphold transubstantiation are idolators and that her interrogators are not biblically literate. Answering indirectly, she seems neither overly eager for death nor fearful, since readers familiar with the biblical allusion would quickly see her answer's import. This conscientious but not reckless stance is very important, as Thomas More recognized when he insisted that martyrs must not die carelessly or unnecessarily (Dillon 24). Asking students to puzzle over Askew's question—"wherfore S. Steven was stoned to death?"—clarifies relevant doctrinal issues as well as the martyr-interrogator dynamic.

Because Askew manipulates gendered expectations with considerable skill, the double-edged uses of gender in Reformation polemic are on clear display. In the "First Examination," a frustrated interrogator asks Askew why she has "so fewe wordes." Askew answers, "God hath geven me the gyfte of knowlege, but not of utteraunce. And Salomon sayth, that a woman of fewe wordes, is a gyfte of God, Prover. 19" (51). Either her interrogators must deny that silence is a feminine virtue, or they must accept her reticence and cease their questioning. More problematic gendered dynamics are evident in the textual relationships between Askew and her male editors; the occasional disjunctions between Askew's words and her editors' are fruitful grounds for discussion and short writing assignments. Particularly useful are those passages concerning her torture on the rack. Askew tersely renders her pain:

> Then they sayd, there were of the counsell that ded mayntene me. And I sayd, no. Then they ded put me on the racke, bycause I confessed no ladyes nor gentyllwomen to be of my opynyon, and theron they kepte me a longe tyme. And bycause I laye styll and ded not crye, my lorde Chauncellour and mastre Ryche, toke peynes to racke me their owne handes, tyll I was nygh dead. (127)

Askew's sentence structure is simple; she uses only a few modifiers, and her matter-of-fact reporting suits her subsequent, astounding claim that after the racking she held her own in a two-hour theological debate. Bale's commentary does not elaborate on this claim; instead, he emphasizes the persecutors' wickedness. Her endurance becomes firm proof that Christ was with her:

> Ryght farre doth it passe the strength of a yonge, tendre, weake, and sycke woman (as she was at that tyme to your more confusyon) to abyde so vyolent handelynge, yea, or yet of the strongest man that lyveth. Thynke not therfor but that Christ hath suffered in her, and so myghtelye shewed hys power, that in her weakenesse he hath laughed your madde enterpryses to scorn. (129)

In vivid prose, Bale stresses her broken, tortured body and physical weakness. Similarly, as Foxe revises his version of her story, the notorious torture episode becomes the primary hook. Asking students to compare the prefaces with her account in Foxe's 1563 and 1570 editions makes this apparent, as do the additions to her story in the 1570 edition, which expand on the torture (Monta, "Inheritance").

In early modern martyrologies, the interplay between prose and visual rhetoric was crucially important. The details in woodcuts adorning early modern martyrologies can speak to contemporary students almost as well as, presumably, they spoke to their first elite and nonelite audiences. The title page to Askew's "First Examination" shows a decidedly feminine Askew (complete with erect nipples) wearing the garb of a Roman matron and holding the palm of a victorious martyr (as in Rev. 7.9). Her head is surrounded by a halo, and she holds a book prominently marked "Biblia" as she treads underfoot a dragon wearing the papal tiara. This woodcut reworks the iconography traditionally associated with Saint Margaret, usually shown trampling a dragon (Dillon 300–03). In the Askew woodcut students may read a number of polemical claims: the connection between persecuted Protestants and early church martyrs, the primacy of the word in defeating Catholic error, the association of the papacy with a beastly Antichrist, and the revision of traditional sainthood to suit sixteenth-century Protestant experience. The title page to Foxe's *Actes and Monuments* provides a similar teaching opportunity. Its parallel columns show opposing Protestant and Catholic forms of worship and sacrifice, offering visually the central arguments of the book. For instance, the opposition of Marian martyrs burning at the stake to tonsured figures celebrating the Mass proclaims the idolatry of the Mass and the proper focus of Protestant martyrs. The martyrs hold trumpets that point toward the top of the woodcut, where Christ is seated in judgment; they clearly praise and glorify the right figure. In contrast, the figures at Mass point their trumpets toward the elevated host in what Protestants considered an idolatrous attempt to repeat Christ's sacrifice and usurp the honor due to him.

Beyond the title page, Foxe's massive work may seem too daunting to tackle in an undergraduate class. But focused examination of a few passages is rewarding. As Foxe's work issued from the presses, English men and women continued to debate what exactly it meant to be Protestant. Recent scholarship has demonstrated that each edition of Foxe's work reflects the changing circumstances of Elizabethan religious politics (Betteridge; Freeman; Lander). The changes each edition makes in response to particular circumstances may be evoked from closely focused comparisons. The revision of Foxe's dedication to Queen Elizabeth I between 1563 and 1570, for instance, challenges traditional views about Foxe's adulation for Gloriana, as Thomas S. Freeman has recently argued; in the classroom, a careful discussion of this revision uncovers the conflicted political valences of martyrology as well as the tricky implication of martyrology in Elizabethan ecclesiastical politics. If either *Early English*

Books Online (*EEBO*) or the *Short-Title Catalogue* (*STC*) microfilms are available, students can easily compare the changes Foxe made to the dedication; the variorum edition of *Actes and Monuments* also provides this material.

In 1563 Foxe's dedication famously compares Queen Elizabeth with the Emperor Constantine, rejoicing that her accession "dispatched" the Marian persecution and encouraging her to imitate Constantine's strong support of the true Christian church:

> [C]onsidering likewyse howe beneficiall, howe carefull, howe bounte-full hee was to the Churche of the Lorde: although the lyke Dona-tions have not yet appeared in giftes geven by youre grace unto the Churche, yet the same care and tendernesse of harte in youre Maiestie hathe not been lackinge. (Bii)[2]

As Freeman has recently argued, however, Foxe's providentialism is a double-edged sword, for if providence has elevated Elizabeth, then she owes a profound debt: she must continue in the godly path for which she has supposedly been rewarded. By 1570, Protestants eager for further reform had begun to lose faith that their Deborah would ever rid the English church of all popish remnants. In the 1563 edition, an elaborate "C" begins the word "Constantine" and inaugurates the dedication's extended comparison; in the 1570 edition, the elaborate "C" forms instead the first letter of "Christ." As the text of the 1570 dedication worries over post-1563 Catholic attacks on Foxe's work, it also subtly demotes Elizabeth. The preamble to the dedication no longer terms her "defendour of the faith, and supreme governour of the saide Realme of Englande and Irelande, next under the Lorde, as well in causes ecclesiasticall, as also to the temporall state appertaining," as in 1563, but instead calls her "defendour of Christes Fayth and Gospel, and principall governour both of the Realme and also over the sayd Church of England and Ireland, under Christ the supreme head of the same." Also in the 1570 text, Christ's office alone merits the adjective "supreme," and the faith that English monarchs since Henry VIII had supposedly defended is first and foremost "Christes." Although Foxe targets Catholic naysayers throughout the dedication, he has another agenda as well; he wishes fervently that his queen might "*speedely* . . . furnish all quarters and countreyes of this your Realme with the voyce of Christes Gospell, and faithfull preachyng of his word"—the wish of a man frustrated that reform has, apparently, stalled (iiv [1570 ed.]; my emphasis). As the changes to this dedication imply, the magisterial impulse behind the Elizabethan dissemination of Foxe's work—as in the Privy Council letter calling the book "a work of very great importance and necessary knowledge both touching religion and other good offices, the matter whereof being very profitable to bring her Majesty's subjects to good opinion, understanding and dear liking of the present government" (qtd. in Freeman 46)—is pointedly in tension with what Richard Helgerson has called martyrdom's "oppositional identity" (268), which contains the potential to bolster opposition to established religion. Other fruitful passages for comparison are the book's concluding sections as well as specific accounts that underwent significant changes, such as those of George Marsh, Thomas Haukes, and Perotine Massey, all available online (Foxe [variorum ed.]). Students can also choose a martyr to follow through the various editions.

Scholars have increasingly called attention to the distortions effected by the exclusion of Catholic writers from English literary history. Placing Catholic martyrologists alongside Foxe, Askew, and Bale provides students with a cross-confessional view of one of the period's most popular prose genres. Catholic martyrologists were extremely prolific, stung into productivity by Foxe's work as well as by the protracted persecutions Catholics suffered. Though the fullest response to Foxe was the Latin work *Concertatio Ecclesiae Catholicae in Anglia*, the *Concertatio* incorporates translations of English language material available through *EEBO* and *STC* microfilms. Robert Miola's new *Early Modern Catholicism: An Anthology of Primary Sources* provides materials on prominent martyrs such as Thomas More and Margaret Clitherow, the first woman to suffer for Catholicism under Elizabeth I. For those interested in juxtaposing Protestant and Catholic visual rhetorics, illustrations from Latin works in Miola's book are invaluable. Because the material on Catholic martyrs is vast and varied, it is both practical and rewarding to focus on the tales of a few.

Edmund Campion, the most prominent of the English Catholic martyrs, makes a good subject for study because the controversy his death provoked was so extensive (see, e.g., Pilarz; McCoog). This controversial literature includes the priest Thomas Alfield's *A True Report . . .* and Anthony Munday's *A Discoverie of Edmund Campion, and His Confederates, Their Most Horrible and Traiterous Practises. . . .* What is at issue between these competing accounts is not necessarily or only what Campion did or said (Gregory 19–20); instead, Alfield and Munday struggle to fix the

intention behind Campion's deeds and statements, and the interpreta-
tional framework into which his final moments best fit. Munday describes
Campion's arrival at the notorious Tyburn:

> First he began with a phrase or two in Lattin, when soone after hee
> fell into Englishe as thus. I am heere brought as a Spectacle, before
> the face of God, of Angelles and of men, satisfying my selfe to dye, as
> becommeth a true Christian and Catholique man. (B4r)

Alfield's version slightly differs:

> [A]fter some small pawse in the carte, with grave countenance and
> sweete voyce stoutly spake as followeth. Spectaculum facti sumus
> Deo, Angeli, & hominibus saying, These are the wordes of S. Paule,
> Englished thus: We are made a spectacle, or a sight unto God, unto
> his Angels, and unto men: verified this day in me, who am here a spec-
> tacle unto my lorde god, a spectacle unto his angels, & unto you men.
> (B6v–C1r)

Alfield records that Campion was interrupted at this point (Munday does
not indicate any interruption). In his version, Munday dismisses Campion's "phrase or two in Lattin," reporting not the Vulgate text but the
English translation Campion "fell" into. Alfield cites the verse first in
Latin and includes a sidenote identifying it as Corinthians 4. 1, a verse
that was a touchstone for Christian martyrdom from at least Origen forward; Alfield implies that Campion was interrupted because to continue
in this vein would be to establish himself firmly in that tradition.

Both authors record that Campion denied committing treason, though
in significantly different ways. Munday writes, "Many indirect aunsweres
he made, as when he was mooved to aske the Queene forgivenesse, and when
the Preacher requested him to shewe some signe of a penitent sinner, when
shortlie he replyed: you and I, we are not of one Religion" (C3r–C3v). Instead of a haughty, evasive convict who speaks "shortlie" and asks for royal
forgiveness only when prodded to do so, Alfield presents a humble, gentle
martyr:

> [P]reparing himself to drinke his last draght of Christ his cup, was in-
> terrupted in his prayer by a minister, willing him to saye, Christ have
> mercy upon me, or suche like prayer with him: unto whom he looking
> backe with milde countenance, humbly saide: You and I are not one in
> religion, wherfore I pray you content your selfe, I barre none of prayer,

only I desire them of the houshold of faith to pray with me . . . he was willed to ask the queene forgevenes, and to praye for her. He meekely answered: wherein have I offended her? In this I am innocent, this is my laste speache, in this geve me credite, I have and do pray for her. (C2r–C2v)

The central point of controversy between the Jesuit's supporters and detractors is clear: Munday's Campion gives unspecified "indirect answers," while Alfield's Campion states meekly but forthrightly that he was innocent and that he prays for the queen. Alfield's allusion to Christ's prayer at Gethsemane links Campion to Christian tradition, inverting the state's attempt to stage a traitor's execution by invoking an image of another supposed criminal whom Christian tradition decidedly redeemed. Neither Munday nor Alfield can lie wildly; the difference in their reportage—indeed, the difference in early modern polemic over true and pseudomartyrs as a whole—is in nuance: in the contexts evoked or suppressed, in the inferences drawn about inward states not readily or easily available in discourse. A similar comparison could be undertaken with the Catholic Adam Blackwood's and the Protestant Robert Wyngfield's accounts of the death of Mary, Queen of Scots, perhaps juxtaposed with Richard Verstegan's illustration of her execution.

One of the most prominent English Catholic martyrs was also one of sixteenth-century England's best prose stylists. As Robert Southwell's work makes clear, the English Catholic community was divided about how to weather persecution. That community is best understood as a continuum, ranging from those sympathetic toward Catholicism to so-called church papists to staunch recusants. Southwell's mission was to encourage what he saw as firm loyalty to the only true church; conformity to the Church of England was for him a flirtation with hell. In *Epistle of Comfort*, Southwell employs his considerable skills to lament the spiritual state of church papists:

Alas poore wretches full litle understand they their owne miserie, carying under the names of Christians, the hartes of Pagans, preferringe pleasure & the future paynes due unto it, before the Crosse of Christ, and the eternall felicitie ensuing after it. (13v–14r)

Southwell uses alliteration and careful parallelism to link "hartes of Pagans" and "pleasure" with "future paynes," as well as "Crosse" with "Christ." His stylistic choices underscore the conceptual argument that a true Christian takes up the cross of suffering in imitation of his or her master:

> We are no better then our maister, who suffered farr more, nor wiser then god himselfe who judged and embraced the distresses of the worlde, as fittest for the passengers therof. Finally we are Christians, whose captayne is a crucifixe, whose stendard the Crosse, whose armoure patience, whose battayle persecution, whose victorye death, whose triumph martyrdome. (41r)

As Southwell enunciates the assumptions undergirding martyrs' sacrifices, he inverts common disparagements of Jesuits as a militant papist vanguard. The reconstitution of militarism in service of passive suffering braces Catholics for the storm firm recusancy could provoke.

In what is perhaps his most poignant and carefully crafted prose piece, the "Epistle unto His Father," Southwell personalizes the arguments in the *Epistle of Comfort* as he attempts to persuade his father to return unambiguously to the Catholic Church. This brief epistle highlights the wrenching personal dimensions of the choices early modern religious minorities faced. Justifying his letter, Southwell asks:

> If in beholding a mortal enemy wrung and tortured with deadly pangs, the toughest heart softeneth with some sorrow, if the most frozen and fierce mind cannot but thaw and melt with pity even when it seeth the worst miscreant suffer his deserved torments, how much less can the heart of a child consider those that bred him into this world to be in the fall to far more bitter extremities and not bleed with grief of their uncomfortable case? (4–5)

Southwell's elaborate if-then structure encodes both the rationale for his writing—a child's natural duty—and his argument: that a gradual descent or "fall" to hellish "bitter extremities" is the trade-off for avoiding earthly pain through craven conformity. The shadow of racked Catholics haunts the first phrase, as does, implicitly, the lack of pity shown by authorities who declared them "mortal enemies" (for Southwell, of course, Catholics most definitely did *not* deserve their torments). These "frozen and fierce" minds who should melt even at the sufferings of miscreants contrast with the Catholic priest's natural and warm filial duty, a duty literally, here, of blood ("bleed with grief"). Southwell's lengthy question skillfully turns its imagined torments from those that are external and judicially imposed (in the opening two phrases) to those that are eternal and to be avoided even at the price of such sufferings hinted at in the earlier portion of the sentence. Southwell's carefully wrought prose encodes the struggle within Catholic families over the degree to which one should conform or uphold strict recusancy, as well as the ways in which even supposedly natural relationships and duties could be conscripted into the era's unforgiving confessional struggles.

A unit on the literature of persecution could range more widely yet, including selections from nonconformist writers such as the Elizabethan separatist Henry Barrow and the Leveller John Lilburne, both skilled manipulators of Foxean tropes; the seventeenth-century best seller *Eikon Basilike* and John Milton's *Eikonoklastes*; and perhaps the early American controversy between Roger Williams (*The Bloudy Tenent, of Persecution, for Cause of Conscience*) and John Cotton (*The Bloudy Tenent, Washed, and Made White in the Bloud of the Lambe*) over whether persecution was an acceptable, Christian, or even effective practice. The Williams-Cotton debate points toward the result of the Reformation most immediately relevant to American students: the exportation of particular strands of English Protestantism to the United States (MacCullough xx). While the relation between church and state in martyrological literature is fundamentally different from that espoused in the constitutions of many modern Western states, it is not so different from that in modern theocracies, and, of course, questions about appropriate boundaries between church and state (to use contemporary parlance) are very much alive in modern American political culture. One of the best reasons for studying the literary products of earlier cultures is that doing so throws our own culture's peculiarities and preoccupations into relief. Martyrologies focus, personalize, and make manageable complex Reformation religio-political struggles, while also casting a wavering light on our own.

Notes

1. Literally *assoyle* means "absolve" or "discharge."
2. Foxe here refers to the supposed Donation of Constantine, a forged document in which Constantine was said to transfer authority over Rome and the Western empire to the pope. Foxe did not give the document any credence.

Works Cited

Alfield, Thomas. *A True Reporte of the Death & Martyrdome of M. Campion Jesuite and Prieste, & M. Sherwin, & M. Brian Priests.* London, 1582. Print.

Askew, Anne. *The Examinations of Anne Askew.* Ed. Elaine Beilin. Oxford: Oxford UP, 1996. Print.

Betteridge, Thomas. *Tudor Histories of the English Reformations, 1530–83.* Aldershot: Ashgate, 1999. Print.

Blackwood, Adam. *The History of Mary, Queen of Scots, a Fragment*. Ed. and trans. Alexander Macdonald. Edinburgh: Maitland Club 31, 1834. Print. Trans. of *Martyre de la royne d'Escosse*. Paris, 1587.

Cotton, John. *The Bloudy Tenent, Washed, and Made White in the Bloud of the Lambe*. London, 1647. Print.

Dillon, Anne. *The Construction of Martyrdom in the English Catholic Community, 1535–1603*. Aldershot: Ashgate, 2002. Print.

Foxe, John. *Actes and Monuments*. London, 1563. Print.

———. *Actes and Monuments*. London, 1570. Print.

———. *John Foxe's Book of Martyrs Variorum Edition Online*. Humanities Research Inst., Univ. of Sheffield. 2006. Web. 28 Apr. 2009.

Freeman, Thomas S. "Providence and Prescription: The Account of Elizabeth in Foxe's *Book of Martyrs*." *The Myth of Elizabeth*. Ed. Susan Doran and Freeman. New York: Palgrave, 2003. 27–55. Print.

Gregory, Brad. *Salvation at Stake: Christian Martyrdom in Early Modern Europe*. Cambridge: Harvard UP, 1999. Print.

Hansford-Miller, F. H. *The 282 Protestant Martyrs of England and Wales, 1555–1558*. London: Hansford-Miller, 1970. Print.

Helgerson, Richard. *Forms of Nationhood: The Elizabethan Writing of England*. Chicago: U of Chicago P, 1992. Print.

Lander, Jesse M. "'Foxe's' *Books of Martyrs*: Printing and Popularizing the *Actes and Monuments*." *Religion and Culture in Renaissance England*. Ed. Claire McEachern and Debora Shuger. Cambridge: Cambridge UP, 1997. 69–92. Print.

MacCullough, Diarmaid. *The Reformation: A History*. New York: Viking, 2003. Print.

McCoog, Thomas M., ed. *The Reckoned Expense: Edmund Campion and the Early English Jesuits*. Rochester: Boydell, 1996. Print.

Miola, Robert, ed. *Early Modern Catholicism: An Anthology of Primary Sources*. Oxford: Oxford UP, 2007. Print.

Monta, Susannah Brietz. "The Inheritance of Anne Askew, Protestant Martyr." *Archiv für Reformationsgeschichte* 94 (2003): 134–60. Print.

———. *Martyrdom and Literature in Early Modern England*. Cambridge: Cambridge UP, 2005. Print.

Munday, Anthony. *A Discoverie of Edmund Campion, and His Confederates, Their Most Horrible and Traiterous Practises, against Her Majesties Most Royall Person, and the Realme*. London, 1582. Print.

The New Testament. Trans. William Tyndale. Antwerp, 1534. Print.

Nuttall, Geoffrey P. "The English Martyrs, 1535–1680: A Statistical Review." *Journal of Ecclesiastical History* 22 (1971): 191–97. Print.

Pilarz, Scott. "'Campion Dead Bites with His Friends' Teeth': Representations of an Early Modern Catholic Martyr." *John Foxe and His World*. Ed. Christopher Highley and John N. King. Aldershot: Ashgate, 2002. 216–34. Print.

Southwell, Robert. *Epistle of Comfort*. London, 1587. Print.

———. "Epistle unto His Father." *Two Letters and Short Rules of a Good Life*. Ed. Nancy Brown. Charlottesville: UP of Virginia, 1973. Print.

Verstegan, Richard. *Theatrum Crudelitatem Haereticorum Nostri Temporis*. Antwerp, 1588. Print.

Williams, Roger. *The Bloudy Tenent, of Persecution, for Cause of Conscience, Discussed, in a Conference betweene Truth and Peace.* London, 1644. Print.
Wyngfield, Robert. *A Circumstantial Account of the Execution of Mary Queen of Scots.* 1587. Clarendon: Clarendon Historical Soc., 1886. Print. Clarendon Historical Reprints 8.

Kate Lilley

Dedicated Thought:
Montaigne, Bacon, and
the English Renaissance Essay

The Renaissance Essay in the Classroom

The digital revolution has made an unprecedented range of early modern printed texts, and sometimes manuscripts, readily available for research and teaching through major initiatives like *Early English Books Online* (*EEBO*) and the Brown University Women Writers Project (WWP). The online edition of the *Oxford Dictionary of National Biography* (*DNB*) provides recently updated and expanded biographical and historical information to use in concert with databases of primary texts. The online *Oxford English Dictionary* (*OED*) and other databases such as *Lexicons of Early Modern English* (*LEME*) allow exploration of the history of words and usage. Along with these licensed sites (which require participating institutional subscriptions), the range and quality of open-access Renaissance resources and e-texts is also multiplying. Of course, such a cornucopia brings with it problems of information management and overload, reminiscent of the mixed excitement and alarm so often expressed by Renaissance authors and readers in the wake of the Gutenberg revolution. The opening up of the archive presents practical difficulties of scale and selection that it has been in many ways the project of canonical literary history (often in the form of the critical essay) to contain by means of an appeal to value and exemplarity. Under the current dispensation, even the most obscure Renaissance text or author can be introduced into the classroom and investigated in student assignments.

In this essay I offer a variety of ways to approach the Renaissance essay, all of which lend themselves to class discussions and presentations as well as to written assignments: the essay as generic name, practice, and orientation; Michel de Montaigne's invention of the informal, personal essay assembled into ongoing volumes as a map of thought, manners, and subjectivity over time; the emergence of the English essay in the early seventeenth century as a popular, humanist genre influenced by Francis Bacon's *Essays*, by John Florio's English translation of Montaigne, and by the patronage of King James I of Great Britain (VI of Scotland); the value of comparing different treatments of similar topics, and of attending to the changing versions of the same essay, as demonstrated by my close reading of Bacon's "Of Great Place"; and the question of gender in relation to the essay as Renaissance genre. For modern teachers, the issues traced here have direct bearing as we ask our students to engage, in oral and written forms, in their own versions of the Renaissance essay, or "assay"; the study of the essay inherently lends itself to the sorts of self-reflexive and reflective, indeed dedicated, thought to which we encourage our students to aspire.

Placing and Displacing the Renaissance Essay

The essay's central place in the history of analytic prose can be traced to its continuous association since the late sixteenth century with "the action or process of trying or testing" ("Essays" [def. 1]). Originally used to describe many different kinds of trial and thinking through, the term *essaying*, or *assaying*, in the sense of both process and product, was used more narrowly over time, until the word *essay* most commonly referred to "a composition of moderate length on any particular subject, or branch of a subject" ("Essays" [def. 8]). If the longevity and ubiquity of the essay as a genre is due, at least in part, to its potential openness literally to all possible varieties of knowledge and experience, in practice the essay has always been both a venue for, and a self-conscious representation of, experiments in thought as a means to self-knowledge. According to its French inventor, Montaigne, who began writing his self-styled *Essais* in the 1570s, while in his thirties, the essay is the genre par excellence of the leisured gentleman's open-ended and periodic reflection on himself and his way of life. Montaigne offered his essays, in all their variety and *copia*, as "an account of the assays of my life" (*Essays* 1224):[1]

> It is a thorny undertaking—more than it looks—to follow so roaming a course as that of our mind's, to penetrate its dark depths and inner recesses, to pick out and pin down the innumerable characteristics of its emotions. It is a new pastime, outside the common order; it withdraws us from the usual occupations of people—yes, even from the commendable ones. For many years now the target of my thought has been myself alone; I examine nothing, I study nothing, but me; and if I do study anything else, it is so as to apply it at once to myself, or more correctly, within myself. (424)

The essayist's "thorny undertaking" necessitates a constant interrogation of the essay's provisional status as well as the relation between theory and practice, precept and example. The Renaissance essay is almost always encountered in single-authored volumes destined to be amplified, revised, reordered, and reissued in a series of editions, as Montaigne's were, in an attempt to keep pace with the changing circumstances of the author and the market, both before and after his death. These collections not only participate self-reflexively in the generic mixing, mobility, and experiment so characteristic of their textual milieu but also in many ways epitomize and thematize the perceived value of piecemeal self-accounting. Réda Bensmaïa characterizes the essay as "an atopic genre or, more precisely, an eccentric one" because its commitment to meta-analysis and formal revision is aligned with the heterogeneity and potential wildness of thought, experience, and textuality itself, in excess of any particular topic, example, or account (96). However, to the extent that essays make a textual place for the serial encounter between the author, his or her own mind, and the minds and texts of others, they can be understood as constituting a heterotopic mirror image, in Michel Foucault's sense:

> The mirror functions as a heterotopia in this respect: it makes this place that I occupy at the moment when I look at myself in the glass at once absolutely real, connected with all the space that surrounds it, and absolutely unreal, since in order to be perceived it has to pass through this virtual point which is over there. (24)

Montaigne's essays move toward a metacritical unfolding, necessarily unfinished, of "the disjunction between how people are said to behave and how they may be observed to behave" (Nichols 55). Stephen G. Nichols aligns this process with what he calls "disnarration," or unsaying, an unsettling of the authority of precedent (what has been said and done) such that "the example continually mediates between doing and saying" (52). This negotiation is destined to be performed, consciously and unconsciously, at every level of the text. For Montaigne, the project of writing, revising, and collecting his *Essais* constitutes an inquiry into the play of difference and similarity, a play that is essential to both the recognition of kind and to the distinction between self and other. Such a project is defined by its reflexive status: "if our faces were not alike we could not tell man from beast: if they were not unalike we could not tell man from man" (1213). This is the exemplary mark of the essay's attempt to (dis)place the relation between the general and the particular and to model the movement of persuasion and dissuasion.

Essays in the Marketplace of Print

Montaigne's essays combine writerly self-portrait with commentary on his reading of other men's texts. In so doing, they cannot fail to show the fraught connections among status, masculinity, and competitive authorship: "there are more books on books than on any other subject: all we do is gloss each other. All is a-swarm with commentaries: of authors there is a dearth" (1212). As Montaigne's first English translator, Florio, put it in 1603: "Al is in the choise & handling" (Florio, "To the Curteous Reader"). In Renaissance England, the overproduction of educated young men seeking place and the gentlemanly associations of the essay attracted new authors and readers but also exposed the new genre to charges of opportunism and inauthenticity. The ungentlemanly Ben Jonson, for instance, regarded the popularity of the essay with a jaundiced eye, seeing its openness as positively inviting the degradation of the emerging model of literary authorship:

> *Some*, that turne over all bookes, and are equally searching in all papers, that write out of what they presently find or meet, without choice; by which meanes it happens, that what they have discredited, and impugned in one worke, they have before, or after, extolled the same in another. Such are all the *Essayists*, even their Master *Mountaigne*. These, in all they write, confesse still what bookes they have read last; and therein their owne folly, so much, that they bring it to the *Stake* raw, and undigested: not that the place did need it neither; but that they thought themselves furnished, and would vent it. (Jonson 585–86)

Jonson's complaint of quantity over quality is echoed not only by contemporaries seeking to distinguish their own productions from the general flood of print but also by most subsequent commentators on the essay. Douglas Bush's succinct survey is a notable exception and remains a valuable guide to a somewhat neglected field. Most of the early English essayists are now forgotten, among them Robert Johnson, Daniel Tuvell, William Cornwallis, Nicholas Breton, John Stephens, Geffray Minshul, John Earle, John Hall, Henry Peacham, Owen Feltham, James Howell, Richard Brathwaite, Richard Flecknoe, Francis Osborne, William Temple, and Joseph Hall.

Extremely miscellaneous in one sense, the essay and its Renaissance kin—pamphlet, treatise, tract, epistle, familiar letter, observations, meditations, advice, counsel, anatomy, discourse, apology, defense, dialogue, character, news, epistle—describe a kind of textual activity and formal orientation that is nonetheless consistent over time. Given the instability of names in general in the Renaissance—even proper names—and the range of those who apply them (authors, printers, readers), it is perhaps surprising that *essay* is used as often as it is, but there is only limited heuristic benefit in insisting on it as generic arbiter. Philip Sidney's famous essay, for instance, appeared in two posthumous editions of 1595, issued by different London printers, William Ponsonby and Henry Olney, entitled "The Defence of Poesie" and "An Apologie for Poetrie" respectively. Thomas Tuke advises readers of his *New Essayes: Meditations and Vowes*:

> Quarrel not with the name, if thou dislike not the nature. . . . If thou dislike the name, call it what thou wilt. Wonder not that new bookes doe still flye abroad: the world is full of new braines; wherefore not of new Bookes? They that are of active sprits, were better do this then nothing. (A6–7)

Even the broad categories on which we now depend—fiction and nonfiction, prose and poetry—cannot be relied on in the Renaissance. It is more helpful to consider, as Alastair Fowler suggests, the shifting alliances between clusters of generic assignations (194).

While the influence of Montaigne's informal, autobiographical mode is evident in the two volumes of "familiar essays" published by Cornwallis in 1600 and 1601, the vogue for essay writing in English is also linked to the patronage of the pragmatic scholar prince, James VI and I.[2] Bacon, who was to become the most celebrated essayist of James's reign, first published his *Essays* in 1597 as a slim volume of ten topics including "Of Studies," "Of Discourse," and "Of Negotiating." As Rosalie Colie suggests, the genre of "[t]he essay is, really, in part a fulfillment of the implications of adage-making; by working from adages into new context, it developed into a form of its own" (36). Like Montaigne, Bacon chose to write in the vernacular of matters that suggest the intertwining of private and public conduct; although both draw on a common reservoir of proverbial wisdom and classical learning, especially the legacy of the Stoic philosophers as mediated by their Latin commentators, the result is quite different. In terms of form and style, Bacon's brief *Essays*, first printed with his *Colours of Good and Evil* and *Religious Meditations* (both originally written in Latin), rejects Montaigne's discursive *copia* in favor of Erasmian aphorism, while sharing a certain humanist curriculum and pedagogical orientation. Brian Vickers makes the important observation that, even at their most pared down, Bacon's essays are designedly "unsystematic": "they would neither foreclose inquiry nor give a premature and spurious coherence to discussions which were not yet definitive" (Vickers xvii). Montaigne and Bacon belong together as the most influential architects of the essay as an experimental genre devoted to representing the movement of thought and, in turn, moving readers to think. The essay's tropological dimension and rhetorical aim are perhaps the best ways to distinguish it from near relations such as the Renaissance "character." Whereas prose "characters" adumbrate conventional types as part of a ready-made satirical social taxonomy, essays weigh the meaning and force of cultural precept while demonstrating the singularity proper to the individual. The essayist thus writes on his own behalf and in his own person—as author and reader, as citizen and discursive subject—while claiming a broader civic utility in helping to guide others and to create the republic of letters.

The versatility and flexibility of the essay are indicated by the range of authors associated with the genre. The essay's central concern, however, remains the ethical and practical deliberation of conduct in everyday life. In "Of Counsel," Francis Bacon writes, "The greatest trust between man and man is the trust of giving counsel" (46), and written counsels, or essays, addressed to the public, are more to be trusted than speech: "books will speak plain when counsellors blanch. Therefore it is good to be conversant in them, specially the books of such as themselves have been actors upon the stage" (49).[3] The association of writing with disinterested advice and considered discourse must, however, be counterbalanced by the ever-present threat of dissimulation. As an admirer of Niccolò Machiavelli, Bacon advocated self-interested dissimulation in certain circumstances. Bacon's explicitly courtly example led to a number of overtly Baconian collections, such as Robert Johnson's *Essaies, or Rather Imperfect Offers* (1601) in praise of "men expert, reall, of a deepe insight, such as are not carried away with appearances" and Nicholas Breton's *Characters upon Essaies, Morall and Divine* (1615).

Montaigne's influence has been particularly associated with the essays of John Donne, William Cornwallis, and, after the Restoration, Abraham Cowley. It would be misleading, however, to think of these lines of descent as antithetical or even truly distinct. Even the most "personal" and "familiar" essays are structured by the interrelation of politics and ethics, public and private benefit. Essays were advice books of a kind, so it is no surprise to find that the authors of popular conduct books also tried their luck as essayists. Brathwaite, best known for *The English Gentleman* (1630) and its companion volume, *The English Gentlewoman* (1631), also published the intriguing *Essaies upon the Five Senses* (1620), described in the prefatory letter as "*Observations*, or what you will, dilating upon the *five Senses . . .* organs of weale or woe, happy if rightly tempered, sinister, if without limit" (A3r). Peacham, a prolific journeyman author and teacher, composer of emblem books and popular advice like *The Compleat Gentleman* (1622, substantially revised in 1627 and 1634), in old age published *The Truth of Our Times Revealed out of One Man's Experience, by Way of Essay* (1638). Picaresque and compulsively readable, Peacham's memoir, disposed into fourteen topics, advises that "all the errors that men commit in their whole lives, is for want of the line and levell of an eaven and true judgement" (58). In his preface, "To the Reader," Peacham explains:

> [T]o say the truth, I have ever found multiplicity of Knowledge in many things to hav beene rather an hinderance, then ever any Way-tending to advancement. Having hereby found much imployment to no purpose. . . . So have I taken paines and deserved well at the hands of many of good ranke, yet got I never any thing. (A5–6)

Montaigne's "Of the Incommoditie of Greatness" and Bacon's "Of Great Place"

The expansive project of Montaigne's *Essays* is rooted in, and reflects on, the enjoyment of his comfortable position and estate as Michel Equem de Montaigne (his discomfort will come from sources other than courtly vicissitude and disappointment, chiefly illness and melancholy). In "Of the Incommoditie of Greatness," Montaigne writes:

> [A] man doth not fall from all heights; divers there are whence a man may descend without falling . . . I have as much to wish for as another, and leave my wishes as much liberty and indiscretion; but yet it never

> came into my minde to wish for Empire, for Royalty, or eminency of
> high and commanding fortunes. I aime not that way: I love my selfe
> too well. (*Essays* [trans. Florio] 550)[4]

Montaigne praises "a quiet easefull life, altogether his owne": "I am dis-
tasted of all mastry, both active and passive." He is, of course, a provincial
master who fraternized with royalty and courtiers when he chose; the estate where he was born, to the title of which he succeeded, is by his own
account "richly plenteous in all manner of commodities and pleasures."
Even so, Montaigne admits that the "interest" he would reject belongs
to subjectivity: "superiority and inferiority, maistry and subjection, are
jointly tied unto a naturall kinde of envy and contestation" (550). Montaigne's discussion centers on the pathos of the sovereign, so cut off from
ordinary pleasures that he "must in begging manner crave some empeach-
ment and resistance" (551), but he also figures courtiers as emasculated
and effeminized. Like "Mithridates his flatterers" who "came to him to
have their members incized and cauterised," so are the souls of courtiers
"a much more precious and nobler part then the body" (552).

Montaigne's "Of the Incommoditie of Greatness" can usefully be studied with and read against Bacon's "Of Great Place," where Bacon writes:

> In the discharge of thy place set before thee the best examples; for
> imitation is a globe of precepts. And after a time set before thee thine
> own example; and examine thyself strictly whether thou didst not best
> at first . . . set it down to thyself as well to create good precedents as to
> follow them . . . ask counsel of both times; of the ancient time, what is
> best; and of the latter time, what is fittest. (24–25)

Here Bacon advises "great persons" of their ethical responsibilities as he
lays out the common "vices of authority": "delays, corruption, roughness,
and facility" (25). "Of Great Place" appeared first in the much enlarged
1612 edition of the *Essays*, published when Bacon was Clerk of the Star
Chamber and the year before he became attorney general. His career flour-
ishing, Bacon gave advice that reads like the counsel of success. Reprinted
with highly significant additions for the final edition of 1625, these same
words bristle with an irony that must have been only too present to Bacon
and his readers. The stricture of Bacon's earlier injunction to "set before
thee thine own example" is now silently brought to bear on its author,
impeached in 1621 after pleading guilty to charges of accepting bribes.
Stripped of his position as Lord Keeper of the Great Seal, the highest legal
office in the land and the post held by his father at the time of Francis's

birth, Bacon was briefly imprisoned and effectively banished from court for the last years of his life. Like other frustrated courtiers before him, notably Sidney, Bacon turned to writing and rewriting. Unlike Sidney, however, whose much-vaunted promise was never highly rewarded in terms of "civil business," Bacon suffered a rise and fall that was spectacular and spectacularly shaming. As Kiernan puts it:

> The role of counsellor was one Bacon craved from his earliest days and one which he performed, often unbidden and still more often unhearkened to throughout his adult life, when he wrote numerous advices, memoranda, drafts of proclamations, and suggested speeches for the King—offered either directly or through the reigning favourite. His impeachment for judicial bribery in 1621 removed him not only from the high position of Lord Chancellor, but forbade him the verge of the court. Though the prohibition was later lifted and he moved back into his lodgings in Gray's Inn in February 1621/2, he never enjoyed the access of counsellor again. (xxvi)

"[U]nbidden and still more often unhearkened to" may seem a surprising description of Bacon's notable public career, but it catches the frustration and anxiety inherent to courtly experience at all levels. The revision and expansion of Bacon's *Essays* over the course of his career in the service first of Elizabeth and then James can be seen as both strategic revisiting—renewed "assay"—and a kind of repetition compulsion generated by the persistence of those problems and desires that underwrite "civil business." A close examination of those revisions and expansions offers an effective way of focusing the study of the Renaissance essay for modern readers.

Whatever his place or lack of it in the hierarchy, "counsel" is Bacon's self-styled civil profession, and the essay in his hands becomes one of its most characteristic genres. In the canonical, final version of Bacon's *Essays* (1625), the rhetoric of magisterial direction and authority is symptomatically at its most forceful, when the counselor himself, now in his sixties, has been publicly reviled, abused as a sodomite, and impeached. He lost his job and his house, and, perhaps most painfully, his propinquity to power. In a surviving draft of a letter to James in 1622—a letter never sent—Bacon mournfully literalizes and rehearses his loss of access to the King's two bodies, James's person and his office: "Your Majesty's arm hath been often over mine in council, when you presided at the table; so near I was" (qtd. in Kiernan xxvii).

The striking fact that Bacon does not mention Montaigne until the 1625 *Essays* may suggest that it is only at this point that he becomes sympathetic to, or is willing to align himself with, Montaigne's retired melancholy. In "Of Adversity," added in 1625, Bacon writes:

> The virtue of Prosperity is temperance, the virtue of Adversity is fortitude; which in morals is the more heroical virtue. . . . We see in needleworks and embroideries, it is more pleasing to have a lively work upon a sad and solemn ground, than to have a dark and melancholy work upon a lightsome ground: judge therefore of the pleasure of the heart by the pleasure of the eye. Certainly virtue is like precious odours, most fragrant when they are incensed or crushed: for Prosperity doth best discover vice, but Adversity doth best discover virtue. (12)

Deprived of office, Bacon takes steps, once again, to demonstrate in writing and through publication on the open market those skills and qualities, the combination of ability, acumen, education, and experience, that allow him to claim the vocation and character of a counselor on his own authority. He addresses his public—conjuring his readers, past, present, and future—in what is not only a tacit defense of the continuity of his good service and advice but also an assertion of such contributions, independence from the favor of the monarch or any civil office. The essays are thus highly charged; it is Bacon's rhetorical task to render his reversion to the essays proof of masculine *virtu* rather than effeminate perseveration.

Bacon returned to the genre of the essay with renewed passion, stressing in his changed title, *The Essays or Counsels, Civil and Moral*, the need to manage and analyze the "commodities" and "discommodities" of private and public life and to demonstrate the utility and persuasiveness of admonitory prose according to his own precepts: "power to do good is the true and lawful end of aspiring" (24). In this way the history of Bacon's *Essays* offers a formal demonstration of their counsel: key experiences and topics must be revisited as a way to gauge and adjust the relations between discourse and performance. The *via activa* requires forensic analysis, intellectual deliberation, and rhetorical demonstration. Especially in its final version, the *Essays* dissects the practice of everyday life to prove that a man makes, or at least participates in, his own fate through successful and unsuccessful negotiation.

In chastened circumstances Bacon sought to claim the moral benefit of "fortitude" and unwavering service: "Merit *and good works* is the end of man's motion; and conscience of the same is the accomplishment of man's rest" (24).[5] The final version of "Of Great Place" and the *Essays* as a whole strive to minimize the gap between "integrity used" and "integrity professed" by trying to reestablish Bacon's rightful "place" as Stoic counselor, "settled and calm" (26). It is notable, however, that Bacon performs this equilibration only implicitly: by allowing earlier passages to stand, and thus asserting the ethical continuity of his career and his texts, and by making certain telling additions to the essay's 1625 text:

> In the discharge of thy place set before thee the best examples; for imitation is a globe of precepts. And after a time set before thee thine own example; and examine thyself strictly whether thou didst not best at first. *Neglect not also the examples of those that have carried themselves ill in the same place; not to set off thyself by taxing their memory, but to direct thyself what to avoid.* . . . For corruption: do not only bind thine own hands or thy servants' hands from taking, but bind the hands of suitors also from offering. For integrity used doth the one; but integrity professed, and with a manifest detestation of bribery, doth the other. And avoid not only the fault but the suspicion. Whosoever is found variable, and changeth manifestly without manifest cause, giveth suspicion of corruption. *Therefore always when thou changest thine opinion or course, profess it plainly, and declare it, together with the reasons that move thee to change; and do not think to steal it.* A servant or a favourite, if he be inward, and no other apparent cause of esteem, is commonly thought but a by-way *to close corruption.* (24–25; my emphasis)

Bacon's 1625 additions ostensibly acknowledge the "suspicion" raised by his own conduct, but they also implicate James I and VI and his favorite, George Villiers, First Duke of Buckingham, to whom Bacon dedicated this last version of the *Essays*: "I doe now publish my *Essayes*; which, of all my other workes, have been most Currant: For that, as it seemes, they come home, to Mens Businesse, and Bosomes" (*Essayes* [ed. Kiernan] 5).[6] In this precarious balancing act of alliance and misalliance, self-examination and vindication, it seems that Bacon accuses himself of both too much and too little "facility," a failure to adequately preserve himself and his place from "mov[ing] violently" (*Essays* [ed. Vickers] 26). But he is always ready to restore rhetorical equanimity with a balancing interpretation. If, as he argues, "[i]t is a strange desire, to seek power and to lose liberty" (*Essays* [ed. Vickers] 24), then Bacon's fall can be construed as at least partly fortunate, gaining liberty by losing power. These essays, he assures Buckingham in the dedication, are "the best Fruits, that by the good Encrease, which God gives to my Pen and Labours, I could yeeld" (*Essayes* [ed. Kiernan] 5). Recuperations notwithstanding, Bacon's sense of the "melancholy" of civil business is already clear in "Of Great State" in the 1612 version, but it is given a more "currant" and personal edge in 1625:

> The standing is slippery, and the regress is either a downfall, or at least an eclipse, which is a melancholy thing. *Cum non sis qui fueris, non esse cur velis vivere.* Nay, retire men cannot when they would, neither will they when it were reason . . . *like old townsmen, that will be still sitting at their street door, though thereby they offer age to scorn.* (24; my emphasis)[7]

Bacon added an entirely new final paragraph to "Of Great State" in its 1625 version:

> All rising to great place is by a winding stair; and if there be factions, it is good to side a man's self whilst he is in the rising, and to balance himself when he is placed. Use the memory of thy predecessor fairly and tenderly; for if thou dost not, it is a debt will sure be paid when thou art gone. If thou have colleagues, respect them, and rather call them when they look not for it, than exclude them when they have reason to look to be called. Be not too sensible or too remembering of thy place in conversation and private answers to suitors; but let it rather be said, "When he sits in place he is another man." (26)

According to the logic of this passage, the Bacon that now returns to the *Essays* should also be "another man," a public counselor returned to himself and the task of negotiating his posterity "like old townsmen, that will be still sitting at their street door" (24). Bacon's simile invokes the Stoic porch as natural auditorium on the cusp of public and private space. As a skilful orator in print, Bacon juggles the familiarity of the stoop with the dignity of the elder statesman. He insists that the exemplary conduct of "great persons" will secure, by emulation, the virtue of the state and its inferior parts, but this exemplarity consists not in the attainment of an impossible perfection or blamelessness but in a continual striving, combined with an ability to consider and judge the results with "discretion." Bacon's counsels are mediated by an impersonal style and an often patently dissimulated rhetoric of objectivity. As Brian Vickers notes, Bacon's 1625 title, *Essays or Counsels Civil and Moral*, stresses the implication of "the *civitas* or public life and the *mores* or behavior of the private individual" (xxv). The different versions of Bacon's *Essays* are the exemplary companion texts of his rise and fall, offered as timely and fit installments, adapted to his own use and those of his imagined readers. Offering himself as a type of conscious striving and tenacity, Bacon urges his readers in his last essays to heed his counsels and think well of him, if not for his sake then for their own: "Use the memory of thy predecessor fairly and tenderly; for if thou dost not, it is a debt will sure be paid when thou art gone" (26).

The Renaissance Essay and the Gender of Knowing

Women tend to figure in accounts of the gentlemanly intimacy of the Renaissance essayist and his readers as facilitators and go-betweens, if at all. Montaigne's first scholarly editor, the fascinating Marie de Gournay (1565–1645), became his protégée after first reading the *Essais* in her teens and declaring herself his "fille d'alliance" (*Proumenoir*). With the approval of Montaigne's widow, she prepared and introduced a number of posthumous editions of the *Essays* over a period of forty years. This is consonant with the kind of ancillary textual labor—as editors, translators, and patrons—most commonly associated with learned Renaissance women such as Mary Sidney, Countess of Pembroke, and Bacon's mother, Anne Cook. On closer inspection these women turn out to be highly accomplished intellectuals and often authors in their own right. The first volume of the first edition of Florio's English translation of Montaigne's *Essays* was dedicated in a long and complex preface to his patrons, Lucy, Countess of Bedford, and her mother, Lady Anne Harrington:

> To my last Birth, which I held masculine, (as are all mens conceipts that are their owne, though but by their collecting . . .) I the indulgent father invited two right Honourable Godfathers, with the One of your Noble Ladyshipes to witnesse. So to this defective edition (since all translations are reputed femalls, delivered at second hand . . .) I yet at least a fondling foster-father . . . would set it forth to the best service I might; and to better I might not, then You that deserve the best . . . as to all, that professe any learning, & do you (but small) steade therein, you and your husbands hand (most bounteous Ladie Harrington) have beene still open, & your hospitable house, my retreate in storms, my reliefe in neede.

Florio's dedicatees are noble women because it is women, here figured indissolubly as wives, daughters, and patrons, who uphold the promise of ideal homosocial commerce between men. There is also a particular motive in addressing courtly women through the topos of the hospitality of the country estate, as Florio does here, because essays are associated with sequestered reflection. As Florio's Montaigne puts it: "At Paris I speake somewhat otherwise then at Montaigne." In his prefatory poem, "To my deere friend M. *John Florio*, concerning *His Translation of* Montaigne," Samuel Daniel praises Florio for the "safe transpassage by his studious care / Who both of him and us doth merit much." Florio's mediation in turn invites Daniel and other readers into "the better world of men / Whose spirits are all of one communitie." Montaigne's text, now doubled with Florio's labor, is figured by Daniel as "most rich pieces and extracts of man," its reader "a guest in gratefulnesse, / For the great good the house yields him within."

The question of women as Renaissance essayists has hardly been broached. The printed record shows that English women's texts are un-likely to be called "essays" until the end of the seventeenth century. The exception is Margaret Cavendish's *The World's Olio* (1655), an extensive collection of short prose opinions in various styles, allegorical or empiri-cal, traversing a wide variety of secular topics concerning manners, privi-lege, institutions, politics, health, warfare, education, history, literary criticism, and natural philosophy. Curiously, in her *Olio* Cavendish uses the generic title "short essayes" only to refer to the 141 numbered entries of book 2, part 2, some titled, some not, ranging in length from a single clause to a sentence to a paragraph. Book 2, part 2, ends appropriately enough with "Of Dilation and Retention. Essay 141":

> A Dilation causeth as much weakness as Contraction; Dilation caus-
> eth weakness by disuniting the United Forces, and setting them at
> too great a Distance; and Contraction binds them up too hard, not
> giving, as we vulgarly say, Elbow room. (S1r)

For all its singularity in the canon of Renaissance women's writing, *The World's Olio* and much else by Cavendish is quite at home in the broadly essayistic discourse of commentary and advice.

Women's (and men's) involvement in the formal defense of women's rational capacity and virtue, such as Rachel Speght's *A Mouzell for Melas-tomus* (1617), published as part of the pamphlet war now known as the Swetnam controversy, is likewise readily interpreted as deterritorializ-ing the gender and genres of knowing.[8] The prose polemics of Speght, Bathsua Makin, Mary Astell, and Judith Drake span the seventeenth cen-tury, but only Drake used "essay" in her title, *An Essay in Defence of the Female Sex* (1696). Genres associated with more decorous female author-ship, such as mothers' advice books and letters, often combined private counsel with public engagement in essayistic form. Catherine Gray has shown that the posthumous publication of Dorothy Leigh's hugely popu-

lar advice book, *The Mother's Blessing* (1616), was a calculated response to
the 1616 edition of King James's *Basilikon Doron*. Elizabeth Grymeston's
advice to her son, *Miscelanea. Meditations. Memoratives* (1604), published
in the wake of the first popular English edition of *Basilikon Doron* in
1603, is modeled in style and structure on essay collections. Averring that
her "desire is, that thou mightest be seasoned with these precepts in thy
youth," she delivers a Baconian lesson: "O levell thy life to the straight-
nesse of the line of thine own portrature" (D4v). Grymeston's last chapter, "Memoratives," consists of a catalog of sententiae somewhat in the
manner of Bacon's 1597 *Essays*: "Opportunity kindleth the fire of concu-
piscence"; "He that leaves his wife a goldefinch, may hap at his returne
finde hir a wagtaile"; "Fortune is always a friend to a forward minde";
"Before thou sleepe, apparel thy remembrance with that thou didst waking." While the subject of women writers as essayists remains unbroached
in scholarship, it need not be so in the classroom, as Cavendish, Grymeston, Speght, and other figures may be productively read in the context of
the Renaissance essay, making visible for students the topographies of the
genres and genders of knowledge.

Essaying the Classroom

The same qualities that made Renaissance essayists so popular among
their contemporaries recommend them to modern readers. Essays are intimately concerned with the minutiae of conduct and the analysis of self
and other, the entanglements of ethics, aesthetics, and politics. They depend on the cultivation of affective and effective links between writers
and readers, mediated by the text as the place of encounter and allegorized
in the drive to rewrite, reread, and reconsider. The idiosyncratic ways in
which particular authors lay claim to the provisional authority of the essay
indicates the heterotopic potential of the genre itself, inviting readers in
their turn to cultivate "the eloquence and wisdom of speech and persuasion" (Bacon 129) and to heed Bacon's call for balanced thought in an
unstable world: "it is not good to look too long upon those turning wheels
of vicissitude, lest we become giddy" (131–32).

Notes

1. All citations are to the translation by Screech except where indicated.

2. The young James published *The Essayes of a Prentise, in the Divine Art of
Poesie* (1584). This treatise on poetics is the first use of "essayes" registered by
EEBO. It makes for a suggestive point of origin in thinking about the history

and historiography of the essay in English, "so long unrecognized as a literary genre although practiced as if it were" (Colie 86). With his self-styled "treatise," *Basilikon Doron; or, His Majesties Instructions to His Dearest Sonne* (1599), James confirmed his patronage of the essayistic mode as one suited to the use of the sovereign as well as his subjects. Printed initially for very limited private circulation, *Basilikon Doron* was reissued in 1603 to coincide with James's accession to the English throne and became immensely popular. The popular essayist William Cornwallis served as one of James's gentlemen of the bedchamber.

3. Except where otherwise indicated, all quotations of Bacon's *Essays* are from the final 1625 version, as reprinted in Vickers's excellent Oxford World's Classics edition. Kiernan's edition is magisterial and highly recommended but less suited to classroom use.

4. In this section I use Florio's 1603 translation of Montaigne's "Of the Incommoditie of Greatness" to better serve the comparison with the 1612 and 1625 versions of Bacon's "Of Great Place" and to prepare the way for the discussion of Florio's project itself. In Screech's modern translation of Montaigne this essay appears as "On High Rank as a Disadvantage." For classroom use, the different versions of Bacon's "Of Great Place" and the relevant parts of Florio's Montaigne can be downloaded from *EEBO*. Reliable free editions of Florio's Montaigne and Bacon's *Essays* (1625) can be accessed at the *Renascence Editions* site (http://darkwing.uoregon.edu/).

5. My italics indicate additions made to the 1625 edition from the 1612 edition.

6. Peltonen argues that "Bacon was not impeached because of the gifts he had taken. Rather, he was a victim of a political campaign directed against monopolies and the king's chief favourite Buckingham" (12). If Bacon wittingly took the fall, he neglected neither to subtly indicate as much nor to cease in his attempts to be returned to favor.

7. Vickers's gloss of the Ciceronian citation is "when you are no longer what you have been, you see no reason why you should wish to live" (166).

8. I borrow the phrase "gender of knowing" from the title of the recent English translation of Le Doeuff's collection of essays, *The Sex of Knowing*.

Works Cited

Bacon, Francis. *The Essayes or Counsels, Civill and Morall*. Ed. Michael Kiernan. Oxford: Clarendon, 1985. Print.

———. *The Essays or Counsels, Civil and Moral*. Ed. Brian Vickers. Oxford: Oxford UP, 1999. Print. Oxford World's Classics.

Bensmaïa, Réda. *The Barthes Effect: The Essay as Reflective Text*. Trans. Pat Fedkiew. Minneapolis: U of Minnesota P, 1987. Print.

Brathwaite, Richard. *Essaies upon the Five Senses*. London: E. G., 1620. Print.

Bush, Douglas. "Essays and Characters." *English Literature in the Earlier Seventeenth Century, 1600–1660*. Oxford: Clarendon, 1962. 192–219. Print.

Cavendish, Margaret. *The World's Olio*. London, 1655. Print.

Colie, Rosalie L. *The Resources of Kind: Genre-Theory in the Renaissance*. Ed. Barbara K. Lewalski. Berkeley: U of California P, 1973. Print.

Daniel, Samuel. "To My Deere Friend M. *Iohn Florio*, Concerning *His Translation of* Montaigne." Montaigne, *Montaigne's Essays*.

"Essay." Def. 1. *Oxford English Dictionary*. 2nd ed. 1989. Print.

"Essay." Def. 8. *Oxford English Dictionary*. 2nd ed. 1989. Print.

Florio, John. "To the Curteous Reader." *Montaigne's Essays*. Trans. Florio. 1603. *Renascence Editions*. 1999. Web. 4 June 2009.

Foucault, Michel. "Of Other Spaces." Trans. Jay Miskowiec. *Diacritics* 16.1 (1986): 22–27. Print.

Fowler, Alastair. "The Formation of Genres in the Renaissance and After." *New Literary History* 34.2 (2003): 185–200. Print.

Gournay, Marie de. *Le proumenoir de Monsieur de Montaigne, par sa fille d'alliance*. Paris: L'Angelier, 1642. Print.

Gray, Catherine. "Feeding on the Seed of the Woman: Dorothy Leigh and the Figure of Maternal Consent." *ELH* 68.3 (2001): 563–92. *Project Muse*. Web. 13 Oct. 2009.

Grymeston, Elizabeth. *Miscelanea. Meditations. Memoratives*. London, 1604. Print.

Johnson, Robert. *Essais, or Rather Imperfect Offers*. London: Barnes, 1601. N. pag. Print.

Jonson, Ben. *"Timber*; or, *Discoveries." Works*. Ed. C. H. Herford, Percy Simpson, and Evelyn Simpson. Vol. 8. Oxford: Clarendon, 1941. 562–649. Print.

Kiernan, Michael. Introduction. Bacon, *Essayes* xix–cxvi.

Le Doeuff, Michèle. *The Sex of Knowing*. Trans. Kathryn Hamer and Lorraine Code. New York: Routledge, 2003. Print. Trans. of *Le sexe du savoir*. 1998.

Montaigne, Michel de. *The Complete Essays*. Trans. M. A. Screech. New York: Penguin, 1991. Print.

———. *Montaigne's Essays*. Trans. John Florio. 1603. *Renascence Editions*. 1999. Web. 4 June 2009.

Nichols, Stephen G. "Example versus Historia: Montaigne, Eriugena, and Dante." *Unruly Examples: On the Rhetoric of Exemplarity*. Ed. Alexander Gelley. Stanford: Stanford UP, 1995. 48–85. Print.

Peacham, Henry. *The Truth of Our Times*. London: Becket, 1638. Print.

Peltonen, Markku. *The Cambridge Companion to Bacon*. Cambridge: Cambridge UP, 1996. Print.

Tuke, Thomas. *New Essayes: Meditations and Vowes*. London, 1614. Print.

Vickers, Brian. Introduction. Bacon, *Essays* xi–xxxvii.

Suggestions for Further Reading

Black, Scott. *Of Essays and Reading in Early Modern Britain*. Basingstoke: Palgrave, 2006. Print.

Breitenburg. Mark. *Anxious Masculinity in Early Modern England*. Cambridge: Cambridge UP, 1996. Print.

Conley, Tom. "Institutionalizing Translation: On Florio's Montaigne." *Demarcating the Disciplines: Philosophy, Literature, Art*. Ed. Samuel Weber. Minneapolis: U of Minnesota P, 1986. 45–58. Print.

Fish, Stanley. "Georgics of the Mind: The Experience of Bacon's Essays." *Self-Consuming Artifacts: The Experience of Seventeenth-Century Literature*. Berkeley: U of California P, 1972. 78–155. Print.

Gournay, Marie de. Apology for the Woman Writing *and Other Works*. Ed. and trans. Richard Hillman and Colette Quesnel. Chicago: U of Chicago P, 2002. Print.

Hutson, Lorna. *The Usurer's Daughter: Male Friendship and Fictions of Women in Sixteenth-Century England*. London: Routledge, 1994. Print.

Jardine, Lisa, and Alan Stewart. *Hostage to Fortune: The Troubled Life of Francis Bacon*. London: Gollancz, 1998. Print.

Johnson, Christopher. "Florio's 'Conversion' of Montaigne, Sidney and Six Patronesses." *Cahiers Elisabéthains* 64 (2003): 9–18. Print.

Lee, John. "The English Renaissance Essay: Churchyard, Cornwallis, Florio's Montaigne, and Bacon." *A Companion to English Renaissance Literature and Culture*. Ed. Michael Hattaway. Oxford: Blackwell, 2000. 600–08. Print.

Lilley, Kate. "Contracting Readers: 'Margaret Newcastle' and the Rhetoric of Conjugality." *A Princely Brave Woman: Essays on Margaret Cavendish, Duchess of Newcastle*. Ed. Stephen Clucas. London: Ashgate, 2003. 19–39. Print.

Miller, John J. "'Pruning by Study': Self-Cultivation in Bacon's Essays." *Papers on Language and Literature* 31.4 (1995): 339–61. Print.

Scodel, Joshua. "Alternative Sites for Literature." *The Cambridge History of Early Modern English Literature*. Ed. David Loewenstein and Janel Mueller. Cambridge: Cambridge UP, 2002. 763–89. Print.

Smith, Gregory G., ed. *Elizabethan Critical Essays*. 2 vols. Oxford: Oxford UP, 1904. Print.

Suzuki, Mihoko. "The Essay Form as Critique: Reading Cavendish's *The World's Olio* through Montaigne and Bacon (and Adorno)." *Prose Studies* 22.3 (1999): 1–16. Print.

Vickers, Brian. *Francis Bacon and Renaissance Prose*. Cambridge: Cambridge UP, 1968. Print.

Wormald, Jenny. "James VI and I, *Basilikon Doron* and the Trew Law of Free Monarchies: The Scottish Context and the English Translation." *The Mental World of the Jacobean Court*. Ed. Linda Levy Peck. Cambridge: Cambridge UP, 1991. 36–54. Print.

Mary Ellen Lamb

Teaching Early Modern Autobiographies and Life Writings

Unlike other writings, life writings demand to be read as reflecting their authors' lives. They are especially engaging to students of early modern literature because they convey a sense, however subjective it might be, that what they describe actually happened. In addition to providing a historical context valuable for understanding other forms of prose writing, life writings are particularly good texts for thinking about the various interpretive lenses—historicist, psychoanalytic, Marxist, feminist—through which we view not only early modern texts but also early modern selves. One goal of the course I describe below was to use the study of early modern life writings to complicate students' notions of what it means to have or to be a self in any period. Ideally, the study of the unfamiliar types of selves shaped by early modern cultural discourses leads to a heightened awareness not only of the cultural discourses of our own time but also of their power over the selves we feel ourselves to be.

This essay brings up issues considered in a graduate class on women's autobiography taught in 2004. We covered life writings by Margery Kempe, Margaret Hoby, Isabella Whitney, Anne Halkett, Anne Clifford, Lucy Hutchinson, and Margaret Cavendish. Toward the end of the semester, we thought about connections between life writings and fictions by Mary

Wroth and Elizabeth Cary. During the semester, each student focused on a particular issue of her or his choice (e.g., sexuality, material goods, children, religion). Students were also encouraged to follow a particular model of the self, or a productive combination of models of the self, chosen from those laid out at the beginning of the semester. To be most useful to teachers of life writings, much of the focus in this essay is on the general questions that arose rather than what was said about specific life writings. These questions represent, for the most part, applications of autobiographical theory. Writings by Hutchinson and Cavendish are contrasted at the end of the essay. The list of life writings at the end provides a sense of the range and richness of available life writings from this period.

The term *autobiography*, literally "self–" (*autos*) "life" (*bios*) "writing" (*graphe*), inevitably brings up complicated questions rendered even more complex by historical distance. *Autos* ("self"): what does it mean to have a self? Students were invited to contribute and then to consider the diverse terms used—*soul, psyche, subjectivity, identity, interiority*—and how all these define the concept of self through disparate discourses, from religion to psychology to cultural studies. Students considered whether it was viable to choose to read early modern lives through a modern concept of self or whether it was preferable to work to discern an early modern model of personhood underlying an autobiographical account. One example introduced and then discussed at more length in a later class involved Cavendish. As we analyzed how the narrator Cavendish seemed to interpret the earlier self of her autobiography, we distinguished the relation between the *I* who is narrating and the *I* who is described in the narrative. Should her self-display be interpreted according to a psychoanalytic frame of a narcissistic personality or through her own desire for "singularity" in the staging of a highly idiosyncratic form of aristocratic status? One student advocated working out a model that accommodates both.

Bios ("life"): what aspects of one's life are worth recording? We discussed interpretations writers (including writers studied in other classes) made of their own experience. Memories of the past are usually elicited by an issue or dilemma in the present. Students responded well to a general discussion of connections they saw between an account of the past and an apparent need or agenda in the present. They became particularly interested in the more political issue of whose lives are worthy of historical record as we looked at the history of the genre of autobiography. In the

1950s, the study of autobiography was mostly limited to a small canon of extraordinary men such as Augustine, Benvenuto Cellini, Jean-Jacques Rousseau, Benjamin Franklin, Henry David Thoreau. The task was to understand, and presumably to attempt to emulate, the processes through which they attained an exemplary self. By expanding autobiography to other forms of life writing such as diaries, other subjects emerged into visibility. The formative power of cultural discourses such as Margaret Hoby's search for signs of assurance of her election and the music tutor Thomas Whythorne's account of his widely varying status in various households rises forcefully to the surface, not only for what aspects of lives are written but also for how early modern lives were actually led.

Graphe ("writing"): what personal or cultural forces empower or compel persons to set down their lives in writing? The writing of one's own life was sufficiently unusual to warrant, in most cases, an explanation or self-justification. Throughout the semester, we discussed how writers justified writing their lives. In most cases, there was substantial information from which to draw conclusions or at least educated speculations. Instead of a transparent transcription, an account of a past event often fosters a particular perception of the present, so that self-writings often resemble rhetorical acts of persuasion of some kind. We analyzed the subject of persuasion to ask about the kind of reader the writer desires us to be, for the invocation and shaping of the reader is an essential component of this persuasive act. For example, Lucy Hutchinson, the widow of a military leader of parliamentary troops in the civil war, writes to those who share her view of God's providence in overturning the royalist forces to institute the government of the commonwealth. While it is not necessary to agree with her worldview, a careful reading of her life writing yields an understanding of how the designs of her text construct us as readers.

In addition to these aspects of autobiography, students took into account how the various forms of narrative affect the kind of life that is written. A memoir is generally retrospective, summing up large portions of a life often according to a certain pattern of events or a specific preoccupation. A confession tends to be more intimate and immediate, elicited by inward or outward forces. A diary may be part of a technique of the self, through which the act of recording daily events may contribute to a heightened self-awareness affecting the actions or thoughts of a subject in process. Travel narratives often describe the writer through encounters with cultural others. In any of these forms, autobiographical writings are distinguished by a distinctive mode of reading. Philippe Lejeune refers to this distinctive relation between author and reader as an autobiographical pact by which, like historians, authors of life narratives present their writings as in some sense true, although this truth may be subjective.

As for any form of historiography, the issue of truth in autobiographical writings has been rendered problematic by the challenges leveled by modern theories against the possibility of objectivity for any self-narrative, including self-narratives of the early modern period. This transformation in the concept of the self has radically changed the field of autobiography from its initial commemoration of the lives of great men. This earlier transhistorical master narrative of the rise of an autonomous self, in full control of its own processes, to prominence in the public sphere derived from Jacob Burckhardt's celebration of the Renaissance as the dawn of individualism. We discussed how, influenced by Sigmund Freud and Jacques Lacan, psychoanalytic approaches eroded this representation of the sovereign subject by questioning the possibility of absolute self-awareness. Freud's subjects were prey to internal psychological forces beyond their control or knowledge. For Lacan, a sense of a unified and coherent self was only an illusion of the mirror stage, a source of initial jubilation followed by inevitable alienation. Marxist approaches similarly undercut the concept of the sovereign self by limiting self-awareness according to a subject's relation to production; and Althusserians have elaborated on this perspective by characterizing any sense of individual agency for subjects, shaped by ideologies that seem to them "natural" or real, as illusory. As students noted, all these approaches provide strategies for reading autobiographical subjects, from ascertaining the operations of repressed desires by identifying the fissures or gaps in self-narratives to determining the effects of a writer's location in class on constructions of the self. Most significantly, the loss of the concept of a sovereign and unified self provides an opportunity for reading for elements or fragments of the self that remain unaccommodated to the subject performed in an autobiographical writing. These questions freed up students for some excellent readings of early modern life writings.

In the 1980s, Stephen Greenblatt and the new historicism focused attention on the power of cultural discourses to shape not only literary texts but also the selves that wrote them. Shaped by contemporary ideologies of gender and class, the self was actively understood as situated in history. For critics such as Paul Smith, agency emerged not through the transcendence of ideology, but through the negotiation of gaps and contradictions between competing ideologies. Michel de Certeau and other cultural historians have stressed the creative potential of individuals to reinterpret and re-create dominant discourses to meet local needs and personal agendas. These movements became particularly important to feminists and scholars of early modern women's autobiographies. Because the theoretical insights they have developed are widely applicable to other social groups, we found it worthwhile to discuss them at length. Early modern male subjects also navigated complex discourses to discover or create a self, and a number of these subjects also maneuvered through an ideological space between the social positions they occupied and cultural ideals of the masculine.

We explored some of the more prominent feminist discussions of autobiography. If this culture represented women as, in Sidonie Smith's words, a "misbegotten man," then how could women negotiate the discourses of their time to express a self in an autobiographical writing (*Poetics* 20–43)? What were the sources of empowerment? We considered how some religious discourses stressed the necessary subordination of women to men because of their supposedly greater responsibility for original sin, as demonstrated by Eve's willful eating of the apple. More generally, religious discourses seemed to enable women—Kempe, Hoby, Hutchinson—to construct a self in writing. In life writings, we looked to see resistances to early modern power structures in institutions as in discourses, and we analyzed the costs of compliance to men as well as to women. As Catherine Belsey has pointed out, the lives of many women provided them with wildly inconsistent subject positions: they were to be efficient managers of their household servants yet docile attendants to their husbands. We worked at creating a more nuanced model through focusing on examples of negotiation and subversion as well as confrontation in the women's narratives.

These gender ideologies were by no means all-powerful. The need for their frequent reiteration suggests women's wide noncompliance, and scholars such as Margaret Ezell have ably demonstrated the very real powers that women retained. Far from uniform, gender ideologies were resisted and adapted, and they were variously inflected across social groups, geographic locations, and time periods. But according to Susan Stanford Friedman, early modern women may still have been generally confronted by a dual consciousness common to subordinated groups, liable to interpret themselves through the perspective of dominant gender ideologies and also to experience alienation from that reflected self. Students found Judith Butler's concept of performativity to provide a usefully complex approach to the relation of women to gender ideology. According to speech-act theory, a performative utterance calls into being that which it utters. For example, in the early modern period a man and a woman who exchange marriage vows become married; the minister's role is to ratify what has happened by virtue of the utterance of those vows. In the early modern Anglican church, the exchange of marriage vows between two people, together with the minister's ratification, attains this power because the vows are citational, or based on many previous pronouncements of the same kind. Butler argues that the enactment of heterosexual gender roles is similarly performative, for it calls into being traits that are then misrecognized as natural to gender, and this power of gender performativity also resides in its citationality, or its congruence with a series of previous such enactments within a culture. As reiterated enactments inevitably produce variations from the modeled act, a sense of dissonance may come to disturb the relation between the woman and her performances. A woman may rebel or identify against a heterosexual gender ideology or simply disengage by disidentifying. Sidonie Smith has extended Butler's model to the practice of autobiography ("Performativity"). Just as gender is performative, or produced through its enactments, so the autobiographical self, for men as well as for women, is similarly performative, or produced through the writing of autobiography. As we looked at life writings then, we considered how, instead of expressing a unified and preexistent self, life writing performs that self, and in the process calls it into being from an inchoate morass of unorganized subjectivity.

Like the gendered self, the autobiographical self also relies on citations of previous models of personhood. In the introduction to their anthology on self-representation in early modern England, Henk Dragstra, Sheila Ottway, and Helen Wilcox assert that early moderns were generally concerned less with individuality than with conformity to a culturally sanctioned model for the self. Even within this drive for conformity, however, the autobiographical act fostered agency in at least two separate ways. First, as Butler has pointed out for gender codes, reiterated enactments of a model of personhood inevitably produce variation. Second, various models of personhood became available to early moderns, especially through the power of the printing press. Not only was some range of choice available, but an autobiographer could also adapt and combine chosen models, together with their underlying ideologies, into diverse admixtures. We discussed how discourses of gender interacted, for example, with religion and politics. Readers of autobiographical writings may look beyond Hutchinson's self-description as her husband's "shadow" to consider the power she derived not only from his military role but also from her recognition that both of them served as agents in a providential design to return an erring England to the purity of a religious vocation as God's chosen nation. Cavendish's choice to clothe herself outlandishly represents a creative variation, verging on parody, that calls attention, whether intentionally or not, to the absurdity of contemporary codes of gender and social status defining subjects by their attire.

Beyond these forms of discursive agency, a woman's decision to write her autobiography itself represented an intervention, or manipulation, of early modern gender ideologies. Perhaps the first issue to explore for any early modern autobiography, whether written by a man or woman, is the author's justification of this act. Because of their opposing positions in the English civil war, Hutchinson and Cavendish provide an especially useful pair to consider together. While Hutchinson depicts herself as a wife in her memoir but not in her autobiographical fragment, in the act of appending their autobiographical writings to their biographies of their husbands, both women construct themselves as wives. But their writings could not be more different. Hutchinson explains her autobiographical fragment as a means of reflection on God's mercies in order to stir up her "thankefulnesse for things past" and her "faith for the future" (278). From her first sentence, she asserts God as "the Almighty Author of all beings." As the author of the events of her life, God is also, in a sense, the author of her life narrative. Her writing presents God as clearly the author of England's narrative, including the victory over the royalist forces. The entanglement of Hutchinson's performance of self in her country's destiny becomes evident in the space devoted to England's history. Only toward the end of this fragment does she relate her own life. She breaks off her account with the birth of her younger sister, whom her mother prefers to her, "I being of too serious a temper" (289).

Cavendish, on the other hand, seldom mentions God, referring to him in reference to the plunderers of their goods, who "would have pulled God out of heaven . . . as they did Royaltie out of his Throne" (48). She fashions an aristocratic self through her long description of her breeding and the excellencies of her family, who endured the ravages of the interregnum with patient dignity. Instead of fostering thankfulness or faith, Cavendish writes to be remembered by a future audience. She represents this remembrance in two very different ways, one grandiose and the other quite humble. Her ambition impels her to aspire to reach "[f]ame's tower, which is to live by remembrance in after-ages" (62). Cavendish's final sentence reduces this ambitious desire for fame to a simpler wish not to be confused with her husband's first wife or, if he should marry again, with his third.

In these autobiographical acts, both Hutchinson and Cavendish perform a number of roles shaped by discourses not only of gender but also of nationalism and class status. Some of the most interesting details seem inconsistent. What do we make, for example, of Hutchinson's account of herself alienating other children by plucking their "babies" or dolls to pieces (33)? How do we interpret Cavendish's extreme bashfulness, which made her inadequate to her role as maid of honor to Queen Henrietta Maria at Oxford? And how does our role, as interpreters, relate to our own models of personhood? As Jerome Bruner has observed, self-perceptions structure not only autobiographical writings but also the lives that writers choose to lead. The same may be said of readers. One benefit offered to us by the study of life writings is a more sensitive and informed perception of these, our own autobiographical projects in process.

Works Cited

Belsey, Catherine. *The Subject of Tragedy: Identity and Difference in Renaissance Drama*. London: Methuen, 1985. Print.

Bruner, Jerome. "Life as Narrative." *Social Research* 54 (1987): 11–32. Print.

Burkhardt, Jacob. *The Civilization of the Renaissance in Italy*. Trans. S. G. C. Middlemore. New York: Harper, 1958. Print.

Butler, Judith. *Bodies that Matter: On the Discursive Limits of "Sex."* London: Routledge, 1993. Print.

Cavendish, Margaret. "A True Relation of My Birth, Breeding, and Life." 1656. *Paper Bodies: A Margaret Cavendish Reader*. Ed. Sylvia Bowerbank and Sara Mendelson. 1999. Orchard Park: Broadview, 2000. 41–63. Print.

de Certeau, Michel. *The Practice of Everyday Life*. Trans. Steven Rendall. Berkeley: U of California P, 1984. Print.

Dragstra, Henk, Sheila Ottway, and Helen Wilcox. Introduction. *Betraying Our Selves: Forms of Self-Representation in Early Modern English Texts*. Ed. Dragstra, Ottway, and Wilcox. New York: St. Martin's, 2000. 1–13. Print.

Ezell, Margaret J. M. *The Patriarch's Wife: Literary Evidence and the History of the Family*. Chapel Hill: U of North Carolina P, 1987. Print.

Friedman, Susan Stanford. "Women's Autobiographical Selves: Theory and Practice." Smith and Watson 72–82.

Greenblatt, Stephen. *Renaissance Self-Fashioning: From More to Shakespeare*. Chicago: U of Chicago P, 1980. Print.

Hutchinson, Lucy. *Memoirs of the Life of Colonel Hutchinson with the Fragment of an Autobiography of Mrs. Hutchinson.* Ed. James Sutherland. London: Oxford UP, 1973. Print.

Lejeune, Philippe. "The Autobiographical Pact." *On Autobiography.* Ed. Paul John Eakin. Trans. Katherine Leary. Minneapolis: U of Minnesota P, 1989. Print.

Smith, Paul. *Discerning the Subject.* Minneapolis: U of Minnesota P, 1988. Print.

Smith, Sidonie. "Performativity, Autobiographical Practice, Resistance." Smith and Watson 108–15.

———. *A Poetics of Women's Autobiography: Marginality and the Fictions of Self-Representation.* Bloomington: Indiana UP, 1987. Print.

Smith, Sidonie, and Julia Watson, eds. *Women, Autobiography, Theory: A Reader.* Madison: U of Wisconsin P, 1998. Print.

Suggestions for Further Reading

Hundreds of early modern autobiographies, diaries, and other life writings are listed in William Matthews, *British Autobiographies: An Annotated Bibliography of British Autobiographies Published or Written before 1951* (1955; Berkeley: U of California P, 1984; print), as well as in his *British Diaries: An Annotated Bibliography of British Diaries Written between 1442 and 1942* (Berkeley: U of California P, 1950; print).

Ashmole, Elias. *Diary and Will.* Ed. R. T. Gunter. Oxford: n.p., 1927. Print.

Baxter, Richard. *Autobiography.* Ed. J. M. Lloyd Thomas. London: Dent, 1931. Print.

Bramston, John. *Autobiography.* Vol. 32. London: Camden Soc., 1845. Print.

Bunyan, John. *Grace Abounding. Grace Abounding with Other Spiritual Autobiographies.* Ed. John Stachniewski and Anita Pacheco. Oxford: Oxford UP, 1998. 1–94. Print. Oxford World's Classics.

Churchill, Sarah. *Memoirs.* Ed. William King. 1930. New York: Kraus, 1969. Print.

Clifford, Anne. *The Diaries of Anne Clifford.* Ed. D. J. H. Clifford. Stroud: Sutton, 1992. Print.

Dee, John. *Private Diary of Dr. John Dee.* Ed. J. O. Halliwell-Phillipps. London: Camden Soc., 1842. Print.

Evelyn, John. *Diary.* Ed. Guy de la Bédoyère. Woodbridge: Boydell, 2004. Print.

Forman, Simon. *Autobiography and Personal Diary.* Ed. J. O. Halliwell-Phillipps. London, 1849. Print.

Fox, George. *Journal.* Ed. Nigel Smith. London: Penguin, 1998. Print.

Gerard, John. *Autobiography of a Hunted Priest.* Trans. Philip Caraman. New York: Pellegrini, 1952. Print.

Halkett, Anne, and Ann Fanshawe. *Memoirs of Anne, Lady Halkett and Ann, Lady Fanshawe.* 1875. Ed. John Loftis. Oxford: Clarendon, 1979. Print.

Henslowe, Philip. *Diary.* Ed. R. A. Foakes and R. T. Rickert. Cambridge: Cambridge UP, 1961. Print.

Herbert, Edward. *Autobiography*. Ed. Sidney Lee. 1906. Westport: Greenwood, 1970. Print.

Hoby, Margaret. *The Private Life of an Elizabethan Lady: The Diary . . . 1599–1605*. Ed. Joanna Moody. Stroud: Sutton, 1998. Print.

Josselin, Ralph. *Diary*. Ed. Alan Macfarlane. London: Oxford UP, 1976. Print.

Machyn, Henry. *Diary*. Ed. John Gough Nichols. 1848. London: n.p., 1963. Print.

Mather, Cotton. *Diary . . . for the Year 1712*. Ed. William Manierre II. Charlottesville: UP of Virginia, 1964. Print.

Mather, Increase. *Autobiography*. Ed Michael G. Hall. Worcester: Amer. Antiquarian Soc., 1962. Print.

Penington, Mary. *Experiences in the Life of Mary Penington Written by Herself.* Ed. Norman Penney. 1911. London: Friends Historical Soc., 1992. Print.

Pepys, Samuel. *Diary*. Ed. Robert Latham and William Matthews. 10 vols. Berkeley: U of California P, 1970–83. Print.

Pilkington, Laetitia. *Memoirs*. Ed. A. C. Elias. Athens: U of Georgia P, 1997. Print.

Pollock, Linda. *With Faith and Physic: The Life of a Tudor Gentlewoman, Grace Mildmay, 1552–1620*. New York: St. Martin's, 1995. Print.

Raymond, Thomas. *Autobiography*. Ed. G. Davies. Vol. 28. London: Camden Soc., 1917. Print. 3rd ser.

Reresby, John. *Memoirs*. Ed. Andrew. Browning. 2nd ed. London: Royal Historical Soc., 1991. Print.

Rich, Mary. *Autobiography*. Ed. Thomas Crofton Croker. London: Percy Soc., 1848. Print.

Rogers, Richard, and Samuel Ward. *Two Elizabethan Puritan Diaries*. Ed. M. M. Knappen. Chicago: Amer. Soc. of Church History, 1933. Print.

Shepard, Thomas. *God's Plot . . . Autobiography and Journal of Thomas Shepard*. Ed. Michael McGiffert. [Amherst]: U of Massachusetts P, 1972. Print.

Thornton, Alice. *Autobiography*. Vol. 62. Durham: Andrews, 1875. Print. Pub. of the Surtees Soc.

Trapnel, Anna. *Cry of a Stone*. Ed. Hilary Hinds. Tempe: Arizona Center of Medieval and Renaissance Studies, 2000. Print.

Whythorne, Thomas. *Autobiography*. Ed. James M. Osborn. London: Oxford UP, 1962. Print.

Christopher Ivic

Reading Tudor Chronicles

In the past, those students of British literature who encountered Tudor chronicles usually did so in classes devoted to early modern drama, in particular, in classes on Shakespeare. Fortunately, teaching chronicle history as the dry stuff that dramatists worked to bring the past alive is on the wane. Invaluable online teaching resources, such as the the Folger Shakespeare Library Web site (www.folger.edu) and the University of Pennsylvania's Schoenberg Center for Electronic Text and Image (SCETI) (http://sceti.library.upenn.edu), have enabled teachers to develop innovative and stimulating approaches to the relations between plays and their chronicle sources. But given that the dominant form of Tudor chronicles is, after all, prose, it is surprising that most students have little or no exposure to chronicle histories in courses covering nondramatic literature of the period. Without the lure of Shakespeare, chronicles have traditionally been cut off from the classroom. How can we, as teachers of early modern prose, come to Tudor chronicles on their own, without Shakespeare as the telos?

First of all, chronicle history needs to be recuperated from the Shakespeare industry. Many students (and teachers) know Tudor chronicles only through Shakespearean resources. A prime example of this is Geoffrey

Bullough's *Narrative and Dramatic Sources of Shakespeare*. Bullough's text contains numerous Tudor chronicles: those of Richard Grafton, Edward Halle, Raphael Holinshed, and John Stow, for instance. The problem, however, is that the excerpts are bardocentric: only passages that Shakespeare drew on are selected for inclusion. Moreover, Bullough's chronicle material is presented in a manner that privileges Shakespeare. The reader thus walks away from the text with an appreciation of how Shakespeare reshaped a historical record that has traditionally been brushed aside as little more than providential narratives intended to legitimize the Tudor dynasty.

No chronicle has suffered more from this bardocentrism than the one that forms the centerpiece of this essay: Holinshed's voluminous *Chronicles of England, Scotland, and Ireland* (1577, 1587). Holinshed's *Chronicles* exist in the shelves of many libraries in the form of modern editions like *Holinshed's Chronicles As Used in Shakespeare's Plays* and *Shakespeare's Holinshed* (two separate editions use the title *Shakespeare's Holinshed*). To appreciate the richness and complexity of Holinshed's *Chronicles*, as literary historians have recently come to do, it is crucial to offer our students the texts as they appeared in print in the latter half of the sixteenth century (which could involve taking into consideration the marginal glosses that appeared in the 1587 volume of Holinshed—but not the 1577 edition—and the numerous woodcuts that adorn the 1577 but not the 1587 volume). Fortunately, a modern edition of Holinshed's *Chronicles* does exist in the form of Henry Ellis's 1807–08 edition, which was reprinted in 1965. Many libraries possess a copy of this reprint, so a lot of students will have the option to use it. Perhaps a better edition for students is the Horace Howard Furness Shakespeare Collection's electronic version, available through the University of Pennsylvania's SCETI site. This electronic version makes Holinshed readily accessible, especially for use in a wired classroom (electronic versions of Halle's *The Union of the Two Noble and Illustrate Famelies* and Stow's *Survey of London* also exist on the SCETI Web site). Furthermore, a handy table of contents affords easy navigation of this rather large, and therefore daunting, text. Since the anthologies that many teachers of early modern literature use—*The Norton Anthology of English Literature* and *The Longman Anthology of British Literature*—do not include excerpts from Holinshed's *Chronicles*, the electronic version is all the more valuable.

To dissociate chronicles like Holinshed's from Shakespeare is to invite a reading of these early modern histories on their own or, from a pedagogical perspective, in relation to other nondramatic texts on one's syllabus. One of the first lessons that we can teach our students is precisely that of early modern reading and writing practices. In the dedication to his *Union of the Two Noble Families of Lancaster and York*, Halle describes his text as "compiled and gathered (and not made) out of diuerse writers" (sig. Aiiv). Instead of perpetuating a traditional dismissal of chronicles as unoriginal and unwieldy compilations, we can use statements like Halle's to remind our students of the ubiquitousness of communal authorship in the sixteenth and seventeenth centuries. The two editions of "Holinshed's" *Chronicles* are a prime example: Holinshed, editor and chief compiler of the 1577 edition, was by no means the sole author; that the expanded 1587 edition was published well after Holinshed's death attests to the collaborative nature of this massive historical compilation. Multiple authorship has serious implications for the text's readership, as Annabel Patterson has pointed out. For Patterson, the heterogeneous inclusivity of Holinshed's *Chronicles* (in terms of both authors and material) resulted in a text that offered early modern readers a complex and often contradictory historical record. Following Patterson, we can ask students to consider the ways in which the writing of Tudor historiography, especially as embodied in Holinshed's *Chronicles*, offered its readership a communal archive that put readers in the position of weighing and considering the past in order to construct their own collective social memory. Directing students (in the classroom or in written assignments) to various and differing accounts of a particular past political event and inviting them to reflect on and account for the variety and differences can be quite productive.

Students will quickly discover that contemporary cultural, political, and social conditions weighed heavily on the construction of the nation's past. The writing, publication, and republication (not to mention censorship) of Holinshed's *Chronicles* coincided with politically charged events for the English nation-state: the execution of Mary, Queen of Scots, and the threat of the Spanish Armada, for example. As signaled by the full title of Holinshed's *Chronicles of England, Scotland, and Ireland*, late Tudor history was the history not simply of the English nation but of the increasingly overlapping and intersecting peoples of the British Isles. Perhaps no section of Holinshed's *Chronicles* bears witness to this more than the Irish volume, especially given its multiple authors/editors. The 1577 volume was compiled mainly by Richard Stanihurst, a Catholic Old Englishman and resident in Dublin; Richard Hooker, a Protestant Englishman, who lived briefly in Ireland and whose contributions to the Irish *Chronicles* give voice to New English aspirations, compiled and contributed to the 1587 volume. The terms *Old* and *New English* will need to be unpacked for students. *Old English* describes the collective descendants of the Anglo-Norman invaders who made a partial conquest of Ireland in the twelfth century and who primarily, though not exclusively, inhabited the area surrounding Dublin, which was under English jurisdiction, known then as the English Pale. With the reconquest and recolonization of Ireland in the sixteenth century, England's closest colony witnessed the arrival of a new wave of Protestant settlers from England, the New English, and this unleashed a political and cultural struggle between the rival colonial groups. While Hooker himself was not exactly a New English settler, his writings adumbrate the hopes and fears of subsequent English colonials in Ireland, most notably Edmund Spenser. The Irish section of the *Chronicles* is one of the pedagogically richest sections of Holinshed, for it gives students a wonderful opportunity to examine how early modern cultural identities were fashioned and refashioned in an expanding English polity. Indeed, the constitutive power of the historical text does well to alert students to the ways in which literature participates, though often subtly, in the production of individual and collective identities.

Stanihurst's "Description of Ireland," which opens both the 1577 and 1587 volumes, provides fertile ground for the study of identity formation. Stanihurst's ethnographic, chorographic, and topographic "Description" is divided into various chapters—including ones devoted to a genealogy of the origins of the native Irish, a pseudo-etymology of the name *Ireland*, a description of the partition of the land and the names of its boroughs, and an account of the language of the people—and this makes assigning select passages easy. Stanihurst's "Description" certainly complements William Harrison's "Description of England," which is housed in the English section of the *Chronicles*; however, by doing an assignment comparing and contrasting the two texts (or parts of them), students uncover precisely how ideologically charged chorographic and topographic descriptions can be, especially when they were being executed in the colonies. Consider, for example, Stanihurst's description of the English Pale:

> There is also another diuision of Ireland, into the English pale, and Irishrie. For when Ireland was subdued by the English, diuerse of the conquerors planted themselues neere to Dublin, and the confines thereto adioining, and so as it were inclosing and impaling themselues

> within certeine lists and territories, they feazed [drove] awaie the Irish; insomuch as that countrie became meere English, and thereof it was termed the English pale: which in ancient time stretched from Dundalke to Catherlagh or Kilkennie. But now what for the slacknesse of marchours, and incroching of the Irish enimie, the scope of the English pale is greatlie impaired. . . . (3)

Reminding students that "meere" in this context means "pure," or "unmixed," will enhance their understanding of the colonial ideology that sustains Stanihurst's "Description." Moreover, soliciting students' responses to the phrase "meere English" is one way to initiate a fruitful discussion of emergent racial or protoracial identities in the early modern period. How Stanihurst's prose qua prose inscribes such ideology should not be overlooked. Indeed, when one teaches Tudor chronicles, one can combine giving information with active learning by having the students engage in textual analysis. On a closer look, students will notice that the second sentence is a remarkable instance of a colonial sleight of hand, for a smooth, graceful, and matter-of-fact narration of the forced flight of the Irish works to efface the violence that underpins verbs like "subdued," "planted," "inclosing," "impaling," and "feazed." The "incroching of the Irish enimie," however, alerts the reader to colonial resistance, even as Stanihurst's use of commas works to maintain the distance between "the English" and "the Irish." Passages such as this allow for a nice analytic balance of form and content.

When teaching the Irish section of the *Chronicles*, I usually assign a short reading, such as the final chapter of Stanihurst's "Description," "The Disposition and Maners of the Meere Irish, Commonlie Called the Wild Irish." This chapter can be retrieved easily on the SCETI's Web site, and it is only one page and a half, or three folio columns. As an ethnography of the "wild Irish," this chapter ostensibly serves to reinforce the "meere" Englishness of the inhabitants of the Pale. The chapter opens, however, with a warning, in the form of a rhetorical commonplace known as anticipation or prevention (*ante occupatio*), whereby the writer at once anticipates the English reader's mistaking the Old English of the Pale for the Gaelic Irish so as to prevent such misidentification. "BEFORE I attempt the vnfolding of the maners of the meere Irish," Stanihurst writes,

> I thinke it expedient, to forewarne thee reader, not to impute anie barbarous custome that shall be here laid downe, to the citizens, townesmen, and inhabitants of the English pale, in that they differ litle or nothing from the ancient customes and dispositions of their

progenitors, the English and Welsh men, being therefore as mortallie
behated of the Irish, as those that are borne in England. (66–67)

Inviting students to read this passage aloud can be productive, especially
if disagreement arises concerning the tone of these lines (arrogant, anxious?). Disagreement can then be channeled into a discussion of whether
the tone sustains or undermines the anticipatory and preventative purpose of the passage. Thus, a passage that serves to foreclose questions ultimately raises them: If the "inhabitants of the English pale" are altogether
unlike the "meere Irish," then why does Stanihurst caution the reader not
to confuse the two? If language, apparel, and customs distinguish the
Old English from the "Irishrie," then why does the distinction between
the "meere Irish" and "mere English" need to be reiterated?

   At this point I inform my students that not all English colonials
"feazed awaie" the Irish. Many colonials, especially those living outside
the Pale, "went native," marrying into Gaelic families, donning Irish
clothing, and speaking Gaelic. I then return to Stanihurst and let him
finish the narrative: while discussing the "present ruine and decaie" of
Ulster's English families, Stanihurst writes:

> They were inuironed and compassed with euill neighbours. Neigh-
> bourhood bred acquaintance, acquaintance waffed in the Irish toong,
> the Irish hooked it with attire, attire haled rudenesse, rudenesse
> ingendered ignorance, ignorance brought contempt of lawes, the
> contempt of lawes bred rebellion, rebellion raked thereto warres, and
> so consequentlie the vtter decaie and desolation of that worthie
> country. (5)

Tudor chronicles are wonderful for at once exhibiting and unsettling the
humanist ideas and ideals that students will have become familiar with,
and this passage is no exception. On the one hand, this passage provides
a memorable instance of a humanist-rhetorical ordering of things, for it is
organized by the rhetorical figure gradation (*gradatio*). "Gradacion,"
writes Thomas Wilson in his *Arte of Rhetorique*, "is when we reherse the
worde that goeth next before, and bryng another woorde thereupon
that encreaseth the matter, as though one should go up a paire of staiers"
(sig. nviii). On the other hand, this passage's rhetorical dexterity, students
quickly notice, struggles to contain or counteract the unnerving account
of "degeneracy." Stanihurst gives voice to a negative gradation: the English settlers, losing first their speech, next their apparel, have gradually
"degenerated" from a state of civility to one of "rudenesse." This also

provides an opportune moment to remind students of the different terminology that we use to describe this period: Renaissance / early modern. Rhetorically, this passage is steeped in the sophisticated classical rhetoric that we associate with the Renaissance; ideologically, this passage bears witness to the cultural anxiety that we see as a signal component of the early modern or early colonial period.

Having students read dedicatory epistles is also instructive, for these epistles offer a bold statement of the purpose of the historical text. One of the finest examples of this is the dedicatory epistle, available in Holinshed, that prefaces John Hooker's 1587 *Conquest of Ireland*—a translation of Giraldus Cambrensis's twelfth-century *Expugnatio Hibernica*. In his dedicatory epistle to Walter Raleigh—who, as an undertaker in the Munster plantation, had a vested interest in Ireland—Hooker supplies a humanist commentary on his translation, reminding his patron that the study of history provides informative lessons for the present. Hooker's stress on the political uses of history is, of course, a Renaissance commonplace. In his *Boke Named the Gouernour* (1531), Thomas Elyot advised English princes to read Julius Caesar, for "therof maye be taken neccessary instructions concernynge the warres agayne Irissh men or Scottes: who be of the same rudenes and wilde disposition that the Suises & Britons were in the time of Cesar" (sig. Eviii). It is precisely this insistence on "necessary instructions" that motivates Hooker's translation. "The promotion of ancient images of virtue as patterns that aim to form or guide readers," Timothy Hampton notes, "is a central feature of almost every major text in the Renaissance," and this is particularly true of historical writings (ix). Indeed, Hooker presents his patron with numerous exemplary figures from the past, including Moses, Alexander the Great, and Caesar. These heroic figures offer Raleigh "a model of excellence, an icon after which [he] is to be formed" (Hampton xi). Take, for instance, Hooker's edifying remarks on Alexander the Great:

> [W]hen he was to inlarge his empire, he gaue himselfe to the diligent reading of Homer, the most exact chronographer of the Troian wars: and so he esteemed that booke, that in the daie time he caried it about him, and in the night time he laid it vnder his beds head; and at all times conuenient he would be reading of it, and in the end was so perfect therein, that he could verbatim repeat the whole without booke; the stratagems, the policies, and the manie deuises vsed in those warres he practised in his owne warres, which stood him in great steed. (102)

Just as Alexander kept a copy of Homer by his side, so too should Raleigh diligently read *The Conquest*. Is it just a coincidence, I ask my students, that the same year in which *The Conquest* was published, Raleigh was granted 42,000 acres in the counties of Cork and Waterford? As the dedicatory epistle makes clear, the "general end" of Hooker's translation is to fashion a colonial gentleman, or to refashion a New English gentleman.

Fitting chronicles (in my case, it is usually Holinshed) into the syllabus of my upper-division Renaissance literature course has never been a problem. I have often introduced the Irish section of *The Chronicles* between study of book 1 and book 2, canto 12, of *The Faerie Queene* and Spenser's *View of the Present State of Ireland*. Alternatively, I have tied the *Chronicles* into readings of "the wider world," to borrow a phrase from the *Norton Anthology* (927). At this point in the course (roughly three to four weeks in), I situate the literary and nonliterary texts being studied within the context of English national self-definition, or what Richard Helgerson calls the Elizabethan writing of England. Read in relation to Spenser, the Irish section of *The Chronicles* is invaluable. Set alongside Spenser's *View*, it not only offers a better understanding of early modern Ireland but also delivers competing and conflicting views of Ireland and the Irish. Such texts also allow students to get a glimpse of the darker side of *The Faeire Queene*'s didacticism as they contemplate the relation between Spenser's knights and their violent deeds and the troubled history of England's colonization of Ireland. Read in relation to New World writing, the Irish *Chronicles* prepares students to consider how the texts of Thomas Hariot and Raleigh, for instance, are less about the New World and its inhabitants and more about England and its inhabitants. In both cases, the Irish section of *The Chronicles* provides a rich investigation of cultural memory and identity formation, topics that are central to any early modern literature course.

Works Cited

Bullough, Geoffrey, ed. *Narrative and Dramatic Sources of Shakespeare*. 8 vols. London: Routledge, 1966–75. Print.

Elyot, Thomas. *The Boke Named the Gouernour*. London, 1531. Print.

Halle, Edward. *The Union of the Two Noble Families of Lancaster and York, 1550*. Facsim. ed. Menston: Scolar, 1970. Print.

Hampton, Timothy. *Writing from History: The Rhetoric of Exemplarity in Renaissance Literature*. Ithaca: Cornell UP, 1990. Print.

Helgerson, Richard. *Forms of Nationhood: The Elizabethan Writing of England*. Chicago: U of Chicago P, 1992. Print.

Holinshed, Raphael. *The Chronicles of England, Scotland, and Ireland.* Schoenberg Center for Electronic Text and Image. U of Pennsylvania Libs. Web. 24
Oct. 2008.

———. *Holinshed's Chronicles of England, Scotland, and Ireland.* Ed. Henry Ellis. 6 vols. 1807–08. New York: AMS, 1965. Print.

The Norton Anthology of English Literature. Ed. Stephen Greenblatt et al. Vol. 1.
New York: Norton, 2006. Print.

Patterson, Annabel. *Reading Holinshed's* Chronicles. Chicago: U of Chicago P,
1994. Print.

Stanihurst, Richard. "Description of Ireland." Holinshed, *Holinshed's Chronicles*
1–69.

Wilson, Thomas. *Arte of Rhetorique.* 2nd ed. London, 1560. Print.

Suggestions for Further Reading

Primary Sources

Camden, William. *Britain; or, a Chorographicall Description of the Most Flour-
ishing Kingdomes, England, Scotland, and Ireland, and the Isles Adioyning.*
London, 1610. Print.

Grafton, Richard. *A Chronicle at Large and Meere History of the Affayres of
Englande and Kinges of the Same.* London, 1569. Print.

Halle, Edward. *The Union of the Two Noble and Illustre Famelies of Lancastre
& Yorke.* London, 1548. Print.

Holinshed, Raphael *The First and Second Volumes of Chronicles.* London, 1587.
Print.

———. *The First Volume of the Chronicles of England, Scotlande, and Irelande.*
London, 1577. Print.

Speed, John. *The History of Great Britaine.* London, 1611. Print.

Stow, John. *A Summarie of Englyshe Chronicles.* London, 1565. Print.

Modern Editions

Camden, William. *Britannia.* Ed. Robert Mayhew. Bristol: Thoemmes, 2003.
Print.

Holinshed, Raphael. *Holinshed's Irish Chronicles.* Ed. Liam Miller and Eileen
Power. Atlantic Highlands: Humanities, 1979. Print.

———. *The Peaceable and Prosperous Regiment of Blessed Queene Elizabeth: A
Facsimile from Holinshed's Chronicles (1587).* Ed. Cyndia Susan Clegg. San
Marino: Huntington Lib. Press, 2004. Print.

Speed, John. *The Counties of Britain: A Tudor Atlas by John Speed.* Ed. Alasdair
Hawkyard. London: Pavilion, 1988. Print.

Stow, John. *A Survey of London: Written in the Year, 1598.* 1912. Ed. Henry
Morley. Dover: Sutton, 1994. Print.

Roger E. Moore

Quaker Writing in the Seventeenth Century

When we speak of Quakers, generally an image of sober, modest, peaceable people with quaint clothing and speech comes to mind. This image, however, emerged in the eighteenth century and does not accurately describe the earliest generation of the faithful, the contemporaries of the founder George Fox who were known as the "first publishers of truth." In the mid–seventeenth century, when the Quakers came into existence, they were obstinate, loud, and disruptive. Quakers were notorious for interrupting church services, for cobbling shoes in pulpits, for burning their belongings in public bonfires of vanities. Whereas many in England desired further reformation of church practice and doctrine, the Quakers called for an end to all of it. For them, Christianity was a strictly inward affair, and they suggested a radical revision of Christian experience. The Quakers were feared by the authorities; in the late 1650s, some believed they were poised to seize control of the government (Reay).

The Quakers played a major role in English life in the latter half of the seventeenth century, and their writings demand our attention. A host of radical sects emerged in mid-seventeenth-century England that proclaimed the inner divinity of the individual and hearkened to his or her mystical and prophetic utterances. The Quakers are the most important representatives of this brand of theology, and their radical claims concerning the nature of the self led to a distinctive prose style. Consider, for example, this selection from William Bayly's *Dreadful and Terrible Day of the Lord God*:

> Howl, howl, howl, ye Inhabitants of the Earth: who have made a Covenant with Death, and with Hell are at an Agreement, the Overflowing Scourge cometh; all your Lyes shall be swept away suddenly, as in a moment, naked and bare must you appear, and stand before the Lamb the Judge of the whole Earth, of the Quick and the Dead. Oh! Oh! What will you do in that day, ye Scoffers, ye Mockers, ye Ranters, ye Wantoners, ye Gamsters, ye Sporters, ye Cheaters, cozeners, deceivers, oppressors, covetous, unrighteous; Tyrants over the witness and witnesses of God, who make merry over it. . . . The great and terrible day of the Lord God, wherein he will arise to judgment, breaks forth upon you suddenly: Oh what will you do ye Hypocrits, ye dawbers, ye painters, ye persecutors, ye whose Silver is become Brass, and Brass, Iron; whose Heavens are become Brass, and Earth Iron. . . .

Bayly writes with conviction about the sinful world he sees around him, and his style is typical of Quaker writing in the third quarter of the seventeenth century. The sentences are long, with clause heaped on clause to heighten the immediacy of his theme. Bayly relies on lists, catalogs, and slightly varied repetitions, in what Jackson Cope long ago identified as an "incantatory" rhetoric (733). Ejaculations ("Howl, howl, howl," "Oh! Oh!") punctuate movements in thought and impart a sense of drama. Although the Quakers, like many other early modern radicals, mistrusted art, their prose writings are imagistically rich. This short passage introduces imagery of storms, floods, whirlwinds, precious metals, and a variety of images of apocalypse (the judging lamb, the "quick and the dead" [2 Tim. 4.1, 1 Pet. 4.5; King James Vers.]). Quaker writers like Bayly use intense imagery to capture the reader in the situation at hand; as the sinful will be "swept away" by the "Overflowing Scourge" on the day of judgment, so too the readers are swept along by the cascades of prophetic denunciation.

As is typical of Quaker authors, most of the imagery is biblical. Quaker writing is known for its densely allusive biblical rhetoric, but the Quakers rarely cite their borrowings or use them as evidence for theological points in the way that sermons and tracts from Anglican or Puritan writers would. Quaker authors write as if they are living in a biblical present: they see no separation between their own spiritual reality and the one recorded in the scriptures, and they thereby communicate a stylistic vividness unique to the prose writings of the Quakers and other religious radicals (Mack 138).

Even nonapocalyptic Quaker texts demonstrate these stylistic characteristics. In a letter to Oliver Cromwell's daughter, Elizabeth, recorded in his *Journal*, George Fox advises his correspondent how to heal her physical malady:

> When art ⟨thou art⟩ in the transgression of the life of God in the particular the mind flies up in the air, and the creature is led into the night, and nature goes out of his course, and an old garment goes on, and an uppermost clothing, and nature leads out of his course, and so it comes to be all of a fire, in the transgression; and that defaceth the glory of the first body.
>
>   Therefore be still awhile from thy own thoughts, searching, seeking, desires and imaginations, and be stayed in the principle of God in thee, to stay thy mind upon God, up to God; and thou wilt find strength from him and <find him to> be a present help in time of trouble, in need, and to be a God at hand. And it will keep thee humble being come to the principle of God, which hath been transgressed; which humble, God will teach in his way, which is peace; and such he doth exalt. (346–47)[1]

Fox's passage shows most of the same features as Bayly's: the long, rambling sentences built on frequent use of coordinating conjunctions, the incantatory lists, the repetitions, the biblical phrasing ("a present help in time of trouble"), and imagery. Although the tone is not apocalyptic, the dualisms of the passage (glorious "first" body versus diseased mortal body, the "transgression" versus the "principle of God in thee") indicate that Fox regards Elizabeth Cromwell's sickness as an instance of the biblical war of good against evil. Quaker writing always highlights the conflict between light and dark so that even a discussion of a seemingly ordinary case of illness is cast as a dense, theological drama.

These stylistic features of Quaker prose did not elicit kind judgments of such writings from others in Restoration society. In 1673, Henry Hallywell claimed that no "sober person" could believe a Quaker was divinely inspired "when he commits endless tautologies and vain repetitions" and gives himself over to a harangue whose "greatest part" is "downright railing" (14). John Locke was the most formidable opponent of enthusiastic sects like the Quakers, and his vilification of those who took the inspirations of their own "overheated" brains as the voice of the spirit contributed to the dismissal of Quaker writings. In an age that demanded simplicity and clarity from its authors, one where the typical Anglican sermon resembled a Senecan moral essay, the tense, emotional, and "incantatory" style of the Quakers seemed oddly alien. The Quakers accepted criticism of their style. They claimed to experience life differently from the masses of the "unconvinced," and their spirituality demanded expression in a new prose style. As trembling, falling, and quaking in a Quaker meeting was partially a protest against the constraints of the body and society, so the disjointed and rambling style of Quaker prose was a protest against the constraints of human language and a declaration of their new inspired existence (Mack 150).

The peculiarities of Quaker theology distinguish Quaker writing from other kinds of nonconformist literature. For the Friends, the inner light, or that "something of God" in each person, was most important. The confidence in the power of the inward light led the Quakers to devalue outward rituals (baptism and the Lord's Supper were spiritual, not physical), ecclesiastical authorities, and even the Bible itself. For them, salvation or "convincement" consisted of recognizing, or waking up to, the divine "seed" or "light" within. After convincement, the Quaker shed his or her old, carnal self, with its obsessions, anxieties, and vices; literally, the saved Quaker had been transformed into what Sarah Chevers called "that which changed not" (183). A Quaker experienced the resurrection inwardly, in the present, and not at the end times of orthodox Christianity. Life after convincement was a perfect union with God. Critics of the Quakers reserved their most bitter invective for this belief in perfection; some accused the Quakers of reviving the ancient gnostic heresy (Hallywell 3–7).

Opponents of the Quakers frequently chastised them for ignoring the historical details of the Bible and for interpreting it as an elaborate allegory of the transformations that occur in each enlightened individual. This criticism was just. Although the Quakers always maintained that they revered the Bible, they viewed it as but one manifestation of the living spirit that spoke in each regenerated person. As Quakers devalued the reality of events recorded in the Bible, so they devalued the details of their own lives; their earthly identity had been swallowed up in the divine. Thus, Quaker texts often demonstrate a surprising slipperiness of authorial identity. Bayly often speaks in the voice of a biblical prophet, indistinguishably mixing his own words and the words of Old Testament prophets. John Perrot signs his works "John of Patmos." Chevers and Katharine

Evans, in the midst of chronicling their incarceration in the Inquisitorial prison in Malta, suddenly find themselves enacting important biblical scenes. Quaker authors seem to regard themselves as players in a cosmic drama, and the stories of suffering and enlightenment—whether in the Bible or in their own lives—are all the same. Most nonconformist writers see themselves as actors located in time. The Quakers, by contrast, see the real import of their life struggles as something transcending time altogether.

The confidence and power of their own regenerated lives led the Quakers to seek every possible means of spreading the truth to a darkened world. Like their spiritual ancestors the Family of Love, the Quakers were quick to use print to further their goals, and a circle of Quaker printers facilitated the publishing of Quaker and other spiritual texts. Quaker writings generally fall into the following categories:

Journals and autobiographies (records of convincements and spiritual development as well as evangelist travel narratives)

Tales of martyrdom and sufferings

Admonitions, prophecies, and apocalyptic works (works that blend the Old Testament prophetic denunciations and speculation on the visions of Revelation with particular reference to the English political situation)

Controversial works (works containing debates and dialogues with religious opponents and "answers" to published attacks on the Quakers)

Imaginative literature (poems, books of proverbs, allegory)

Quaker authors help illuminate many of the important themes of seventeenth-century English literature. One of the most important issues in the seventeenth century was the construction and identity of the self. In my upper-level class in seventeenth-century literature, I organize our readings around the various "selves" dominating the era: the erotic self, the melancholy self, the spiritual self, the mortal self, the gendered self, and the mystical self. Of course, in analyzing the introspective strategies at work in the period, we spend a good deal of time with the canonical prose works—Thomas Browne's *Religio Medici*, Robert Burton's *Anatomy of Melancholy*, John Bunyan's *Grace Abounding to the Chief of Sinners*. But I also include selections from Fox's *Journal* and Lawrence Clarkson's *The Lost Sheep Found* (Clarkson was only a Quaker for one period of his life, but his autobiography owes much more to the radical understanding of self than to Puritan understandings). The inclusion of the Quaker writings allows the students to see that there is more than just an "Anglican" and a "Puritan" way of characterizing the self and suggests the considerable variety of doctrinal positions on the nature of the self, its relation to God, and its ultimate destination.

I was surprised at how well the students responded to Clarkson. The story of a young man whose search for religious truth leads him to an antinomian acceptance of licentious behavior certainly catches the attention of undergraduate students. In a couple of lively class discussions, many of the students indicated that Clarkson's spiritual restlessness resonated with their own uncertainty about ultimate truth. These comments provided an excellent teaching opportunity. I could emphasize to students how individual struggles over truth, like their own, led to powerful changes in the seventeenth century. As a result of reading Clarkson, students claimed to perceive the spiritual confusion of the era in a tangible way.

Quaker women writers also provide a necessary supplement to the discussion of the status of women. In class we study selections from non-Quaker works like Aemilia Lanyer's *Salve Deus Rex Judaeorum*, including "Eve's Apology," and the poems of Anne Bradstreet. With these I teach Margaret Fell's *Women's Speaking Justified*. Fell was an early convert to Quakerism who later became the wife of Fox; her home at Swarthmoor Hall became the center of the movement. *Women's Speaking Justified* is a controversial tract that refutes those who interpret too literally Saint Paul's injunctions against the involvement of women in the church. In class, we consider a number of questions about these works. How differently do these women handle adversity? How do they employ biblical material? On what bases do these writers argue for the significance of women?

Fell resembles other seventeenth-century women in that she uses many of the same biblical examples to prove that Christ respected women and that women were essential to the success of the early church, but this biblical evidence leads her to promote very different ends for women. Fell wants to move beyond the question of gender entirely. For her the differences between male and female are merely distinctions in the material world. The spirit extends to all souls, male and female, and therefore Fell's plea for women's speaking enjoins listening to the spirit in every speaking form. Reading Fell along with the other women makes it possible for students to see the multiple, complex agendas pursued by women facing similar prejudices and limitations in early modern society.

Fell's preoccupation with women's speech is particularly interesting. Because England experienced such social and religious turmoil in the seventeenth century, many of its writers longed for quiet, silence, and solitude; one of the most popular biblical texts for sermons in the last half of the century is 1 Thessalonians 4.11, "Study to be quiet" (King James Vers.). In class, we examine the desire for silence in Burton, Andrew Marvell, John Milton, and others. *Women's Speaking Justified* plays a role in the cultural discussion of silence because Fell sees the silencing of women, and of all those who bear the inward light, as the work of the spirit of darkness. Although the Quakers, whose worship consisted of silent waiting on the Lord, valued silence probably more than any other group in the era, Fell flouts the zeitgeist by insisting on a role for inspired speech that leads to radical transformation.

Fell's tract also helps articulate a seventeenth-century idea of truth. I begin the semester by proposing that probably the most pressing issue for England in the 1600s was distinguishing truth from falsehood. In an age that witnessed many challenges to established political, religious, and philosophical authorities, the yearning for truth was especially intense. Fell's *Women's Speaking Justified* emblematizes an English Protestant search for truth. Fell sees all human history as a cosmic battle between truth and falsehood, and she imagines this battle in multiple forms—as a conflict between the woman's seed and the serpent, between the children of the bondwoman and the freedwoman, between the letter and the spirit, between the woman clothed with the sun and the whore of Babylon. Fell's text provides a thorough introduction to some of the most salient and pervasive imagery of Protestant discourse, and the relative brevity of the work makes it an especially good tool for introducing students to a Protestant understanding of human history.

The Quaker authors were popular among students in the seventeenth-century-literature class and inspired some of the most thoughtful, animated discussions. The immediacy and vividness of Quaker prose appealed to them, and they found the Quaker challenge to authorities compelling. They were particularly captivated by Fell's critique of male authority and found her text relevant to contemporary debates about women. *Women's Speaking Justified* led us into a valuable discussion about the possibility of speaking about seventeenth-century "feminism." For their final essay, students were asked to choose from a list of broad topics (solitude, paradise, liberty, mortality, and authority) and to refer to at least four authors from the syllabus; a significant number of students included Fell or Clarkson in their papers.

One of the most interesting Quaker texts is a short prose allegory by Stephen Crisp, *A Short History of a Long Travel from Babylon to Bethel*. Crisp (1628–92) is a major Quaker figure; he distinguished himself as a writer of controversial works, and we even possess published copies of some of his sermons (which is rare since Quakers valued extemporaneous inspiration of the spirit and eschewed the commission of such utterances to print). His allegory is in the style of Bunyan's *Pilgrim's Progress*. In the text, the main character, a native of Egypt who grows up in Babylon and who is "spiritually called" searches for a way to God's house (23). He engages two different guides to lead him on his path. The first, a thinly disguised Anglican, is unfamiliar with the way, and, although he keeps consulting a book, he gets lost and cannot lead our pilgrim onward. The second guide is a sectarian, most likely a Baptist, who leads the pilgrim through a deep river to an attractive house that is dirty and full of contentious people (7–12; Wright 139). Almost in despair, the pilgrim leaves the house and sets out on his own. At his darkest moment, while sitting in a "vast howling Wilderness" after a great storm, the pilgrim perceives a light near him, which he decides to follow (12). Despite numerous difficulties on the way, the pilgrim finally arrives at the house of God, where he is stripped of his old clothes and given white raiment.

The text is a succinct account of the Quaker experience of salvation; the individual transcends all outside mediators as he looks to the light within. The tale is rather crudely written and is no match for the style and execution of *Pilgrim's Progress*, but Crisp's text makes a worthy addition to undergraduate classes. In a British literature survey class, Crisp's text can provide a useful companion to Bunyan's masterwork by deepening inquiry about allegory and the ways that narrative was used to tell the Christian story in nonconformist circles. Students are often wary of allegory, but looking at two competing versions of the Christian pilgrimage helps them perceive the form's rich possibilities.

In an upper-level undergraduate class in seventeenth-century literature, the inclusion of *A Short History* furnishes students an opportunity to place Bunyan's work in its historical context. Bunyan was a great opponent of the Quakers, and some of his earliest and most powerful controversial works were written against them. The character Ignorance in *Pilgrim's Progress*, who is cast into hell in the last moments of the work, is thought to represent the Quakers (Hardin). Reading Crisp's text alongside Bunyan's strengthens students' understanding of the doctrinal disagreements motivating Bunyan to write *Pilgrim's Progress*; it also enables them to see at least one competing imaginative account of Christian salvation. Crisp's and Bunyan's texts are but two of the many versions of the pilgrimage motif to appear in the early modern period, and grouping these works with the journey poems of George Herbert or Henry Vaughan, for instance, would provide students with a useful compendium of Christian spiritual speculation in the period and suggest the centrality of Quakerism in the imaginative life of the seventeenth century.

Note

1. The angle brackets appear in the edition of George Fox's journal here cited, where the editor, John L. Nickalls, uses them to indicate that text has been taken from a source other than the main manuscript he consulted.

Works Cited

Bayly, William. *The Dreadful and Terrible Day of the Lord God, to Overtake This Generation Suddenly; Once More Proclaimed*. London, 1665. Print.

Chevers, Sarah, and Katharine Evans. *This Is a Short Relation of Some of the Cruel Sufferings*. 1662. *Hidden in Plain Sight: Quaker Women's Writings, 1650–1700*. Ed. Mary Garman, Judith Applegate, Margaret Benefiel, and Dortha Meredith. Wallingford: Pendle Hill, 1996. 171–209. Print.

Clarkson, Lawrence. *Lost Sheep Found*. London, 1660. Print.

Cope, Jackson I. "Seventeenth-Century Quaker Style." *PMLA* 71.4 (1956): 725–54. Print.

Crisp, Stephen. *A Short History of a Long Travel from Babylon to Bethel*. 1691. London, 1711. Print.

Fell, Margaret. *Women's Speaking Justified, Proved, and Allowed by the Scriptures*. 1666. *Lay By Your Needles, Ladies, Take the Pen: Writing Women in England, 1500–1700*. Ed. Suzanne Trill, Kate Chedgzoy, and Melanie Osborne. Oxford: Oxford UP, 1997. 217–20. Print.

Fox, George. *The Journal of George Fox*. Ed. John L. Nickalls. Rev. ed. Philadelphia: Religious Soc. of Friends, 1997. Print.

Hallywell, Henry. *An Account of Familism as It Is Revived and Propagated by the Quakers*. . . . London, 1673. Print.

Hardin, Richard F. "Bunyan, Mr. Ignorance, and the Quakers." *Studies in Philology* 69 (1972): 496–508. Print.

Locke, John. *An Essay concerning Human Understanding*. Ed. Peter H. Nidditch. Oxford: Clarendon, 1979. Print.

Mack, Phyllis. *Visionary Women: Ecstatic Prophecy in Seventeenth-Century England*. Berkeley: U of California P, 1992. Print.

Reay, Barry. *The Quakers and the English Revolution.* New York: St. Martin's, 1985. Print.

Wright, Luella M. *The Literary Life of the Early Friends, 1650–1725.* 1932. New York: AMS, 1966. Print.

Suggestions for Further Reading

Journals and Autobiographies

Bayly, William. *A Short Relation or Testimony of the Working of the Light of Christ in Me from My Childhood.* London, 1659. Print.

Crook, John. "A Short History of the Life of John Crook." 1706. *Grace Abounding with Other Spiritual Autobiographies.* Ed. John Stachniewski and Anna Pacheco. Oxford: Oxford UP, 1998. 157–69. Print. Oxford World's Classics.

Ellwood, Thomas. *The History of the Life of Thomas Ellwood.* New York: Routledge, 1885. Print.

Mulliner, John. *A Testimony against Periwigs and Periwig-Making, and Playing on Instruments of Musick among Christians. . . .* London, 1677. Print.

Penington, Mary. "A Brief Account of Some of My Exercises, from My Childhood. . . ." *Hidden in Plain Sight: Quaker Women's Writings, 1650–1700.* Ed. Mary Garman, Judith Applegate, Margaret Benefiel, and Dortha Meredith. Wallingford: Pendle Hill, 1996. 210–32. Print.

Prophecies, Admonitions, and Apocalyptic Works

Bayly, William. *The Life of Enoch Again Revived, in Which Abel's Offering Is Accepted, and Cain's Mark Known.* London, 1662. Print.

Ellwood, Thomas. *An Alarm to the Priests; or, A Message from Heaven to Forewarn Them of the Dreadfull Day of the Lord Which Will Suddenly Overtake Them. . . .* London, 1660. Print.

A Controversial Work

Fisher, Samuel. *Rusticus ad Academicos . . . the Rustick's Alarum to the Rabbies. . . .* London, 1660. Print.

Imaginative Literature

Perrot, John. *A Sea of the Seed's Sufferings.* London, 1661. Print.

Secondary Works

Bauman, Richard. *Let Your Words Be Few: Symbolism of Speaking and Silence among Seventeenth-Century Quakers.* Cambridge: Cambridge UP, 1983. Print.

Carroll, Kenneth L. *John Perrot: Early Quaker Schismatic.* London: Friends Historical Soc., 1971. Print.

Corns, Thomas N., and David Loewenstein, eds. *The Emergence of Quaker Writing: Dissenting Literature in Seventeenth-Century England.* London: Cass, 1995. Print.

Hazleton, Meiling. "'Mony Choaks': The Quaker Critique of the Seventeenth-Century Public Sphere." *Modern Philology* 98.2 (2000): 251–70. Print.

Keeble, N. H. *The Literary Culture of Nonconformity in Later Seventeenth-Century England*. Athens: U of Georgia P, 1987. Print.

Smith, Nigel. "Exporting Enthusiasm: John Perrot and the Quaker Epic." *Literature and the English Civil War*. Ed. Thomas Healy and Jonathan Sawday. Cambridge: Cambridge UP, 1990. 248–64. Print.

———. *Perfection Proclaimed: Language and Literature in English Radical Religion, 1640–1660*. Oxford: Clarendon, 1989. Print.

Mary Beth Rose

A Voyage on a Dangerous Sea: Marriage as Heroism in Early Modern English Prose

The extraordinary thing about early modern English prose concerning marriage is the fact of its existence, along with its urgency, proliferation, and exuberance. It is not that theologians, lawyers, philosophers, and moralists had entirely disavowed the struggle to define marriage in earlier centuries: they did undertake it, although not very thoroughly or very well. Their efforts to consider marriage as an institution were vague and without enthusiasm. To contemplate marriage as a relationship beyond and including the reproductive one was hardly worth the effort. Before the Protestant Reformation in England, sexual union between a man and a woman with the purpose of producing children did not seem the noblest of human endeavors; it was distinctly lacking in prestige. "He that hath wife and children hath given hostages to fortune; for they are impediments to great enterprises, either of virtue or mischief," Francis Bacon wrote in "Of Marriage and Single Life," with a skepticism about heterosexuality that is both belated and perennial (81). While Bacon's fears focus on the precarious nature of life in the world, Saint Paul's view of marriage as merely a necessary evil is more notorious and even more pessimistic in its dismissal of erotic desire and the heterosexual act itself, even for purposes of procreation, as products of human weakness and sin. "For I would that all men were even as I myself [celibate]," Paul wistfully tells the Corinthians; "It is good for them if they abide even as I. But if they cannot contain, let them marry: for it is better to marry than to burn" (1 Cor. 7.7, 9 [King James Vers.]).

When I began my research about early modern marriage, I was astonished by the negative press that institution has received until (taking the long view) fairly recently in Western history. I have found that students, like me the products of the idealization of marriage—even given the currently precarious state of that institution—share my surprise at the low prestige it embodied until the sixteenth century. At that time an ebullient discursive effort arose among Protestant Reformers to raise the cultural status of marriage, to re-create it as vital to securing human relationships and as an institution essential to the state instead of a somewhat shameful vehicle designed to accommodate human sensuality and to legitimize the inheritance of property. In his 1977 work *The Family, Sex, and Marriage*, the historian Lawrence Stone characterized a long and gradual shift in the early modern centuries that saw marriage (among the upper classes) transform from an arrangement among extended kin groups primarily for the purpose of consolidating and transmitting property to a union between two people who had the option of choosing each other and forming a nuclear familial core in which the new marital goal of personal happiness conjoined with the traditional goal of social stability. Stone's work has been criticized, augmented, and refined, primarily because his coverage of social class is for the most part restricted to the elite and his views of emotions and psychology are naive and inaccurate. Nevertheless subsequent scholarship has never superseded the large pattern of transformation in the institution of marriage that he establishes.[1] Early modern English prose about marriage is well worth studying for its adamant participation in the ideological aspects of this transformation. The importance of ideological shifts in conceptions of marriage is clearly registered in the development of literary forms in the period. In terms of the lyric, Edmund Spenser's *Amoretti* and *Epithalamion* (for example) would have been quite different without changes in the prestige of marriage; *Othello*, *The Duchess of Malfi*, and *Paradise Lost* would be unimaginable. Romantic comedies (to cite another instance) did not conclude with marriages that conjoined happiness and stability, symbolizing the wished-for society (a pattern still very much in evidence in the twenty-first century) until well into the 1580s. Early modern prose about marriage, then, is important both in its relation to other literary texts and in its participation in effecting cultural change.

Many famous Renaissance prose writers contribute to the larger discussion about marriage: as we have seen, Bacon weighs in, as do Erasmus, Marguerite de Navarre, John Luis Vives, Michel de Montaigne, and John Donne.[2] For the most part (with the partial exceptions of Marguerite de Navarre and Erasmus) their discussions of the subject advocate what were in the sixteenth century conservative values, including arranged marriages, unquestioned privileging of property, and pessimism about heterosexual love. Because I am arguing that the main reason to study prose about marriage as a genre in itself is its contribution to ideological change and its impact on and interaction with literary forms, I concentrate in this essay on the outpourings of the Protestant Reformers in England. As historians have shown, many of the themes in Protestant marital discourse are derivative: the frequent analogy of marriage and family relationships to the political organization of the state, for example, is brought into view by Aristotle (see Jordan 43–44). Nevertheless the emphasis, elaboration, and wide distribution certain issues achieve in Protestant Reformers' tracts are completely new. It is the power, popularity, and accessibility of the early modern idealization of marriage that establish its relevance and importance.

In their ideological campaign to promote the importance of marriage and the family, the Protestants (addressing middle as well as upper classes) continually define the family as an institution that is private but nevertheless distinguished by its connections to political and spiritual life. With urgent solemnity, the Protestants' prose insists on the public dignity and cosmic significance of marriage, viewing it as the heroic arena in which salvation and damnation are determined for husband and wife. Whether these writers stress the obstacles or rewards inherent in marriage, the configuration on which all their arguments depend is their careful, fervent elaboration of the ancient analogy connecting the family, society, and the spiritual realm. "Commonwealths I say," Alexander Niccholes declares, joining his colleagues in explaining that the husband is to the wife as the magistrate is to the subject, are to marriage as Christ is to the church (qtd. in Rose, *Expense* 119).[3]

Extending the idea of the family as a model of the church and the state gives a newly momentous significance to individuals' domestic actions. An important innovation of early modern prose about marriage is the emphasis on marriage not simply as a matter of doctrine or law but as a relationship involving two people with complicated emotions and distinctive roles. This view could be said to be institutionalized in 1549, when the Book of Common Prayer added companionship as a third reason for marriage, in addition to the traditionally acknowledged motives of reproduction of offspring and avoidance of fornication (*First and Second Prayer Books* 252–58). In subsequent analyses, a number of issues previously taken for granted come up for scrutiny: should a husband and wife choose each other, or is parental consent needed? what are the parameters of wifely obedience? how important should property relations be in the forming of a marriage? what is the place of sexual love? should happiness be expected? must husband and wife be from the same social class?

No doubt readers of this essay will recognize these issues as animating much of the literature of the period, especially the drama, and will also recognize the persistence of some of their disturbing ironies into the present day. The analysis of these issues embodies (often without the consciousness of the authors) the contradictions between mutuality and hierarchy that characterize the Protestant idealization of marriage, permeating the prose. How can an institution that enforces inequality, subordination, and wifely obedience as defining components of its existence—legalized in the doctrine of coverture—also aspire to loving companionship and fulfillment between spiritually equal spouses? As I will show, these paradoxes and contradictions are often unacknowledged and are always left unresolved.[4]

Assigning the "Homily of the State of Matrimony" is a good way to introduce students both to the issues and themes mentioned above and to the disturbing contradictions inscribed within them. This sermon is the eighteenth in a series of sermons that were required to be read by parsons every Sunday from 1562 onward, so it is a well-known and widely accepted Elizabethan formulation of marriage and a good place from which to expand outward with comparison to other texts. The homily begins with the three reasons for marriage, interestingly giving first priority to companionship ("the intent that man and woman should live lawfully in a perpetual friendly fellowship" [501]). Presenting marriage as a place of potential salvation for both spouses, the text quickly introduces a grammatical slippage that points to the unresolved status inconsistency between husband and wife:

> [B]oth of you stand in the fear of God, and abhor all filthiness. For
> that is surely the singular gift of God; where the common example
> of the world declareth how the devil hath their hearts bound and en-
> tangled in divers snares, so that they in their wifeless state run into
> open abominations without any grudge of their conscience. (501)

"They" and "both of you," the couple, rather quickly if unintentionally transform into the husband ("they in their wifeless state"), thus echoing the paradoxical legal truism of coverture: husband and wife are one person in law and that person is the husband, itself a problematic interpretation of the biblical ideal of man and wife as one flesh.[5]

The homily goes on to elaborate at length the proper duties for husband and wife, clearly establishing the husband as "the leader and author of love" and admonishing him to tolerate and forgive his—according to this writer—inevitably annoying wife. Although wife beating is discouraged but not forbidden in the marital texts, in the homily the husband is explicitly told he should not beat his wife. Women, pointedly, repeatedly, and characteristically termed the "weaker vessels," in turn must obey their husbands, enduring even their extreme "sharpness" (508). Thus the well-known components of hierarchy and subordination in early modern marriage are established in the elaboration of spousal roles.

There are two striking aspects to the discussion of marital roles in the homily and elsewhere that exceed the intricately defined parameters of inequality, an unaccountable excess that appears in varying forms and different degrees in all the marriage prose. The fact that marriage has the potential for human dignity and noble endeavor that allows it to become the arena for heroism is a striking and new phenomenon, one that belies easy assumptions about the ways in which the development of separate spheres by the end of the seventeenth century denigrated the importance of "private" life.[6] Describing the perils involved in the heroic marriage and suggesting their remedies, commentators rely frequently on military metaphors of conquest and self-defense:

> [F]or it is in this action as in a stratagem of war: "Wherein he that errs can err but once, perisheth unrecoverably to all after-advice and relief." (Niccholes)

> [A] valiant soldier doth never repent of the battle, because he meets with strong enemies; he resolves to be conqueror, and then the more and stronger his foes, the greater his honor. (Whately)

> [[D]omestic] authority is like a sword, which with over much using will be blunted, and so fail to do that service which otherwise it might when there is most need. A wise, grave, peaceable man, may always have his sword in readiness, and that also very bright, keen, and sharp: but he will not be very ready to pluck it out of his scabberd. (Gouge)[7]

Although spouses are viewed in these tracts as heroic, the terms of their heroism have changed. The marital virtues adduced are in noticeable contrast to those of a warrior aristocracy, who were exhorted to exuberant, hands-on, violent aggression. Heroes of marriage are, indeed, soldiers: they must pass through dangers and adversity, but to do so successfully, they must be armed not with quick-witted, assertive domination but with patience, endurance, and tolerance. Further, these characteristics are equally essential to both husband and wife. Thus while busily defining women as inferior, weak, and subordinate, these writers simultaneously open up the possibility for female heroism in terms identical to those prescribed for men.

The unresolved paradoxes of the wifely position, particularly in terms of obedience, are as visible in the homily as they are in many other discussions. At first the obedience hierarchy seems clear; while a wife is required to obey her husband, her children must obey her: "To obey is another thing than to control or command, which yet they may do to their children, and to their family: but as for their husbands, them must they obey, and cease from commanding, and perform subjection" (505). Yet two pages later, the author of the homily collapses the category wife into the category servants and children, when exhorting wives to obey. That is, in contrast to the passage just quoted above, the obedience of wives suddenly becomes identical to, not distinguished from, that of children and servants:

> For when we ourselves do teach our children to obey us as their parents; or when we reform our servants, and tell them that they should obey their masters, not only at the eye, but as to the Lord; if they should tell us again of our duties, we would not think it well done. (507)

While fervently proclaiming and defining the subjection of women, the idealizers of marriage provide the necessary material for its subversion. After lionizing wifely obedience, for example, William Gouge urges women never to obey husbands who want them to do what "is forbidden by God." In a similar vein, after demanding obedience and subjection (rising against husbands is the equivalent of rising against God), writers including Gouge, John Dod and Robert Cleaver, and Samuel Hieron, urge women not only to disobey but also actively to seek to correct erring husbands. Furthermore they define wives' subjection as merely temporal, temporary. Woman's place is one of "inferiority and subjection, yet the nearest to equality that may be," Gouge offers unhelpfully (121–22).

Many of the marriage tracts are simply misogynistic, but in others women assume a striking and positive prominence. Edmund Tilney's *Flower of Friendship* (1568), a dialogue clearly modeled after Baldassare

Castiglione's *The Courtier* (1528), distinguishes itself from its predecessor by including women not merely as mediators but as protagonists in the debate. Instead of concentrating solely on the need for female chastity, Gouge's *Of Domesticall Duties* inveighs against the sexual double standard, insisting that both partners in a marriage must remain chaste and arguing for equality of sexual desire: "Their power also over one another in this respect is alike" (125). Gouge spends a virtually equal amount of time enumerating husbands' and wives' duties and responsibilities in marriage. Of the marriage tracts I have studied, though, William Whately's *A Care-Cloth* treats women with the greatest interest and imagination. Whately not only gives women equal time in his considerations of marriage but also recognizes a distinctly female point of view and attempts to enter into it. Clearly, Whately has tried to imagine what it is like to be a woman: "What if he lie thus by me groaning and tossing, many days, weeks, months, and some years?" he asks, taking on the role of a desperate housewife. He continues:

> What if bringing forth be so tedious and painful, that I never become a mother, but by going through the torment of a hundred deaths in one, besides a long weakness after? . . . How shall I bear headache, heartache, backache, stomach ache, retching, casting, longing, loathing, . . . pangs, swoonings, and twenty deaths a day? (125)

The tone of the homily is similarly bleak; marriage is harness to a yokefellow, a trial to be endured with unending patience: "And by these means all things shall prosper quietly, and so we shall pass through the dangers of the troublous sea of this world," the writer offers, sadly resigned ("Homily" 514). Much of the marital prose is pronounced in its distrust of heterosexuality, viewing marriage as a solemn duty, but happiness as a dangerous delusion. "Likely none do meet with more crosses in marriage, or bear their crosses more untowardly, than those that most dream of finding it a very Paradise," warns Whately (121). Other tracts are considerably more optimistic, confident of the possibility of happiness and self-knowledge: "The very name . . . should portend unto thee merryage . . . for marriage awaketh the understanding as out of a dream" (120–21). In his rhapsodic *The Crown Conjugal* (1632), John Wing finds the location of happiness to be "the worth of a gracious wife," although he does regard that source of bliss as "both frail and inferior" (qtd. in Rose, *Expense* 124–25).[8] While the Protestant preachers (which they almost always are) express a wider variety of views and approaches than is commonly recognized, they do reach consensus in making the crucial point that the marriage relationship constitutes the arena in which the individual can struggle and meet death or defeat, triumph or salvation. As Niccholes writes, "marriage is an adventure, for whosoever marries, adventures; he adventures his peace, his freedom, his liberty, his body; yea, and sometimes his soul too." Furthermore, undertaking this quest, "the means either to exalt on high to preferment, or cast down headlong to destruction" becomes "this one and absolutely greatest action of a man's whole life," requiring the unwavering commitment characteristic of the hero and assuming the properties of inevitable destiny: "as thereon depending the future good or evil of a man's whole after-time and days." Marriage is a perilous odyssey, a voyage on a dangerous sea, "wherein so many shipwreck for want of better knowledge and advice upon a rock" (121).

In this perilous adventure spouses enjoy spiritual equality, a fact that is not acknowledged to contradict the rigid hierarchical differences attributed to every other aspect of their identities, which are nevertheless supposed to be linked. Other areas of concern in the marriage prose—class, status, age, money, and parental consent—are all treated with the same seriousness and disregard of inconsistency.

> An equal yoke-fellow should be taken, of due proportion in state, birth, age, education, and the like, not much under, not much over, but fit and correspondent . . . the rich and noble will likely despise, or set light by the poorer and meaner: so will the younger do the aged,

observes Whately. When a marriage is socially unequal, however, it turns out to be the husband's identity that determines the social status of the couple, and gender will trump even class. If a man "of mean place be married to a woman of eminent place," she must nevertheless acknowledge him as her superior: "It booteth nothing what either of them were before marriage . . . for in giving her self to be his wife, and taking him to be her husband, she advanceth him above her self, and subjecteth her self unto him" (127). A similarly irreconcilable set of assertions are offered about the matter of parental consent to a marriage. Time and again the Protestant idealizers vehemently protest the common phenomenon of parents forcing their children to marry against their will; yet they are equally resistant to the idea of children marrying without parental consent. "No man can pass away another's right, without his liking," Whately asserts in seeming defense of individual choice of a spouse; yet he immediately adds that a couple marrying without parental consent is living in sin until "they have procured an after-consent, to ratify that which ought not to have been done before the consent" (129, 130).[9]

Absolute spiritual and social equality between the sexes, coexisting with the equally absolute subjection of women that is decreed and then subverted, and issues of class difference and parental consent that are deemed both irrelevant and consequential—the logical inconsistencies that now appear so glaring, particularly given their consequences, seem never to have occurred to the producers of this prose. These contradictions and paradoxes permeate not only the conceptualization of women but also all matters concerning love, marriage, and sexuality. Busily seeking to separate the present from the past and participating in the abstract and visionary formation of an ideology, these writers appear not to be aware of the contradictions they were articulating. The value of this prose does not lie in its self-consciousness or its prescience. Rather, because of its historical position, Protestant marriage ideology in the sixteenth and seventeenth centuries provides a remarkable index of the ways in which modern marital values were being created, terms were being constructed, and conflicts were taking shape: an ideology observable at the moment it is being formulated. Both in its differentness and its continuities, early modern prose about marriage combines the familiar with the strange. Particularly given twenty-first-century quandaries about the family, this discourse provides students a direct way to observe the ongoing legacy of the past.

Notes

1. See Stone, *Road to Divorce*. For an early critique of Stone's work that offers the objections I mention, see Wrightson.

2. See Erasmus 40–64; Marguerite de Navarre; John Luis Vives; Montaigne 510; and John Donne's three sermons on marriage (2:17, 3:11, 8:3).

3. See also in Rose, *Expense*, Niccholes 178; Gouge 2, 17, 219–20, 260–61; Whately 38; Perkins 669; Dod and Cleaver, sig. A4; Hieron 469. The Puritan analogies among the family, the state, and the church are discussed in Haller and Haller and in Hill 443–81.

4. See Rose, *Expense*, esp. 119–77, for the ways in which the unresolved paradoxes in English Renaissance marital prose relate to the representation of marriage in tragedy. Three excellent analyses that deal directly with the historical consequences of these unacknowledged contradictions are Harris; Erickson; and Pateman.

5. The best early modern source on coverture is T. E.

6. See Pateman; Rose, *Gender*; and Shoemaker.

7. See 121–22 in Rose, *Expense*. Quotations from Niccholes, Gouge, and Whately are taken from Rose, *Expense*, unless otherwise noted. For other uses of

the heroic-military idiom in constructing marriage, see Wing 63, 74, 125–33; Whately 25–26, 42, 46–48, 58–59, 68, 72–74, 76–77, 80.

8. Also see Dod and Cleaver, sig. K3; Gouge 225, 227; and Smith.

9. See also Hieron, who speaks strongly against "the buying & selling of children among parents," the "forced marriages, which mostly have the same issue of extreme loathing," and the unequal yoking "of an ox and an ass together" (405). See also T. E.: "It is now received a general opinion that the good will of parents is required, in regard of honesty, not of necessity, according to the Canons which exact necessarily, none other consent but only of the parties themselves, whose conjunction is in hand, without which the conclusion of parents is of none effect" (53).

Works Cited

Bacon, Francis. *The Essays*. Ed. John Pitcher. Harmondsworth: Penguin, 1985. Print.

Dod, John, and Robert Cleaver. *A Godlie Form of Household Government*. London, 1598. Print.

Donne, John. *The Sermons of John Donne*. Ed. George R. Potter and Evelyn M. Simpson. 10 vols. Berkeley: U of California P, 1953–62. Print.

Erasmus, Desiderius. "An Epistle to Persuade a Young Gentleman to Marriage, Devised by Erasmus in the Behalf of His Friend." Trans. Thomas Wilson. *The Art of Rhetoric*. By Wilson. London, 1580. Print.

Erickson, Amy Louise. *Women and Property in Early Modern England*. London: Routledge, 1995. Print.

The First and Second Prayer Books of Edward VI. 1549. London: Dent, 1949. Print.

Gouge, William. *Of Domesticall Duties*. London, 1622. Print.

Haller, William, and Malleville Haller. "The Puritan Art of Love." *Huntington Library Quarterly* 5 (1941–42): 235–72. Print.

Harris, Barbara J. *English Aristocratic Women, 1450–1550: Marriage and Family, Property and Careers*. Oxford: Oxford UP, 2002. Print.

Hieron, Samuel. *The Sermons of Master Samuel Hieron*. London, 1635. Print.

Hill, Christopher. *Society and Puritanism in Pre-revolutionary England*. New York: Schocken, 1964. Print.

"An Homily of the State of Matrimony." *Sermons, or Homilies: Appointed to Be Read in Churches in the Time of Queen Elizabeth*. New York: Swords, 1815. 501–15. Print. Early Amer. Imprints, 2nd ser., 34346.

Jordan, Constance. *Renaissance Feminism: Literary Texts and Political Models*. Ithaca: Cornell UP, 1990. Print.

Marguerite de Navarre. *The Heptameron*. Ed. and trans. P. A. Chilton. London: Penguin, 1988. Print.

Montaigne, Michel de. "Upon Some Verses of Virgil." *The Essays*. Trans. John Florio. London, 1603. Print.

Niccholes, Alexander. "A Discourse of Marriage and Wiving." London, 1615. *The Harleian Miscellany: A Collection of Scarce, Curious, and Entertaining Pamphlets and Tracts . . . from the Library of Edward Harley. . . .* Ed. William Oldys. Vol. 2. London: White, 1808–13. Print. 10 vols.

Pateman, Carole. *The Sexual Contract*. Stanford: Stanford UP, 1988. Print.

Perkins, William. *Christian Economy; or, Household Government.* London, 1631. Print.

Potter, George R., and Evelyn M. Simpson, eds. *The Sermons of John Donne.* 10 vols. Berkeley: U of California P, 1953–62. Print.

Rose, Mary Beth. *The Expense of Spirit: Love and Sexuality in English Renaissance Drama.* Ithaca: Cornell UP, 1991. Print.

———. *Gender and Heroism in Early Modern English Literature.* Chicago: U of Chicago P, 2002. Print.

Shoemaker, Robert B. *Gender in English Society, 1650–1850: The Emergence of Separate Spheres?* London: Longman, 1998. Print.

Smith, Henry. "A Preparative to Marriage." *The Works of Henry Smith.* Ed. Thomas Fuller. Vol. 1. Edinburgh: Nichol, 1866. 1–40. Print.

Stone, Lawrence. *The Family, Sex, and Marriage in England, 1500–1800.* New York: Harper, 1977. Print.

———. *Road to Divorce: England, 1530–1987.* Oxford: Oxford UP, 1990. Print.

T. E. *The Law's Resolutions of Women's Rights; or, The Law's Provision for Women.* London, 1632. Print.

Vives, John Luis. *Instruction of a Christian Woman.* Trans. Richard Hyrde. 1529. London, 1557. Print.

Whately, William. *A Care-Cloth.* London, 1624. Print.

Wing, John. *The Crown Conjugal; or, The Spouse Royal.* London, 1632. Print.

Wrightson, Keith. *English Society, 1580–1680.* New Brunswick: Rutgers UP, 1982. Print.

Gary Schneider

Teaching Early Modern Letters

One advantage of exploring early modern letters with students is that the continuing practice of letter writing—be it only in e-mails—offers students an unmistakable point of reference. Yet students' familiarity with present-day modes of immediate, long-distance communication such as telephone, radio, cell phones, and text messaging often obscures the recognition that before the advance of electronic communications, even the simplest message had to wait days, even weeks, to be transmitted by the frequently unreliable postal systems of the sixteenth and seventeenth centuries. Once students appreciate that the only other means of personal communication in the early modern era besides face-to-face conversation was epistolary contact, an exploration of early modern letters and letter-writing practices becomes a study of its practical and material elements— how letter exchange served as a primary mode of communication, how specialized rhetorical strategies sustained epistolary communication, and how the nature of the post threatened it. Yet, at the same time, exploring early modern letters allows investigation of crucial conceptual issues, including how social ties were formed and managed by epistolary means, how women employed the genre, and how letters constituted literary documents—all of which come into sharp focus when we study the epistolary writing of the period.

Epistolary Communities, Letters as Vehicles of Communication

The primary function of letters in this period was communicative; that is, letters were sociotexts exchanged within epistolary communities to share information and affect, news and emotion. The variety of epistolary communities was of course great, ranging from letters circulated in court environments to those circulated in domestic contexts. Individuals established and maintained epistolary communities chiefly for official business, shared concerns, and mutual interests.

Letters circulating within court constitute official, political correspondence—letters whose content may be bureaucratic and administrative, yet also complimental and courtly, sometimes resembling the familiar letter and using the language of sincerity, emotion, and friendship. Patronage relationships were commonly transacted by letters in this environment. Such letters allowed the prospective client an opportunity to approach a patron he or she otherwise might not have access to, and these letters often highlight the rhetoric of service and duty. One must bear in mind that the language of compliment was an *expected* language in this milieu—that politics were often negotiated in the language of love and friendship. Hence, when the Earl of Essex was imprisoned by Elizabeth and denied her presence, he negotiated with such epistolary sentiments:

> Haste paper to that happy presence, whence only unhappy I am banished; kiss that fair correcting hand which lays new plasters to my lighter hurts but to my greatest wound applieth nothing. Say thou comest from pining, languishing, despairing,   ESSEX.
> (Devereux 2: 120)

Language such as this, though seemingly trite and clichéd, was a prerequisite in certain sociocommunicative contexts.

Domestic, family, and intimate circles form another common sort of epistolary community. These letters tend to contain quotidian, often mundane matter but nevertheless demonstrate how intimate social affiliation was sustained by way of epistolary contact. These letters also sometimes commented on the news and political events of the moment. Both domestic and court letters, it should be underscored, were occasionally composed by multiple writers, sometimes intended for multiple readers, and often (owing to low literacy rates) read aloud to others. While many letters were indeed meant to be private, others were meant to be shared; hence, a modern perception of privacy and dyadic transmission must be adjusted somewhat in discussing the composition, circulation, and reception of early modern letters.

The exchange of news and intelligence was a crucial function of letters in this period. Numerous letters among state officials and administrators, as well as among family members and friends, had as their primary purpose the transmission of information. These sorts of letters are most productively studied by considering not the content of the information they exchanged but *how* and *why* the information was exchanged. Such factors determined the framing, composition, and reception of the report. For instance, news had to be "worthy" of a correspondent, and often letter writers requested secrecy. Furthermore, the language of affect and duty often accompanied relays of news and intelligence. The rhetoric of affection and the transmission of news, in fact, functioned synergistically in early modern letters, since news also had a significant social (as opposed to a strictly informational) role in early modern society and was used to bind correspondents by way of common values and joint interests. Henry Wotton, for instance, writes to Thomas Edmondes:

> [Y]our Lordship's letters coming but every fortnight unto me, I do thereby lose either the whole or a great part of their fruit and benefit, except the testimony of your affection; for all that your Lordship doth advertise me of that Court [at Brussels] doth here arrive before. . . . Therefore, since your love will well bear it, I could wish that your Lordship would be pleased hereafter to write weekly. (Smith 1: 435)

Wotton emphasizes the timely reportage of news, yet he also indicates that "affection" and "love" too are often fundamental components of epistolary news exchange.

Letter writers often maneuvered "body language" as a persuasive tool. Because early modern society generally held face-to-face speech as more reliable and trustworthy, letter writers employed figures of orality, aurality, and bodily presence to assure correspondents that the same emotional authenticity and communicative veracity of face-to-face interaction existed in letters. Katherine Paston, for instance, textualizes speaking, seeing, and hearing in her letter: "I see [by your letters] that thow hast a desire to heer often frome me . . . to speake offten withe me, and thy good desire to see me onc[e] a day" (72). Kneeling and kissing hands—requisite behaviors in many face-to-face social encounters—were also inscribed. Other strategies, like the "letter as nuisance" tactic, were used by letter writers to textualize politeness or humility, as in John Donne's statement to Thomas Roe: "it were an injury to trouble you with a busie Letter" (41–42). Declarations like Donne's *inscribe* the deference and humility obligatory in face-to-face interaction.

Studying the rhetorical strategies in letters demonstrates to students how social ties were initiated, negotiated, and consolidated by way of letters. Since letters in many social environments mediated interpersonal contact, the manner in which letters served as communicative tools shows to students the value and purpose of letters in pre–Industrial Revolution societies.

The Postal System

Postal systems were notoriously unstable during the period, even after the official establishment of a public post in 1635 and the Penny Post in 1680. These conditions determined the practice of letter writing in significant ways. To sustain epistolary contact in an era of letters commonly lost, intercepted, and misdirected, certain epistolary strategies were vital. Many of these concerned epistolary continuity, repair mechanisms initiated to mend real or imagined breaks in epistolary communications. Even inscribing the date of a letter's composition was a continuity strategy, since this, as well as recording the date of a correspondent's previous letter, attempted to ensure an unbroken circuit of transmission. Including dates also ensured letter delivery was prompt. A sender might inscribe his or her location for similar reasons, since from this information the recipient could determine if delivery was timely.

Other specialized rhetorical strategies common in letters attempted to assure correspondents of the integrity of political, social, or intimate ties. Often this rhetoric drew on the mechanics of the post itself, letter writers frequently blaming carriers for delays that could harm or even destroy a correspondence. Anne Conway, for instance, blames the bearer when she writes to her husband that "[y]ou must impute it to the negligence of the carriour that you had not a letter from me laste week" (Hutton 67). A strategy maneuvered to maintain active correspondence is used in Dorothy Osborne's letter to William Temple: "You must not forgett

that you are some letters in my debt besydes the Answer to this"
(Osborne 117). Here Osborne reminds her correspondent of his "debt"
to her, thus encouraging epistolary reciprocity. Robert Dudley, First Earl
of Leicester, writes to Francis Walsingham, "I pray you giue credit to this
berer, he can informe you of all things" (Dudley 236)—a common epistolary strategy meant to save the effort of writing complicated information or to preserve the secrecy of the information in case a letter was
intercepted.

All these epistolary strategies were designed to keep social ties strong
against the dangers of interception, delay, and miscarriage. Investigation
of these strategies demonstrates to students not only that the language of
letters served a crucial pragmatic purpose but also that letters shared with
other more "literary" genres similar persuasive and rhetorical tactics.

Letters and Print Culture, Literary Objectives

Personal letters in English began to be published with frequency in the
last half of the seventeenth century. The growing body of letters published
during this time testifies to an increasing valuation of vernacular letters
in print, and the availability of ProQuest's *Early English Books Online*
(*EEBO*) makes using these printed letter collections in the classroom extremely convenient, since students can locate and print the required material
on their own.

One of the most important collections of the period is James Howell's *Epistolae Ho-Elianae; or, The Familiar Letters of James Howell* (1645,
with three volumes following). When originally printed, Howell's letters
were intended to be received and understood as real. Scholarship in later
centuries, however, has generally concluded that many of the letters were
fabricated when Howell was imprisoned, though some may be real letters
that were sent to their addressees. Howell's collection essentially initiated the vogue for printing personal letters and includes letters from the
entire epistolary spectrum: letters of news, familiar letters, homiletic let-
ters, prison letters, travel letters, and scientific letters. Examples of posthumously published letters are in John Donne's *Letters to Severall Persons
of Honour* and Tobie Mathews's *A Collection of Letters*. The former was
published by John Donne, Jr., principally for patronage purposes; yet
the letters themselves can be explored for the fascinating ways Donne
engages epistolary theory and epistolary communication. Additionally,
many of his finely wrought letters could indeed be considered literary doc-

uments in that aesthetic values were surely borne in mind by Donne when he composed them. The Mathews collection presents a variety of letters from several well-known personages to establish the primacy of English letter writing and was perhaps published to double as a composition manual. Several printed letter collections are in fact quite nationalistic, emphasizing the superiority of English letters compared with their Continental (especially French) counterparts. The distinction between posthumously and nonposthumously published letters also requires highlighting: while posthumously published letters represented the everlasting literary monuments of dead writers, living letter writers could not use this publication strategy and were forced to justify their letter collections by other frames.

Other motives for letter publication existed. *The Kings Cabinet Opened* exemplifies letters published for political purposes—in this case, to demonstrate King Charles's duplicity. *Familiar Letters Written by the Right Honourable John, Late Earl of Rochester and Several Other Persons of Honour and Quality* is a collection in which multiple letter writers are gathered and is the sort of compilation that characterized late-seventeenth-century Grub Street epistolary publication. The collection mixes a variety of epistolary styles, tones, and subjects; real and fictional letters; letters of the dead with those of the living. Instead of having strictly literary motivations, these publications had principally commercial and entertainment purposes.

The letters published during the sixteenth and seventeenth centuries had a variety of motivations and intentions. They were published as propaganda, as literature, as entertainment, for money, for fame, and for instruction. Their increasing publication demonstrates to students that letters were, during this time, becoming a more important cultural discourse.

Gender

Women generally used the same epistolary and rhetorical strategies as men, though by comparison fewer women wrote letters during this era because of their lower literacy rates, among other sociocultural factors. However, letters constituted a relatively acceptable medium of personal, emotional, and intellectual self-expression for women. The letters of Arabella Stuart, Dorothy Osborne, and Elizabeth Cary, for example, contain numerous articulations of epistolary emotion, including complaints, resentments, and anger. These letters may indeed be considered therapeutic, allowing women a vent for their emotions in a society more intent on civility, self-control, and manners—common societal expectations that were more stringent for women.

Women of social position took advantage of letters in a wide range of situations. Stuart and Cary exploited letters in court contexts and for official business, composing carefully constructed letters of suit to accomplish their ends. Conway wrote manuscript letters to debate philosophical and religious matters, while others such as Honor Lisle used letters to manage a substantial household and maintain connections with friends, associates, and retainers. Several examples exist of women's interest in news and politics and in circulating information. Joan Barrington demonstrates a deep interest in domestic and foreign news (see Searle), while Brilliana Harley exchanged news in her letters to her husband and son and took an active interest in politics. Studying letters by women allows us to hear voices that are absent in other discourses and genres.

Rarely did personal letters by women find their way into print during the seventeenth century. Margaret Cavendish's *Sociable Letters* dramatizes a fictional correspondence between "two ladies, living at some short distance from each other" (42). It treats topics including marriage, gambling, religion, music, science, and friendship. Mary de la Rivière Manley's *Letters Writen by Mrs. Manley*, a collection of living letters, and Katherine Philips's *Letters from Orinda to Poliarchus*, which was posthumously published, also deserve study. These collections demonstrate to students that women shared with men the pursuit of scientific, literary, pleasurable, even commercial goals in publishing letters, although during this time it was generally deemed an impropriety for women to publish their letters.

Works Cited

Cary, Elizabeth. *Elizabeth Cary, Lady Falkland: Life and Letters*. Ed. Heather Wolfe. Cambridge: RTM, 2001. Print.

Cavendish, Margaret. *Sociable Letters*. 1664. Ed. James Fitzmaurice. New York: Garland, 1997. Print.

Devereux, Walter Bourchier, ed. *Lives and Letters of the Devereux, Earls of Essex . . . 1540–1646*. 2 vols. London: Murray, 1853. Print.

Donne, John. *Letters to Severall Persons of Honour*. London, 1651. Print.

Dudley, Robert. *Correspondence of Robert Dudley, Earl of Leycester*. Ed. John Bruce. 1844. New York: AMS, 1968. Print.

Familiar Letters Written by the Right Honourable John, Late Earl of Rochester, and Several Other Persons of Honour and Quality. 2 vols. London, 1697. Print.

Harley, Brilliana. *Letters of the Lady Brilliana Harley*. 1854. Ed. Thomas Taylor Lewis. New York: AMS, 1968. Print.

Howell, James. Epistolae Ho-Elianae: *The Familiar Letters of James Howell*. Ed. Joseph Jacobs. 2 vols. London: Nutt, 1892. Print.

Hutton, Sarah, ed. *The Conway Letters: Correspondence of Anne, Viscountess Conway, Henry More, and Their Friends*. Rev. ed. Oxford: Clarendon, 1992. Print.

The Kings Cabinet Opened; or, Certain Packets of Secret Letters & Papers Written with the Kings Own Hand, and Taken in His Cabinet at Nasby-Field, June 14. 1645. London, 1645. Print.

Manley, Mary de la Rivière. *Letters Writen by Mrs. Manley to Which Is Added a Letter from a Supposed Nun in Portugal to a Gentleman in France in Imitation of the Nun's Five Letters in Print by Colonel Pack*. London, 1696. Print.

Mathews, Tobie, ed. *A Collection of Letters*. London, 1659. Print.

Osborne, Dorothy. *Dorothy Osborne, Letters to Sir William Temple*. Ed. Kenneth Parker. New York: Penguin, 1987. Print.

Paston, Katherine. *The Correspondence of Lady Katherine Paston, 1603–1627*. Ed. Ruth Hughey. [Norfolk]: Norfolk Record Soc., 1941. Print.

Philips, Katherine. *Letters from Orinda to Poliarchus*. London, 1705. Print.

Searle, Arthur, ed. *Barrington Family Letters, 1628–1632*. London: Offices of the Royal Hist. Soc., 1983. Print.

Smith, Logan Pearsall, ed. *The Life and Letters of Sir Henry Wotton*. 2 vols. Oxford: Clarendon, 1907. Print.

Stuart, Arabella. *Letters of Lady Arbella Stuart*. Ed. Sara Jayne Steen. New York: Oxford UP, 1994. Print.

Suggestions for Further Reading

Beale, Philip. *A History of the Post in England from the Romans to the Stuarts*. Aldershot: Ashgate, 1998. Print.

Daybell, James. *Women Letter-Writers in Tudor England*. Oxford: Oxford UP, 2006. Print.

Ellis, Henry, ed. *Original Letters, Illustrative of English History*. 3 vols. 1824–46. New York: AMS, 1970. Print.

Gardiner, Dorothy, ed. *The Oxinden and Peyton Letters, 1642–1670*. London: Sheldon, 1937. Print.

———, ed. *The Oxinden Letters, 1607–1642*. London: Constable, 1933. Print.

Kirby, Joan, ed. *The Plumpton Letters and Papers*. Cambridge: Cambridge UP, 1996. Print.

Lodge, Edmund, ed. *Illustrations of British History, Biography, and Manners*. 2nd ed. 1838. 3 vols. Westmead: Gregg, 1969. Print.

McClure, Norman Egbert, ed. *The Letters of John Chamberlain*. 1939. 2 vols. Philadelphia: Amer. Philosophical Soc., 1962. Print.

Moody, Joanna, ed. *The Private Correspondence of Jane Lady Cornwallis Bacon, 1613–1644*. Rev. ed. Madison: Fairleigh Dickinson UP, 2003. Print.

Robinson, Howard. *The British Post Office: A History*. [Princeton]: Princeton UP, 1948. Print.

Schofield, Bertram, ed. *The Knyvett Letters, 1620–1644*. London: Constable, 1949. Print.

Appendix:
A Sample Course Pack

I have used this course pack in the past (over four to five class hours) to explore not only the topics I outline in the essay but also other pertinent issues—all of which illuminate the critical cultural value of letters in the early modern period. Since letters occurred in almost all facets of early modern life, exploring this typically ignored genre allows an innovative approach to early modern culture: letters are a vital structuring principle of early modern communicative and social interaction, as well as an important mode of personal and literary expression. When I teach early modern letters, my students come away with an enhanced understanding of the wide range of early modern epistolary situations, of how letters were a crucial means of social interaction during this period, and of the significance of letters and the function of letter writing in a society before the advent of electronic communications.

Braunmuller, A. R., ed. *A Seventeenth-Century Letter-Book: A Facsimile Edition of Folger MS. V.a. 321*. Newark: U of Delaware P, 1983. Print.

    Letters dating from c. 1580s to 1610s

    See 76–81, 130–34, 162–65, 370–71, 376–81.

    Topics: handwriting, letters of suit, patronage, prison letters, female letter writing

Byrne, Muriel St. Clare, ed. *The Lisle Letters*. 6 vols. Chicago: U of Chicago P, 1981. Print.

    Letters dating from 1530s

    See 1: 484–85; 3: 156–71, 564–71.

    Topics: the nature of exchange (gifts and letters), function of the scribe, female letter writing, epistolary news exchange, uses of specialized epistolary strategies, letters as sociotexts

Donne, John. *Letters to Severall Persons of Honour*. London, 1651. Print.

    Letters dating from roughly first quarter of the seventeenth century

    See 22–26, 104–09, 114–16, 120–27, 140–43, 240–41.

    Topics: patronage and letters, epistolary theory, nature of posthumous letters, letters as sociotexts, letters compared with face-to-face contact, uses of specialized epistolary strategies, letters as literature

Harley, Brilliana. *Letters of the Lady Brilliana Harley*. Ed. Thomas Taylor Lewis. New York: AMS, 1968. Print.

    Letters dating from 1625 to 1643

    See 8–20.

    Topics: female letter writing, signatures, epistolary news exchange, letters of advice, nature of the post, uses of specialized epistolary strategies, letters as sociotexts

Howell, James. *Epistolae Ho-Elianae.* Ed. Joseph Jacobs. 2 vols. London: Nutt, 1892. Print.

Letters from 1618 through the first half of the seventeenth century

See 1: 13–15, 17–25, 44–46; 2: 411–12, 495.

Topics: nature of print letters, nature of familiar letters, epistolary theory, letters as sermons, travel letters, letters of advice, prison letters, exchanges of news, letters as literature

Hutton, Sarah, ed. *The Conway Letters: Correspondence of Anne, Viscountess Conway, Henry More, and Their Friends.* Rev. ed. Oxford: Clarendon, 1992. Print.

Letters dating from 1640 to 1679

See 51–55, 61–69, 77–79, 163–64.

Topics: female letter writers, uses of specialized epistolary strategies, letters as philosophical discourses, nature of the post, news exchange, letters as sociotexts

James I. *The Letters of King James VI and I.* Ed. G. P. V. Akrigg. Berkeley: U of California P, 1984. Print.

Letters dating from the mid 1570s to 1624

See 71–72, 127–36, 154–58, 253–54, 316–17.

Topics: court letters, uses of specialized epistolary strategies, letters of suit, letters and politics, letters compared with face-to-face contact

More, Thomas. *The Correspondence of Sir Thomas More.* 1947. Ed. Elizabeth Frances Rogers. Freeport: Books for Libs., 1970. Print.

Letters dating from 1501 to 1535

See 488–91, 507–11, 540–47.

Topics: prison letters, uses of specialized epistolary strategies, letters and politics, letters as sermons, letters as propaganda

Nicolas, Harris, ed. *Memoirs of the Life and Times of Sir Christopher Hatton.* London: Bentley, 1847. Print.

Letters dating from 1572 to 1594

See 17–19, 25–27, 97–98, 229–30.

Topics: court letters, patronage, nature of familiar letters, letters of suit, uses of specialized epistolary strategies

Eric Sterling

Teaching Gascoigne, Deloney, and the Emergence of the English Novel

Although I enjoy using *The Norton Anthology of English Literature* when I teach my course Survey of English Literature 1 (from *Beowulf* through the Enlightenment), I am disappointed by the anthology's omission of Renaissance fiction. It is important, of course, for students to read Renaissance nonfiction prose, such as Francis Bacon's *Essays* and *The Advancement of Learning*, selections from Baldassare Castiglione's *The Courtier*, or Thomas Elyot's *The Book Named the Governor*. Although these significant works have much to teach students about Renaissance moral codes and views of learning and education, they tend to idealize people, to present concepts abstractly, and to focus solely on members of the upper class. Thomas Deloney's prose fiction work *Jack of Newbury*, on the other hand, contains characters deriving from the lower classes and the emerging middle classes who provide viewpoints concerning courtship, marriage, the economy, and royalty that differ significantly from the opinions of the aristocrats in nonfiction works such as *The Courtier*, thus exposing readers to new perspectives on Renaissance society. I believe, therefore, that students also need to read Renaissance prose fiction works, in which characters of different social classes—from the poor to the wealthy—are often portrayed as complex human beings, complete with imperfections and foibles, in sophisticated narratives.

Prose fiction works such as George Gascoigne's *A Discourse of the Adventures of Master F. J.*, Robert Greene's *Pandosto*, and Deloney's *Jack of Newbury* provide students with valuable Renaissance perspectives on love, jealousy, and courtship involving characters of various social classes. Gender issues play a significant role in these works. Complex female characters such as Elinor, in Gascoigne's *Adventures of Master F. J.*, act (rather than passively respond to the actions of male characters). Early modern fiction thus provides students a broader perspective on various aspects of the culture and gives them the opportunity to learn about the evolution of English prose fiction from its exciting beginning. Consequently, I have supplemented *The Norton Anthology* with Paul Salzman's *An Anthology of Elizabethan Prose Fiction*, an inexpensive paperback that contains five works of fiction, including, perhaps, some of the first English novels ever written.

After my class has read *Beowulf*, *Sir Gawain and the Green Knight*, Geoffrey Chaucer's Wife of Bath's Prologue and Tale, various English and Scottish ballads, sonnets by Thomas Wyatt and Henry Howard (Earl of Surrey), and selections from Castiglione's *The Courtier* and Thomas More's *Utopia*, we read two works of fiction from Salzman's book. I usually select Gascoigne's *A Discourse of the Adventures of Master F. J.* (1573), which originally appeared in the anonymous *A Hundreth Sundry Flowers*, and Deloney's *Jack of Newbury*, although I have also assigned Thomas Nashe's *Unfortunate Traveller*. I use these Elizabethan novels to discuss genre and to compare them with other works in regard to structure and theme. But I do not teach Elizabethan fiction simply to discuss it in relation to other literature, because these novels are themselves outstanding and culturally significant prose works; they merit attention, therefore, not merely for what students can learn by reading and discussing them in relation to other works but also because of their inherent excellence. Gascoigne's biographer, C. T. Prouty, claims that many

> critics have failed to recognize Gascoigne's most important work, the first original prose narrative of the English Renaissance. . . . Gascoigne's rendition of the [love] theme is unique in the literature of the English Renaissance and finds no equal until well over a hundred years after its publication. In other words, its importance lies less in its plot than in its method of narration. (191–99)

Because these works are arguably the first English novels ever written, they teach students a great deal about the early stages and the initial development of the English novel. Students learn how early modern English fiction evolved from other genres and from fiction of other nations and how this genre influenced subsequent prose fiction writers.

The narration of Gascoigne's *Adventures of Master F. J.* begins with the exchange of letters between F. J., G. T., A. B., and H. W. that precedes and contextualizes the initiation of the plot—letters that students often find obscure. When I taught the novel for the first time in the literature survey, I came to class hoping that most of the students would possess at least an adequate understanding of the work; I was disappointed when many students complained about the difficulty of the text and mentioned that they had given up early in their reading. Because the class is a core requirement and invariably contains only one or two English majors, I recognize now that the students need to possess some essential information regarding the prefatory material that initiates Gascoigne's work; they need to know the roles that F. J., G. T., A. B., and H. W. play in the text. I show them that F. J. is the author of the fourteen poems and is the lover who, in a castle in northern England, has related the story of his love for and courtship of a married woman to G. T., who in turn has edited F. J.'s adventures, surrounded F. J.'s poems with his narration, and provided the manuscript to H. W., who surreptitiously has copied the work and forwarded it to A. B., who has published it. It should be clear from this complicated and extensive last sentence why some students are initially nonplussed by Gascoigne's work. When students understand the significance of this elaborate prefatory material, their comprehension of the fictional work increases dramatically, as does their confidence in their ability to interpret the work. The implication in the prefatory letters that this fictional work might derive from actual events also piques their curiosity. Readers of Gascoigne's introductory letters learn not only about the prefatory material but also about the supposed publication history of a significant work of Renaissance prose fiction and its implications for attitudes toward publication in the Renaissance.

When I taught Gascoigne's work the following semester, I prepared the students at the end of the previous class by telling them about this complex prefatory material, explaining the roles of F. J., G. T., H. W., and A. B. I also told them that men of the noble class in the sixteenth century generally considered it beneath their dignity to publish their own works of literature. Thus the purpose of Gascoigne's elaborate introductory letters might be that if Gascoigne were identified as the author, he could protest that the work was written in part by G. T. and published without his permission by A. B.—unidentified people distanced from him. This defense could prove invaluable because of the strong implication that Gascoigne was writing about scandalous events involving real people, including himself. An anonymous letter to the Privy Council objected to his election to Parliament because Gascoigne was a "deviser of slaunderous Pasquelles againste divers personnes of greate callinge" (Great Britain). Gascoigne's work did, in fact, create a stir. In the second edition, which appeared in a miscellany entitled *The Posies of George Gascoigne* (1576), the author for the first time took credit for the work. He mentioned that he was revising *The Adventures of Master F. J.* and changing the name to *The Fable of Ferdinando Jeronimy* because of strong objections from various people who "have presumed to think that the same [the plot that contained scenes involving debauchery] was indeed written to the scandalizing of some worthy personages whom they would seem to know thereby" ("Epistle" 3). Although Gascoigne revised the action so that it would be set in Italy, rather than northern England, and provided the characters with Italian names, copies of *The Posies* were confiscated, suggesting that some influential nobles were disturbed because scandalous events in their private lives were published in Gascoigne's work.

When I teach Renaissance prose fiction, I, along with my students, make connections between these short novels and other writings that we have discussed, for these fictions owe a literary debt to works of various genres. We discuss the argument between Jack of Newbury and his first wife (Jack, a servant, has married his master's wealthy widow). He has locked her out of the house because she revels every night with her gossips; the feisty and clever wife turns the tables on Jack by gaining entrance into the house and then locking him out. He finally acquiesces and promises her that she will thereafter always get her way: "[F]rom henceforth I will leave you to your own wilfulness, and neither vex my mind nor trouble myself to restrain you, the which if I had wisely done last night I had kept the house in quiet and myself from cold" (Deloney 333). Students readily correlate this episode with the Wife of Bath's struggles and tribulations with her husbands and with her quest for marital dominance that is detailed in her prologue and alluded to in her tale when the knight capitulates by allowing the old woman he married to make her own choice. I stress that there is no evidence that Deloney borrows directly from Chaucer's Wife of Bath's Prologue and Tale for *Jack of Newbury* and that both authors derive their stories from the same tradition. I mention that Deloney might also have been influenced by Italian fiction writers such as Giovanni Boccaccio (*The Decameron*) and by jestbooks such as the anonymously authored *A Sackful of News*. In male-dominated cultures, authors of comic works create humorous situations by allowing their female characters to outsmart and dominate their male counterparts; the laughter derives from the inversion of the normal cultural portrayals that the readers have come to expect.

Similarly, when we discuss Dame Pergo's and Dame Frances's stories during the game played in *The Adventures of Master F. J.*, many students, having read *Beowulf*, recognize the significance of the tales. When we discuss *Beowulf*, some readers initially consider certain stories, such as Hrothgar's narration concerning Siegmund and Heremod, to be digressions, histories irrelevant to the main plot. I stress that in literary texts, every incident and scene contains significance. The histories of Siegmund, Heremod, and other leaders before Beowulf are integral to the story because they manifest Beowulf's potential—the potential to become a great and beloved king or a selfish, greedy, and ignoble leader. These "digressions" also clarify what qualities Beowulf's society considered essential in a hero. Because of our class discussion concerning meaningful but seemingly extraneous textual material in *Beowulf*, when we study Gascoigne's work, most students readily discern the importance of Pergo's and Frances's stories to the novel.

Dame Pergo relates her history: a gentleman fell in love with her and courted her for seven years, yet she, without reason, rejected him; for the next seven years, she loved him, yet his love transformed into disdain because she had rejected him for so long. F. J., who plays the judge in this game, declares that Pergo must bear more blame than the man for the failed courtship: "[G]reater in my judgement hath been both the wrong and the grief of the knight in that, notwithstanding his deserts, which you yourself confess, he never enjoyed any guerdon of love at your hands. . . . [Y]ou enjoyed his love seven at the least, but that ever he enjoyed yours we cannot perceive" (57). F. J.'s attitude illustrates a male-chauvinist perspective, one that accuses women of coy cruelty; students found this perspective in the poetry of Wyatt and Surrey. Readers connect Pergo's story to F. J.'s affair with Elinor, partly because of the woman's initially coy behavior and partly because in both stories, a strong desire in a courtly love relationship transforms into hate. Readers thus believe that Gascoigne employs Pergo's "history" to foreshadow the disintegration of F. J.'s relationship with Elinor. I add in class that F. J.'s judgment against Pergo is significant because it demonstrates how the lover dismisses Pergo's right to choose a man, suggesting that the protagonist believes that if a man pines for a woman, she is obligated to return his affection. Pergo's refusal to accept the gentleman's love dutifully causes F. J. to judge against her. Readers perceive that F. J. is more lenient toward the courtier's subsequent refusal to return her love during the second seven years. F. J.'s judgment should be important to students because it displays his views on women and relationships, further illuminating his character and moral views.

F. J.'s and G. T.'s views on women became more apparent to me in class one day when we discussed the immediate aftermath of the protagonist's rape of Elinor. I asked my students what they thought of the fact that after Elinor is raped, she sleeps well—what point was Gascoigne trying to make? One student claimed that it was not a fact that she sleeps well. He found the following passage to contradict my suggestion that Elinor sleeps well after being raped: "[H]aving now recovered her chamber, because she found her hurt to be nothing dangerous, *I doubt not* but she slept quietly the rest of the night—as F. J. also . . ." (61–62; emphasis mine). Although I have invariably interpreted the passage to mean that Elinor sleeps well, my student corrected me, claiming that the passage signifies that G. T. and F. J. assume that she sleeps well. Perhaps they believe that because F. J. is not disturbed by the rape and thus sleeps well, the same must hold true for her. G. T. and F. J. assume that the rape is not hurtful or malevolent, that the victim is unaffected by it. The student argued convincingly that G. T.'s narration about Elinor's sleep manifests a great deal about Renaissance male attitudes toward women and, in particular, the victimization of women.

To encourage students to place these works in a literary history of prose fiction, I ask them what constitutes a novel. Most students consider a novel to be an extensive prose work that narrates a fictional story with a plot. When I ask whether *The Adventures of Master F. J.*, which contains poems and letters, is a novel, some state that the work is a combination of genres; others assert that because Gascoigne had no concrete model for a novel—*The Adventures of Master F. J.* being arguably the first—he was experimenting with a new style. Students also combine these views, observing that it would make sense for the first of a new genre to incorporate various attributes of different literary forms. G. T. asserts that he has received the poems and built a prose narrative around it. Perhaps Gascoigne is experimenting with a new form—a combination of extended narrative prose and poetry, a miscellany. Although the prose complements the verse, students invariably focus on the former while realizing that the poetry embellishes the plot and elucidates F. J.'s character for the reader.

I then ask my students to demonstrate how Gascoigne's and Deloney's works compare with, or differ from, Castiglione's and More's prose. Students quickly distinguish the novelistic fictional works of Gascoigne and Deloney from More's *Utopia* and Castiglione's *The Courtier*. They assert that Gascoigne creates an extended and cohesive narrative tale about F. J.'s relationships with Elinor and Frances and that Deloney's work, although episodic and lacking the tight cohesion of *The Adventures of Master F. J.*, presents a sustained "history" of Jack of Newbury; thus, argue my students, both works may be classified as novels. The students create a rigid demarcation between such works of fiction and *Utopia* and *The Courtier*, labeling the latter two as political, non-novelistic prose tracts. The students believe that these works are polemical, but they also doubt whether More considers his fictional society to be truly utopian, since he was a devout Catholic and since the Utopians are not religious. Students see More's work as a prose treatise about a promising but imperfect society that More wanted his readers to compare and contrast with England. Thus readers view the work as an ideological treatise, not as a work of fiction. The same holds true for Castiglione's work, a dialogue among several distinguished people about their views of the courtier. My students see this work as a conduct book, a treatise about the ideal courtier in which Castiglione presents his views, through the voices of Pietro Bembo and his group, about grace, love, and other qualities. Students who have read Gascoigne and Castiglione are quick to point out that in *The Adventures of Master F. J.*, Gascoigne narrates a plot-driven tale that portrays the actions of a courtier, F. J., in a variety of dramatic situations and dilemmas, while in *The Courtier*, Castiglione elaborates his views about courtiers, never including a plot or character development; there is dialogue in *The Courtier* but no action.

Although verse plays a larger role in Gascoigne than in Deloney, students regard *The Adventures of Master F. J.* as more of a novel than *Jack of Newbury*. Deloney's work is disjointed and fragmentary, lacking a cohesive plot; the only thread keeping the text together as a unit is the presence of Jack of Newbury. For instance, chapter 6, which concerns the restrictions on free trade for English cloth makers, has no relation to the following chapter, which deals with the lustful and immoral Italian, Benedick.

I mention to the students that perhaps the celebration of the cloth-making profession and the life of Jack of Newbury, the didactic plot, political and religious commentary, and the readers' approval—not a cohesive narrative structure—represent Deloney's true concerns in penning the novel. The author follows the jestbook tradition, borrowing from desultory sources, and he wishes to glorify the clothiers and make the book accessible to them:

> Wherefore to you, most worthy clothiers, do I dedicate this my rude work, . . . and in a plain and humble manner that it may be the better understood of those for whose sake I take pains to compile it. That is, for the well-minded clothiers, that herein they may behold the great worship and credit which men of this trade have in former time come unto. (313)

As with *The Adventures of Master F. J.*, I show the students the significance of the prefatory material, a dedication that most students overlook. The introductory material reveals Deloney's purpose, concerns, targeted audience, and reason for using plain language. This novel was the first attempt at a sustained narrative by the author, who previously was a popular ballad writer. As did Gascoigne, Deloney inserted poetry into his narrative, such as "The Maidens' Song"—a ballad from "Child, no. 9, preserved solely by Deloney" (Salzman 408n).

By reading the fictional pieces, students learn both about narrative and about rhetorical strategies during the Renaissance. Readers are sometimes nonplussed by rhetorical devices in lines by Wyatt and Surrey. The last line of Wyatt's sonnet "The long love that in my thought doth harbour," for instance—"For good is the life ending faithfully"—changes normal English word order, displaying the rhetorical device called hyperbaton. They wonder whether the speaker is sincere or merely employing the rhetoric of the courtly lover. When we read F. J.'s love letters, poems, and flowery conversation, students gain another perspective with which to consider the lyric voices of Wyatt and Surrey. Most of my students realize that F. J.'s humble words to Elinor about his unworthiness are false rhetoric—assumed humility intended to flatter and patronize the object of his desire. F. J.'s use of manipulative rhetoric perhaps represents Gascoigne's satire of the courtly love tradition, and perceptive students observe that immediately before raping and controlling Elinor, F. J. humbly declares his subjugation to her: "I must confess that in receiving that guerison at your hands I have been constrained to fall into an ecstasy through the galding remembrance of mine own unworthiness" (60). He claims to be at her mercy but then apparently rapes her; a huge discrepancy exists between his rhetoric and his actions. I bring into class a quotation from Ronald C. Johnson concerning his views on F. J.'s language:

> Nearly every time F.J. speaks, his words are so stilted, so formal, so filled with compliment and manners, so emptied of feeling—in short, so courtly—that, given the situation, they provide immediate laughter. For example, as F.J. is on the brink of his first amorous experience with Elinor, . . . [t]he lady, of course, pays no attention to his words but proceeds directly to her goal. . . . We see [during the rape scene] that none of the highly idealistic sentiments of love which he has been writing and saying are of the slightest value to him. His all-important acts of love are determined by blind emotions and passions, not by publicly stated and socially accepted laws of conduct. (124–25)

Another student suggested that F. J.'s words concerning love are insincere because he idealizes—and renders abstract—the emotion, calling it Love, as in Venus or Cupid, not love; for this student, F. J.'s feelings, like those of Wyatt's narrator, are rather abstract and based on literary conventions of the era.

After I teach Gascoigne's and Deloney's works, I break the students into groups and assign each group one of the following questions:

> Which book, Gascoigne's or Deloney's, is more of a novel? Why? Define your conception of a novel and discuss how well these books conform, or don't conform, to that definition.
>
> Discuss the role of the narrator in these books. Does the narrator in one work play a more significant role than in the other? In what ways do the narrators contribute to these works?
>
> Discuss the importance of verisimilitude (or the lack of it) in these two works. Does realism contribute much to these works?
>
> Discuss the role of love and gender in these works. Both works focus specifically on a courtship and deal extensively with love and gender issues. Compare and contrast the themes of love and gender in these two works. For instance, do the titular characters treat women in similar ways or does Jack of Newbury have more respect for women than does Master F. J.?
>
> What kinds of reading audiences do you believe that Gascoigne and Deloney are addressing? How do those audiences play a role in these texts? For instance, does Jack of Newbury's respect for his workers and the paintings that he chooses to display in his house

contain added significance because of the reading audience that Deloney targets?

It is essential that each group receive a specific task or goal to stay focused. Group members need not reach a consensus; disagreements often are illuminating and lead students to a better understanding of the texts while allowing them to appreciate their complexity. After each group details for the class what its members have discussed, other classmates join in; thus students ultimately participate in the discussion of all five topics. The group assignments work well and encourage shy students to share their ideas freely in small groups, speaking usually to people with whom they feel comfortable (students choose their own groups and thus select people who sit near them).

By the conclusion of the semester, students possess a greater understanding of genre and the evolution of the English novel from *Adventures of Master F. J.* to Jonathan Swift's *Gulliver's Travels.* When we discuss *Gulliver's Travels,* they pay close attention to the beginning of the work, where Swift includes a letter from Captain Gulliver to his cousin Richard Sympson and a letter from the publisher (Sympson) to the reader. In the captain's missive, Gulliver complains about the publication of the book, and in the publisher's letter, Sympson attests to the veracity of the manuscript and discusses why he chose to have it published. Readers are intrigued by these two letters because the missives remind them of similar ones in Gascoigne's work. We discuss the inclusion and the purpose of such letters in Renaissance fiction and subsequently in Swift's work. Readers believe that Gascoigne employs the letters of G. T., H. W., and F. J. to endow the novel with a sense of verisimilitude; that the letters confer on the fictional work a sense of realism lacking in nonfictional prose; and that F. J. must exist, perhaps as a nom de plume, to mask the identity of a historical gentleman who narrates actual events.

Gascoigne was clearly affected emotionally by events mentioned by C. T. Prouty, who claims that Gascoigne decided to relate these private events to the public, even if—or perhaps because—he knew that his book would embarrass the participants; he thus gave narrative form to the intrigues with which he was intimately involved:

> To a variety of events, some casual, some amusing, some, at least to him, highly dramatic or deeply emotional, Gascoigne gave a pattern. He remembered his summer in the North; he had preserved the letters and poems, as does every young lover, but when he came to tell

the story he realized the function of the artist by imposing form on the shapeless mass of remembered events. In so doing he did not destroy the complete picture of a summer's interlude; instead, he created a verisimilitude which today gives us a story with the full flavor of Elizabethan country life and which has the added distinction of being not only the first novel, but indeed the first psychological novel. (201)

Some readers of the fictional work might consider the letters, which discuss how the book has fallen into the hands of A. B. (the publisher), unnecessary unless the account were real and the author needed to suggest that he was not responsible for its publication. Some students concur that the elaborate fiction at the beginning of the novel creates a sense that the fictional story is historical fact. They then compare these prefatory letters with the ones that begin *Gulliver's Travels*. Although they correlate the two sets of introductory materials, they consider Gascoigne's an attempt to shield the author's identity and create a sense of verisimilitude; they perceive Swift's letters as satirizing such attempts at verisimilitude (though of course Swift may not have known of Gascoigne's work). The study of the evolution of the English novel helps students prepare for the second part of a survey course, when they might read a novel by Jane Austen, Charles Dickens, or one of the Brontë sisters. In addition, teachers of Renaissance literature courses for English majors might use Gascoigne's and Deloney's works to debate the very idea of the novel.

Works Cited

Deloney, Thomas. *Jack of Newbury*. Salzman 311–92.

Gascoigne, George. *A Discourse of the Adventures of Master F. J.* Salzman 1–81.

———. "The Epistle to the Reverend Divines." *The Complete Works of George Gascoigne*. Ed. John W. Cunliffe. Vol. 1. Cambridge: Cambridge UP, 1907. 3–8. Print. 2 vols.

Great Britain. Public Record Office. State Papers, Domestic Series of the Reign of Elizabeth 86, no. 59. Print.

Greene, Robert. *Pandosto: The Triumph of Time*. Salzman 153–204.

Johnson, Ronald C. *George Gascoigne*. New York: Twayne, 1972. Print.

Nashe, Thomas. *The Unfortunate Traveller*. Salzman 207–309.

Prouty, C. T. *George Gascoigne: Elizabethan Courtier, Soldier, and Poet*. New York: Columbia UP, 1942. Print.

Salzman, Paul, ed. *An Anthology of Elizabethan Prose Fiction*. 2nd ed. Oxford: Oxford UP, 1998. Print.

Wyatt, Thomas. "The long love that in my thought doth harbour." *Sir Thomas Wyatt: The Complete Poems*. Ed. R. A. Rebholz. New Haven: Yale UP, 1981. 76–77.

Part III

Teaching Selected Authors

Donald Stump

Reforming the Greek Tragic Hero: Narrative Trickery and Gender Reversal in Sidney's Old *Arcadia*

There are few better introductions to the literature of the English Renaissance than Philip Sidney's *Arcadia*. Often regarded as the first novel in English, it was one of Shakespeare's favorite sources, not just in the late romances, but also in *As You Like It*, *King Lear*, and other plays. It inspired works of fiction by Robert Greene and Thomas Lodge and provided plot ideas for Francis Beaumont and John Fletcher. It helped popularize in England many forms in vogue on the Continent, including Hellenistic romance, Italian and Spanish romantic epic and pastoral, the sestina, and the epithalamion. *Arcadia* was also among the earliest English works to adapt Greek principles of tragic design, a fact from which I begin when I teach it (Stump, "Greek and Shakespearean Tragedy").

Since the revised (or new) *Arcadia* is too long and too Byzantine to work well in the three and a half weeks that I usually have available for Sidney, I assign the original version in Katherine Duncan-Jones's modern-spelling paperback edition, skipping many of the eclogues that serve as interludes between the work's five "books or acts." A good way to bring the romance to life is to explore its implicit views of gender. These come to the fore when the main heroes (Pyrocles and Musidorus) dress as an Amazon princess and a shepherd to penetrate the pastoral retreat in which

King Basilius has sequestered his wife (Gynecia) and his daughters (Pamela and Philoclea) in a vain attempt to circumvent an ominous Delphic oracle. Before the implications of Pyrocles's gender crossing can be evaluated, however, students need to puzzle out the curious tone and trajectory of the work. Although both the narrator and the characters generally treat the action as "tragic," its first three acts actually follow a pattern derived from Roman new comedy. Charming and ingenious young lovers, separated from the women they desire by the strictures of an overweening father, circumvent his will through disguise and trickery. Only in acts 4 and 5 do the tragic implications of Pyrocles's dressing in women's clothing to penetrate the royal retreat fully emerge.

My first aim is to teach students the subtle techniques by which the first three books of the romance lull us to sleep so that we do not anticipate the calamity that lies ahead. These techniques include not only Sidney's use of comic conventions to mislead the reader but also his unreliable observations as a narrator and his cunning use of stylistic tricks that provoke us to laugh at behavior that will later prove disastrous. My second aim is to encourage students to puzzle out for themselves what Sidney accomplishes by tricking the audience in this way. A final aim is to consider whether Pyrocles's cross-dressing is simply a passing comic device or part of a serious interrogation of traditional gender roles. Musidorus's inversion of class roles is, of course, nearly as important in the economy of the work as a whole, but one cannot do everything. If students show interest in Musidorus's role in the main action and that of Dametas's family and the Arcadian shepherds, those elements can make good subjects for paper topics and exam questions.

Act I

Because classical tragedy and comedy are such important genres for Renaissance writers, I use part of the class period before students begin *Arcadia* for a minilecture on the two forms. Besides obvious distinctions in emotional effect and outcome and in the social ranks of the characters and their styles of speech, I stress points of special relevance to *Arcadia*:

Happy endings are fairly common in Greek tragedy, particularly in the late plays of Euripides that influenced the Hellenistic romances that Sidney was imitating.

The justice of the gods, always a central issue in tragedy, is often worked out not just through oracles and prophetic dreams but through *daimōnic* possession, by which the higher powers send *atê* (delusion or madness) to afflict the minds of those who are guilty of *hubris* (unjust defamation of a god or another person) and so bring about their *nemesis* (divine retribution).

Although comedy and tragedy were rarely mingled in antiquity, they have much in common. Both frequently turn on a *hamartia* (a mental error or blunder) involving a failure to recognize relatives or other key figures at crucial moments in the action (Stump, "Sidney's Concept").

With these bits of lore in mind, I assign students act 1 of *Arcadia*, asking that they mark references to the drama as they read and think about the kind of play Sidney had in mind as he crafted his prose romance. When they come to class, I begin by fielding reading questions, working through a few key passages that are hard to follow and sorting out the basics of the plot before I begin the main discussion. Since Sidney's syntax is long and difficult and throws even the best students, it helps to begin each day's work slowly. As one goes through the book, I also recommend breaking into small groups once in a while, so that students can compare notes on the assigned homework before having to speak in front of the entire class. It is useful to ask the less vocal students to report for their groups so that everyone has opportunities to contribute.

On the question of the dramatic genre that Sidney was imitating in act 1, most of the evidence points to tragedy. The setting is in ancient Greece; the action begins with an oracle; act 1 ends with two foreign princes infiltrating the royal family in disguise; and it seems likely that the fulfillment of the oracle will involve errors about the princes' identities. Sidney's first use of the term *tragedy* is worth lingering over. After Pyrocles first confesses his infatuation with Philoclea, Musidorus warns him not to "overthrow all the excellent things you have done, which have filled the world with your fame," and so "mar the last act of [your] tragedy" (17). The difficulty is to decide whether his friend is right to reproach him for allowing a woman to distract him from a life of action. Students tend to be divided on the issue. Though they feel the tug of Musidorus's lofty ideals, most are put off by his view of women and are inclined to side with Pyrocles in his pursuit of love. It is important not to let them off the horns of the dilemma too easily.

If we set aside for a moment Musidorus's demeaning view of the opposite sex, we see that there are good reasons to side with him instead of his friend. Cross-dressing and deceiving a troublesome father to gain access to his daughter are amusing, and they are standard fare in comedy, but comedy does not generally take place in royal households, where the fate of a country may turn on a marriage alliance or the legitimacy of a royal heir. The force of Musidorus's arguments can also be brought home by calling attention to the larger context of the action, in which Pyrocles's father, Euarchus, is struggling to defend Greece against powerful foreign enemies. Observant students may also notice that the narrator tends to side with Musidorus, calling the love that seizes Pyrocles—and, because of him, all the other major characters—an "infection," an enchantment, a form of bondage, a "folly" (e.g., 37, 41, 44).

This is a good time to begin probing the views of the narrator, and I like to start with his rejection of Musidorus's low opinion of women. On the opening page, he observes that "nature is no stepmother to that sex, how much soever the rugged disposition of some men . . . hath sought to disgrace them" (4). Musidorus is clearly just such a "rugged" man, who argues that women have "idle heads" and "weak hands" and that to love them "doth . . . womanize a man" (18–19). On such views, Mary Ellen Lamb's work on the gender biases instilled in sixteenth-century humanist classrooms is illuminating. It is curious that the narrator should side with Musidorus in treating love as demeaning and at the same time defend the worthiness of women.

How, then, are we to evaluate the great debate in act 1? By now, the students generally haven't a clue, having received so many mixed signals from the author. Mikhail Bahktin's notion of the dialogic imagination is enlightening here. I also like to show the importance of the debate by pointing out famous analogues to the dilemma facing Pyrocles. Achilles is particularly apposite, since his mother, Thetis, dresses him as a girl and secludes him in Scyros to circumvent an oracle foretelling his death in the Trojan War. Discovered by the Greek commanders, who know that they cannot win the war without him, Achilles is faced with the choice between living long in obscurity or dying young in glory. In his encounter with Dido, Aeneas faces a similar choice between private fulfillment and public honor. Unlike these ancient heroes, however, Pyrocles sets heroism aside, choosing to dress as a woman to pursue Philoclea. What, one wonders, was Sidney's point in upending the priorities of such venerable authors as Homer and Vergil? Since developing a plausible answer takes time, I ask students to keep the question in mind as they read further. It is made more intriguing by the fact that Sidney made much the same choice in 1579–80, when he set aside martial ambitions in the Netherlands and retired for a time from court, living quietly with his sister at her rural estate and writing the old *Arcadia* for her and the women in her circle (3).

Acts 2 and 3

In discussing act 2, I begin by asking whether students stand by their initial hunches that the book is modeled on Greek tragedy. There is good reason now to think it a comedy or even a farce. The besotted king courts Pyrocles, thinking him a woman. The more perceptive queen does the same, thinking him a man. The naive Philoclea errs as her father has, worrying that she is a lesbian. And Musidorus woos Pamela by making love to oafish Mopsa. Even though the characters continue to talk as if their loves are tragic, it is difficult to take them seriously, and I press the class to look beyond the absurdities of the plot to find out why.

A good passage to examine closely features Philoclea in reverie over a white stone, where, before falling in love, she had written a vow that her "virgin life no spotted thought [should] stain" (95–98). Having broken her oath in desiring Cleophila, she struggles with guilt. Students generally find the passage interesting, with its stress on adolescent self-doubt and worries over sexual orientation. The point that is most relevant to the question of dramatic genre is not so much Philoclea's confusion as her curious style. So artificial is her way of speaking and so odd her lapses into poetry that it is hard to believe that anyone in the grip of powerful emotion would actually talk as she does. Here, Ben Jonson's wickedly funny comment that, in *Arcadia*, Sidney made "everyone speak as well as himself" comes to mind (132). Other details also help render her lamentations more charming than compelling: the narrator's patronizing tone, Philoclea's improbable degree of naïveté, and the tension between her exquisitely refined feelings and her absurd situation. A glance at other incidents in act 2 reveals similar tricks of style and tone that undercut our sense that the action is tragic.

This is a good time to introduce a point from Aristotle's *Poetics*. Aristotle defines the laughable as "some blunder or ugliness that does not cause pain or disaster" (1449a). Pity, by contrast, arises from a mistake or ugliness that does. In lyrical passages such as Philoclea's reverie by the white stone, Sidney lulls us into forgetting the terrible harm that her infatuation may bring. Only at the end of act 2, in the attack of the Phagonian rebels, does he allow us a glimpse of the dangerous ramifications of Basilius's withdrawal to the country and Pyrocles's penetration of his retreat. Even in act 3, Sidney continues to emphasize the comic. Musidorus's diversion of Pamela's rustic guardians, Dametas, Miso, and Mopsa, comes straight out of the fabliau tradition, and Pyrocles's device to get Basilius and Gynecia out of the way so that he can elope with Philoclea is an old trick from comedy.

　　Asked about the tone, many students are uneasy with Musidorus's plan to elope with Pamela and return with an army to enforce his will on Basilius. They are even more troubled by his near rape of her in the forest and by Gynecia's bitter jealousy of her daughter Philoclea. Yet the narrator's reactions continue to distract us from the seriousness of what is about to happen. In remarking on Pyrocles's bedding of Philoclea, for example, the narrator repeats none of his earlier warnings about the "infection" of love and seems as happily engrossed in the lovemaking as they are (211). He is also curiously blind to the faults of his young heroines. For the moment, at least, he does not condemn Philoclea for agreeing to act as a go-between in her father's attempt to seduce Pyrocles; he offers no comment on the political implications of her illicit union with the prince; and he has nothing bad to say about Pamela's even more astonishing betrayal of her father and her country to a foreign power. As act 3 comes to an end, the narrator seems almost as blind to the implications of the events he is describing as the lovers themselves.

Acts 4 and 5

In discussing act 4, I raise for the last time the question of tone. The unexpected savagery of several incidents is startling, particularly the narrator's gleeful account of Musidorus's grisly killing of three Phagonian rebels (266–67) and Philanax's order that Dametas and his family be chained and "cruelly whipped" every third hour (250). Pyrocles's attempted suicide (252–54) and Gynecia's lament over the body of Basilius (242–43) are also genuinely tragic. Along with these darker elements, however, act 4 includes long stretches of farce involving Dametas and his family. Sidney's condemnation of the "mongrel tragicomedy" in his *Apology for Poetry* (135–36) may not entirely rule out such juxtapositions of the serious with the absurd, but it certainly makes them more puzzling.

　　The opening of act 4 offers a particularly striking instance of the shifty mood of the romance and the unpredictable stance of its narrator. Having been sympathetic at the end of act 3—refusing to describe the lovemaking of Pyrocles and Philoclea "lest my pen might seem to grudge at the due bliss of these poor lovers" (211)—he suddenly becomes judgmental, invoking the "everlasting justice" that makes "our own actions the beginning of our chastisement, that our shame may be the more manifest, and our repentance follow the sooner," and noting with apparent approval the determination of the gods that the contemptible Dametas should be the one "by whose folly the others' wisdom might receive the greater overthrow" (230).

When one probes these remarks in class, it is revealing to ask students about the role of the gods elsewhere in the work. Basilius's false belief that the Delphic oracle has been fulfilled in the rebellion of act 2 deserves attention (117–18), as do his blasphemous song "Phoebus farewell" (155–56) and his "Hymn to Night" (238), which show his gradual descent into delusion and contempt for Apollo. Students who have not yet tumbled to the fact that the comic elements of the book have all along concealed a Greek tragic structure generally do now. A king consults the priestess of Apollo and attempts to evade her oracle. Thinking that he has succeeded, he treats the god with *hubris*; *atê* comes over him, clouding his judgment; and *nemesis* follows. The entire progression turns on a *hamartia* involving the identity of a close relative—his nephew Pyrocles—and is played out in a traditional five-act structure, with the king erring in act 3, when he agrees to meet Cleophila in the cave. In act 4, when he finds that he has actually spent the night with his own wife, he goes through the painful process of recognition and reversal that Aristotle makes so much of in his theory of Greek tragedy, and the death of the protagonist is the apparent result.

Such tidy formal arrangements belie the complexity of what Sidney is doing, however, and one way to show that is to ask students briefly about the valences of key terms: the narrator's stress on "repentance" in the opening paragraph of act 4; Musidorus's earlier remarks on his "tragical pilgrimage" (39); the narrator's reference to the "devils" possessing Gynecia (107); and Boulon's description of human beings as "worms" in relation to the gods (130). The first three are, of course, Christian instead of pagan, and the last reveals a Calvinist strain in Sidney's thought (Elton 34–63). This is a good time to quote the famous statement in the *Apology for Poetry* on the "accursed fall of Adam" and the universal conflict between the "erected wit" and the "infected will" (101). Students have, of course, already encountered this dichotomy in the debate of act 1, where Pyrocles concedes the rightness of Musidorus's reasoning but does not heed it because he is in the grips of the "pestilent fever" of love (22).

Prepared in this way, students should now be ready for a productive discussion of the function of Sidney's plummet from comedy into tragedy. I encourage them to suggest their own theories, tossing out an idea or two myself if discussion stalls. Several points are worth bringing up at such moments. First, Sidney is clearly interested in the tipping point between laughter and pity, delight and horror, and he frequently holds his readers' interest and intensifies their reactions by swinging rapidly from one to the other. Students often become fascinated with a discussion of the ease with which such contrary pairs of emotions mingle and transmute into each other. Asking them about their own experiences of tears during weddings and laughter during minor disasters usually provokes an interesting discussion.

Second, by tempting us to regard the early parts of the work as a comedy, Sidney implicates his readers in the delusions and errors of the characters and thus instantiates one of his most important views—namely, that all human beings suffer from myopic inner vision and an "infected will." The great divide between the ancient Greco-Roman stress on education and his own Christian stress on repentence, sanctification, and communion as the first steps to take in improving society is lurking in that telling phrase from the *Apology for Poetry*.

Third, by heightening the contrast between the wisdom of the higher powers and the blindness of mortal beings, Sidney reinforces a second point that is central to the work—his distrust in things human and reliance on divine providence. Here, discussion of students' expectations for their futures can help start a productive exchange. Though some are optimistic, many assume that their own efforts to secure safe and happy lives for themselves are not sufficient to the task and that forces beyond their control will ultimately determine their destinies. The great question, of course, is whether there is any "uninfected will" at work in such forces or whether they are as blind as we.

Late in my exploration of *Arcadia*, I turn to the other main question that I have been pursuing: what are we to make of Pyrocles's reversal of the choice of Achilles? I further ask whether his cross-dressing is simply a comic device or part of a serious interrogation of gender roles. Helpful here is Jean Howard's "Sex and Social Conflict," which discusses the "recuperation" of the status quo that commonly follows episodes of cross-dressing in plays of the period. A good point to begin with in examining whether Sidney arranges such "recuperation" is Pyrocles's relationship with Philoclea. I ask whether, in his debate with her about suicide in act 4,

Pyrocles shows any signs of being "womanized," as Musidorus had predicted. On close reading of the passage (which, here as elsewhere, I generally ask the students themselves to do aloud), it soon becomes apparent that Philoclea dominates him, first mounting arguments every bit as subtle and skillful as his own, and then, when he will not listen, forcing him to relent by threatening to do terrible things. A sixteenth-century audience would almost certainly have judged her the winner of the debate because of her argument that "since neither we made ourselves, nor bought ourselves, we can stand upon no other right but [God's] gift" (258). In adopting this essentially Christian position—based on the notions that God has bought us with a price and that our very lives are consequently in his gift (Rom. 5.14–21; 1 Cor. 6.20)—she rescues Pyrocles from himself and determines their course for the remainder of the romance.

In discussing this passage, I point out that it is important that the violent heroism of Pyrocles is founded on a philosophy very different from the patient sufferance of Philoclea. His is an ethic of self-reliance and what Reformed theology calls "works." Since he regards himself as "master" of his own life (257–58), he feels justified in committing suicide to protect her. As she points out, however, "The uttermost instant is scope enough for [God] to revoke everything to one's own desire" (258). In urging the "authority of love" over his "rules of virtue" (259), she turns out to be wiser than he, for in Basilius's revival in act 5, God does indeed "revoke everything" to the characters' desires.

In the light of the religious view that wins the day in the debate of act 4 and in the outcome of act 5, the earlier debate of act 1 looks very different from the way it did when the students first encountered it. In that exchange, the self-reliance of the princes is set over against the dependence forced on them by *eros*. In taking on the subordinate positions of a woman and a shepherd in pursuit of love, Pyrocles and Musidorus have been forced to accommodate their own wills to those of Philoclea and Pamela and, in doing so, have also submitted to the promptings of nature and the will of the higher powers, as revealed in the oracle. Even though Pyrocles does not entirely accept Philoclea's arguments in their debate in act 4, the very fact that he complies with her desires shows that he has come to accept the "authority of love" over the "rules of virtue," and that is a major change in outlook. As students often observe, moreover, there is no evident "recuperation" at the end of the book, no sign that Philoclea will give up her share in that authority once they are married.

A memorable passage on which to end is the narrator's reflection that "in such a shadow or rather pit of darkness the wormish mankind lives that neither they know how to foresee nor what to fear, and are but like tennis balls tossed by the racket of the higher powers" (333). The "womanizing" of Pyrocles has led to goods that neither he nor Musidorus could have foreseen in their initial, self-reliant blindness. In the process, the wisdom of the "higher powers" has been revealed as greater than that of "wormish mankind." As the narrator considers all that has happened to the characters, the tragic reversals they have suffered are subsumed in something more like a divine comedy—a game of tennis that, for all its volleys back and forth, ends in delight.

The strategy I adopt in teaching *Arcadia* leaves out many parts of the romance that I wish I could linger over, including most of the plot involving Musidorus and Pamela, all the pendant episodes and side narrations, and most of the eclogues. It has the advantage, however, of teaching students about unreliable narrators, introducing them to the lively process of reevaluation in which the best writers are always engaged when they appropriate traditional literary forms, and filling in some missing knowledge of early modern debates over gender roles. It also engages students in moving from close reading to exploration of life issues of considerable scope and importance. To have given them a glimpse of the fundamental divide between classical culture, based in ideals of *paideia*, and Sidney's implicitly Christian assumptions, based in hopes of inner rebirth, is worth the effort all by itself.

Works Cited

Aristotle. *The Poetics. Aristotle:* The Poetics; *Longinus:* On the Sublime; *Demetrius:* On Style. Trans. W. Hamilton Fyfe. Cambridge: Harvard UP, 1932. 1–118. Print.

Elton, William R. King Lear *and the Gods*. San Marino: Huntington Lib., 1966. Print.

Howard, Jean. "Sex and Social Conflict: The Erotics of *The Roaring Girl*." *Erotic Politics: Desire on the Renaissance Stage*. Ed. Susan Zimmerman. New York: Routledge, 1992. 170–90. Print.

Jonson, Ben. *Ben Jonson*. Ed. C. H. Herford and Percy Simpson. Vol. 1. Oxford: Clarendon, 1925. Print. 11 vols.

Lamb, Mary Ellen. "Apologizing for Pleasure in Sidney's *Apology for Poetry*: The Nurse of Abuse Meets the Tudor Grammar School." *Criticism* 36 (1994): 499–520. Print.

Sidney, Philip. *An Apology for Poetry*. Ed. Geoffrey Shepherd. New York: Barnes, 1965. Print.

————. *The Countess of Pembroke's Arcadia (The Old* Arcadia*).* Ed. Katherine Duncan-Jones. Oxford: Oxford UP, 1985. Print.

Stump, Donald V. "Greek and Shakespearean Tragedy: Four Indirect Routes from Athens to London." *"Hamartia": The Concept of Error in the Western Tradition.* Ed. Stump et al. New York: Mellen, 1983. 211–46. Print.

————. "Sidney's Concept of Tragedy in the *Apology* and in the *Arcadia.*" *Studies in Philology* 79 (1982): 41–61. Print.

Leah S. Marcus

Speech Made Visible: The Writings of Queen Elizabeth I

In a striking episode from *Gargantua and Pantagruel*, book 4, Pantagruel sails in the Arctic Sea and encounters frozen words hovering in the air from a battle that had taken place the previous winter. Some of the words are brightly colored like blown glass—red, green, blue, yellow—and some of them are sharp and ugly. As the frozen words thaw, he hears a cacophony of battle sounds, as well as more mellifluous noises produced by words of bright red. His companion expresses a desire to save some of the most beautiful words "by putting them in oil, as you preserve snow and ice, storing them under good clean straw." But Pantagruel sees no need for such a rescue operation, since he and his companions can always produce more of the happy, eloquent "bright red words" of the type his companions covet (Rabelais 496–97). In fact, the fantasy of frozen sound captures one of the functions that the written record of *Gargantua and Pantagruel* imagines itself as performing: it preserves the wildly abundant outflowings of speech among the heroic orator and his friends as though they were fact, not fiction, so that they can be "thawed" and appreciated after the fact with the immediacy of actual events by readers.

One of the most interesting challenges in teaching early modern prose is to get students to imagine a culture for which written language was thought of less as "prose" in our relatively inert sense of the term than as a written record of speech. And not of speech in our emptied-out and enervated modern sense, as we might consider an aging politician droning on before a nearly empty Senate chamber, but of speech as a dynamic, energizing activity that produces vivid, palpable material effects. In early modern culture, speech still held primacy over writing in most people's minds, even for highly intellectual activities like debate and scholarly argument, and writing was regularly conceptualized as the afterimage of speech. The writings of Queen Elizabeth I cannot vie with the vivid, racy "bright red words" of *Gargantua and Pantagruel,* though occasionally they come close. But her writings are particularly useful in the pedagogical endeavor of getting our students to understand the bias toward orality in early modern uses of language, because the most compelling of her writings began as speeches.

Most of Elizabeth's speeches were delivered before Parliament or parliamentary delegations, but a few were delivered at Oxford and Cambridge, at court, or during royal progresses to various parts of the realm. Occasionally, she gave extemporaneous speeches in Latin, as well as in her more customary English. For example, on 25 July 1597, after an ambassador from the king of Poland took an offensively high and combative tone in a Latin speech before her at court, she cut him down to size in a Latin response of her own that caused Lord Burghley to report in astonishment to the Earl of Essex, "I swear by the living God . . . her majesty made one of the best answers *extempore* in Latin that ever I heard."[1] In making this comment, Burghley had momentarily forgotten what he and others already knew. Well before the 1590s, Elizabeth had earned a reputation as a brilliant public speaker, quite apart from the charisma that one would expect to surround the presence and utterances of a ruling monarch. Contemporaries began to try to preserve the brilliance of her oral performances in writing just as Pantagruel's followers sought to preserve the most compelling of the frozen words by packing them in straw.

Part of Elizabeth's success as an orator came from the aura of spontaneity with which she delivered her speeches. Usually their timing could not be predicted in advance, and I know of no case in which a speech by the queen was announced or publicized in advance. Unlike her more verbose successor, James I, Elizabeth delivered speeches that were short, pithy, and to the point—and she did so apparently without notes or any visible written text. Very few of her speeches ever actually existed before their delivery as "prose" as we tend to think of it today—a text that is not poetry and that is composed and recorded in writing by an identifiable author. She seems as a rule to have spoken extemporaneously. Indeed, she often could not have done otherwise because (as in her Latin rebuke to the Polish ambassador) she was responding to remarks made in an unfolding situation that she could not have anticipated, though she may well have followed the advice of contemporary rhetorical manuals by memorizing and mentally organizing her likely topics in advance. For some speeches that we know the queen delivered, no known written record has survived. In the very few cases in which we have manuscript evidence of Elizabeth's composition of her speeches, it is more than likely that her written text postdated the actual delivery of her thoughts to her audience. More typically, when her speeches were turned into prose, they were recorded in writing not by the queen herself but by some other party— perhaps an official agent of her government or a courtier or quite possibly another auditor with little or no connection to the court.

Thus, while the analogy of Rabelais's frozen words works well as a general description of an early modern bias toward the primacy of speech over writing, it does not work well as a predictor of early modern writing's fidelity to that which has been previously spoken. In *Gargantua and Pantagruel*, the frozen words, when thawed, deliver their message of sound unchanged—Pantagruel and his companions can hear the noise of battle as vividly as if it were taking place in the air around them. The written record of Elizabeth's speech is not nearly so reliable a reproduction of what she may actually have said. For speeches that exist in only one relatively trustworthy contemporary copy—like Elizabeth's first speech at Hatfield House to members of her incipient government on 20 November 1558, even before she was crowned queen (Elizabeth I 51–52), or her final speech before Parliament, delivered 19 December 1601 (346–51)— it is easy enough for us to convince ourselves that the fullest available contemporary manuscript faithfully reproduces the speech as she gave it. But for speeches that exist in multiple early versions, we are frequently confronted with several possible texts of a speech, all of which can plausibly claim to be the speech as the queen delivered it.

Given the exigencies under which such manuscripts were produced— almost always after the fact and from memory, since it is unlikely that Elizabeth's subjects would have risked taking down her words in her presence unless she was offering formal dictation—the variations among versions are not surprising. Early modern auditors were formally trained to remember sermons and other addresses, and their mnemonic capacities were generally far greater than ours are now. Nevertheless, transcribers of

Elizabeth's speeches frequently included a caveat in their headings warning those among whom they circulated the manuscript that their memories may have failed them at certain points. Often, the transcribers protested that they had not been able to hear every word. And then there was the emotional toll taken by the frisson of actual attendance at one of her infrequent oratorical performances. An auditor of Elizabeth's final speech before Parliament protested of his attempted transcription of it, "For besides I could not well hear all she spake, the grace of pronunciation and of her apt and refined words, so learnedly composed, did ravish the sense of the hearers with such admiration as every new sentence made me half forget the precedents [the preceding sentences]" (351).

The most prominent example of the textual uncertainty surrounding Elizabeth's speeches is provided by her most famous speech of all—Elizabeth's Golden Speech, delivered before Parliament on 30 November 1601. There are three major contemporary versions of this address, all with significant differences, not counting other copies with minor variants; and each of the three major versions had its own afterlife in terms of manuscript copies and even printed reproductions. But what is most perplexing about the Golden Speech is that the "official" published version of it, which appeared in print shortly after the speech was delivered and with the royal arms as its frontispiece, is by far the least "golden" of the three early versions in terms of its language and sentiment. It is short and offers bald summary of some of the passages that contemporary auditors found most affecting and uplifting. (All three versions are included in *Elizabeth I*, along with excerpts from the preceding parliamentary debate [335–46].)

There are various possible reasons for this oddity, if one assumes that the published version was indeed issued under the auspices of the court. Lacking, of course, the queen's own manuscript, since such a manuscript did not exist, government officials may have sought out the best version they could find, unaware that better transcriptions had been made by other auditors. Or perhaps there was some politically pressing reason why the government did not want the fuller, more "golden" version circulating in print. Or conceivably, the better texts of the speech were produced after the publication of the official version was printed: transcribed from memory or notes by auditors who were dissatisfied with the printed version as a record of the actual event.

However we may wish to deal as scholars with multitextual issues such as these, we need to consider how, if at all, they can be dealt with in the classroom. To what degree will students—particularly undergraduate students with no special expertise in the period—respond with interest to a presentation of the textual complexities of the queen's prose, and to what degree will the whole vexing matter simply cause them to tune out completely? Arguably, one version of a speech by Elizabeth is enough to throw at most students, particularly if time constraints require us to choose between, say, teaching three versions of the Golden Speech and teaching that speech in one version along with two other speeches that are equally worth studying. In the edition of the "works" of Elizabeth I that I edited with Janel Mueller and Mary Beth Rose—which we could not call "writings" precisely because her speeches did not quite qualify as writing—my coeditors and I offered multiple versions of many of the speeches to enable readers and teachers of her work to wrestle with the interesting conundrum of what might constitute a reliable text. But the seventh edition of the *Norton Anthology of English Literature*, volume 1, which features Elizabeth on its cover but gives her writings only a scant seven pages on the inside, offers only single versions of two of her speeches. Though there are plans to considerably expand the selection of Elizabeth's writings in the next edition, *Norton* will probably still offer only single versions of the speeches. The simplest solution to the multiple-text problem, and one that is particularly appropriate for the British literature survey courses for which anthologies like the *Norton* are typically assigned, is simply to choose a single text to teach. That way, students are insulated from the fluid circumstances of sixteenth-century speaking and writing in dealing with Queen Elizabeth's prose just as they are typically insulated from the same uncertainties in dealing with other genres of the period such as the drama, both Shakespearean and otherwise.[2]

In upper-level courses, and as we encounter particularly gifted undergraduate students and graduate students, however, we can hope to do better. In her Elizabethan portraits, the queen appears almost always as a static icon, a figure of seemingly inscrutable power and authority. Exposing students to different versions of a speech by Elizabeth I effectively breaks down some of that iconicity and demonstrates the provisionality of political utterance, even when it comes from the lips of a monarch. In teaching Elizabeth's writings, I sometimes have undergraduate students read her speeches aloud in much the same way and for the same reasons that we expose students of Shakespeare to performed versions of the plays. By "performing" aloud one of Elizabeth's speeches—or portions of it—students can often come closer to understanding what she was trying to convey and how a speech might strike auditors differently. Often, the variations among transcriptions of a given speech can be correlated with political and other differences, and pointing out those correlations helps enliven students' perceptions of sixteenth-century prose by showing them specific ways in which it is immersed in cultural and political cross-currents of its time. Sometimes, as in Elizabeth's two 1586 speeches on the execution of Mary, Queen of Scots (186–204), we can follow a speech from the vehemence and directness of its original extemporaneous delivery (assuming of course that the contemporary transcriptions are true to its original tone) through a process of revision at court that alters its meaning and leads eventually to a more formal, guarded version of the queen's views for publication. By coming to understand the complexities of the rhetorical situation surrounding Elizabeth's speeches and the processes of revision that sometimes came after their delivery, students can get a much richer sense of the dynamism and ferment of Elizabethan discourse in general. They can also get a sharpened sense of the different levels of sixteenth-century rhetoric and the ways in which prose could be revised up or down a register of stylistic formality to suit specific circumstances.

Another way in which the study of textual differences can be enlivened in the undergraduate classroom is through a re-creation of the textual circumstances that helped create those differences. One student can play the queen and deliver a speech at normal speed while other students, the queen's auditors, attempt to transcribe her words as she speaks them—discreetly, so as to preserve an aura of respectful attention that masks their scribal activities. Or students can hear a speech, then attempt to record its language after the fact, which is more likely to be the way in which successful transcriptions were made during Elizabethan times. The very different texts that result from these exercises help introduce students to a lost world of orality in which people relied much more on memory than we do now. In performing this exercise, students discover firsthand some of the conditions that caused Elizabeth's speeches to circulate in different versions. To the extent that transcriptions by Elizabeth's contemporaries tend to preserve many key elements and even whole paragraphs intact from one version to another, while modern student versions tend to vary much more widely, students can also come to appreciate how far our own culture has traveled from the mnemonically and aurally trained culture that originally received Elizabeth's speeches and writings.

Until the publication of *Elizabeth I: Collected Works*, the version of Elizabeth's speeches most readily available for possible adoption in the classroom was often the more formal published version instead of the contemporary version that was closest to the speech as the queen delivered it. At least in terms of our twenty-first-century aesthetic standards, Elizabeth usually comes off considerably better as an orator if we study her remarks in their original, relatively spontaneous wit and freshness instead of in the drier and more orotund published versions. Sometimes our dependence on early modern published versions has led us seriously astray. Scholars still cite William Camden's versions of Elizabeth's speeches as though they were accurate renditions, even though Camden himself notes that, in typical humanist fashion, he has freely altered and compressed her speeches to suit his own narrative purposes. It is still common to find scholars citing Camden's version of Elizabeth's first speech before Parliament, 10 February 1559, which claims that Elizabeth fended off demands that she marry by showing her auditors a ring and averring, "I am already bound unto an husband, which is the kingdom of England" (59). But that lovely flourish is Camden, not Elizabeth. Early copies of the speech do not include the episode. She did say something similar, however, in a conference with the Scottish ambassador William Maitland two years later (65). In this single instance, Camden's embellishment may have improved on Elizabeth's speech as given, but in general Camden flattens out most of her subtlety and rhetorical finesse. If we read his version of the 1559 speech alongside a transcription made close to the time of its original delivery by a parliamentary auditor, we will likely find the more contemporaneous version more complex, more interestingly nuanced—in fact, much better all around. (See Elizabeth I, *Collected Works*, which reproduces both versions for comparative purposes [56–60].)

To appreciate the nuance, of course, we need some sense of the immediate context of a speech. An element of early modern prose that students have difficulty understanding is its persistent dialogism: its preference for debate over monologue, its tendency to think of problems dialectically instead of in terms of single, unitary solutions. Many of Elizabeth's speeches were specifically designed as answers to previous speeches or petitions, and in turn her speeches were sometimes at least implicitly answered by other speeches or documents. In the edition of her writings, my coeditors and I made a point of including some of these other materials when we could find them, so that readers could get a clearer sense of the context within which Elizabeth made her arguments. Exposing students to this material can often give them a much sharper sense of what she was trying to accomplish with a particular line of argument or in many cases what she was attempting to accomplish through her evasion of a particular line of argument. Not surprisingly, she developed various strategies for attempting to close down the persistent dialogism of contemporary discourse when it tried to coerce her into adopting a specific position that she did not want to endorse in public. In a speech before Parliament in 1576, for example, she responded to a request for specific religious reforms with a general, almost mystical speech about the progress of her life and rule, which one of its auditors described as "a very eloquent and grave oration" but which few of her listeners could fathom (167–71). Why on this particular occasion did she desert her usual relative directness? How do we interpret the speech now, and why was it so difficult for its auditors to understand? Was she using Tacitean indirection as a deliberate strategy to deflect continuing debate? These are questions that can best be explored in a class that has been supplied with at least snippets of the swirling ferment of talk and writing that surrounded the issues she addressed. Students, in reading Elizabeth within the context of such materials, often find it more illuminating to recognize what elements of contemporary debate she ignores or adroitly sidesteps than to recognize the elements that she takes on directly.

Some of Elizabeth's letters, like her speeches, may have existed as oral documents before they were written, since Elizabeth often dictated letters for her secretaries to record. However, the letters she penned herself are generally the most colloquial in tone and closest to the combined intimacy and majesty of her speeches. They also have the advantage of giving us the queen's words in a less mediated form than do most existing manuscripts of the speeches, since they are preserved in her own hand. Full-length letters in her hand are invariably addressed to fellow monarchs: the queen observed a careful hierarchy in correspondence that calibrated her degree of participation in terms of actual penmanship to the rank of the recipient and the favor in which that recipient was held. On commoners she bestowed only her signature, if that; aristocrats she sometimes rewarded with a superscription or postscript all in her hand, as in two letters to George Talbot, Earl of Shrewsbury, in which she warmly expressed her gratitude for his solicitude over her severe case of smallpox in 1572 and for his careful custody of Mary, Queen of Scots, in 1577 (212–14, 228–30).

Occasionally, we can observe Elizabeth withholding her penmanship as a sign of disfavor. In an indignant 1574 letter of instructions to her ambassador in Paris during her intermittent negotiations with the French king over her possible marriage to François, duc d'Alençon, Elizabeth expressed her frosty reception of the king's previous missives:

> You shall also say to the king that though the contents of his letters seemed strange to us for the reasons before alleged, yet it did much content us to receive the letter written wholly with his own hand, for the which we do heartily thank him, and pray him at this time to hold us for excused that we do not acquit him with the like. The cause thereof being in that our hand was at the time of this depeach [dispatch] somewhat strained, that we could not write. (227)

It is, of course, possible that her hand was indeed strained; it is much more likely that she was refusing reciprocity and imposing the barrier of a secretary between herself and the French monarch as a sign of her anger at his overzealous attempts to push the marriage forward. By such subtle means, she turned her letters into extensions of the silent indications of favor and disfavor that accompanied face-to-face diplomacy.

Letter exchanges are inherently dialogic, and Elizabeth's epistolary debates with James VI of Scotland (later James I of England) are particularly valuable for illustrating the period's habitual dialogism for modern students in the classroom. *Elizabeth I: Collected Works* includes a particularly choice exchange between Elizabeth and James from the 1590s. Elizabeth made a habit of beginning her letters to James with a highly indignant exclamation, as in the opening of a 1593 letter: "Wonders and marvels do so assail my conceits" at the "approach of your state's ruin, your lives' peril, and neighbors' wrong . . ." (365–66), or in the first sentence of another letter from a few months later: "To see so much, I rue my sight that views the evident spectacle of a seduced king, abusing Council, and wry-guided kingdom" (372). James's response from April 1594, saucily parodies Elizabeth's habitual openings and her most recent letter in particular:

> So many unexpected wonders, madame and dearest sister, have of late so overshadowed my eyes and mind and dazzled so all my senses as in truth I neither know what I should say nor where at first to begin. But thinking it best to take a pattern of yourself since I deal with you, I must, repeating the first words of your last letter, only these changed, say "I rue my sight that views the evident spectacle of a seduced queen." (375)

James goes on to threaten Elizabeth with the dark floods of Acheron should she fail to deliver on her promised support, and he uses wrathful Juno's threat against Aeneas in the *Aeneid*: "I trust ye will not put me in balance with such a traitorous counterpoise, nor willfully reject me, constraining me to say with Virgil, *Flectere si nequeo superos, Acheronta movebo*" ("If I am unable to sway the gods above, I will stir up Acheron" [376–77; my trans.]).[3]

In her next missive, Elizabeth reproaches him: "[You] shall never need a threat of hell to her that hath ever procured your bliss" (378). James responds, nervously, with an elaborate (and hilarious) explication of his intended political allegory that denies the meaning implied by the queen and exempts him from the charge of threatening hell against her (381). By studying this lively epistolary exchange, modern students can learn a great deal about how educated early modern people thought and debated. James's explication of his allegory is noteworthy as an example of the many-layered ways in which prose writers of the period could understand allegory, and the exchange has much of the character of oral academic and political debate.

In her own time, Elizabeth was very highly valued as a prose stylist, in part because she combined an aura of conversational intimacy with a capacity for extreme subtlety and indirection. To study her speeches and letters closely is to realize that the history of English prose style needs to be rewritten. Three decades ago, when I was a graduate student, we were taught that a major innovation of seventeenth-century English prose was its "Senecan amble," as we termed it—its tendency to construct sentences, whether short and pithy or long, loose, and exploratory, that attempted to follow the human mind and emotions in the process of developing a thought instead of presenting that thought prepackaged in a perfectly balanced complex sentence with a Latinate structure resembling that of the most formal orations by Cicero.[4] To discuss the history of early modern English prose as a sixteenth-century Ciceronian phase followed by a seventeenth-century anti-Ciceronian Senecan phase is no doubt to oversimplify a much more complex set of stylistic developments. Nevertheless, to the extent that seventeenth-century prose did grow away from the orotund style then associated with Cicero, it owed a strong debt to the highly influential style of Queen Elizabeth I. That debt has not been acknowledged by modern scholarship. Even in her earliest writings, we find her resisting the highly formal stylistic preferences of her early humanist teachers for a style that is more colloquial and closer to the rhythms of everyday speech. By giving Elizabeth's speeches and writings the attention they deserve as part of a broader study of her era, we can begin to recognize the magnitude of her impact on subsequent English prose—even though, in her speeches at least, she cannot quite be said to have written prose herself.

Notes

1. Quoted in Elizabeth I's *Collected Works* 335. Citations to Elizabeth's works are from this edition.

2. See my earlier pedagogical article, "Texts That Won't Stand Still."

3. See *Aeneid*, book 7, line 312.

4. See in particular Croll.

Works Cited

Camden, William. *History of the Life and Reign . . . of Elizabeth*. London: Fisher, 1630. Trans. of *Annales rerum Anglicarum et Hibernicarum regnante Elizabeth*.

Croll, Morris. *"Attic" and Baroque Prose Style: The Anti-Ciceronian Movement*. Princeton: Princeton UP, 1969. Print.

Elizabeth I. *Elizabeth I: Collected Works*. Ed. Leah S. Marcus, Janel Mueller, and Mary Beth Rose. 2000. Chicago: U of Chicago P, 2002. Print.

Marcus, Leah S. "Texts That Won't Stand Still." *Approaches to Teaching English Renaissance Drama*. Ed. Karen Bamford and Alexander Leggatt. New York: MLA, 2002. 29–34. Print.

The Norton Anthology of English Literature. M. H. Abrams and Stephen Greenblatt, gen. eds. 7th ed. Vol. 1. New York: Norton, 2000. Print.

Rabelais, François. *Gargantua and Pantagruel*. Trans. Burton Raffel. New York: Norton, 1990. Print.

Margaret W. Ferguson

Thomas Nashe: Cornucopias and Gallimaufries of Prose

Like William Shakespeare and François Rabelais, Thomas Nashe was a prodigious verbal experimenter who enriched the lexicon and played with the syntactic possibilities of the English language emerging as a "national" tongue in Nashe's era. Through teaching his prose as a field of verbal experimentation that would have challenged his sixteenth-century readers in some of the same ways it challenges modern students, I consider Nashe's work in relation to modern and early modern debates about the shifting and porous borders among languages, dialects, and stylistic as well as social levels.[1] Nashe lards his vernacular texts with foreign and newly coined words, learned allusions, wildly inventive tropes, and dizzying shifts of rhetorical tone. He frequently invites his contemporary readers to question their assumptions about social and literary conventions. Nashe's most famous narrator, Jack Wilton, for example, addresses his "Gentle Readers" but then immediately questions the convention of the complimentary apostrophe ("looke you be gentle now I have cald you so").[2] Nashe challenges modern readers to think about their own literary tastes as well as their practices in both writing and speaking what counts today as "standard" English.

Nashe added about 800 new words to what linguists consider early modern English. Only Shakespeare, with some 1,700–2,000 new words to his credit (depending on who is counting), enriched English more than Nashe did.[3] Nashe boasts of his "Italionate coyned verbes all in Ize" (e.g., *mummianize, anagrammatize, tyrannize*) and explains his "compound-ing" of words (e.g., *life-expedient, thought-exceeding, eare-agonizing*) by comparing his practice to that of "rich men who, having gathered store of white single money together, convert a number of those small little scutes into great peeces of gold" (2: 184).[4] It's not surprising that many literary historians think that Shakespeare credited his fellow wordsmith's talents by portraying him under the name of "Master Moth"—with a bilingual pun on *mot*, the French word for *word*—in *Love's Labour's Lost*.[5]

Unlike Shakespeare, Nashe wrote only one play (*Summers Last Will and Testament*), although he probably helped Christopher Marlowe with *The Tragedie of Dido Queen of Carthage*, and he had to flee London for his part in writing, with Ben Jonson, an offensive satirical drama, *The Isle of Dogs*, which is now lost through censorship. Nashe wrote a few poems too; among the ones my students like best are an erotic tour de force about a woman's preference for a dildo's prowess over that of the poem's male speaker (*The Choice of Valentines*) and the short poem beginning, "Adieu, farewell earths bliss," which is often included in modern antholo-gies, divorced from its original context. Nashe's character Will Summer, in the witty play mentioned above, requests that the poem (titled "The Song") be sung to him with lute accompaniment to "complaine my neere approaching death" (3: 282). With its powerful alternation between a re-peated personal lament ("I am sick, I must dye") and a communal, prayer-like refrain ("Lord, have mercy on us"), this poem works brilliantly in the classroom as a paratext for the graphic description of the plague in Nashe's novella, *The Unfortunate Traveller*.[6] Although that text, Nashe's best-known work today, includes lyric and dramatic moments that show his virtuosity in different genres, there is no question that Nashe's preferred medium was prose.

His favorite prose genre can fairly if paradoxically be called the cor-nucopian hybrid or—to use a popular Elizabethan metaphor—the galli-maufry, a stew or hodgepodge of different styles and discursive genres. In Nashe's works, the mix ranges from the mock oration, sermon, historical chronicle, and bombastic heraldic description to the mock epic and the melodrama.[7] Almost all his works contain elements of satire—a term that derives from the Latin word signifying *medley*, or, more literally, *full*, as in the phrase *satura lanx*, "a mixed or full platter of food."[8] Since Nashe typically displays generic conventions in miniature and in parodic forms, he is a good choice for teachers desiring to introduce students to a variety of genres and rhetorical modes in a short space of time. Most of Nashe's writings are highly self-reflective and display a fiery, self-advertising wit of a kind that Nashe himself associated with a foreign source of inspiration: the satiric works of the Italian writer Pietro Aretino, "one of the wittiest knaves that ever God made," a man whose "pen was sharp pointed lyke a poinyard" and who valued "libertie of speech" above all other things (2: 264–65).[9] Praising Aretino's ability to "set on fire all his readers," Nashe chose prose—and, more specifically, the prose pamphlet—as his major vehicle for engaging his readers' thoughts and feelings, including, whenever possible, feelings of generosity toward the writer.

The eponymous hero of *The Unfortunate Traveller; or, The Life of Jack Wilton* (1594) gives students a fascinating portrait of the Elizabethan writer as a rogue seeking his fortune through his facility with words. Usually classified as picaresque fiction, *The Unfortunate Traveller* is called a "pamphlet" by Nashe's own first-person narrator, Jack. The term *pamphlet* as Nashe uses it seems to denote a relatively short work of prose (still a key meaning of *pamphlet* in modern English): "I must not," Jack says, "place a volume in the precincts of a pamphlet" (2: 227).[10] But there is much irony in this distinction between a volume and a pamphlet. The clause ostensibly signaling the writer's desire to abide by the pamphlet's boundaries, its "precinct," begins a sentence that goes on to condense a long historical narrative of two sieges of French cities by Henry VIII into an "hour or two" of sleep that the narrator kindly gives to the reader in lieu of the tedious chronicle; the mention of the pamphlet, moreover, marks the point in the text where Nashe's own narrative of "travel" (punning on "pain" and "journeying") expands from its joke-book beginnings to a mock-epic, border-crossing narrative (stuffed with incident and more like a volume than a pamphlet) in which the reader follows the rogue hero from France, where the story begins, back to a plague-ridden England and from thence across Europe to an Italian landscape where Jack experiences an upside-down version of Dante's epic journey.[11] Instead of traveling from hell to purgatory to paradise, Jack goes from an artificial Roman paradise (a summer banqueting house) to various "purgatorial" adventures in Florence and Venice to an "inferno" (darkly represented by Jack's falling into a Jew's cellar). The infernal part of the story includes various experiences of near death and of dire spectatorship as an increasingly impotent Jack watches a rape and an execution of a villain, Cutwolfe. The "tragical" episodes of the story occur in a plague-infested Rome that recalls the plague in England from which the hero fled early on. He finally ends up back in France where he began; few readers have felt that an uplifting moral message of any kind emerges from this bleak and disjointed story, which has been described both as "grotesque" and as "realistic" by critics attempting to make sense of it.[12]

When Nashe (or Jack) describes *The Unfortunate Traveller* as a *pamphlet* threatening to spill beyond its limits into a *volume*, we see that the former term connotes something more than a brief type of discourse. In fact, Nashe places the very idea of the pamphlet into a large field of cultural inquiry, and conflict, that includes reflections on the educated but penurious English writer's uncertain place in his own society and in relation to authority figures—literary, religious, and political—from other places and times. In Nashe's hands, the pamphlet form displays ambivalence about what his "poor hungerstarved Muse" makes him do either to chase a stingy patron or to sell a manuscript to a stationer (publisher) for a fee rarely above two pounds (3: 225). Although pamphleteering according to Sandra Clark "was an occupation with a low status and a bad reputation" when it emerged as a distinct mode of writing for a living in the late-sixteenth century (27), the pamphlet was nonetheless a flexible, even an inspirational, genre for Nashe; as Charles Nicholl remarks, the term *pamphleteer* is right for Nashe "precisely because of its looseness. A pamphleteer writes pamphlets, and a pamphlet is whatever the reader will pay . . . three pence for" (5). The pamphlet as Nashe variously defines and illustrates it—from *Pierce Pennilesse His Supplication to the Devil,* in which the writer begs the devil for a loan, to *Nashe's Lenten Stuffe,* which contains a comic version of the Hero and Leander story—involves frequent mixings of historical fact with fiction as well as a lively interest in the emergent discourse of international news, a discourse requiring travel, real or imagined, for its production.

The poet John Berryman defined Nashe's prime imaginative concern as being with "his medium, with prose itself" (8). Teachers can use selections from Nashe's prose works as rich materials for exploring a variety of topics such as the history of the novel; the history of "creative nonfiction"; first-person narrators in the early era of what Benedict Anderson calls "print capitalism" (43–46); relations between literature and journalistic discourses; travel literature; kinds and concepts of literary genre in the

Elizabethan era; kinds of English sentence and what sentence structures—
including specific choices of syntax and diction—may tell us about a
writer's interest in readers of different social ranks and degrees of education; and last but not least (this list is not exhaustive), English prose as a
multicultural medium in the early modern period—a medium that challenged the idea of national borders even as it helped promote international
rivalries and create national stereotypes.[13]

According to one of his contemporary readers, a man of letters named
Gabriel Harvey whom Nashe notoriously attacked in a series of pamphlets
and whom he satirized as a "bursten belly inkhorn Orator called Vander-
hulke" in *The Unfortunate Traveller*, being the victim of Nashe's pen was
a viscerally alarming experience that required description in terms of ex-
travagant, transnational comparisons. Nashe, Harvey writes,

> layeth about him with . . . [his] quill, as if it were possessed with the
> sprite of *Orlando Furioso*, or would teach the clubb of Gargantua to
> speake English . . . Pore I must needes be plagued; plagued? Na brayed
> and squised to nothing, that am matched with such a Gargantuist, as
> can devoure me quicke in a sallat. (qtd. in Brown 49)

Harvey resorts again to food metaphors in an effort to describe his opponent's style: it contains "nothing but pure Mammaday [dialect word
meaning a sweet made of milk] and a few morsels of fly blownc Euphuism, somewhat nicely minced for puling stomackes" (qtd. in Clark 238). If
good discourse was aimed, according to humanist doctrine, at providing
"nourishment" for the mind and soul, Nashe's discourse provides something else altogether, though it often looks as if it is aiming at the reader's
moral improvement.

Nashe used the still relatively new medium of print to fashion various
innovative but morally and epistemologically difficult personae; in *The
Unfortunate Traveller*, he punningly refers to his narrator Jack Wilton as
a "page."[14] The pun defines the narrator both as a servant seeking advancement ("Page Sb.1") and as a printed sheet ("Page Sb.2"), a material
object with the potential to become "waste paper" or, more nobly, to
confer an afterlife on the author.[15] Rabelais had used the same pun on
page to describe the hybrid nature of his narrator in the *Œuvres* he began
to print in 1532; Rabelais shared Nashe's fascination with the modes of
carnivalesque discourse and with the relation among oral, written, and
printed modes of communicating—or with dramatically failing to

communicate, as in the famous battle of mostly obscene hand gestures that Rabelais's Panurge engages in with an English scholar in chapter 18 of *Pantagruel*. Like Rabelais in this respect, and like Shakespeare too, Nashe uses his pen to mimic but also to transform popular forms of gesture and speech, including the insult.[16]

Nashe frequently addresses us directly—"O my Auditors" (2: 219)—as if we could hear the words coming from a speaker's always-thirsty mouth: "soft, let me drinke before I go anie further . . . there's great virtue (I can tel you) to a cup of sider" (209, 210); but Nashe never lets us forget for long that we are readers being constantly challenged to decipher printed signs made from a pen. "[E]xercise thy writing tongue" is the paradoxical command made by one character in Nashe's *Have with You to Saffron Waldon* (3: 33). As Lorna Hutson remarks, Nashe's narrative "I" is typically so

> disarmingly frank about the ongoing processes and hazards of writing that the act of composition itself becomes vividly present behind the printed words: "now my penne makes blots as broad as a furd stomacher," he confides in the middle of a discourse on apparitions, "and my muse inspires me to put out my candle and goe to bed." (1)[17]

Nashe's words are sent to us, like ghostly letters of solicitation, by a series of narrators who evidently resemble the author but who also differ from him in ways that anticipate the mind games made and played by modern unreliable narrators and their creators. In *The Unfortunate Traveller*, dominated though it is by the voice of Jack, the reader's knowledge is not wholly governed by Jack's point of view; we "hear" other voices speaking, and though they are all ostensibly filtered through Jack's memory, various techniques of metaphor and symbolic parallelism invite us to notice and ponder things Jack does not see: his gradual change, for instance, from a prankster actively using his "lying tongue" in order to castrate his enemies (he zestfully compares his triumph over the cider merchant to that of a hunter who pursues a beaver to "bite off" its "stones" [2: 215]) to a spectator impotently watching a villain rape a Roman matron. Reading what Nashe and his ambiguous male narrators offer is not easy. My students complain of being bored and offended by certain parts of the *Unfortunate Traveller*, and they find that text's plot so hard to follow that I've drawn up a summary that I'd be happy to share with fellow teachers. Nashe himself acknowledges that his often haranguing voice may be hard for readers to "digest" (2: 32)—but a taste for Nashe is nonetheless worth encouraging. It exercises the mind, expands the vocabulary, and bracingly frustrates those who like their literary categories neat.

The difficulty of digesting Nashe's prose would have existed for many of his contemporary readers, particularly those who lacked the university education he conspicuously advertises with his use (and abuse) of Latin phrases. But his tonal shifts, his interest in criminal cant, and his delight in coining words from the "Greek, French, Spanish, and Italian" when he finds the "English tongue" too poor for his needs because it "swarmeth with the single money of monasillables" (2: 184) would have provided interpretive challenges to well-educated readers too. When modern students entertain the idea that Nashe was deliberately setting out to challenge readers of different social classes to think about what was licit or illicit in the (changing) sphere of "English," the difficulties of his prose can seem interesting instead of simply numbing. If we look carefully at passages in which he borrows, mangles, or, in his favorite economic metaphor, "coins" new words (and values) from different sources, we can see his prose as a heady international mix of flavors. Several times a month "when my conduit of incke will no longer flowe for want of reparations," confesses one of Nashe's favorite personae, Piers Pennilesse, "I follow some of these new fangled *Galiardos* and *Senior Fantasticos*, to whose amorous *Villanellas* and *Quipassas* I prostitute my pen in hope of gaine" (3: 30–31).

Pursuing gain, fame, and what Nashe calls "a new stile" in the letter dedicating *The Unfortunate Traveller* to the Earl of Southampton (2: 202), he compares his writing, in that same letter, to "goods uncustomed" (2: 201). The punning analogy between his writings and commodities brought illicitly from abroad (as if in the "unfortunate traveller's" knapsack) suggests that his pages may enrich the natives of England and expand their knowledge; but his pages may also cause offense—and provoke censorship—by challenging as "mere" customs or conventions what has previously been considered natural.[18] "I know not what blinde custome methodicall antiquity hath thrust upon us, to dedicate such books as we publish to one great man or other," Nashe remarks to his noble reader at the beginning of the novella starring Jack Wilton. Here, the author's impudent voice anticipates that of the servant-page who mocks, praises, impersonates, steals from, and ultimately—after begging and receiving forgiveness for his errors—parts from his master as a successful traitor, in contrast to that master himself, who is modeled on the historical Earl of Surrey, executed for treason in 1547. Surrey, like the "banished earl" who lectures Jack on the uselessness of travel at the end of the story, shares his rank with the man Nashe addresses as a desired master or patron at the beginning of the work. Such a noble reader should perhaps beware of taking gifts from this writer.

Nashe's habits of verbal innovation clearly owe something to the humanist ideal of rhetorical "copiousness," an ideal taught in grammar schools through the practice of double translation (from Latin to English and English to Latin). Copiousness, as William Kerrigan explains, was usually understood as "the ability to say the same thing, clothe the same body, in a multitude of fashions"; training in copiousness was thought to guarantee a "fulsome, ready, plenitude of speech" (qtd. in Simons 18). Nashe seems to illustrate the ideal, but he does so in a "special way," as Louise Simons aptly puts it (18). Nashe's way tends to challenge the widespread early humanist belief that good words and good "matter"— eloquence and moral virtue—are two sides of the same coin or, in Roger Ascham's formulation in *The Scholemaster* (1570), are like partners in a happy marriage that is critical to the health of the individual and the state:

> For good and choice meats be no more requisite for healthy bodies, than proper and apt words be for good matters. . . . Ye know not what hurt ye do to learning, that care not for words, but for matter; and so make a divorce betwixt the tongue and the heart. (101)

While humanist teachers like Ascham acknowledge but deplore the possibility of a divorce between words and truths (including the truth claims of the heart), Nashe relishes the role of the talented but wild schoolboy who sees the divorce occurring in acts of rhetorical translation and imitation of many texts, including the Bible. Fascinated with themes of treason to God the father and to his earthly representative, the monarch, Nashe repeatedly plays at the level of style with modes of doubling in which one word or phrase—a translation or a metaphor or even an apparent synonym—competes with another. Jack Wilton, for example, tells his fellow "pages" that he will play a game with them called "*novus, nova, novum*, which is in English, newes of the maker" (2: 207); the Latin adjectives of different genders become a noun in a phrase that plays (as Erasmus does in his famous title *Encomium Moriae* [*Praise of Folly*]) with an ambiguous genitive: is this game giving us new things made by the author or information of (about) that author-maker? Nashe invites students to think in new ways about how modes of translation work within a language as well as between languages. This is so in part because the sphere of translation overlaps historically and conceptually with that of metaphor. The Greek verb *metapherein* ("to transfer" or, literally, "to carry" [*pherein*] "beyond" [*meta*]) is often translated into Latin as *transfero*; the past participle of this verb is *translatus*, commonly rendered into English as "translated." And when we see Nashe boasting of his ability to "use more compounds than simples, and graft wordes as men do their trees to make them more fruitfull" (2: 184), we should keep in mind the old Italian proverb, *Traddutore, tradditore.*

To illustrate this point further, let me adduce another example of how Nashe mangles and thus makes new the meaning(s) of phrases he ostensibly translates from Latin to English. "Well, tendit ad sydera virtus," says Jack Wilton as he's about to trick a cider merchant into dispensing his precious liquid freely (2: 210). Apparently translating the Latin saying "virtue extends to the stars," Jack wrangles the Latin "sidera" into a play on the English "cider"; in so doing, he appropriates a classical notion of manly virtue for his own narrator's (roguish) purposes. His style invites us to wonder whether what counts culturally as a "virtue" can be counterfeited by words rather than expressed or faithfully conveyed by them. This is the kind of question Nashe often poses by the very shape and rhythm of his sentences as well as by his handling of nouns and adjectives denoting "customary" kinds of virtues. During the same early episode of *The Unfortunate Traveller* describing the cider merchant's duping, Jack describes his way of playing with his gullible auditor in a complex sentence that begins this way: "I, being by nature inclined to Mercie (for in deede I knewe two or three good wenches of that name) bad him harden his eares, and not make his eies abortive before theyr time" (2: 213). *Mercy*, an English word with French and Latin roots and analogues, suddenly becomes the proper name of a girl, or, rather, of several girls "known" by Jack. One could easily use this sentence to launch a discussion of the paradoxes of the very concept of the "proper" name and how it works as a signifier.

One could also use this and many other sentences by Nashe to think with students about how to order a sentence's elements for various rhetorical effects, including irony. Although the Anglo-American pedagogical tradition stresses "clarity" as a supreme compositional virtue, Richard A. Lanham has bracingly challenged that tradition (in his aptly titled *Style: An Anti-textbook*) by urging students and teachers to analyze and imitate writers who do not model clarity—or its moral analogue, sincerity. Nashe's festive or carnivalesque prose, according to Hutson and other recent readers, often works precisely to disrupt ordinary practices of communication in educational, theological, and economic spheres. Hutson writes of Nashe as the producer of a discourse that is "disingenuously, ironically inefficient" as it "transforms its rhetorical conventions and strategies into the comically palpable objects of literary experience" (127). The same qualities that make Nashe "inefficient" from a moralist's or a capitalist's perspective are, however, what may make him exciting to teach. Consider, for instance, using the following sentence from *Christ's Teares over Jerusalem* to discuss how syntactic parallelism and vivid diction work to create an image of something at once repellent and fascinating— the body's decomposition in the grave: "As many iagges, blysters, and scares, shall Toades, Cankers, and Serpents, make on your pure skinnes in the grave, as nowe you have cuts, iagges, or raysings, upon your garments" (2: 138). A triadic direct object precedes a triadic subject to heighten the horror of the basic comparison this sentence constructs between the dead body's pure skin and the living body's clothes. With this sentence, students can see why analogy requires understanding of dissimilarity as well as likeness and also why word-order inversion can be an effective rhetorical technique even in prose, where rhyme and meter do not require the breaking of the "ordinary" English pattern of subject / verb / direct object. The effect of death, the triadic "object" of a force— the grammatical subject—represented here by toads, cankers, and serpents, is the main point of the sentence, its conceptual "subject," as it were. The writer asks us to think about how the body's covering, its once "pure" skin, will be made after death into jags, blisters, and scars just as (but also not just as) the clothes we wear are made fashionable, interesting, and by implication enticing to "impure" thoughts, by the cuts, jags, or raisings on a piece of fabric. Have students look up *jag* as a noun in the *OED*; there they will discover that among the several meanings of this word relevant to the sentence in question is the following: "a slash or cut made in the surface of a garment, to show a different colour underneath." The choice of this vividly colloquial word indicates that Nashe is comparing skin to clothes even before the terms of the analogy are made explicit.

Teaching a medley of Nashian sentences or selected short passages may be an effective way of introducing students to this major (but also, in terms of the Renaissance canon, minor) writer. His corpus lends itself well to dissection. The lack of unity or coherence lamented (or laboriously refuted) by some critics of Nashe's works, especially of his novella, may be a pedagogical asset in those many courses in which we are always teaching composition and rhetoric even when our subject, ostensibly, is literature of the past. Nashe himself was fascinated by the links he saw between the processes of proto-scientific dissection, of juridical torture, and of interpreting texts; modern students who attempt to dismember one of Nashe's complex sentences may find the experience oddly rewarding, even eerily surprising, as was the case when, recently, I asked a class to work in small groups on the description of the "sweating sickness" from the *Unfortunate Traveller* (2: 228–31). One student, a biology major, did research that showed (persuasively) that the symptoms Nashe describes in grotesque detail—and which he also describes as beyond the reach of any doctor's "impotent principles" (230)—are those that modern scientists ascribe to anthrax poisoning.

Teachers can devise exercises that start with close readings of Nashe's prose and that move on to a cornucopia of strange topics (or strangely familiar ones like anthrax). His writings readily illustrate the three basic stylistic registers or levels as these were understood by classical and Renaissance rhetoricians. The categories are enlivened for modern students by Nashe's habit of mocking instances of the high and middle styles; among the variants of the "decorated middle style" parodied in *The Unfortunate Traveller* are the "Ciceronian, Euphuistic, Arcadian, homiletic, sententious, [and the] epigrammatic"; Nashe parodies the more lofty "elegiacal" or "tragic" style in the novella's concluding episode of Esdras and Heraclide (Kaula 50). The parody emerges through juxtapositions of passages in low and higher styles, with the former often spoken by Nashe's narrator Jack in sentences that are typically shorter and blunter in their description of physical desires than are the passages in the higher styles. Although I don't agree with David Kaula's claim that Jack's "true speaking voice" is the "low style" (that is to impute a dubious psychological essence to Jack), I regularly borrow from (and give credit to) Kaula's brilliant and detailed exposition of a stylistic contrast between low and high through two passages comparing a horse and a woman, respectively, to an ostrich in *The Unfortunate Traveller* (Kaula 50–52). The passages in question, which occur several pages apart (2: 261, 273), can be taught together as an ideologically provocative contrast between styles that both may be used to advance the narrator's erotic and economic goals through argument by analogy. The first passage uses the ostrich to describe the sexual charms of Diamante, a woman whom Jack efficiently steals from the verbose and ideologically confused Surrey, represented as not realizing that he cannot win Diamante's favors while ostensibly pining in Petrarchan angst for Geraldine. The second passage, cleverly playing on our memory of the first, compares Surrey's horse to an ostrich as part of Nashe's bravura mimicking—and deflation—of the outdated aristocratic rituals and language epitomized in the tournament that Jack's "master," a version of the historical Surrey, stages in Florence, birthplace of Surrey's beloved Geraldine and scene for Nashe's "vivid exhibition of chivalry in its final, decadent phase" (Kaula 50).

In teaching Nashe's prose, I have found over the years that less is more. Working with a medley or gallimaufry of passages, some from *The Unfortunate Traveller*, others from prefaces such as that to *Christ's Teares over Jerusalem*, where Nashe vividly explains his tactics for making English a richer language, many of my students have developed a taste for this writer's prose and for the questions it raises about what counts, now and in the past, as legitimate (much less "good") English. Nashe, who crossed the boundaries of what some powerful people in his own society considered the "precinct" of decorum, offers students numerous opportunities to reflect on their own writing and speaking styles as these are fashioned in a language that was and is never "English only."

Notes

1. My approach to Nashe in this essay is inspired by Terence Cave's *The Cornucopian Text* and by Mikhail Bakhtin's influential work on carnivalesque and heteroglossic discourses. I draw also on ideas I developed in an earlier essay, "Newes of the Maker."

2. *Works* 2: 217. All citations of Nashe are from *Works*, edited by McKerrow. Teachers wanting a modern-spelling version of this narrative and a selection from Nashe's other writings should consider using Steane's edition of The Unfortunate Traveller *and Other Works*. Teachers wishing to assign Nashe's *The Unfortunate Traveller* in the context of other Renaissance English prose, including Deloney's *Jack of Newbury* and Lyly's *Euphues*, should consider the collection edited by Paul Salzman.

3. For Nashe's additions to English, see Crystal 328 and Crewe 65–66. For Shakespeare's additions to the language and examples thereof, see Nevalainen 340–41. Some of Nashe's inventions are still alive (at least in books), for example: *duncify, abhorrent, adumbrate, multifarious,* and *finicality*. But many of Nashe's verbal coinages, like Shakespeare's wonderful words "dispropertied" and "superdainty," have gone to the graveyard of scholars' footnotes. Among "lost Nashisms" lamented by Crystal (328) are "bodgery" ("botched work"), "tongueman" ("good speaker"), "chatmate" ("person to gossip with"), and "collacrymate"

(tearful). Wells marks words that Nashe evidently invented in the useful "Glossarial Notes and Index" included in his edition of Nashe's selected works.

4. Cited and discussed in Crewe 65–66.

5. For the evidence for reading Moth as Nashe, see Nicholl 161; Hilliard, in contrast, finds the parallels "too general to be conclusive" (215).

6. Many of my students enjoy doing a homework assignment that asks them to interpret Nashe's description of plague symptoms in the light of modern medical knowledge.

7. The dedication to Spenser's *Shepherdes Calendar* by "E. K." describes the English language itself as a "gallimaufry"; see the *Oxford English Dictionary* for this and other early uses of the word in literary contexts.

8. On this etymology—not generally accepted until 1605—see Waddington 661–62.

9. See also the praise of Aretino in the preface to *Lenten Stuffe*, Nashe 3: 152. For an incisive discussion of Aretino as Jack's "inspiration," see Linton 143.

10. On Nashe as a pamphleteer see Clark; Raymond; and Halasz.

11. For the Italian portion of the narrative as an inversion of Dante's journey, see Ferguson 178.

12. For a discussion of Nashe's style as "grotesque," see Rhodes 5 and 43–44; for a discussion of the early and mid-century critical tradition that saw Nashe's *The Unfortunate Traveller* as the first "realistic" novel in English, see Kaula 43. Davis; Kaula; and Rhodes offer valuable overviews of Nashe's mixing of generic modes.

13. I have experimented with various photocopied "readers" made from McKerrow's edition, which makes many graphic puns visible because of its use of the original spelling. Nashe's prefaces are especially interesting to include in such readers. My students generally need more help with syntax and with what Nashe himself jokingly calls his "huge words" (3: 152) than modern editors such as Steane provide.

14. Jack plays on the term *page* in the author's prefatory address to "the dapper Mounsieur Pages of the Court" (2: 207). For useful discussions of the difficulties generated by this narrator, see Raymond; Stephanson; and Hyman.

15. For Nashe's innovation in using "page" to mean "printed sheet," see Simons 21. On the significance of Nashe's vision of his pages as "waste paper" that can best fulfill the humanist ideal of doing "service" to their "countrie" by kindling tobacco (2: 207), see Hutson 147. On Nashe's fascination with print and with the labor of making books, see Mentz 18–32.

16. In the prologue to *Pantagruel*, Rabelais defines his narrator, Alcofribas Nasier, as one who has served for wages ever since he grew out of his "pagehood" ("j'ay servy à gaiges dès ce que je fuz hors de page . . ." (1: 219). Nashe uses "Gargantuan" as a term of comic abuse in his attack on Gabriel Harvey (3: 34). For useful discussions of the stylistic similarities between Rabelais and Nashe, see Rhodes; Weimann; Jones.

17. Hutson here cites Nashe 1: 384.

18. Before he died at around age 34, Nashe had been imprisoned (probably for debt) and had fled London under threat of arrest for having coauthored *The Isle of Dogs*, censored by the authorities for its "seditious and sclanderous matter"; for an account of this affair, see Nicholl 242–57. For a discussion of the problems attending various critics' efforts to interpret Nashe's works in the context of the "meagre" facts known about his life, see Hutson 1–11.

Works Cited

Anderson, Benedict. *Imagined Communities: Reflections on the Origins and Spread of Nationalism*. 1983. Rev. ed. London: Verso, 1991. Print.

Ascham, Roger. *The Scholemaster*. Ed. R. J. Schoeck. Don Mills: Dent, 1966. Print.

Ashley, Robert, and Edwin M. Moseley, eds. *Elizabethan Fiction*. 1953. New York: Holt, 1962. Print.

Berryman, John. Introduction. *The Unfortunate Traveller; or, The Life of Jack Wilton*. By Thomas Nashe. New York: Putnam, 1960. 7–28. Print.

Brown, Huntingdon. *Rabelais in English Literature*. Cambridge: Harvard UP, 1933. Print.

Cave, Terence. *The Cornucopian Text*. Oxford: Clarendon, 1979. Print.

Clark, Sandra. *The Elizabethan Pamphleteers: Popular Moralistic Pamphlets, 1580–1640*. Rutherford: Fairleigh Dickinson UP, 1985. Print.

Crewe, Jonathan V. *Unredeemed Rhetoric: Thomas Nashe and the Scandal of Authorship*. Baltimore: Johns Hopkins UP, 1982. Print.

Crystal, David. *Stories of English*. London: Lane, 2004. Print.

Davis, Walter R. *Idea and Act in Elizabethan Fiction*. Princeton: Princeton UP, 1969. Print.

Ferguson, Margaret. "Nashe's *The Unfortunate Traveller*: The 'Newes of the Maker' Game." *English Literary Renaissance* 11.2 (1981): 165–82. Print.

Halasz, Alexandra. *The Marketplace of Print: Pamphlets and the Public Sphere in Early Modern England*. Cambridge: Cambridge UP, 1997. Print.

Hilliard, Stephen S. *The Singularity of Thomas Nashe*. Lincoln: U of Nebraska P, 1986. Print.

Hutson, Lorna. *Thomas Nashe in Context*. Oxford: Clarendon, 1989. Print.

Hyman, Wendy. "Authorial Self-Consciousness in Nashe's *The Vnfortvnate Traveller*." *Studies in English Literature, 1500–1900* 45.1 (2005): 23–41. Print.

"Jag. *Sb.* 1." Def. 1. *The Oxford English Dictionary*. 2nd ed. 1989. Print.

Jones, Ann Rosalind. "Inside the Outsider: Nashe's *Unfortunate Traveller* and Bakhtin's Polyphonic Novel." *ELH* 50.1 (1983): 61–81. Print.

Kaula, David. "The Low Style in Nashe's *The Unfortunate Traveller*." *Studies in English Literature, 1500–1900* 6.1 (1966): 43–57. Print.

Lanham, Richard A. *Style: An Anti-textbook*. New Haven: Yale UP, 1974.

Liebler, Naomi Conn, ed. *Early Modern Prose Fiction: The Cultural Politics of Reading*. New York: Routledge, 2007. Print.

Linton, Joan Pong. "Counterfeiting Sovereignty, Mocking Mastery: Trickster Poetics and the Critique of Sovereignty in Nashe." Liebler 130–47.

Mentz, Steve. "Day Labor: Thomas Nashe and the Practice of Prose in Early Modern England." Liebler, *Early Modern Prose Fiction* 18–32.

Nashe, Thomas. The Unfortunate Traveller *and Other Works.* Ed. J. B. Steane 1972. Harmondsworth: Penguin, 1978. Print.

———. *The Works of Thomas Nashe.* Ed. R. B. McKerrow. 1910. 5 vols. Ed. F. P. Wilson. Oxford: Blackwell, 1958. Print.

Nevalainen, Terttu. "Early Modern English: Lexis and Semantics." *1476–1776.* Ed. Roger Lass. Cambridge: Cambridge UP, 1999. 332–458. Print. Vol. 3 of *The Cambridge History of the English Language.* Richard M. Hogg, gen. ed. 6 vols. 1992–2001.

Nicholl, Charles. *A Cup of Newes: The Life of Thomas Nashe.* London: Routledge, 1984. Print.

"Page. Sb.1." Def. 3. *The Oxford English Dictionary.* 2nd ed. 1989. Print.

"Page. Sb.2." Def. 1a. *The Oxford English Dictionary.* 2nd ed. 1989. Print.

Rabelais, François. *Oeuvres complètes.* 1532. Ed. Pierre Jourda. 2 vols. Paris: Garnier Frères, 1962. Print.

Raymond, Joad. *Pamphlets and Pamphleteering in Early Modern Britain.* Cambridge: Cambridge UP, 2003. Print.

Rhodes, Neil. *The Elizabethan Grotesque.* London: Routledge, 1980. Print.

Salzman, Paul, ed. *An Anthology of Elizabethan Prose Fiction.* Oxford: Oxford UP, 1998. Print.

Simons, Louise. "Rerouting *The Unfortunate Traveller*: Strategies for Coherence and Direction." *Studies in English Literature, 1500–1900* 28.1 (1988): 17–38. Print.

Stephanson, Raymond. "The Epistemological Challenge of Nashe's *The Unfortunate Traveller.*" *Studies in English Literature, 1500–1900* 23.1 (1983): 21–36. Print.

Waddington, Raymond B. "A Satirist's Impresa: The Medals of Pietro Aretino." *Renaissance Quarterly* 42.4 (1989): 655–81. Print.

Weimann, Robert. "Fabula and Historia: The Crisis of the 'Universal Consideration' in *The Unfortunate Traveller.*" *Representations* 8.4 (1984): 14–29. Print.

Wells, Stanley. "Glossarial Notes and Index." *Thomas Nashe.* By Nashe. Ed. Wells. Cambridge: Harvard UP, 1965. 335–74. Print.

P. G. Stanwood

Community and Context
in Richard Hooker's Prose

Richard Hooker is "[o]ne of the great masters of English prose" (718),
the writer of "perhaps the [Elizabethan] period's most sonorous and elegant prose" (638), say the editors of *The Longman Anthology of British
Literature* and of *The Norton Anthology of English Literature*. There are
similar assessments by other modern commentators on Richard Hooker.
C. S. Lewis is typical in calling Hooker's style "for its purpose, perhaps
the most perfect in English" (462). Richard Hooker (1554–1600) has
also been described as having invented prose in English and as the theological descendant and interpreter of Augustine and Thomas Aquinas.
Such homage ought to assure for him a large readership of his long (but
not his only) work, *Of the Lawes of Ecclesiastical Polity* (1593, 1597). Although he has not been much read in recent years except by a few determined students of church history and politics and by some fewer still who
appreciate his literary and rhetorical skill, Hooker's importance to the
development of English religious thought as well as to English prose style
deserves emphasis in our classrooms. The common notion that Hooker is
an obscure writer of long sentences on subjects of remote interest to modern students must be addressed and vigorously confronted with attractive
truths.

In reaching out to the writers and thinkers of earlier times, contemporary students wish to know how their efforts to explore a different age, one that describes itself in an unfamiliar style, might still be significant and timely. Hooker is an author who does repay close attention, for he was a philosopher, historian, and theologian with a brilliantly analytic mind packed with a great deal of the knowledge of the centuries before him. How does one convincingly condemn folly and advance truth, allowing little room for refutation? Hooker knows how to define difficult issues and argue tenaciously for his position. He may not be easy to read, nor are later generations of controversialists, like Milton, transparent to the impatient reader. Hooker, however, offers rich rewards to those who enjoy the intellectual challenge of lively discourse and who like to see how an astute writer and thinker can demolish his opponents.

Hooker is remembered for his central place in the development and defining of the English church. As an apologist for the Elizabethan settlement and a defender of the church, his work responds to the intense religious controversies of his age. He tries at once to discriminate what he saw as unchanging and divinely bestowed from that which is ephemeral or humanly established. He begins his major work by warning us of his grand and overall intentions:

> Though for no other cause, yet for this; that posteritie may know we have not loosely through silence permitted things to passe away as in a dreame, there shall be for mens information extant thus much concerning the present state of the Church of God established amongst us, and their carefull endevour which woulde have upheld the same. (1: 1)

"Thus much"— Hooker opens his massive *Lawes of Ecclesiastical Polity*. We must know, he is suggesting, what is best in our past; at the same time, he wants us to understand how the present can preserve the past. Hooker wants to uncover the religious and social foundations of his day—therein lies his wish for "unity." He writes also of the disturbances and upheavals that surround and contaminate his world. The points of past and present complement each other, connecting politics and religion.

Hooker may be approached for the comprehensiveness of his thought as much as for his style. He upheld tradition, but also challenged it. John Booty, one of his most discriminating readers, nicely describes this paradox:

> Hooker assesses that which is received from the past in terms of purposes and ends, but also in relation to changing times and circumstances. On the one hand, we find in Hooker devotion and humility,

and on the other evaluation and advice concerning things to be defended and things to be changed. (3)

Hooker distinguishes between material and humanly made laws and what he recognizes as the unchanging spiritual laws that govern all creation. He appeals to the "natural law," by which he means the universal law implanted by the creator in nature and discernible by all rational creatures through the light of reason (Milton called this intellectual capacity "right reason").[1] The natural law appears thus to be the basis of all morality— the highest good beyond human beings. Human society may formulate codes and laws of conduct; it may not, however, contravene this greater law. The social community may only reinforce good action and avoid whatever is evil or injurious to the common happiness.

Hooker introduces contemporary readers into a culture with assumptions about community that differ greatly from our own. He lived and wrote in an age that still assumed a community of beliefs and values—a largely homogeneous social order in which unchecked individualism was considered wrong. Any attack against community and the willful opposition to the natural law had awful consequences. Perversion or breaking down of the social order was a common theme of his age. Gloucester's complaint in Shakespeare's *King Lear* is a poignant and familiar reminder of what happens when individuals ignore the bonds of harmonious affinity and the natural order:

> Love cools, friendship falls off, brothers divide: in cities, mutinies; in countries, discord; in palaces, treason; and the bond crack'd 'twixt son and father. . . . We have seen the best of our time. Machinations, hollowness, treachery, and all ruinous disorders follow us disquietly to our graves. (1.2.106–14)

Hooker might have said that this wretched state is the condition of a society that has turned away from right order in defiance of the natural law.

One of the most commonly quoted passages from Hooker's *Lawes* recognizes the wholeness of creation and of the divine or natural law that ties all creation together. Against such right government stands Gloucester's aberrant world, but Hooker has described the ideal world where nature has its proper sway:

> Now if nature should intermit her course, and leave altogether, though it were but for a while, the observation of her own lawes: if

those principall and mother elements of the world, wherof all things in this lower world are made, should loose the qualities which now they have, if the frame of that heavenly arch erected over our heads should loosen and dissolve it selfe: if celestiall spheres should forget their wonted motions and by irregular volubilitie, turne themselves any way as it might happen: if the prince of the lightes of heaven which now as a Giant doth runne his unwearied course, should as it were through a languishing faintnes begin to stand and to rest himselfe: if the Moone should wander from her beaten way, the times and seasons of the yeare blend themselves by disordered and confused mixture, the winds breath out their last gaspe, the clouds yeeld no rayne, the earth be defeated of heavenly influence, the fruites of the earth pine away as children at the withered breasts of their mother no longer able to yeeld them reliefe, what would become of man himselfe, whom these things now do all serve? See we not plainly that obedience of creatures unto the lawe of nature is the stay of the whole world? (1: 65–66)[2]

Hooker assumes that nature is indeed holding its accustomed course. How could that be otherwise? But is this, for our world, an impossibly nostalgic and unrealistic view? What has changed since Hooker's time—human beings, the political order, the universe? These would be useful questions to ask of a group of contemporary students.

Hooker naturally reflects his own time, and he responds to its ecclesiastical and political situation; yet in introducing his work one may have little time to explore the Elizabethan Settlement (1559), the admonition controversy, or the myriad of problems and disputes of the early modern period. But one must urge that Hooker was writing in an age of controversy, in support of Queen Elizabeth and of John Whitgift, her last archbishop. Hooker directed his *Lawes* partly against those who wanted to reform (and upset) the church and state. Such persons spoke stridently in *An Admonition to Parliament* (1572), and they advocated an end to the episcopacy—the government of the church by bishops—and at the same time urged a radical restructuring of the justice and political system. Certainly it is desirable to discuss Hooker's description of the natural law as the source of man-made, civil law, to query the meaning and source of authority—*any* authority, to question also the constitution and meaning of a social community and of individual rights, to review the use of tradition and how to reject or modernize it. Do we still believe—or can we believe—in absolutes, in the fundamental natural law, whose "seate is the bosome of God, her voyce the harmony of the world" (Hooker 1: 142)? Hooker wishes to accommodate a traditional view of divine order with human society and government. Exactly how these seeming oppositions may be reconciled continues to vex succeeding generations from Thomas Hobbes, John Locke, and beyond, even to our own day.

Hooker should be introduced to his unfamiliar and likely wary reader with explicit directions. Everyone must be encouraged to ask questions, even if they are difficult to answer—or if an answer must be deferred. Why did Hooker title his long work as he did? What does the title mean? "Of the lawes" has special significance reminiscent of ambitious classical treatises, notably Cicero's *De legibus*. Teachers should explain the plan of Hooker's work—its eight books, the first four on general principles, the last four on specific applications. It should become clear that Hooker is writing about the human, or man-made, law in its variety of situations; the natural law governs all others and gives shape and meaning to the entire book. One might broadly relate Hooker's work to the controversies that it set out to address and then, depending on local circumstances and time, take up in some detail Hooker and the English Reformation.

I have found that the best way of introducing Hooker is to concentrate on two issues: the defining of *law* and of *style*. For the first, students need to understand the terms *ecclesiastical* and *polity*. Of course, fundamental to any discussion of Hooker is the first question to ask: What do we mean by *law*? Can you tell how Hooker defines it? Then students can be asked to help list what they understand by *law*, including rules against various kinds of behavior, from no speeding in a school zone and no cutting of trees in public parks to more serious breaches of conduct, like assault and murder. What is the difference between these kinds of infractions—some minor, others major? Is there a hierarchy of law? And who decides what it is and how it should be arranged? This discussion can easily lead to Hooker's careful distinction between different kinds of law, and especially to his view of the wholeness and coherence of society and the construction of social and human community.

For the second issue, I like to hear what students understand by *style* and how they would characterize Hooker's mode. Many very general observations will likely be forthcoming, and I might introduce the broad definition of style that Erasmus gives: "The term style comprehends . . . a multiplicity of things—manner in language and diction, texture . . . thought and judgment, line of argumentation, inventive power, control of material [and] emotion . . . , and within each one of these notions a profusion of shadings" (78). Some selectiveness is obviously in order, and my concern is to demonstrate Hooker's mastery of various features—especially of irony, one aspect that many readers can easily miss.

Sometimes Hooker is expansive and forthright, as we have seen in the famous passage quoted above; but at other times he is detailed, ambivalent, generally vigorous, and frequently humorous. Opportunities abound for analyzing his style. Deservedly known for his long sentences, he frequently constructs great periods, that is, he holds in suspension the finite verb until nearly the end of the statement, anticipating the conclusion with a series of compound-complex clauses. One should not overlook his supremely ironic and witty manner, as well as his skill with the apothegmatic and moralistic statement. Examples of proverbial statements abound. He says early in the first book that "the lawes of well doing are the dictates of right reason" (1: 79) and that "we all make complaint of the iniquitie of our times: not unjustly; for the dayes are evill" (1: 98). Wittily, he states, "I am perswaded, that of them with whom in this cause we strive, there are whose betters amongst men would bee hardly found, if they did not live amongest men, but in some wildernesse by themselves" (1: 140). Later, he remarks that "he that will take away extreme heate by setting the body in extremitie of cold, shal undoubtedly remove the disease, but together with it the diseased too" (1: 298) and that "[n]o man which is not exceeding partiall can well denie, but that there is most just cause wherefore we should be offended greatly at the Church of Rome" (1: 302), this last comment employing the ironic understatement that is typical of much of Hooker's writing.

We meet such irony in many places, especially, for example, in book 4 (1: 276–77), where he is answering the admonitionist objection that the Church of England lacks "ancient Apostolicall simplicitie." With irony, he writes critically:

> For it is out of doubt that the first state of thinges was best, that in the prime of Christian Religion faith was soundest, the scriptures of God were then best understood by all men, al partes of godlines did then most abound: and therefore it must needes follow, that customes lawes and ordinances devised since are not so good for the Church of Christ, but the best way is to cut off later inventions, and to reduce things unto the auncient state wherin at the first they were.

And he further writes to the same point:

> It is not I am right sure their meaning, that we should now assemble our people to serve God in close and secret meetings, or that common

brookes and rivers shoulde be used for places of baptisme, or that the Eucharist shoulde bee ministred after meate, or that the custome of Church feasting shoulde be renewed, or that all kinde of standing provision for the ministerie shoulde be utterly taken away, and their estate made againe dependent upon the voluntary devotion of men. (1: 278)

Students may be asked to consider particular sentences to discover how they are constructed and how that construction may shape the meaning. Periodic sentences occur on almost every page of the *Lawes*, and we have already seen one instance. The long and important tenth chapter of book 1 details the formation of human laws through reason. The organization of another particularly arresting sentence begins with a kind of prologue: "That which plaine or necessarie reason bindeth men unto may be in sundry considerations expedient to be ratified by humane law: for example. . . ." It then continues with three adverbial "if" clauses, each with dependent clauses (here separated by a space):

if confusion of blood in mariage, the libertie of having many wives at once, or any other the like corrupt and unreasonable custome doth happen to have prevailed far and to have gotten the upper hand of right reason with the greatest part, so that no way is left to rectifie such foul disorder without prescribing by lawe the same thinges which reason necessarilie *doth* enforce but is not *perceyved* that so it doth,

or if many be grown unto that, which thapostle did lament in some, concerning whom he wryteth saying, that *Even what things they naturally know, in those very thinges as beasts void of reason they corrupted them selves;*

or if there be no such speciall accident, yet for as much as the common sort are led by the swaye of their sensuall desires, and therefore do more shun sinne for the sensible evils which follow it amongst men, then for any kinde of sentence which reason doth pronounce against it:

At the end of the third "if" clause, Hooker introduces the long-awaited independent clause: "this verie thinge is cause sufficient. . . ." But this "cause sufficient" is a temporary conclusion, for not only does it complete one sentence but also it provides the pivot upon which rests a further succession of dependent clauses:

why duties belonging unto ech kinde of vertue, albeit the law of reason teach them, shoulde notwithstanding be prescribed even by humane law. Which lawe in this case wee terme *mixt*, because the matter

whereunto it bindeth, is the same which reason necessarily doth require at our handes, and from the law of reason it differeth in the
maner of binding onely. (1: 105–06)

This elaborate sentence is typical of the *Lawes*. Here, Hooker uses the
earlier part of the sentence to anticipate the later part and to reflect grammatically two sides, even as he is carefully discriminating "mixt" laws or
defining the conjunction of human (or positive) law with natural (or divine) law. The effect is expressive of Hooker's logical method, with its
suspension of opposing ideas in a steadying equilibrium of confident
poise. I like to analyze and diagram a few sentences to emphasize both
Hooker's habits of argument and his style. Further, one should certainly
read Hooker aloud and encourage students to do the same, for oral
reading of difficult yet accurate prose helps reveal its force and clarify its
sense. And Hooker never writes an ungrammatical statement or one
whose meaning cannot with close attention be unlocked. In spite of—or
because of—its elaborateness, Hooker's language is keenly critical, evalu-
ative, and often ironic. Hooker shows how to write prose that is complex,
clear, and cogent.

The enduring interest and importance of Hooker's work can be understood and emphasized with only a few passages—probably more than
most anthologies provide, yet it is easy to copy additional selections or to
assign sections to individual students. I've found that, in addition to the
passages discussed above (and those noted in my appendix), the concluding chapter of book 1, especially the first section on the several kinds of
law and much of what follows, reveals Hooker's mischievous, ironic humor
and the method of his argumentation. Hooker's ideas may be helpfully
studied and compared, along with his prose style, with those of other writers, such as Francis Bacon, John Donne, Thomas Hobbes, and John Milton. For this reason, I find it especially helpful to teach Hooker in courses on
early modern prose, as well as in more general early literature surveys. It is
impossible to pass over Richard Hooker lightly, for he does illuminate current issues of social involvement and the significance of law. Hooker may
even help us discover unity in the discord of the world around us.

Notes

1. See Milton, *Paradise Lost*, 6.42; cf. *Areopagitica* 999, where Milton describes reason as "the Image of God."

2. Hooker paraphrases the fourth-century Arnobius of Sicca (see Gibbs).

Works Cited

Booty, John E. "Richard Hooker." *The Spirit of Anglicanism: Hooker, Maurice, Temple.* Ed. William J. Wolf. Wilton: Morehouse-Barlow, 1979. 1–45. Print.

Erasmus, Desiderius. *Patristic Scholarship: The Edition of St. Jerome.* Ed. James F. Brady and John C. Olin. Toronto: U of Toronto P, 1992. Print.

Gibbs, Lee W. "The Source of the Most Famous Quotation from Richard Hooker's *Laws of Ecclesiastical Polity.*" *Sixteenth Century Journal* 21.1 (1990): 77–86. Print.

Hooker, Richard. *Of the Lawes of Ecclesiastical Polity.* Ed. W. Speed Hill et al. *The Folger Library Edition of the Works of Richard Hooker.* 7 vols. Cambridge: Belknap-Harvard UP, 1977–98. Print.

Lewis, C. S. *English Literature in the Sixteenth Century Excluding Drama.* Oxford: Clarendon, 1954. Print.

The Longman Anthology of British Literature. Ed. David Damrosch et al. 2nd ed. New York: Longman, 2002. Print.

Milton, John. *Areopagitica. The Riverside Milton.* Ed. Roy Flannagan. Boston: Houghton, 1998. 997–1024. Print.

———. *Paradise Lost.* Ed. Merritt Y. Hughes. New York: Odyssey, 1957. Print.

The Norton Anthology of English Literature. Ed. Stephen Greenblatt et al. 8th ed. New York: Norton, 2006. Print.

Shakespeare, William. *King Lear. The Riverside Shakespeare.* Ed. G. Blakemore Evans et al. Boston: Houghton, 1974. 1255–1305. Print.

Appendix:
Further Reading

Hooker's works, especially the *Lawes,* are now available in *The Folger Library Edition* (see above), the definitive modern edition, which should be in many libraries, but not necessarily on the shelves of many students and teachers. The well-known Everyman's Library edition (2 vols.; London: Dent, 1907) gives only the first five books and it follows John Keble's edition of 1888. The most accessible and best selection of Hooker is an edition by Arthur Stephen McGrade in the series of Cambridge Texts in the History of Political Thought. McGrade gives the preface and books 1 and 8 (Cambridge: Cambridge UP, 1989), basing his text on the Folger edition (but in a modernized form) and providing a useful introduction and notes. In a course where discussion of Hooker may be limited, I have made copies (usually from the Folger edition) of the preface, chapters 1–3, and the final page that describes the plan of the whole work (bk. 1, ch. 3; bk. 5, ch. 1, parts 1–5; bk. 5, ch. 8, parts 1–5; and bk. 5, ch. 67, parts 1–13). Now in its eighth edition, *The Norton Anthology* offers selections from the *Lawes* (ed. Stephen Greenblatt et al.; New York: Norton, 2006), currently in a section called "Faith in Conflict," with several additional excerpts available on *Literature Online.* *The Longman Anthology* gives an excerpt within a contextualizing section called "Perspectives," on government and self-government (ed. David Damrosch et al.; 2nd ed.; New York: Longman, 2002).

Philip B. Secor has written a popular and readable biography, *Richard Hooker: Prophet of Anglicanism* (Tunbridge Wells: Burns, Anglican Book Centre, 1999). A number of excellent essays concerned with reason, law, and rhetoric appear in *Richard Hooker and the Construction of Christian Community* (ed. A. S. McGrade; Tempe: Medieval and Renaissance Texts and Studies, 1997). There is a very full bibliography and much helpful commentary in *Richard Hooker and the English Reformation* (ed. W. J. Torrance Kirby; Dordrecht: Kluwer, 2003) and also in *A Companion to Richard Hooker* (ed. W. J. Torrance Kirby; Leiden: Brill, 2008).

Elizabeth Hodgson

"Amorous Metaphors": John Donne's Prose

In his voluminous scholarly and sacred prose works (sermons, devotions, polemical tracts, letters, disputations), John Donne (1572–1631) is a self-consciously social wooer of souls. With the self-aware narrative voice so familiar from his poetry, Donne in his prose establishes a similarly change-able, dynamic presence. With that voice Donne creates the illusion of that "spontaneous overflow of . . . feelings" prized by both some noncon-formists of his own day and later generations of Romantics (Wordsworth 163–64). Intensely relational "amorous . . . metaphors" of dependence and devotion also distinguish Donne's prose style (Donne, *Sermons* 7: 86). His imagination relies on the metaphoricity of affection, especially as a sign of spiritual communion and community.

Witness these dynamics in a passage from one of Donne's marriage sermons:

> This Lamb and I (these are the Persons) shall meet and mary; there is the action. . . . But this is a mariage in that great and glorious Con-gregation, where all my sins shall be laid open to the eys of all the world, where all the blessed virgins shall see all my uncleannesse, and all the Martyrs see all my tergiversations, and all the Confessors see

all my double dealings in Gods cause; where *Abraham* shall see my faithlesnesse in Gods promises; and *Job* my impatience in Gods corrections; and *Lazarus* my hardness of heart in distributing Gods blessings to the poore; and those virgins, and Martyrs, and Confessors, and *Abraham*, and *Job*, and *Lazarus*, and all that Congregation, shall look upon the Lamb and upon me, and upon one another, as though they would all forbid those banes, and say to one another, Will this Lamb have any thing to doe with this soule? (*Sermons* 3: 253–54)

This sentence's length emphasizes the distance between the human "I" and the Lamb, a gap reinforced by the descent in diction from terms like "tergiversations" to the sentence's final monosyllables. The sentence's dramatic and conversational voice seeks to bridge that gap, though, as the speaker overhears the gossip of the "great and glorious Congregation" of heaven to suggest the amorous intimacy of spiritual conversation that Donne prizes so highly.

This social mind in motion of Donne's is also pedantically intricate and mercurial, simultaneously exhilarating and exhausting. Donne is certainly not immune to the scholastic fussiness of his era's homiletic style, for instance; in fact, his fascination with the inner workings of the soul often matches a similar fascination with the inner workings of a word, a phrase, or a metaphor that seems as self-obsessive or tortured as any Puritan diarist's examination of conscience. What is most difficult for the modern reader to grasp is that for Donne, these tortured but loving dissections (of soul, of self, of text) are often a key element in the Donnean speaker's projects of creating *social* discourse. Donne's prose texts often link dramatically solipsistic moments directly with the community building of which he is so enamored. Donne imagines that convoluted inwardness can and should beget a doctrine of community in the strikingly engaged (and egotistical!) sociability at the heart of much of his work. One example from the *Devotions*, as the speaker finds himself ill, alone, and bedridden:

I lye here, and say, *Blessed are they, that dwell in thy house*; but I cannot say, *I will come into thy house*; I may say, *In thy feare will I worship towards thy holy Temple*, but I cannot say in thy holy *Temple*: And, *Lord, the zeale of thy House, eats me up*, as fast as my fever; It is not a *Recusancie*, for I would come, but it is an *Excommunication*, I must not. But *Lord*, thou art *Lord of Hosts*, & lovest *Action*; Why callest thou me from my calling? *In the grave no man shall praise thee;* In the doore

of the grave, this sicke bed, no Man shal heare mee praise thee.
(*Devotions* 17)

This frenetic pastiche of scriptural passages reinterpreted for his particular illness reveals the Donnean speaker at his most self-pitying. The
grounds of his plaintive address to God, though, are that he cannot serve
God in the larger community while he is ill. The social soul is the subject
of his solitary debate. As Ramie Targoff says, "for Donne . . . the public
space of the church is the site for achieving selfhood . . . for realizing
the individual 'I' not in spite of, but precisely because of, a collective
act" (53).

Just where this leaves the modern reader, teacher, or student is a real
question. Donne's insistence on dependence and interdependence does
serve his own pastoral and polemical authority. His defenses of spiritual
and political hierarchies are both implied and explicit, no less worrisome
to many modern sensibilities because so impassioned and persuasive.
Likewise, his praise of maternal nurturing or marital sacrifice does not
translate into praise for wives or mothers per se. But Donne refuses to
abide by the public-private divide so frequently applied to early modern
literature, and for this alone, even aside from his stylistic virtuosity and
dramatic intensity, he is important to our understanding of the period.
Donne's prose in particular, with its self-consciousness about occasion,
about patronage, and about social forms, can give us a much clearer sense
of his deep concern with how to be a social, a communal, individual. If
we really want to challenge easy assumptions about the private "I" in Renaissance literature, Donne's prose, intensely personal and very political
at the same time, is an excellent place to begin.

Donne's *Devotions upon Emergent Occasions* is probably the logical
starting point for teaching his prose. This work is the most accessible of
Donne's prose works, partly because of his intense desire to generate
a spiritually communal world even at the brink of a solitary death. The
twenty-three short sections of the *Devotions* are all framed as dialogues
between the narrator and God; each includes a meditation (a personal
reflection on Donne's "emergent occasions"); an expostulation (in which
he addresses God to plead, to demand, to complain, and to confess); and
a prayer (a humbler address to God). The emergent occasions of the title
are the stages of a serious illness of Donne's in the winter of 1623, considered in a concrete, autobiographical, and dramatic form.[1] The prose style
is varied, complex, and often powerful, particularly in meditation 1

("O miserable condition of Man") and in 17, the source of the famous "no man is an island" passage.

The *Devotions* combines the speaker's concern with his physical health with a spiritual self-examination in a format original to Donne. Puritan and Ignatian examinations of conscience certainly inform the *Devotions*'s stylistic method, but Donne's tripartite dialogues, using his own illness as the point of departure for his conversations with the divine, are unique. Donne deliberately emphasizes the immediate drama of his discourse by using dramatic present tenses and vocative forms.[2] He is conscious that his illness is potentially fatal and likely contagious, so the *Devotions* constantly communicates, in form and content, a fear of being silenced or isolated, of being cut off from others. Donne speaks about being unable to speak—or about not being heard.

As spiritual meditations on an illness, the *Devotions* carries on a running debate over the speaking sign of the body itself, a sign sometimes platonic and sometimes metonymic. Donne seeks to understand the nature of divine judgment of the body and the soul, the interventionist power of God in human illness, and the edifying or pathogenic effects of illness on the human spirit. With all these questions the speaker attempts to reach beyond his solitary deathbed to speak to others and to be spoken to. Often, for instance, the metaphor of spiritual sickness becomes for Donne a question of his role in the community. Likewise, his fear of divine judgment is translated, especially in the famous meditation 17, into an attempt to re-create Donne's own pastoral role over his flock through a claim (a plea) for human connection, enacted in his prayers for other dying souls.

The *Devotions* fulfilled this social agenda in many respects. The work was published shortly after Donne recovered from his illness;[3] it was dedicated to Prince Charles, and Donne sent complimentary copies to James I's daughter Elizabeth as well as the Duke of Buckingham (Raspa xviii). The *Devotions* was quite popular, with five editions published by 1638 (Raspa xliv). Donne was, after all, a senior divine, dean of Saint Paul's Cathedral in London, and several of his polemical works had previously been printed. The "privacy" of the text's described experiences, then, exists in the context of this very public text and author.

This is clear in the work when Donne explicitly defends public church and Christian doctrines on hermeneutics and the sacraments, especially the Eucharist (meditations 7, 19); on social inequity, wealth, and poverty (7, 8, 20); and on liturgical politics (16, 17). Such discussions, though wide-ranging and polemical, consistently refer to personal agonies and debates, layering and conflating social and individual voice. "No prayer is so truly, or so properly mine as that that the Church hath delivered . . . to me" (*Sermons* 9: 218–19), says Donne, and in the *Devotions* his political comments often tend to mutually reinforce church authority and his own voice.

I find meditations 1 (with its microcosm rhetoric), 5 (with its political critiques), and 17 (with its social theory) the most productive to teach, in both first-year and upper-level classes. Because meditation 17 contains the most well-known passage ("no man is an island"), it is often the most immediately engaging. A close reading of the speaker's rhetorical techniques (e.g., sentence length and how it varies, images and what they suggest) alongside the real situatedness of the meditation is often very productive: what is the speaker saying, and to whom? What point is he making about the bell, and how does it relate to his own situation? Because this meditation is so deeply personal and so acutely aware of social interdependence, it is a great text for making Donne's ideology clear. I also often assign one of the sentences from the *Devotions* for memorization, so that Donne's lyrically structured prose can get into the students' ears and so that students can begin to understand how sentence structure creates and illustrates meaning.

Certain of the *Sermons* also work well to illustrate the typical dynamics of Donne's prose as well as several themes (gender, postcolonialism) of current interest. In Donne's many extant sermons, Donne speaks much more confidently than in the *Devotions* as an active pastor to his flock. He is also quite explicitly responsive to the homiletic genre, with its highly structured form and its overlapping scholarly, pastoral, and patronage constraints (on teaching sermons as a genre, see Lori Anne Ferrell's essay in this volume).

These constraints are evident in the provenance of the sermons. Donne's 160 extant homilies were written over fifteen years, from Donne's first posting at Saint Dunstan's in 1615/16 through his appointment as dean of Saint Paul's Cathedral in London (1621) until his death in 1630/31.[4] As a Roman Catholic turned Anglican, Donne came late to the ministry, urged into it by James I himself; Donne's promonarchical politics (whether cause or effect of this royal patronage) are thus evident in many of his sermons. Of the twelve to fourteen sermons he preached annually, he gave two to four each April as chaplain-in-ordinary to the royal court. Donne's other sermons also respond to particular liturgical, seasonal, and ceremonial occasions, from christenings to the death of James I, from prebendary sermons on the Psalms to meditations on high holy days such as Easter and Christmas. Some of these were cathedral sermons, others parochial sermons at Saint Dunstan-in-the-West, and still others commissioned on special occasions. In all these instances the intersecting authorizing narratives of liturgy, preacher, occasion, and audience render the sermon a complex rhetorical conversation.

Connections to community in tension with the solitary voice of saint or sinner are still the mainstay of Donne's endeavors, though. For instance, Donne's sermons speak explicitly through the authority of the echo so privileged in early modern rhetorical practice. As he says in one of his sermons, "to that Heaven which belongs to the . . . Church, I shall never come, except I go by the way of . . . former Ideas, former examples, former patterns" (*Sermons* 7: 61). Donne's sermons respond deferentially to voices of authority and learning, constantly citing patristic and Protestant authorities alongside a web of biblical passages. Donne demonstrates his scholarly fluency in several biblical translations (Vulgate, Genevan, Authorized Version) as well as Hebrew to show his deference to "former patterns." He also echoes the respected traditions of Jacobean homiletics, relying heavily on *divisio*, the popular word-by-word analysis of a particular scriptural verse.

This bowing to authority in scholarly conversation, along with Donne's microanalysis of individual words (jazzlike riffs that can go on for several pages), generates soliloquies that can verge on the abstruse. The effect of these excursions is mediated, though, by Donne's powerful "applications" of his exegeses. Here Donne speaks quite directly to and of himself or to the occasions and to the auditors of his sermons. These dramatic addresses, along with his amorous metaphors, aim to generate communal response and interaction, a move most apparent in Donne's occasional sermons. Virtually all his sermons are titled according to their liturgical circumstances, but the special occasion of an aristocratic marriage or the death of a king can render Donne's dramatic voice and social sensibility still more strikingly evident.

It is telling that the most commonly read and taught of Donne's sermons is his most oddly occasional work. "Deaths Duell" (*Sermons* 10: 229–48) is certainly Donne's most famous sermon, and it is the last one Donne wrote before his death, though in it he never refers to his own illness. "Deaths Duell" was first published with a preface announcing that it was "by Sacred Authoritie, stiled the Authors owne funeral Sermon" (*Sermons* 10: 229), and that characterization has continued to be popular. The sermon is considerably complex and autobiographical, though it is clearly a sermon by a gravely ill man on a highly relevant subject: death and how death's power is destroyed.

The contemplation of death for Donne always generates a crisis, a fear of being completely cut off and isolated from others. Donne therefore often concentrates with great intensity on the communal elements of an individual death, whether that community be divine or human. "Deaths Duell" imagines death as the opposite of solitary: as a common human condition, accompanied by the divine presence and prepared for by divine example. "Unto God the Lord belong the issues of death" is the sermon's text, and Donne argues for three meanings of this phrase: God delivers us "*a morte, in morte, per mortem*, from death, in death, and by death" (10: 231). Donne says that God frees us from death, especially the "manifold deathes of this world" (233); that God delivers us in death by controlling "the disposition and manner of our death" (230); and that God delivers us "through the death of this God our Lord Jesus Christ" (231).

The sermon's *divisio* concentrates on the social image of the *danse macabre*, the vision of death as the great common chain linking beggars and rich men. The metaphors Donne uses are not original to him, but his tropes are dramatic and highly suggestive: "we have a winding sheete in our Mothers wombe . . . and this whole world is but . . . our common grave" (10: 233). The sermon's "application" likewise concentrates on de- pendent connections, as it dramatically re-creates Christ's passion: "behold how that Lord which was God yet could dye, would dye, must dye, for your salvation" (244). Donne details the day before Christ's death, imag- ining Christ in each moment and comparing the congregation to his dis- ciples: "Now thy Master . . . looks back upon thee, doe it now" (246–47). The preacher directly challenges the congregation: "art not thou too con- formable?" (246). The final lines personalize the challenge and reenlist metaphors of childlike dependence: "there wee leave you in that blessed dependancy, to hang upon him that hangs upon the Crosse . . . there suck at his woundes, and lye downe in peace in his grave, till hee vouch- safe you a resurrection . . ." (248). Like George Herbert and other more baroque writers, Donne here blurs matter and "mater" in his metaphors of pastoral devotion. He speaks himself into a "blessed dependancy" that keeps at bay the solitary silence of death.

This sermon is often treated as an entirely and obviously autobio- graphical text, but in the classroom I find it more productive to resist that temptation, to look instead at how insistently Donne brings the congregation into his personal drama. Examples of the *danse macabre* tradition (woodcuts in particular) are often helpful in making this point, as are discussions of the very weird images at the beginning and end of the sermon (worms, winding sheets, wounds, sucking blood). Asking students to consider which deaths are and are not present in the sermon, making them consider the functions of those graphic images, and examining the purposes of the "j'accuse" section of the sermon can help them see the metonymic and metaphoric use of dying bodies in this very public and social form.

A more argumentatively political conversation, but one that still invokes the importance of "blessed dependancy," is the sermon for "the Honourable Company of the Virginian Plantation" preached and published in 1622 (*Sermons* 4: 264–82). Donne spoke at a special fund-raising dinner held in the Merchant Taylors' Hall in London for the company that had founded a plantation near present-day Raleigh, Virginia. Donne had considerable interest in the Virginia Company; in 1609 he had sought appointment as secretary of Virginia (*Sermons* 4: 37–38). He might have been grateful by 1622 that he had not been offered the post, since the company was financially troubled and beset by famine, disease, and attacks from without and squabbles within; on the occasion of this banquet "many of the nobilitie and counsaile were invited but few came" (Chamberlain qtd. in Potter and Simpson, Introduction 36n98). Tobacco and Pocahontas seemed to be the company's only exports of note, along with starving settlers' children sent back to England.

Donne assumes the voice of nationalist prophet in response to the company's situation; he repeatedly argues that submission and interdependence will yield both spiritual and political power. To this end he is careful to rearticulate the legal authority of the plantation, implying that it can only operate because of authoritative codes that define how unimproved, uncultivated, or abandoned land can be settled and how colonizers in need can expropriate territory. He also argues that mutual submissiveness can heal the rifts within the company. Donne insists likewise on proper deference to the monarch:

> [I]f those that goe thither, propose to themselves an exemption of
> lawes, to live at their libertie, this is to . . . devest *Allegeance* . . . and
> if those that adventure thither, propose to themselves present benefit,

and profit, a sodaine way to bee rich, . . . this is to bee sufficient of themselves. (4: 269)

To be "sufficient of" oneself is one of the most damning errors Donne can imagine.

Perhaps not surprisingly, Donne critiques self-sufficiency and self-interest most forcefully when he questions the colony's spiritual priorities, arguing repeatedly that if his hearers are looking more for mercantile profits than for spiritual conversion, they will be disappointed. "O, if you would be as ready to hearken at the returne of a *Ship*, how many *Indians* were converted to *Christ Iesus*, as what Trees, or Druggs, or Dyes that Ship had brought, then you were in your right way, and not till then" (4: 269). Donne argues that this spiritual understanding of the mission will also reinforce English *nationalist* interests:

> [Y]ou shall have made this *Iland*, which is but as the *Suburbs* of the old world, a Bridge, a Gallery to the new; to joyne all to that world that shall never grow old, the Kingdome of heaven, You shall add persons to this Kingdome and to the Kingdome of heaven. (281)

His argument constantly shifts between the "kingdom of heaven" and the kingdoms of the world, in the end arguing for their metonymic connection. References to the Red Sea and Noah's Ark suggest that the colonizers resemble the chosen people. Donne supports this connection by describing the colony as a child or a younger sister to England (267, 270, 271, 276) or as a body (282) or part of the body (272) contributing to English glory. The kingdom of England, like the body of Christ, is an interconnected, organic unit that offers communal benefits (spiritual and political) to all its members if they resist singular, self-interested, or independent action.

When teaching this sermon, I find it helpful to discuss how much Donne feels he needs to make the case for colonization. Students often assume that there were no debates, no troubled consciences, no legal difficulties over European imperialist projects, but this sermon helps dislodge that assumption. Here I often focus on Donne's discussions of *potestatem* (4: 274) and ask students to identify the different models of authority in the sermon, so that they can see how Donne not only denigrates earthly authority while championing spiritual powers but also supports the one with the other when it comes to land claims. It is also often productive to teach Donne's sermon alongside other writings on the colonies (Raleigh's more explicitly exploitative arguments in part 5 of his *Discovery of the . . . Empire of Guiana*, for instance).

Other prose works need careful excerpting to be assigned to students but repay the investment. Many of Donne's works elucidate his social individualism, some very accessibly. Three other sermons particularly illustrate the complex social dependencies of the Donnean homiletic worldview. The "Sermon of Commemoration of the Lady Danvers [Magdalen Herbert]" (8: 61–93), an elegy for George Herbert's mother, offers a fascinating example of Protestant hagiography, its culturally gendered collective metaphors and narratives. The commemorative sermon for James I (6: 280–91) ironically and strategically downplays the king's power and celebrates maternal substitutes (Christ, earth, church) for the dead king, while the marriage sermon for Margaret Washington (3: 241–55) compares human marriage to divine, applying "amorous metaphors" to their most direct cultural occasion. *Biathanatos* is a polemical debate on suicide that invokes powerful tropes of collective subjectivity, martyrdom, and the maternal power of the church as well. Finally, for a less theological, more directly socioeconomic view of Donne's sociability, the *Letters to Severall Personages of Honour* is another critical treasure trove.

There are a number of ways to introduce and layer these texts in the classroom. *Biathanatos* compared with John Foxe's *Acts and Monuments* can generate lively discussions of martyrdom, saints, and heroes in the period. In *Biathanatos*, the opening discussions on martyrdom as suicide and the fascinating accounts of Perpetua's gendered death pair nicely with a discussion of Foxe's women of Guernsey, with their hypergendered martyrdom, and with the interplay of passive and active death in Foxe's woodcuts and in his account of Hugh Latimer's death. Donne's *Letters* can initiate discussions of patronage, of social and literary networks (including women's roles in the same), and of the coterie cultures in which Donne and his colleagues were involved. It's often effective to place Donne's letters to Henry Goodyer alongside his patronage poems (including the dedicatory poem "To E. of D. with Six Holy Sonnets," or the verse letters to Goodyer himself). Such a comparison often makes it clear how persistent and how carefully constructed is Donne's presentation of himself as a liminal member of a community.

Donne's prose constitutes such a major part of his literary output and was so significant to his reputation in his lifetime and in succeeding centuries that it would be a grave misrepresentation of his writing to ignore it. The intense energy and complexity of his prose and the synthesizing of individual and society in which it so strongly engages provide a strong counterweight both to his seemingly solipsistic verse and to the "public

versus private" freight that many critics unhelpfully carry into their readings of the period. When one teaches these works to students, it also
doesn't hurt that in the most unexpected contexts, Donne's "amorous
metaphors" abound.

Notes

1. Donne does not specify the precise nature of the illness, though critics
agree that he was probably suffering from some combination of a "rheum," ty-
phus, and a relapsing fever (Raspa xiv–xv).

2. Donne later said that he wrote the *Devotions* during his convalescence
(qtd. in Raspa xvii).

3. The work was entered in the stationers' register on 9 January 1623/24
(Raspa xviiin18).

4. Only eight sermons were published during his lifetime (Potter and Simpson, "General Introductions" 50); the rest were gathered together by his son and
published in three folio editions over a period of thirty years after Donne's death.
Donne memorized his sermons from extensive notes that he later "exscribed"
into the texts we have now ("General Introductions" 48), texts that he at least
partly prepared for publication himself.

Works Cited

Donne, John. *Devotions upon Emergent Occasions*. 1624. Ed. Anthony Raspa.
    New York: Oxford UP, 1987. Print.
———. *The Sermons of John Donne*. Ed. George R. Potter and Evelyn M. Simp-
    son. 10 vols. 1955. Berkeley: U of California P, 1984. Print.
Potter, George R., and Evelyn M. Simpson. "General Introductions." Donne,
    Sermons 1: 1–108.
———. Introduction. Donne, *Sermons* 4: 1–41.
Raspa, Anthony. Introduction. Donne, *Devotions* xii–lvi.
Targoff, Ramie. *Common Prayer: The Language of Public Devotion in Early Mod-
    ern England*. Chicago: U of Chicago P, 2001. Print.
Wordsworth, William. "Preface to *Lyrical Ballads*." *The Norton Anthology of En-
    glish Literature*. Ed. M. H. Abrams et al. New York: Norton, 1979. 160–75.
    Print.

Appendix:
Donne's Works: A Short Bibliography

Editions

Sermons

The Sermons of John Donne. Ed. George R. Potter and Evelyn M. Simpson.
    10 vols. 1955. Berkeley: U of California P, 1984. Print.†

Devotions

Devotions upon Emergent Occasions. 1624. Ed. Anthony Raspa. New York: Oxford UP, 1987. Print.[†]

Devotions upon Emergent Occasions *and* Death's Duel: *With the Life of Dr. John Donne by Izaak Walton.* Pref. Andrew Motion. New York: Vintage, 1999. Print. Vintage Spiritual Classics Series.[‡]

Letters

Letters to Severall Persons of Honour. 1651. Introd. M. Thomas Hester. Delmar: Scholars' Facsimiles, 1977. Print.

Selected Letters. Ed. P. M. Oliver. Manchester: Fyfield, 2002. Print.[‡]

Other Works

Biathanatos. Ed. Ernest W. Sullivan. Newark: U of Delaware P, 1984. Print.[†]

Ignatius His Conclave; or, His Inthronisation in a Late Election in Hell. 1611. Norwood: Johnson, 1977. Print. English Experience Series 868.

Paradoxes and Problems. Ed. Helen Peters. New York: Oxford UP, 1980. Print. Oxford English Texts.

Pseudo-Martyr. Ed. Anthony Raspa. Montreal: McGill-Queen's UP, 1993. Print.[†]

Collections

The Complete Poetry and Selected Prose of John Donne. Ed. Charles M. Coffin. New York: Modern Lib., 2001. Print.

John Donne. Ed. John Carey. Oxford: Oxford UP, 1990. Print. Oxford Authors.[‡] [includes many short selections from the prose works]

One Equall Light: An Anthology of the Writings of John Donne. Ed. John Moses. Grand Rapids: Eerdmans, 2004. Print.[‡]

Selected Prose. Ed. Neil Rhodes. New York: Penguin, 1987. Print.[‡]

Biographies

Bald, R. C. *John Donne: A Life.* Ed. Wesley Milgate. Oxford: Clarendon, 1970. Print.[†]

Flynn, Dennis. *John Donne and the Ancient Catholic Nobility.* Bloomington: Indiana UP, 1995. Print.[†]

Electronic Resources

John Donne. Luminarium: Anthology of English Literature. www.luminarium .org/sevenlit/donne. 29 Jan. 2007. Web. 5 May 2009. [Scholarly electronic versions of selected prose works, including the complete *Devotions* and excerpts from several sermons. Also a range of criticism and biographical information, some trustworthy.]

[†]standard scholarly edition
[‡]good textbook version

Sheila T. Cavanagh

The Long and Winding Road: Teaching Lady Mary Wroth's *Urania*

Lady Mary Sidney Wroth's *Countesse of Mountgomery's* Urania (1621) provides an incomparable opportunity for students to gain insight into female contributions to the early modern prose tradition. Wroth's romance, the first prose narrative published by a woman in English, includes significant examples of a consciously gendered text, raises important questions about class and ethnicity during the early modern period, models literary experimentation with its unconventional prose style and its interpolation of poetry into its narrative, and promotes a reexamination of our presumptions about women writers during this period. From its pastoral opening to its abrupt ending, *Urania* offers a work filled with rich textual and cultural material. Although readers new to the text sometimes misinterpret it as an adaptation of Philip Sidney's *Arcadia* because of its conventional pastoral beginning and Sidneyan conclusion, Wroth's text is not merely a literary tribute to her famous uncle. As I argue at length elsewhere (*Cherished Torment*), in fact, *Urania* offers a significant literary and intellectual contribution to early modern studies in its own right. Its examination of social topics in the period, for instance, including miscegenation, illegitimacy, and spiritual deviance, can make it a valuable component of many investigations of early modern literature and cultural studies. It also offers an unusual example of an extended, experimental prose piece penned by a woman during this period.

Given space constraints, I include one brief example of *Urania*'s style and content to demonstrate ways it could be useful in a course on prose from this era. This section comes from the text's manuscript continuation and features the dark-skinned King of Tartaria, who later marries the main female character, Pamphilia:

> The King was sett and all his Princes when the great Tartar came in: A brave and Comly Gentleman, shaped of body so curiously as noe art cowld counterfett soe rare a proportion, of an excellent stature neither to high nor of the meanest stature, his hands so white as wowld have become a great Lady, his face of curious and exact features, butt for the couler of itt, itt plainely shewed the sunne had either liked itt to much, and so had too hardly kissed itt, or in fury of his delicacy, had made his beames to strongly to burn him, yet cowld nott take away the perfect sweetnes of his loveliness. (*Second Part* 42)

As this lengthy, dense sentence indicates, Wroth's style compresses a multiplicity of literary allusions and cultural commentary into the introduction of this figure. Characteristically, Wroth incorporates traditional elements of the blazon and sonnet traditions, as well as a meandering sentence structure to fashion an elegant yet vexed character who will figure prominently in her text. At the same time, however, the "white" hands that "wowld have become a great Lady" that are part of this dark-skinned character's body, whose face was "too hardly kissed" by the sun, provide a startling moment in what might otherwise be seen as a conventional description. The interpolation of a blazon that would typically be focused on a fair-skinned lady with the reminder that this passage describes a dark, male ruler from an exotic country demonstrates the way that fissures in the text regularly open up avenues for further investigation. Faculty members wishing their students to investigate seventeenth-century attitudes toward race and gender, in addition to considerations of prose style, therefore, will find in Wroth's text an abundance of pertinent material. Other, similarly intriguing, passages in *Urania* can be found that fit within the parameters of numerous courses on early modern literature and culture.

The challenges associated with teaching Wroth's *Urania* are readily apparent, however, to anyone considering this prospect. The two volumes, published separately by the Renaissance English Text Society (RETS), are, together, extremely long (1,396 pages in total) and thus expensive. Apart from a graduate seminar devoted to Wroth or some similarly specialized venue, there are presumably few courses where faculty members could justify the investment of time and money that would be necessary for students to study the complete *Urania*. At the same time, although a few excerpts of the romance appear in anthologies, such truncated texts necessarily limit the scope of the pedagogical enterprise in ways largely predetermined by the compiler of the anthology. Since *Urania* is a complicated narrative, it is hard for anthologies to include anything more than a glimpse of Wroth's expansive text. In addition, it is so difficult initially to keep track of the *Urania*'s many characters and to adapt to Wroth's convoluted narrative style that students may have difficulty acquiring an appreciation for the romance if they only read a brief selection.

What I propose in this essay, therefore, is one approach designed to offset the impediments of time, money, and length of text that make it difficult to include *Urania* in early modern courses. At the same time that it accommodates these practical constraints, moreover, the approach can expand student research, oral presentation, and critical thinking skills in ways that can benefit their further studies.[1] My suggestion will not alleviate the limited familiarity gained by students who do not read the entire romance, of course, but it can introduce them to an intellectually rich and vibrant narrative, while building their expertise in literary investigation. This approach is fashioned to have students learn how to frame a topic, ask questions, and raise hypotheses about a text in ways that differ in form and content from those they typically encounter in undergraduate classes.

My proposal is geared specifically toward use of the RETS volumes (edited initially by Josephine Roberts, then completed by Suzanne Gossett and Janel Mueller) because of their extensive scholarly apparatuses, which offer students the opportunity to become familiar with the characters, issues, and themes of *Urania* even before reading the text itself. These editions of *Urania* offer a series of detailed and sophisticated essays, invaluable charts of main figures and their relationships, and a character index that orients and guides both new and regular readers. While students often give short shrift to the materials that surround a text, in Wroth's *Urania* the learned apparatus that frames the narrative makes it possible for this text to reach a much larger audience than would be feasible through the use of other versions, such as the Early Modern Women facsimile edition or the electronic texts available through *Early English Books Online* (*EEBO*) and the Brown University Women Writers Project.[2]

Although these editions can be extremely useful, they offer limited assistance for students reading *Urania* in standard classroom settings, and they do not include the second part of the *Urania*.[3] Facilitating student access to *Urania* through creative use of the RETS volumes, however, provides a way to incorporate significant segments of this important prose work into a variety of classroom environments. While it would be ideal for the faculty members undertaking this kind of assignment to be personally conversant with the complete *Urania*, my proposal does not presume such knowledge. Instead, although the course segment described below requires the teacher to read the material assigned to the students, as well as a selection of critical works regarding Wroth,[4] I am assuming that the faculty member's familiarity with Wroth will grow as she or he guides this student research and as time and repeated reading increase his or her expertise.[5]

The first volume of the RETS edition contains a series of introductions, each addressing the literary, political, social, or personal contexts of the narrative. At the end of the volume, one finds an account of the textual apparatus; commentary on individual words and episodes; genealogical tables; and indices of characters, places, and first lines of poems in the relevant portion of *Urania*. Since Roberts died before completing the second volume, this part does not contain the contextual introductions she had planned. It does, however, provide a description of the manuscript and details of the editing process, as well as textual notes; commentary; genealogical tables; and indexes of characters, places, and first lines of poems in this part of the romance. Making this material available to students, to the extent that resources allow, will provide them with information for a range of research agendas.

As the critical introduction, prefaces, and commentary to *Urania* make clear, Wroth's text contains episodes dealing with concerns that might find a place in a twenty-first-century classroom. A course focusing on literary genres in the early modern period, for example, might guide students to read the pastoral opening of the narrative in conjunction with some of the text's more distinctly romantic or poetic passages,[6] so that the class could discuss ways that Wroth both follows and alters the literary styles of her predecessors and contemporaries. For example, the students could read *Urania* in conjunction with the works of Sidney and Edmund Spenser, contemporary Continental romance writers, and other early modern authors of sonnet sequences. A class considering a broader chronological range could be directed to some of the passages that experiment with the kind of conversational verisimilitude that we more commonly expect to find in forms such as the novel.[7] Such discussions demonstrate Wroth's continual manipulation of narrative forms and styles, particularly in part 2 of her narrative, which seems not to have been intended for publication. Students attracted to history and political science could learn about the importance of the Holy Roman Empire in Wroth's literary imagination through Roberts's section on political contexts (Roberts xxxix). They would also be exposed to the activities of Wroth's cousin/lover, William Herbert, in the politics of the day. Depending on their individual interests, then, students could use the character index to follow the political career of Amphilanthus (who is largely based on Herbert) or use the index of places to follow events such as the expansion of the empire.[8] At the same time, since Amphilanthus's role in the narrative is so multifaceted, reading through "his" section of the index will alert students to many details about his love life, his genealogy, and his military career, as they search for citations that are relevant to their projects. As they subsequently read through the sections of the text that were identified through the index, students will also become aware of some of the many intersecting tales that appear within the story of Amphilanthus. They will not achieve total proficiency in the romance through this procedure, of course. Nevertheless, by creating a presentation and an essay that bring together different parts of *Urania* in a cohesive fashion, students will gain a valuable perspective on Wroth's literary accomplishments.[9] The work of these students, when combined with the work of their colleagues in the class, will allow for a broader understanding of the text than would be possible through readings in an anthology.[10] A pair of students could work together on Amphilanthus, for example, dividing their responsibilities between the first and second volumes of the narrative. Given the scope of the text, there is no obvious limit to the kind of collaborative efforts that might be devised.

I would recommend that faculty members whose institutional resources allow rely on electronic-reserve collections to make ancillary materials, such as the indexes, as widely available as possible. Since the prohibitive cost for typical students of the complete *Urania* is a guiding impulse behind this assignment, libraries would need to be prepared to keep at least two copies of the complete text on print reserve, so that students could share these volumes during their reading of the narrative proper.[11] Print reserves often put restrictions on usage, but careful planning by faculty members and students should ensure that all students handle the original books sufficiently to complete the assignment. Electronic reserves, in contrast, can provide different students with access to the same materials simultaneously, often from remote locations, even when the physical library is closed. This expanded dissemination of critical parts of the texts will enable students to plan their work more conveniently, even when they live off campus or have other commitments that impede their use of the library.[12] Individual libraries have their own interpretations of "fair usage" under current copyright laws; faculty members should thus consult with the library staff at their institutions to determine how much of *Urania* they can make available electronically. This assignment will be most effective if liberal use of the scholarly apparatus is possible, since students will be best served if they are able to read all the introductory materials as well as the indexes, and if they can keep at hand a copy of the charts detailing familial relationships in the narrative.

Many of the other literary and cultural interests contained within *Urania* can perhaps be best illuminated through a description of the class module under discussion here. Once students are acclimated to the text through limited lecturing and a careful reading of prefatory materials, they can be sent for a detailed reading of the indexes, in preparation for a class presentation and paper, whose parameters can be set according to the level of the students and the time available for this project. In general, however, each student will be expected to use the indexes to help identify a topic of interest that she or he will then explore through a close reading and analysis of select portions of the romance. If possible, it is best to assign both an oral presentation and an essay for this project, to give the entire class as full a sense of the narrative as possible and to help the students find different ways to give shape to what they are reading. Presumably, students will hone in on a range of topics and sections of the text, which can be fruitfully shared with their colleagues. The project can easily accommodate group or individual efforts. The main goal is to get students involved in the story so that they learn how to work with unfamiliar materials and research methods, from whatever perspective will best suit them or the aims of the course. Adjusting the assignment to suit their syllabi, faculty members can be more or less restrictive in the instructions that they offer to their students.

Since the indexes included with *Urania* offer unusually detailed information about the content of the narrative, this strategy is far more interesting than a similar endeavor would be using a text equipped with a more conventional index.[13] In fact, many readers will find that the indexes are essential aids to their reading; the text contains so many characters and episodes and covers such diverse geographic spaces that it is not easy to navigate the narrative without this assistance. Unlike Spenser's epic, which is divided into distinct legends that can help readers situate themselves, Wroth's text does not contain clearly demarcated sections, and its convoluted prose style and indistinct use of pronouns increase the possibility of readerly confusion.

While even reading the index aimlessly could prove to be fruitful, students who have read the introductory materials will be able to map out a more profitable route through the back of these texts. Topics as wide-ranging as female friendship, literary coteries, diverse marital patterns, colonial expansion, politics, religion, the relations between gender and sovereignty, supernatural encounters, leadership, life after death, and ethnic diversity are among the many themes and issues that can be explored in the pages of this narrative. By following the adventures of a major figure, such as Pamphilia or Amphilanthus; by focusing on lesser yet interesting characters, such as the addled poet Antissia or the "sex slave" Selarinus; or by remaining alert to the ramifications of racial identity in the stories of dark-skinned characters, such as Rodomondro and Follietto, students gain the opportunity to delve into a portion of the narrative more deeply than a typical assignment from an anthology generally allows. Other students in the class could follow different paths through the narrative. Someone wishing to investigate the characteristics of early modern romance, for instance, could look in the index to the second volume and find any number of captivating romantic characters, including Duardo the dwarf, the giants Lamurandus and Lofturado, and the unnamed "Female Spirit who haunts Selarinus" (Wroth, *Second Part* 561). Another student could track the progress of the plentiful missing children and attempt to sort out the many stories of lost offspring that are told in *Urania*, part 2, while yet another might become intrigued by the fate of the numerous female writers described in the romance or the historical and intellectual underpinnings of the text. So long as the students are well versed in the introductory materials and guided through the process of reading and assimilating textual information in this new way, they should be able to construct projects that will enhance their understandings of the narrative while strengthening their abilities to grapple with material that could initially appear overwhelming.

Students, by subsequently sharing their findings in class, benefit the entire class by fostering an expanded understanding of the text that each student reads only partially. The class presentations also facilitate conversations about the strengths and weaknesses of this pedagogical approach and whether it can successfully make a virtue out of the necessity of reading in excerpts. Engaging students in discussions about the methods they undertake in various forms of literary study, including this one, further enhances the strength of the exercise, since it offers an important opportunity for both faculty members and students to reflect on the literary enterprise and their individual and collective goals in this project. As recent research on brain-based learning has revealed, the most effective pedagogies allow time for reflection and discussion about the reasons for learning. In addition, using the variety of skills that is needed to complete this exercise supports the types of learning many educational leaders believe are crucial for our era.

Although this module is partly fueled by financial and pedagogical necessity, inquiry is at its heart. Guiding students to compile their own anthology of excerpts and analyses from a text as lengthy and complex as Wroth's *Urania* will not compensate for all the inevitable disadvantages of reading a literary work only partially. Nevertheless, having students find their own ways through a text like this—with faculty and print guidance—can enhance their ownership of the material and of their educations, while introducing them to substantial portions of a significant piece of early modern literary history.

Notes

1. Recent research on brain-based learning and problem-based learning indicates that assignments such as those included here can increase levels of student engagement and retention of knowledge. For information about brain-based research, see Zull; Caine and Caine. See Evansen and Hmelo for descriptions of problem-based learning. In addition, the Association of American Colleges and Universities released a 2007 report entitled *College Learning for the New Global Century* that emphasizes the importance of the kind of student research described here (30).

2. The Brown University Women Writers Project electronic edition is available by subscription only. *EEBO* is also available through subscription only.

3. Although the electronic versions can be useful because of their search capacities, the length of the text makes it difficult to read on computer, while the lack of an index impedes novice Wroth readers. In addition, only volume 1 of *Urania* is available electronically. Similarly, the facsimile edition only includes volume 1 and does not offer an index. Mary Ellen Lamb is currently working on an

abridged version of the text that should alleviate some of these problems, although it will still leave faculty members without an uncomplicated way to teach the entire work. Presumably, the entire text will eventually be online. Once that happens, there will be new pedagogical possibilities for this text, although the introductions available in Roberts's edition are likely to remain invaluable.

4. Space precludes mentioning all the Wroth criticism available, but since the publication of the RETS volumes, such resources are proliferating.

5. While this idea may be startling to many educators, it fits well within the "tutor" or "guide" model espoused by problem-based learning, which leaves the burden for acquiring expertise primarily with the student.

6. The poems of Pamphilia and others can readily be found through the indexes, just as many of the episodes drawing heavily from the romance tradition should be fairly accessible through this medium.

7. The discussions with the " 'Merry' Marquise of Gargadia," for example, fit this pattern (see, e.g., Wroth, *Second Part* 30).

8. The character index contains considerably more detail than the index of places, which is likely to be of most use to students with well-defined, relevant projects.

9. Cohesion, of course, is not always a hallmark of this text. Still, having the students bring some structure to the narrative will facilitate their analysis.

10. Anthologies are obviously useful tools, and I do not wish to discount their importance in the classroom, although I am offering an alternative pedagogical strategy for *Urania*.

11. Students should be encouraged to buy the texts for individual use, of course, but it remains implausible to require this.

12. The materials in question may also be made available through standard reserve procedures, as individual or institutional circumstances warrant.

13. Having read both parts of *Urania* before, then after, the indexes were available, I acknowledge my own deep gratitude to Josephine Roberts and Micheline White for compiling these guides. Teaching this narrative without these resources would be immeasurably more difficult.

Works Cited

Association of American Colleges and Universities. *College Learning for the New Global Century: A Report from the National Leadership Council for Liberal Education and America's Promise*. Washington: Assn. of Amer. Colls. and Univs., 2007. Print.

Caine, Renate Nummela, and Geoffrey Caine. *Making Connections: Teaching and the Human Brain*. New York: Addison-Wesley, 1994. Print.

Cavanagh, Sheila T. *Cherished Torment: The Emotional Geography of Lady Mary Wroth's* Urania. Pittsburgh: Duquesne UP, 2001. Print.

Evansen, Dorothy H., and Cindy E. Hmelo. *Problem-Based Learning: A Research Perspective on Learning Interactions*. Mahwah: Erlbaum, 2000. Print.

Hutchings, Bill. "Problem-Based Literature Course?" *National Teaching and Learning Forum* 15.2 (2006): 6–8. Print.

Roberts, Josephine A. Introduction. Wroth, *First Part* xv–cii.

Wroth, Mary. *The First Part of the Countess of Montgomery's* Urania. Ed. Josephine A. Roberts. Binghamton: Center for Medieval and Early Renaissance Studies, State U of New York at Binghamton, 1995. Print. Medieval and Renaissance Texts and Studies 140. Renaissance English Text Soc., 7th ser., 17.

———. *The Second Part of the Countess of Montgomery's* Urania. Ed. Josephine A. Roberts, completed by Suzanne Gossett and Janel Mueller. Tempe: Arizona Center for Medieval and Renaissance Studies, 1999. Print. Medieval and Renaissance Texts and Studies 211. Renaissance English Text Soc. 24.

Zull, James E. *The Art of Changing the Brain: Enriching the Practice of Teaching by Exploring the Biology of Learning*. Sterling: Stylus, 2002. Print.

Deborah E. Harkness

Francis Bacon's
Experimental Writing

When teachers are faced with a pile of Francis Bacon's scientific works on the one hand and his slim volume of essays on the other, it is no wonder that most reach for the *Essays* when searching for examples of Francis Bacon's prose (on Bacon's essays, see Lilley, in this volume). Bacon's *Essays* receives far more attention than *The Advancement of Learning* (1605) or English translations of his *Instauratio Magna* (*Great Instauration*) of 1620, which was published to begin the process of replacing the deficient human arts and sciences with a new system of learning based on natural history. Bacon's minor works that shed light (however obliquely) on his efforts to read the book of nature—such as the *Sylva Sylvarum*'s collection of receipts and experiments or the fabulous *Wisdom of the Ancients*—are even less familiar. When an exception is made and one of Bacon's scientific works is assigned to undergraduates, the special case is usually the *New Atlantis,* a strange hybrid of an adventure story, utopian political treatise, and scientific wish list published posthumously in 1627.[1]

Yet there are strong incentives for considering Bacon's scientific writing in the context of early modern prose, all of which cluster around the notion of experimental writing. Bacon faced real challenges when it came to conceptualizing how his natural philosophical work should be couched and framed. There were two prominent, elite intellectual models available to him: the Latin dialogue, popular in ancient philosophy and still used throughout the early modern period by contemporaries such as Galileo in his *Dialogue on the Two Chief World Systems*, and the Latin commentary, which juxtaposed ancient and medieval authoritative texts and combined them with the author's own critiques and emendations on the subject. The dialogue became especially popular among early modern authors writing in the vernacular—Galileo's *Dialogue on the Two Chief World Systems* was first published in the vernacular under the title *Dialogi sopra I due massimi sistemi del mondo* (1632)—while the commentary remained a predominantly Latinate endeavor. At the time that Bacon was writing, author commentaries were fast outstripping the texts they were critiquing, and Nicolaus Copernicus and Johannes Kepler both produced original works of natural philosophy that were rooted in the commentary tradition but went well beyond it and advanced new theories and philosophical arguments. At a more popular level of publication, however, Bacon's options for prose models were less limited. During the sixteenth century, English students of nature published a wide range of treatises concerned with the natural world. Almanacs, books of basic mathematical and technical instruction, compendiums of medical remedies, translations of Continental works, editions of alchemical treatises in prose as well as verse—all were available to eager readers. These books were chatty, newsy, informative, illustrated, and largely printed in the vernacular.

Considering Bacon's scientific prose in conjunction with the vernacular books printed in England on scientific, medical, and technical subjects opens up new possibilities for teaching. First, late sixteenth- and early-seventeenth-century England emerges as a site for prose experimentation as authors grappled with the complexities of presenting information about nature that was increasingly based on experiment and observation. Second, the prose itself can be examined for its stylistic components, namely the use of a complex vernacular scientific idiom and a plain and direct voice well suited to conveying information. Finally, Bacon can be put in a more satisfying context—not as a single voice speaking out on behalf of a new science but as one of many who were trying to bridge the widening gap between ancient, authoritative approaches to the study of nature and new, experimental modes.

The gulf that opened up between the elite prose models taught in the university and the popular science publications of the Elizabethan period put Bacon in an especially difficult position, however. Unlike some of his

contemporaries who wrote works on nature, Bacon wanted not only readers but patrons who would support his vision of what the natural sciences
could be. As a result, he found himself at a crossroad, where his intellectual and political agendas met up with the burgeoning business of books
and a very different set of reader expectations among literate men and
women familiar with popular science books. This difficult position between genres, audiences, and agendas made it problematic for Bacon to
settle on a suitable voice for his scientific work, as well as a suitable genre
for the new, experiment- and observation-based study of nature that he
wished to promote. The brisk, straightforward pithiness of his *Essays* is
nowhere apparent in his scientific prose. Instead, his voice is hesitant, ten-
tative, and experimental. Bacon's scientific works strike this reader as a set
of ideas in search of a genre that could both advance his agenda and appeal to the developing interest in the natural world found among his
contemporaries.

Bacon's troubles finding a voice and a vehicle for his ideas were compounded by the twists of fortune that took him from an assured place in
the Elizabethan political system and brought his future and his livelihood
into doubt. Bacon was born just outside London's walls to Nicholas Bacon, a gifted Tudor administrator, and Anne Cooke, a well-educated
woman known for her learning and incisive mind. At the age of twelve
Bacon went to Trinity College, Cambridge, where he read widely in classical and contemporary authors and received his undergraduate degree.
At fifteen, he continued his education at London's law schools, the Inns
of Court. After a hiatus spent in the retinue of the English ambassador to
France, where he was introduced to the complexities of real politics as opposed to theoretical models, he returned to England to practice the law.
Nicholas Bacon's unexpected death in 1579 left Francis Bacon's future
unsettled, since Nicholas had not settled property and money on his
younger son to ensure his financial well-being. Francis, still a young man,
now found it necessary to make his own way in the world, with only his
intelligence, his education, and his family's name to his credit.

With the help of his maternal uncle William Cecil, Bacon began the
painstaking work of entering into the crowded world of the Elizabethan
court and its politics. His progress was made more difficult because most
of Bacon's contemporaries either loved him or hated him. Nevertheless,
Bacon won a seat in Parliament and began participating in the political
maneuverings of the day, such as the trial and execution of Mary, Queen
of Scots. Still, Bacon's entry into the inner echelons of power was slow in
coming. In 1592, at the age of thirty-one, Bacon felt that he was washed

up politically and had little hope of further advancement. It was then that he decided to embark on a career in natural philosophy and announced his intention to take "all knowledge" as his "province." Bacon told Cecil that if he could only rid natural philosophy of "two sorts of rovers," namely "frivolous disputations" and "blind experiments," he would be able to reform the discipline into something that could boast of its "industrious observations, grounded conclusions, and profitable inventions and discoveries" (Bacon, *Letters* 1: 108–09).

The trials and tribulations of Bacon's life partially explain his need for experiments in writing. Bacon was perpetually in search of gainful employment, and he restlessly sought fame, fortune, and recognition. When one strategy failed to appeal to the queen or her courtiers or another did not win favor with the university dons, Bacon simply changed tack and tried something else. In the crowded and competitive environment of the late Elizabethan and Jacobean courtly circles, he proved to be remarkably flexible at trying out new approaches to win royal favor and popular acclaim. Bacon's experimental writing thus can be viewed from two different vantage points, each of which opens up new vistas for a better understanding of his prose. First, because the traditional genre conventions of natural philosophy (such as the dialogue) could not meet all Bacon's goals for the advancement of learning, he found it necessary to experiment with different prose styles to discover what might be most effective (Vickers, Introduction xv–xliv, xxii). Second, because no genre Bacon experimented with was ever perfectly suited to his purpose or to his anticipated audience, his prose was often published in incomplete and unpolished form. There are few early modern authors for whom so many fragments, drafts, and revisions are accessible to modern students and teachers. Bacon's scientific prose writings thus give students an opportunity to examine how early modern authors were grappling in new ways both with studying nature and with writing about nature. They show a man who was struggling to find the proper voice for expressing the new authority of science, as well as a man who was striving to locate the most effective way to convey scientific information to his readers.

Ideas in Search of a Genre

Some of the best evidence we have to support the notion that Bacon was faced with the challenge of finding a genre that was appropriate to his ideas comes from the comparison of one of the earliest works, the *Gesta Grayorum* (1594), and one of his posthumously published works, *The*

New Atlantis. When his proud boasts to his uncle failed to win him a government position, Bacon turned to dramatic entertainments in the hopes of catching the queen's eye. His *Gesta Grayorum* was one of a number of entertainments that have survived from the period and that record the annual productions put on by lawyers and students to celebrate the holiday season. Prominent court figures were usually in attendance, which made the productions a venue for winning patronage and employment. Bacon's *Gesta Grayorum* was staged as a debate among six men— including a philosopher, a warrior, and a sportsman—each of whom defended his way of life. The philosopher, arguing on behalf of the scholarly way of life, exhorted his listeners to pursue the study of nature and construct for their use a library, a garden, a cabinet of curiosities, and a laboratory to explore the potential utility of the natural world. The *Gesta Grayorum* was not enthusiastically received by Bacon's audience, and, when it failed to win him a position, he turned to writing essays in hopes that they would manage both to instruct and entertain. Brief, succinct, and provocative, Bacon's *Essays* covers subjects of interest to a wide range of readers, and the skeletal outlines of topics he would return to in his lengthier scientific works can be found in a far more digestible and direct form in his essays "Of Travel," "Of Cunning," "Of Regiment of Health," "Of Gardens," and "Of Studies." Buoyed by their success, Bacon ventured once more into experimenting with philosophical and scientific writing, only to return to the safer shores of history and translations of the Psalms toward the end of his life.

Around 1623, however, Bacon took up again the central ideas of the philosopher's way of life first explored in the *Gesta Grayorum* masque and touched on lightly in the *Essays.* Stripping these ideas from their original dramatic context, he gave them a prominent place in his utopian adventure story *The New Atlantis.* This work, too, draws on a well-established genre that extends back to Plato's *Republic* and forward to the early modern period and the work of Thomas More, François Rabelais, and Tommaso Campanella. At the end of *New Atlantis,* Bacon describes a remarkable institution called Salomon's House, which, according to his literary executor, was "a model or description of a college instituted for the interpreting of nature and the producing of great and marvelous works for the benefit of men" (qtd. in Wortham 185). At Salomon's House the *Gesta Grayorum*'s small clutch of scientific spaces—library, garden, cabinet, and laboratory—were expanded into a complex as sprawling as any university. Specially equipped caves were dug into the earth to simulate natural mines and accommodate refrigeration experiments, and observation towers were erected for studying the heavens. Hospitals and distillation apparatuses were built to foster the study of useful medicinal cures. Orchards and gardens were planted to provide ample opportunities for botanizing, grafting, viticulture, and agriculture. Sound houses, perfume houses, bakehouses, brewhouses, and enginehouses emitted a cacophony of sounds and a sneeze-inducing set of aromas, all in pursuit of natural knowledge.

While modern readers may consider Bacon's description entirely fantastic, his contemporaries would have had concrete examples drawn from their own lives and experiences that would have suggested that Salomon's House already existed, at least in part. One way to encourage students to think through Bacon's rhetorical strategies in presenting Salomon's House as a utopian fantasy is to juxtapose these often-quoted passages from *New Atlantis* with a few pages of Hugh Plat's *The Jewel House of Art and Nature* (1594). Plat and Bacon were contemporaries and shared an interest in natural history. Both were also avid promoters of the benefits that the natural sciences could bring to the commonwealth. But while Bacon left the issue of what men and women were to actually do in the houses of knowledge open to conjecture, Plat spelled out their activities in detail and included recipes and instructions on how to make toothpaste, build a bridge, construct a lamp that could not be extinguished in high winds, and make a variety of medicines.

We can glean additional insights into Bacon's notions about the hands-on work of science from other examples of his prose. Bacon wrote about experiments in his manuscript notebooks, and he also recorded some of his observations in a compendium of receipts published posthumously in an incomplete state called *Sylva Sylvarum; or, A Naturall Historie in Ten Centuries*. Writing about his hands-on inquiries into nature was, in Bacon's view, as important to making knowledge as actually doing the experiments, and, although his accounts of experiments are often brief, a close examination of them can shed light on the development of scientific and technical prose and on the ways in which writing was an activity of making and doing in the early modern period. Any page of the *Sylva Sylvarum* immerses the reader instantly into a world of instructions on how to perform experiments, reports of other experiments, and attempts to draw scientific conclusions from these activities. At the same time, the prose is strained, and the how-to descriptions cursory. Conveying scientific information was not an easy business.

Passages in the *Sylva Sylvarum* and the other works he classified as natural history, such as his numerous treatises on the prolongation of life or his work on the tides, also shed light on why the reform of natural knowledge depended on these disciplines. We see that as Bacon struggled to capture in writing the complicated workings of nature, he tried to achieve a balance between the particular and observable and between the generalized and abstract. Natural history, with its basis in the study of natural objects such as fossils, plants, and animals, provided a better opportunity for resolving the tension than did disciplines such as astronomy or mathematics. For Bacon the problem with natural history as it was practiced in the Elizabethan and Jacobean periods was that its practitioners had not exercised sufficient choice and judgment in sorting out appropriate and inappropriate objects of study. To redress this situation Bacon intended to construct a natural history "as may be fundamental to the erecting and building of a true philosophy, for the illumination of the understanding, the extracting of axioms, and the producing of many noble works and effects." These efforts would replace "those natural histories, which are extant . . . gathered for delight and use, [and which] are full of pleasant descriptions and pictures, and affect to seek after admiration, rarities, and secrets" (*Sylva* Av). Bacon concluded that the compilers of these contemporary natural histories had "no knowledge of the formulary of interpretation, the work whereof is to abridge experience and to make things as certainly found out . . . in short time, as by infinite experiences in ages" (*Valerius* 246–47). Exploring these tensions in works such as *New Atlantis* and the *Sylva Sylvarum* along with Bacon's efforts to reconcile the observable and the abstract can help students see Bacon's contributions to early modern prose in a less self-assured light.

There is no evidence, however, that Bacon's prose could live up to his own promise. His *Sylva Sylvarum* offers examples of his efforts in the field of natural history—but they were a pale reflection of the rigors of the discipline as it was being practiced at the time. The book's contents were drawn from reported facts and generalizations taken from anonymous "daily experience" and contained a few anecdotal reports about Bacon's successful medical treatments. These snippets were not evaluated systematically to assess their success or applicability. Instead, they seem like the kernel of one of Bacon's essays—jottings on discrete topics that might eventually have been drawn into something more axiomatic. Bacon's literary executor, William Rawley, admitted in the preface to the *Sylva Sylvarum* that his master had in fact been reluctant to publish the work, "For it may seeme an Indigested Heap of Particulars; And cannot haue that Lustre, which Bookes cast into Methods haue" (Ar). In the *Sylva Sylvarum* Bacon had not been able to find his ideal middle way between theory and practice, nor had he found it possible to use the "formulary of interpretation" that he assured his readers was in his grasp. Comparing individual entries in the *Sylva Sylvarum* with those of his essays related to scientific topics and the call to arms on behalf of a new science in *New Atlantis* can help students see the ways in which all three seemingly distinct genres overlap and blur into one another, without being successfully integrated into a single, unified mode of writing. Students could be asked to write a Baconian account of a modern scientific discovery or idea for a general reader and to further explore the porous boundaries between instruction, entertainment, and novelty.

Bacon clearly valued both the practical and theoretical aspects of natural knowledge, but he often found it difficult to explain their proper relationship. He criticized William Gilbert for making "a philosophy out of the observations of a loadstone," for example, though this empirically grounded effort would seem to be a model of the reformed philosophy he was trying to promote (*Advancement* 30). Caught between accounts of experiments—which seemed fragmentary, vulgar, and incomplete—and the philosophical discussions that struck him as empty and unfruitful, Bacon was stumped about how to best draw together the experimental and the philosophical into a single prose genre.

The Never-Ending Story: Bacon's Prose Drafts

Bacon's search for an effective genre for his scientific ideas can also be seen in his inability to conclude, polish, and complete most of the major works that he composed that had to do with the natural sciences. As early as 1605, Bacon was already deeply alarmed at the state of knowledge in general and natural knowledge in particular. Unable to attract influential patrons with his prescriptive remarks about what the sciences should be in the *Gesta Grayorum*, he turned to make a vitriolic critique of the current state of the study of nature. Drawing together years of notes, unfinished treatises, letters, and unpublished manuscripts, he laid out his scheme for the reform of the natural sciences in *The Advancement of Learning* (1605).

In the work, the seams of the patchwork process are often evident. Bacon's criticisms of the current state of natural knowledge, for example, typically took two forms: sometimes he claimed there was scant interest in the natural world; at other times he argued that there was abundant interest in nature but that the wrong people were using methods of inquiry that were shoddy, muddled, confused. As Bacon waffled back and forth between criticizing people for using the same practices that he suggested would ultimately reform natural knowledge and deploring the lack of interest in the empirical study of nature, he became wildly inconsistent and terribly confusing. Studying an example of Bacon's most polished scientific works and emphasizing the disconnects and inconsistency one finds in them challenges the widely held notion that he knew what the new science should be and that he knew how the new science should be presented.

A comparison of Bacon's *Thoughts and Conclusions* (*Cogita et Visa* [1607]), a preliminary version of ideas later featured in another of Bacon's works on the philosophy of science, with the later *Novum Organum* (1620) reveals similar inconsistencies and evidence of work still in progress. In *Novum Organum*, a work that would become influential among early members of the Royal Society, Bacon not only set out a new inductive method for the study of nature that would replace Aristotelian models but also criticized the study of nature being undertaken at the time. Even Bacon's contemporaries found his dual approach to the issue confusing. In a letter thanking Bacon for the gift, Thomas Bodley praised him for prompting every student "to look more narrowly to his business . . . by aspiring to the greatest perfection, of that which is now-a-days divulged in the sciences" and also by "diving yet deeper . . . into the bowels and secrets of nature" (41). Yet Bodley urged Bacon to adopt a more circumspect tone and to give credit where credit was due for work already being undertaken. In his letter to Bacon, Bodley wrote, "We profess a greater holdfast of certainty in your science, than you by your discourse will seem to acknowledge" and defended both the contributors and the contributions already being made by students of nature (39–40).

According to Bodley, Bacon spoke longingly of acquiring "a knowledge [of nature] more excellent than now is among us, which experience might produce, if we would but essay to extract it out of nature by particular probations." But, Bodley pointed out, this only admonished readers to do that which "without instigation, by a natural instinct men will practice of themselves." There already were "infinite [numbers of people] in all parts of the world" undertaking just such an inquiry "with all diligence and care, that any ability can perform." Hundreds of inventions and discoveries were "daily brought to light by the enforcement of wit or casual events," which proved to be of enormous use and benefit to humanity. Bodley was particularly aggrieved by Bacon's harsh characterization of the activities of physicians and alchemists. The practice of medicine, for example, flourished "with admirable remedies . . . taught by experimental effects." These experimentally derived remedies, Bodley said, already provided "the open high-way to knowledge that you recommend" (40). There was therefore no need to do as Bacon suggested and start afresh, abandoning all supposed knowledge and the ill-advised experiments from which they were sometimes derived in a quest for new and more certain information. Such a plan "would instantly bring us to barbarism," Bodley countered (40), and leave the natural sciences with fewer substantive and correct theories than were already known.

Seeing how Bacon stitched earlier treatises, new ideas, and ancient theories together into a work of science shows students how much the writing of science was still an experimental project in the early modern period. Plat, comfortable with his experimental accounts, as exemplified in *The Jewel House*, did not take the prose risks that Bacon did in the *Novum Organum* or *The Advancement of Learning*. Plat's object was not to overhaul or replace the existing canon of scientific literature; Bacon's object was to do precisely that. Bacon's drafts, revisions, and cut-and-paste work are a testament to how difficult—and ultimately unsuccessful—that task would be.

Writing Experiments

The evidence from Bacon's scientific prose suggests that he attempted to create a new way of writing about science rather than the new science he is so often credited with conceiving. With such models available as Socratic dialogues and scholastic commentaries, Bacon turned instead to other genres—drama, travel writing, exposition, receipt books, fables, and essays—to find the best vehicle for the display of natural knowledge and its discussion. It is interesting finally to consider, then, the current fate of the remaining artifacts of Bacon's experimental writing. The *Gesta*

Grayorum is considered a curiosity. The *Sylva Sylvarum* is hardly ever read. The *Advancement of Learning* is referred to but seldom read, and that fate is shared by the *Novum Organon*. Of all the prose works Bacon wrote, the one that has most influenced what people think of his idea of science is his *fiction*—the utopian travel story of *New Atlantis*. Even in the case of the *New Atlantis*, however, students seldom read the entire text but instead only encounter the passages on Salomon's House in anthologies of English literature.

I think the reasons Bacon's prose is seldom taught, or taught only in snippets, are related to the reasons they are such fascinating examples of early modern prose: they are writing experiments that defy easy categorization or interpretation. Like many modern writers, Bacon in his prose works set out to accomplish a great deal but had difficulty achieving his goals. His scientific writing weaves through genres, taking on useful framing devices and stylistic tics but avoiding wholesale adherence to any one expository convention. For all these reasons, however, Bacon's scientific prose provides a fascinating glimpse into the difficult work of writing. Students who struggle with writing academic prose often get more out of Bacon's work when the image of a confident spokesman for science is set aside in favor of the experimental writer in search of a voice that can convey the excitement and concerns Bacon had about the study of nature at a time of enormous change and transformation.

Notes

I am indebted to Margie Ferguson and Susannah Monta for inviting me to participate in this volume and for their generous and invaluable assistance with earlier versions of this article.

1. See, for example, *The Norton Anthology of English Literature,* which includes excerpts from *The New Atlantis, Novum Organum, Essays,* and *The Advancement of Learning* and the *Longman Anthology of British Literature,* which includes selections from the *Essays* and an excerpt from *The Advancement of Learning.*

Works Cited

Bacon, Francis. *The Advancement of Learning.* Ed. Michael Kiernan. Oxford: Clarendon, 2000. Print. The Oxford Francis Bacon 4.

———. *Letters and Life of Francis Bacon.* Ed. James Spedding. 7 vols. London: 1861–74. Print.

———. *New Atlantis.* Vickers, *Francis Bacon* 457–89.

———. *Sylva Sylvarum; or, A Naturall Historie in Ten Centuries.* London, 1627. Print.

———. *Valerius Terminus. The Works of Francis Bacon.* Ed. James Spedding, Robert Leslie Ellis, and Douglas Denon Heath. 7 vols. London: Longman, 1859–64. 3: 215–52. Print.

———. *Works of Francis Bacon.* Ed. Basil Montague. 17 vols. London: Pickering, 1830. Print.

Bodley, Thomas. "Sir Thomas Bodley's Letter to Sir Frances Bacon, about His 'Cogitata et Visa.'" Letter 98 of *The Works of Lord Bacon.* Vol. 2. London: Ball, 1838. 39–41. Print.

Harkness, Deborah. *The Jewel House: Elizabethan London and the Scientific Revolution.* New Haven: Yale UP, 2007. Print.

The Longman Anthology of British Literature. Ed. Barbara Damrosch et al. Vol. 1. New York: Longman, 2006. Print.

The Norton Anthology of English Literature. Ed. Stephen Greenblatt et al. Vol. 1. New York: Norton, 2006. Print.

Plat, Hugh. *The Jewel House of Art and Nature.* London: Short, 1594. Print.

Vickers, Brian. Introduction. *Francis Bacon: A Critical Edition of the Major Works.* 1996. Ed. Vickers. New York: Oxford UP, 2008. xv–xliv. Print.

Wortham, Simon. "Censorship and the Institution of Knowledge in Bacon's *New Atlantis.*" *Francis Bacon's* New Atlantis: *New Interdisciplinary Essays.* Ed. Bronwen Price. Manchester: Manchester UP, 2003. 180–98. Print.

Appendix:
Bibliographic Notes

While early modern editions of Francis Bacon's scientific works are available online through scholarly resources such as *Early English Books Online*—and his works do appear in noted anthologies of English and British literature—Oxford University Press's ongoing project to publish a modern critical edition of all Bacon's works under the direction of Graham Rees deserves notice. Thus far, six volumes have been completed, including those containing *Essays, The Advancement of Learning, Instauratio Magna* ("Great Instauration"), *Historia Naturalis* ("History of Nature"), and *Historia Vitae* ("History of Life"). These editions include superb, detailed commentary and an explanation of how the works were printed. Instructors will find them invaluable when seeking to understand how the texts came into being and how Bacon drew on earlier drafts and textual fragments to complete the works.

For students, there are edited texts and collections of texts that are available in paperback. Chief among them, in terms of scholarly rigor and readability, is Francis Bacon's *The New Organon*, edited by Lisa Jardine and Michael Silverthorne. A wider range of texts can be found in the second edition of Brian Vickers's *Francis Bacon: The Major Works.* The most complete listing of reliable online editions of Bacon's major works—including several no longer in print such as *The New Atlantis*—is located at the University of Pennsylvania's *Online Books Page.*

For a telling comparison between Bacon and one of his early modern contemporaries, consult Plat. A full analysis of the comparison, and further examples drawn from Elizabethan scientific, medical, and technical literature, can be found in my *The Jewel House: Elizabethan London and the Scientific Revolution*. While it is fairly common to draw a comparison between Thomas More's *Utopia* and Bacon's *New Atlantis*, a more provocative contrast can result from the juxtaposition of *New Atlantis* with Margaret Cavendish's *The Description of a New World, Called the Blazing World* (1666). Cavendish's work also shows a writer still very much experimenting with the utopian genre in order to express her scientific creativity and interests.

Stephen M. Fallon

Discovering Milton
in His Prose

In *The Reason of Church Government*, the thirty-three-year-old John Milton paused to observe that, were he looking for fame, "I should not choose this manner of writing, wherein knowing myself inferior to myself, led by the genial power of nature to another task, I have the use, as I may account it, but of my left hand" (*Complete Poetry* 839). Despite this disclaimer, Milton wrote a great deal of prose, filling eight large volumes in the standard Yale edition. And while we may ask our students to read it because of Milton's poetry, the prose, bristling with vivid and sometimes overpowering language and imagery, stands up surprisingly well on its own. Milton realized this. A moment after the passage disparaging his prose, he observes that discriminating readers found that his style, whether "prosing or versing, . . . by certain vital signs it had, was likely to live" (*Complete Poetry* 840).

The prose can be read to flesh out Milton's perspective on central themes in his poetry, including the operation of free will, the tyranny of institution and custom, the freedom of the individual and of conscience, and the relation between man and woman. In addition, with its frequent autobiographical digressions, Milton's prose tantalizes readers with clues to the inner life of the poet. Milton apparently could not resist an opportunity

to write about himself. He integrates substantial autobiographical portraits into, for example, an attack on episcopacy (*The Reason of Church
Government*) and a Latin defense of the English revolution and Oliver
Cromwell's government (*Second Defence of the English People*). Milton,
Coleridge writes, "is himself before himself in every thing he writes"
(1: 129–30). Thomas Newton, one of Milton's eighteenth-century editors, quotes Voltaire on Milton's penchant for autobiography:

> I cannot but own that an author is generally guilty of an unpardon-
> able self-love, when he lays aside his subject to descant upon his own
> person: But that human frailty is to be forgiven in Milton; nay, I am
> pleased with it. He gratifies the curiosity he has raised in me about his
> person. (Milton, *Poetical Works* 3: 135)

While sharing Voltaire's gratitude, I want to suggest that Milton's self-
representations in his prose offer us more than liner notes or valuable additional information on the artist. In the prose one can witness the manner in which argument is inflected and sometimes distorted by the author's
self-investment.

Milton's prose career falls into several distinct segments. His earliest
published prose works are five so-called antiprelatical (i.e., antiepiscopal)
tracts (*Of Reformation*, *Of Prelatical Episcopacy*, and *Animadversions*, all
from 1641, and *The Reason of Church Government* and *An Apology for
Smectymnuus*, both from early 1642). In the mid-1640s Milton wrote
what he would subsequently label in the *Second Defence* works on "domestic or personal liberty" (*Complete Poetry* 1094), including his most
famous prose work, *Areopagitica* (1644), a defense of the free exchange
of ideas; his tractate *Of Education* (1644); and four books advancing a
view of marriage as a spiritual conversation between man and woman and
arguing for the permissibility of divorce: *The Doctrine and Discipline of
Divorce* (1643; rev. and expanded in 1644), *The Judgement of Martin
Bucer concerning Divorce* (1644), *Tetrachordon* (1645), and *Colasterion*
(1645). After a brief lull appeared several works of political controversy.
Writing on his own initiative, Milton in *The Tenure of Kings and Magistrates* (1649), which appeared within two weeks of the execution of
Charles I, defended a people's right to depose and execute a tyrant. Tak-
ing note, Cromwell's new Council of State commissioned Milton to write
Eikonoklastes (*Image Breaker* [1649]), a response to Charles's posthumous
Eikon Basilike (*The King's Image*), and several Latin works defending the
execution of the king to a European audience, *A Defence of the English*

People (1651), *The Second Defence of the English People* (1654), and *The Defence of Himself* (1655). In 1659 Milton published two significant works on the relations between church and state: *A Treatise of Civil Power in Ecclesiastical Causes*, in which he argued that civil government should not dictate religious observance, and *The Likeliest Means to Remove Hirelings from the Church*, in which he argued against compulsory tithes. In 1660 Milton, undaunted by the inevitability and imminence of the restoration of Charles II, courageously published a final plea to his compatriots to reject monarchy, *The Ready and Easy Way to Establish a Free Commonwealth*. His final prose work, published the year before his death, is *Of True Religion* (1673), a plea for toleration among Protestants and continued opposition to popery. Other works, less topical in nature, were published well after the conjectured dates of composition, several after Milton's death in 1674: a Latin grammar (1669), the history of Britain (1671), a Latin *Art of Logic* (1672), a collection of Latin correspondence from Milton's time as secretary for foreign tongues during the interregnum (1676), *A Brief History of Muscovia* (1682), and, most notably, the learned and unorthodox Latin *Christian Doctrine* (1825), which, had it not been suppressed in his lifetime, would almost certainly have called down the wrath of Milton's contemporaries for its anti-Trinitarianism and other heresies.

Milton's prose style, as Thomas Corns has demonstrated, develops over time and varies in response to rhetorical situation (*Development*). In his first published prose book, *Of Reformation* (1641), sentences often run to several hundred words, with the concatenated clauses brimming with elaborate metaphors. Undergraduate students will likely need a modernized version to make such a text palatable (in editing *Of Reformation* for *The Complete Poetry and Essential Prose of John Milton*, I broke down the tract's 375-word third sentence into three sentences divided between two paragraphs). *Of Reformation* continues to be read, despite its difficult prose, for the brilliance of its imagery and the force of Milton's zealous voice. The poet's right hand is manifest in torrents of graphic depictions of the bishops' bestial nature and the disease and deformity of a bishop-ridden church. Typical is his charge that under episcopal government "the obscene and surfeited priest scruples not to paw and mammock the sacramental bread as familiarly as his tavern biscuit" (*Complete Poetry* 812). In the most famous set piece in the work, Milton compares episcopacy to "a swollen tumor," "a bottle of vicious and hardened excrements," "a heap of hard and loathsome uncleanness" (*Complete Poetry* 822).

Milton's language for the glory of true reformation is as exalted as his language for his opponents is abusive:

> [W]hen I recall to mind . . . how the bright and blissful reformation (by divine power) struck through the black and settled night of ignorance and antichristian tyranny, methinks a sovereign and reviving joy must needs rush into the bosom of him that reads or hears, and the sweet odor of the returning gospel imbathe his soul with the fragrancy of heaven. (*Complete Poetry* 809)

In *Of Reformation*, as in Milton's "Nativity Ode" or *Paradise Lost*, the author takes center stage, where he oscillates uncertainly between welcoming and attempting to displace the Son of God. At the very least, the author or heroic singer is responsible for the national reformation auguring the Son of God's return for his millennial reign. The blessing and curse at the end of the work come at least as much from the singer Milton as they do from the "shortly-expected King." The closing is savagely eloquent:

> [T]hey . . . that by the impairing and diminution of true faith . . . aspire to high dignity, rule, and promotion here, after a shameful end in this life (which God grant them) shall be thrown down eternally into the darkest and deepest gulf of hell, where, under the despiteful control, the trample and spurn of all the other damned . . . , they shall remain in that plight forever, the basest, the lowermost, the most dejected, most underfoot, and downtrodden vassals of perdition. (*Complete Poetry* 834)

God, Milton hopes, will grant his enemies a shameful death, but it seems that it is as much Milton as God who pronounces the curse that will send them to perdition. Corns has remarked that the peculiar brilliance of Milton's earliest prose results from "the friction of genius and genre, as Milton the poet redirected his energies in the limiting medium of prose" (*Development* 195).

Fairly quickly, Milton's prose becomes, especially from our perspective, more disciplined and readable. The sentences become shorter (though still long by modern standards), and the relation of clauses clearer. And when Milton assumes the role of spokesperson for the victorious party of Cromwell in 1649 and the early 1650s, his tone becomes more temperate, although the fire returns as the interregnum's republican experiment dies at the end of the decade.

Undergraduates are most likely to meet Milton's prose in anthology excerpts, perhaps in the *Norton Anthology*'s fourteen pages of excerpts from

The Reason of Church Government and *Areopagitica* or in the *Longman Anthology*'s seven-page excerpt from *Areopagitica* or in the *Broadview Anthology*'s printing of *Areopagitica* and excerpts from *Eikonoklastes*. Taken together, the two excerpts in the *Norton Anthology* give students a window on what kind of person Milton was (or at least what kind of person he wanted us to think he was) and on what he thought about several themes central to his poetry. The preface to the second book of *The Reason of Church Government* is a condensed autobiography designed to purchase authority for a young and relatively unknown author challenging learned and elder bishops. It is at least as fascinating for the manner in which Milton frames and constructs his self-representation as it is for what we learn about his life. As often when writing of himself, Milton begins defensively:

> [A]lthough a poet soaring in the high region of his fancies with his garland and singing robes about him might without apology speak more of himself then I mean to do, yet for me sitting here below in the cool element of prose, a mortal thing among many readers of no empyreal conceit, to venture and divulge unusual things of myself, I shall petition to the gentler sort, it may not be envy to me. (*Complete Poetry* 839)

The soaring poet, despite being presented in the third person, seems to be Milton's deeper, or "natural," self. This self speaks of himself without apology, as opposed to the speaker of the digression, who speaks about himself voluminously but with profuse apology. The self writing now ("for me sitting here below") is a "mortal thing" bared before vulgar readers, "of no empyreal conceit," divulging "things of myself." Embedded in the sentence are the "I" ostensibly not writing but who dresses the text (and himself) in poetic figures and the "I" ostensibly writing who is often treated as an object instead of a subject of contemplation. When Milton appeals to "the gentler sort" that his self-revelation "may not be envy to me," it is difficult to discern who this "me" is—the poet, the prose writer, or Milton himself.

For the rest of the preface of the *Reason*, Milton alternates between offering promises of future achievement (which read like uncannily prescient literary autobiography) and nervously defending his doing so. He announces his intention to "leave something so written to aftertimes, as they should not willingly let it die" (*Complete Poetry* 840), adding that "what the greatest and choicest wits of Athens, Rome, or modern Italy, and those Hebrews of old did for their country, I, in my proportion, with this over and above of being a Christian, might do for mine" (*Complete Poetry* 840). Milton can match the great poets (or nearly, he suggests with unusual but tactful modesty) in what he calls the "critical art of composition" (*Complete Poetry* 841), but he will surpass them inasmuch as he has access to the truth.

Having made this remarkable claim, Milton again pauses to defend his digression:

> Time serves not now, and perhaps I might seem too profuse to give any certain account of what the mind at home in the spacious circuits of her musing hath liberty to propose to herself, though of highest hope and hardest attempting, whether that epic form whereof the two poems of Homer and those other two of Virgil and Tasso are a diffuse, and the book of Job a brief model. (*Complete Poetry* 840)

Milton goes on to provide precisely the account that, he acknowledges here, is untimely. As in other moments when he anxiously frames self-representation, Milton splits himself, here into the "I," the "mind at home," and that mind's "self." The multiplication of selves highlights the self-dramatization or the mediated nature of the self of the representation. Milton frames and constructs himself before our eyes.

Milton insists that the ability to write what he anticipates writing is "the inspired gift of God rarely bestowed, but yet to some (though most abuse) in every nation" (*Complete Poetry* 841). The poet requires moral purity along with poetic craft and a true subject, as this tale of the loss of inspiration to abuse implies. Abilities are granted to few. This group is further winnowed by abuse of the gift. Those left can boast both a divine gift and acquired merit. If he is among them, Milton joins the great poets mentioned in his preface, much as Dante ranks himself with his great classical predecessors in *Inferno*. But these predecessors drop away as well, since true poets lead their compatriots in celebrating hymns to God and teach them the "holy and sublime" truths of religion, something only Milton, "with this over and above of being a Christian," can do. In a typically Miltonic move, a bid for inclusion in a select group ends in a stringent sorting that leaves, arguably, a set of one.

Nearing the end of his preface to the second book of the *Reason*, Milton yet again apologizes for dwelling on himself. He characterizes his self-representation as a premature birth:

> The thing which I had to say, and those intentions which have lived within me ever since I could conceive myself anything worth to my

country, I return to crave excuse that urgent reason hath plucked from me by an abortive and foredated discovery.
(*Complete Poetry* 843)

The phrase "conceive myself" carries a hint of self-generation; Milton makes himself as he contemplates and represents himself. The process as described in this passage is fraught with anxiety, and the sense is compressed to the point of obscurity. Returned from where? Crave excuse from whom? The uncertainty is a measure of Milton's unease about his belatedness in producing the promised poetic works. It is appropriate that this passage and a similar one—"Although it nothing content me to have disclosed thus much beforehand" (*Complete Prose* 1: 821)—frame another promise of prophetic achievement in its proper time:

> Neither do I think it shame to covenant with any knowing reader, that for some few years yet I may go on trust with him toward the payment of what I am now indebted, as being a work not to be raised from the heat of youth or the vapors of wine, like that which flows at waste from the pen of some vulgar amorist or the trencher fury of a rhyming parasite, nor to be obtained by the invocation of Dame Memory and her siren daughters, but by devout prayer to that eternal Spirit who can enrich with all utterance and knowledge, and sends out his seraphim with the hallowed fire of his altar to touch and purify the lips of whom he pleases. To this must be added industrious and select reading, steady observation, insight into all seemly and generous arts and affairs, till which in some measure be compassed, at mine own peril and cost I refuse not to sustain this expectation from as many as are not loath to hazard so much credulity upon the best pledges that I can give them. (*Complete Poetry* 843)

If he is, as he was, relatively late among those attacking the bishops, he is ahead of himself in promises of poetic achievement. He borrows from the beginning of Shakespeare's sonnet 129 ("Th' expense of spirit in a waste of shame / Is lust in action . . ."), a pun on waste/waist to declare that the fury of love will not be his muse. His muse, now as in *Paradise Lost*, is the spirit of God, who will touch his lips as Isaiah's were touched (Isaiah 6.6). As in all the prophetic passages, Milton meets this divine favor halfway, working tirelessly to acquire the learning and skills necessary for the poet-prophet. He ends this brief passage with knotted syntax, clotted with negatives and with terms suggesting more diffidence and tenuousness than one might expect from a writer whose lips are about to kiss the sacred coal.

Teaching the *Norton* excerpt from *The Reason of Church Government* not only gives students a sense of the springs of *Paradise Lost* and the personality of its author, it also makes it possible to raise questions of voice and authorship, of the layers of self in self-representation, of the manner in which anxieties shape sentence structure and imagery. The excerpt from *Areopagitica* also has something to tell us about Milton's self-construction; see, for example, a description of England that reads like a self-description of the author ("a nation not slow and dull, but of a quick, ingenious, and piercing spirit, acute to invent, subtle and sinewy to discourse, not beneath the reach of any point the highest that human capacity can soar to" [*Complete Poetry* 956]) or the author's outraged reaction to the prospect of being treated as a pupil instead of a teacher, needing an *imprimatur* to "appear in print like a puny with his guardian" (*Complete Poetry* 947). The excerpt is particularly valuable, however, for the power and beauty of its prose and its expression of several of Milton's central themes, such as the defense of free will, the provisional nature of any articulation of truth, and fierce opposition to tyranny.

Some students respond to the idealism and extraordinary beauty of passages such as Milton's passionate defense of books:

> For books are not absolutely dead things, but do contain a potency of life in them to be as active as that soul was whose progeny they are; nay, they do preserve as in a vial the purest efficacy and extraction of that living intellect that bred them. I know they are as lively and as vigorously productive as those fabulous dragon's teeth, and, being sown up and down, may chance to spring up armed men. And yet, on the other hand, unless wariness be used, as good almost kill a man as kill a good book. Who kills a man kills a reasonable creature, God's image, but he who destroys a good book kills reason itself, kills the image of God, as it were, in the eye. Many a man lives a burden to the earth, but a good book is the precious lifeblood of a master spirit, embalmed and treasured up on purpose to a life beyond life.
> (*Complete Poetry* 930)

Milton has come a long way from the sometimes unruly prose of *Of Reformation*. The sentences of *Areopagitica* are measured, balanced, and clear, without losing any of the vitality of the earliest works.

Areopagitica's argument illuminates the poems in which the free choices of characters (and the reader) take center stage, including the great poems of Milton's maturity, *Paradise Lost, Paradise Regained*, and *Samson Agonistes*. Foreshadowing words he will put in the Father's mouth in his epic ("reason also is choice" [bk. 3, line 108; *Complete Poetry* 364]), Milton says in his own voice, "reason is but choosing" (*Complete Poetry* 944). He presents a world in which "Good and evil . . . grow up together almost inseparably" (*Complete Poetry* 938) and in which the "lovely form" of the "virgin Truth" has been cut "into a thousand pieces, and scattered . . . to the four winds" (*Complete Poetry* 955). In this world, true heroism means discerning and choosing the good from a welter of deceiving appearances and gathering up the scattered limbs of truth.

At the center of *Areopagitica* lies the defense of free will fundamental to the theodicy in *Paradise Lost*:

> Many there be that complain of divine providence for suffering Adam to transgress. Foolish tongues! When God gave him reason, he gave him freedom to choose, for reason is but choosing; he had been else a mere artificial Adam, such an Adam as he is in the motions. We ourselves esteem not of that obedience, or love, or gift, which is of force. God therefore left him free, set before him a provoking object, ever almost in his eyes; herein consisted his merit, herein the right of his reward, the praise of his abstinence. Wherefore did he create passions within us, pleasures round about us, but that these rightly tempered are the very ingredients of virtue? (*Complete Poetry* 944)

In *Areopagitica*, Milton draws a portrait of the "true wayfaring Christian" (or "true warfaring Christian" as hand-corrected presentation copies read), who exhibits not "a fugitive and cloistered virtue" but an active engagement with the world and struggle against evil that characterizes the hero (Adam and Eve? the Son? Milton? the reader?) of *Paradise Lost* (*Complete Poetry* 939).

If one has the luxury of teaching from complete texts and more substantial excerpts available in several of the one-volume Milton collections, for example, the old warhorse Merritt Hughes edition (*Complete Poems*) or the 2007 *Complete Poetry and Essential Prose*, edited by William Kerrigan, John Rumrich, and Stephen Fallon, a particularly promising pedagogical avenue is the exploration of tensions and conflicts. The older picture of the univocal Milton is rapidly giving way to a picture of a tenser, more divided figure, in no small part because of his prose.

In *Areopagitica*, students may respond on their own to the inspiring calls for freedom of thought and speech. At the same time, one can direct them to the tension between Milton's assertion that no book is bad to a good reader and his acknowledgment that bad books should be disciplined.

Just before the ringing passage on the life of books, Milton writes, "I deny not but that it is of greatest concernment in the church and commonwealth to have a vigilant eye how books demean themselves as well as men, and thereafter to confine, imprison, and do sharpest justice on them as malefactors" (*Complete Poetry* 930). Already there is a false note, as the church is supposed to have punitive power, a notion Milton elsewhere soundly rejects. As the argument proceeds, moreover, the rationale for "sharpest justice" dissolves, except in the case of libel (and Milton's predilection for ad hominem attack, common in seventeenth-century polemic, suggests he would give wide latitude to character assassination). Even bad books can serve good ends:

> Wholesome meats to a vitiated stomach differ little or nothing from unwholesome, and best books to a naughty mind are not unappliable to occasions of evil. Bad meats will scarce breed good nourishment in the healthiest concoction, but herein the difference is of bad books, that they to a discreet and judicious reader serve in many respects to discover, to confute, to forewarn, and to illustrate. (*Complete Poetry* 937–38)

What can we make of this contradiction? The answer may lie in the self-referentiality pervasive in Milton's works. Some books required disciplining, but Milton cannot or will not break out of the charmed circle of his own experience and plans. Books may need watching, but he refuses to countenance having his own books watched. His argument for admissibility of postpublication punishment for pernicious books disintegrates in the face of his repudiation of anyone's right to limit his writing and reading.

Milton's two main divorce tracts, *The Doctrine and Discipline of Divorce* and *Tetrachordon*, have drawn increased attention in recent decades, in part because they embody Milton's ambivalence about gender and foreshadow the ambiguities of *Paradise Lost*. These works champion a vision unusual in its time, a vision of marriage as a meeting of near equals. Where others followed Augustine's lead in suggesting that were it not for the need for procreation, God would have given Adam a man as a companion, Milton argues in *Tetrachordon* that the soul finds its best company "where the different sex in most resembling unlikeness, and most unlike resemblance, cannot but please best and be pleased in the aptitude of that variety" (*Complete Poetry* 998). Because marriage should be a union of what he calls "fit conversing soul[s]" (*Complete Poetry* 875), Milton

argues vigorously for the permissibility of divorce for mutual incompatibility, as opposed to the far more restrictive and physically focused canon-law
criteria, still in force in Protestant England, of adultery and nonconsum-
mation. Some couples, because of natural, innocent, but incompatible tem-
peraments, are unable to join in true marriage, and they should be allowed
to separate.

When teaching the divorce tracts, I begin by laying out this argument. Students quickly see that Milton's argument foreshadows our own
time's acceptance of no-fault divorce. Things become more complicated
and interesting when I ask students to focus on tensions and contradictions in the works. For even as Milton mounts this humane and nearly
egalitarian argument for divorce, he lashes out at women for disappoint-
ing the spiritual hopes of men. Within pages of arguing that divorce is
necessary because some couples, through no fault of their own, find their
innate tempers to be incompatible, Milton insists on the need "to separate upon extreme urgency the religious from the irreligious, the fit from
the unfit, the willing from the willful, the abused from the abuser," with
the second half of each binary occupied by the woman. Bad marriages, he
continues, "bind and mix together holy with atheist, heavenly with hellish, fitness with unfitness, light with darkness, antipathy with antipathy,
the injured with the injurer" (*Complete Poetry* 1013). Milton's own sense
of injured merit arising from his failed marriage with Mary Powell
swamps his argument for blameless mutual incompatibility. Marriages
now fail because of the woman's willful and sinful opposition to the husband. Milton's dispassionate argument for liberalizing the grounds for
divorce is disrupted by his passionate and self-regarding outbursts (Fallon
110–36).

The divorce tracts seethe with unresolved tensions. Milton articulates
an ideal of nearly egalitarian, companionate marriage, and at the same
time he insists, following 1 Corinthians 11.3, that man is "the head of
the other sex which was made for him" (*Complete Poetry* 915). He holds
out a vision of chaste, redeemed sexuality and describes loveless copulation in degrading terms ("instead of being one flesh, they will be rather
two carcasses chained unnaturally together or . . . a living soul bound to
a dead corpse" [*Complete Poetry* 903]). It is precisely Milton's idealism
about the marriage bond and married sexuality that makes the loveless
copulation of an unfit couple so abhorrent.

The tensions in the tract arise from and illustrate something Milton
has all but acknowledged as driving his writing on divorce, "the spur of

self-concernment" (*Complete Poetry* 860). The *Doctrine and Discipline* is punctuated by descriptions of the virtuous young man who, like Milton, has delayed sexual gratification only to be mistaken in his choice of a mate and robbed of divinely sanctioned corporeal and spiritual intimacy. In the antiprelatical tracts and in his early poems, Milton had constructed a self-image in which prophetic gifts and prospective literary greatness are tied to his unspotted virtue and specifically his chastity. Now he contemplates the possibility of alienation from God under the weight of an unhappy marriage, and in his compatriots' response to his arguments on divorce he finds himself vilified as a libertine. Hoping for an idealized marriage as offered by God in Genesis 2.18, Milton finds himself trapped in wedlock with a woman whom apparently he does not love and with whom as a result copulation is a grinding slavery (*Complete Poetry* 878–79) instead of a "fountain" of "the pure influence of peace and love" arising from "the soul's lawful contentment" (*Complete Poetry* 873). The *Doctrine and Discipline* embodies both the idealized hope and the bitterness of failed expectations. One can read the traces of the *Doctrine and Discipline*'s wrestling with gender relations through *Paradise Lost* and beyond. The assertion of male superiority found in the epic and the first divorce tract, however, is the common coin of Milton's time (and of the Bible). Milton's signature contribution, a vision of marriage built around the spiritual conversation between man and woman, informs his portrayal of Adam and Eve at its deepest levels. The vision is lyrically expressed, significantly by Eve, in one of the loveliest speeches in the poem (book 4, lines 639–56; *Complete Poetry* 404–05).

An essay such as this one must be selective, for Milton's prose is vast and contains many riches: the autobiographical digressions in *An Apology for Smectymnuus* and the *Second Defence*; *The Tenure of Kings and Magistrates*, with its arguments for the dignity of the republican citizen and the inevitable tyranny of monarchy; *The Ready and Easy Way*, in which Milton attempts to stem the irresistible tide of restoration and in which he claims again what is paradoxically his most congenial role, the lone prophet ignored by his compatriots; and the idiosyncratic, intellectually adventurous, courageous, and deeply heretical *Christian Doctrine*. In his poetry Milton celebrates the lone voice of truth, perhaps most notably in the opposition of Abdiel to the devils in *Paradise Lost* and of the Son of God to Satan in *Paradise Regained*. In the prose, one can witness Milton trying on that role for himself, sometimes succeeding and sometimes becoming entangled in snares of his own devising.

Works Cited

Coleridge, Samuel Taylor. *Specimens of the Table Talk of the Late Samuel Taylor Coleridge*. Ed. Henry Nelson Coleridge. 2 vols. London, 1835. Print.

Corns, Thomas N. *The Development of Milton's Prose Style*. Oxford: Clarendon, 1982. Print.

Fallon, Stephen M. *Peculiar Grace: Milton and Self-Representation*. Ithaca: Cornell UP, 2007. Print.

The Longman Anthology of British Literature. Ed. David Damrosch et al. 2nd ed. New York: Longman, 2002. Print.

Milton, John. *Complete Poems and Major Prose*. Ed. Merritt Y. Hughes. New York: Odyssey, 1957. Print.

———. *The Complete Poetry and Essential Prose of John Milton*. Ed. William Kerrigan, John Rumrich, and Stephen M. Fallon. New York: Modern Lib., 2007. Print.

———. *Complete Prose Works*. Don M. Wolfe, gen. ed. 8 vols. New Haven: Yale UP, 1953–82. Print.

———. *The Poetical Works of John Milton, with Notes of Various Authors*. Ed. H. J. Todd. 6 vols. London, 1826. Print.

The Norton Anthology of English Literature. Stephen Greenblatt, gen. ed. 8th ed. New York: Norton, 2006. Print.

Shakespeare, William. *The Riverside Shakespeare*. Ed. G. Blakemore Evans et al. Vol. 2. Boston: Houghton, 1974. Print.

Suggestions for Further Reading

Achinstein, Sharon. *Milton and the Revolutionary Reader*. Princeton: Princeton UP, 1994. Print.

Cable, Lana. *Carnal Rhetoric: Milton's Iconoclasm and the Poetics of Desire*. Durham: Duke UP, 1995. Print.

Corns, Thomas N., ed. *A Companion to Milton*. Oxford: Blackwell, 2001. Print.

———. "Milton's Prose." *The Cambridge Companion to Milton*. 1989. Ed. Dennis Richard Danielson. Cambridge: Cambridge UP, 1999. 84–99. Print.

Fish, Stanley. *How Milton Works*. Cambridge: Harvard UP, 2001. Print.

Kranidas, Thomas. *The Fierce Equation: A Study of Milton's Decorum*. The Hague: Mouton, 1965. Print.

Loewenstein, David. *Milton and the Drama of History: Historical Vision, Iconoclasm, and the Literary Imagination*. Cambridge: Cambridge UP, 1990. Print.

Loewenstein, David, and James Grantham Turner, eds. *Politics, Poetics, and Hermeneutics in Milton's Prose: Essays*. Cambridge: Cambridge UP, 1990. Print.

Claire Preston

Stand-Up Browne:
Religio Medici
in the Classroom

Undergraduates often favor stories with strong narrative energy and boldly drawn characters with whom they can identify, characters struggling with moral and emotional issues that speak to their own conditions and sensibilities. Faustus, Hamlet, and Milton's Satan are especially attractive, and drama or the dramatic, especially if tragic, which have the advantage of speaking voices and mimetic representation, also fare well. Even a prose romance like Philip Sidney's *Arcadia* can be surprisingly popular because of its charismatic teenagers speaking in elaborate rhetorical patterns. The early modern essay, however, rarely includes any of these features, and most of us who teach the period are all too familiar with resistance to or impatience with the more abstract expository writing of major figures like Francis Bacon, Robert Burton, Thomas Browne, and the nonpoetic John Milton. The expectation of either crusty theology or scholastically detailed controversy is widespread, and it is an unusual undergraduate who can immediately sense and enjoy the tone of even so bold a work as the *Defence of Poetry*. Yet *voice* is perhaps the most obvious feature of the Renaissance essay. If students can be encouraged to hear the early modern prose voice not as antique and unintelligible but rather as emanating from specific sensibilities and personalities, they can begin to find their way into the genre.

Young writers or their poetic personae or their precocious young fictional characters are given to ostentatious self-declaration. Philip Sidney, Percy Shelley, Huck Finn, Jay Gatsby, Robert Lowell, and Holden Caulfield formulate apparently reckless manifestos, personal philosophies, confessions of brilliance, ambition, uncertainty, and self-accusation. Such voices combine humility, swagger, informality, impudence, and frankness in a winsome blend of prematurity, virtuosity, and arrogance. So, too, the early modern essay, although purportedly difficult and remote, with its themes and modes of expression that seem to have little resemblance to those of twenty-first-century readers, is in fact often the vehicle for similarly appealing displays of youthful exuberance. The essay claims the additional privilege of speaking, apparently in propria persona, the views of the writer not obviously occulted by character.

Yet although *Religio Medici* is his "junior" work, probably written before Browne was thirty, he fails to advertise its season of juvenile brilliance; he seems instead to have rejected the obvious empathetic intimations of hindrance, frustration, and youthful precocity. *Religio Medici*'s purpose and subjects are contemplative and abstruse, its voice interesting but difficult to interpret, its conclusions—such as they are—obscure and far from definitive; and glory and sentimental passion are far from Browne's "general and indifferent temper" (135; pt. 2, sec. 2).[1] Indeed, his querulous wish that we might procreate like trees instead of fooling around with the opposite sex and his churlish claim to detect no difference between the beauty of women and horses (149; pt. 2, sec. 9) would be aggressively ungallant if they were not so amusing. Such gaffes, if gaffes they be, may be attributed to inexperience, but they may also be deliberate self-revelation that lacks the intensity of Milton in his seventh sonnet but does not quite achieve the maturely mannered eccentricity of Burton. *Religio Medici* is not, in other words, very obviously a young man's style or subject.

For this reason it is always taken too seriously: virtually all the critical writing about it, at least since Samuel Taylor Coleridge and probably earlier, has admired its aphorisms, its sententiousness, its grand and graceful formulas and summations. Always an astute reader, however, Coleridge did understand that *Religio Medici* must be "considered as in a *dramatic* & not a metaphysical View" (758). The early modern essay is a genre that, despite the playful influence of Montaigne, attains a gravity in the works of Bacon and Milton seemingly inimical to its ludic precursor, and *Religio Medici* has suffered by association with this tonal evolution. Reverence for its word-music and its grave formulations has disguised its true nature and obscured the youthfulness and even the humor of Browne's poses and vocal antics. For it is through these devices—both the comic and the grave— that we can detect a Browne quite as self-dramatizing, quite as preposterous, as some of his great contemporaries. One way, therefore, for new students of seventeenth-century prose to gain some purchase on this quirky and seemingly wayward statement of a doctor's religion is to look for its impersonation of voice; to read it as a species of animated, junior dramatic monologue; and to discuss its expression of youth and age.

Religio Medici was, according to Browne, an accidental publication. It was written, apparently for private purposes, between 1633 and 1635, when Browne was still completing the medical training that was to cap virtually an entire young life of study. It seems to have circulated in manuscript for some years, until, in 1642, a copy reached a London printer who brought out an anonymous, unauthorized edition. It had instant notice, and a further impression appeared. In 1643, as Browne explains in his preface, he was compelled to authorize a corrected version. What we read now as the *Religio Medici* of 1643 is in fact mainly a juvenile work of nearly a decade earlier, with a contemporary preface and some new material attached. Composed when Browne was perhaps twenty-eight and unestablished in his profession, it did not appear until he was in his late thirties and long since practicing as a doctor.

This troubled history of its appearance is described in Browne's 1643 preface, "To the Reader." Prefaces, as Kevin Dunn has shown so well, have richly manipulable conventions that betray much about their writers despite their seemingly formulaic cast. Thus, if an aperture into the character and personality of the writer is the key to teaching *Religio Medici* successfully to undergraduates, the 1643 preface is a crucial element: its tone of controlled resentment makes a signal contrast with the easygoing latitude of the body of the work and allows even the beginner to sense a competitive, antiphonal pair of attitudes. Asking the undergraduate reader to consider the nature of such a preface, and possibly to think about it in the light of other early modern examples of such confessional writing—for example, Milton's seventh sonnet, as already mentioned, or Sidney's exordium in the *Defence of Poetry*—can be an extremely fruitful exercise. The two voices are flagged in the preface, where Browne entreats us to recall at the outset that what we are about to read is "the sense of my conceptions at that time . . . and therefore there might be many things therein plausible unto my past apprehension which are not agreeable unto my present self" (60). As a framing device for the whole essay, it suggests a fall from carefree naïveté into weathered acceptance of slights and knocks; it enacts the journey from innocence to experience by indicating the passage of time and the evolution of the adult personality through the imposition of public cares and the inevitable contact of the untoward and the uncomfortable that heralds the end of youth. The essay, he laments, has been sullied by handling and public exposure—"it became common unto many, and was by transcription successively corrupted until it arrived in a most depraved copy at the press"—almost as if the physical book were a talisman of defiled personal innocence (59). The prefatory declaration that *Religio Medici* "was the sense of my conceptions at that time, not an immutable law unto my advancing judgement at all times" (60) is one that simply could not have been made by the callow Browne of the 1630s, the writer who airily advises us of "having in my riper years and confirmed judgement, seen and examined all" (61; pt. 1, sec. 1). The preface is the voice of undeceived, even cynical, maturity.

The preface, however, is but one element of the relatively small part of the authorized edition to have been added in 1643; the greater part consists of the lightly edited original version of the 1630s. And that earlier, more audible voice does two things: it displays some of the emotional gaucheries of youth, and it plays with our sense of Browne's true age. For example, the Browne of apparently "riper years" who has "seen and examined all" impersonates advanced age when he says, echoing Macbeth, "I have outlived myself, and begin to be weary of the sun . . . the world to me is but a dream or mockshow . . ." (112; pt. 1, sec. 41), and asserts with the authority of lengthy experience, "I would not live over my hours past, or begin again the thread of my days. . . . I find in my confirmed age the same sins I discovered in my youth . . ." (113; pt. 1, sec. 42). He loves, in other words, to ventriloquize some elderly sensibility, contentedly acknowledging the wisdom of "settled years" (144; pt. 2, sec. 7). And yet, disconcertingly, he is careful to declare his actual juniority, his "miracle of thirty years" (153; pt. 2, sec. 11) or less (112; pt. 1, sec. 41). These tropes of youth are even more disconcerting because we know that, along with the puerile remarks about sex and women, they could have been excised or recast in the authorized edition of 1643 along with those sections that were corrected or inserted anew. That they were not suggests that Browne wished at least to preserve that sense of juvenility in order to demonstrate, and even to heighten, the bivocality of his former and his present self, to magnify the essay's dramatic quality. If this is true, we must read *Religio Medici* as a *performance* of youth against age, of immaturity against wisdom, of optimism against cynicism.

Browne also mimics age in another way, in the most celebrated feature of *Religio Medici*—its sententiousness, its gloriously succinct and often poetic maxims. "There is no deformity but in monstrosity" (80; pt. 1, sec. 16), he instructs us; "the world was made to be inhabited by beasts, but studied and contemplated by man" (75; pt. 1, sec. 13); "God hath not made a creature that can comprehend him" (72; pt. 1, sec. 11); "we term sleep a death, yet it is waking that kills us," he announces (155; pt. 2, sec. 12). The apothegmatic is, like the senescent, a very odd intonation from a young man just emerging from his years of study, not yet one score and ten. For the adage, maxim, or aphorism—staple of the humanist curriculum and product of "authorities" from Quintilian to Erasmus—is not normally associated with youth. It is the carefully crafted product of distilled experience and is convincing only from the mature and the wise. When, therefore, Browne proclaims that "it is a brave act of valour to contemn death, but where life is more terrible than death, it is then the truest valour to dare to live" (115; pt. 1, sec. 44), this neo-Stoic precept, once we notice that it is uttered from the greenest understanding of a privileged and relatively sheltered youth, can sound almost hilarious. These maxims of age and experience oddly superimposed on youth and inexperience are a feature of the work that offer a useful starting point for class discussion, from which the undergraduate reader can go on to assess Browne's voice more fully.

The nature of his revisions in 1643 gives us good reason to regard this confusion of age and voice as an adopted pose, artful, perhaps even slyly humorous, and certainly self-dramatizing. This pose becomes even more evident in his self-contradictions. He regards himself as "full of rigour, sometimes not without morosity" (63; pt. 1, sec. 3) and indisposed for "the mirth and galliardize of company" (154; pt. 2, sec. 11), but that Malvolian misanthropy gives way to self-indicting humor when, having congratulated himself on avoiding the sin of pride, he lists his wide competence in foreign languages ("besides the jargon and patois of several provinces I understand no less than six languages" [147; pt. 2, sec. 8]) and his encyclopedic acquaintance with many "ologies." His subsequent advice, to be content with "a modest ignorance" (148; pt. 2, sec. 8), is thus surely waggish, a playful oscillation between humility and vainglory that is strongly reminiscent of Burton's Democritus Junior in *The Anatomy of*

Melancholy. These vocal pranks seem far too clever for a work that Browne insists is unironic and "junior," arising out of "first studies" (148; pt. 2, sec. 8).

Religio Medici is a relatively informal, only scantly biographical account of the meditations and conclusions of an individual. It is thus unclear whether that individual is a young or an old man. Is he droll or serious? Is this a summa of a lifetime's thought or the momentary illumination of an immature sensibility? It is difficult to tell. Beyond a few disjointed hints, there is no life-narrative or ordered rehearsal of intellectual development; instead, it is an account of certain beliefs, a tally of selected considerations, proposed with what seems a deliberately confusing impersonation of self. With its loosely jointed thematic sections, one following another with only the merest contingency, *Religio Medici* reads like the early modern equivalent of a postmodern stand-up routine, not gag driven but instead a series of conceits, jeux d'esprit, observations, and pronouncements about the state of the world and Browne's take on it. The antiphon of youth and age, the variations of voice that strongly hint at impersonation, suggest that *Religio Medici* is a rudimentary dramatic monologue or epistolary harangue, forms derived from Theocritus, Ovid, Seneca, and Propertius and now more usually associated with much later Augustan and Romantic poets.

Both epistolary writing (with its affinity to the early modern essay) and the dramatic monologue share the implication of a second party, the former directly addressed to a real or imagined reader (usually identified), the latter implying a dialogue, or what has been called a dialectical performance of readership as well as authorship. Seneca's letters to the young Lucilius are framed as a conversation in which only one voice is actually heard directly; Bacon's essays, with their abrupt, almost conversational lacunae and transitions, often replicate the give-and-take of colloquy with an inaudible interlocutor. Thus the opening gambit in "Of Truth"—"What is truth, said jesting Pilate, and would not stay for an answer" (61)—seems to mock the powerlessness of the unheard second party of the dramatic monologue by initiating and then refusing dialogue. Some of the great nineteenth- and twentieth-century verse monologues—Alfred, Lord Tennyson's "Ulysses" and T. S. Eliot's "Prufrock," for example—linger on the interplay of an elder voice and its younger precursor, two distinct authorial selves in conversation.

These features—bivocality and agedness—of the dramatic monologue and its cognate forms are clear in *Religio Medici*, where the latent

Tennysonian world-weariness after long life and great care is anticipated and where Browne's 1635 self, dominant in terms of sheer page presence in the essay, is not only curtailed and subverted by the older Brownean voice of 1643 but even made to seem ventriloquized by it, as if the young Browne were an adopted persona of the older, without actual existence. And indeed that 1635 Browne has, as his older voice insists in the preface, no substance: the self of the past, in his rendition of a dramatic conversation between his two personae, is always irrecoverable, not merely lost but virtually fictional.

Browne's maintenance of this sensibility is a concerted effort of the two voices instead of specific only to one. The "then" voice of the 1630s and the "now" voice of the 1643 preface and additional passages are explicit and differentiated: although both are emphatic, the younger voice is of its moment and age, often rashly peremptory but ultimately inconclusive, self-contradictory; the older voice is developed, sterner, authoritative, assisted by hindsight. In this respect the younger voice is subordinate: belonging to a lost past, the young Browne is naive because unacquainted (so to speak) with his older self. The elder 1643 voice is dominant and corrective, with its advantage of belatedness and achieved wisdom. This alienation of the authorial sensibility from its earlier incarnation is a generically established memento mori and, moreover, a "memorial unto me." We are constantly passing away as older selves tread down younger ones. Like Montaigne's philosophizing, Browne's essayistic self-scrutiny is a rehearsal for death. If the compositional and publishing history of *Religio Medici* unavoidably fractured the authorial sensibility into two parts, Browne finds a way to use that bifurcation to narrate the drama of personal development.

The sequence of part 1, sections 20–26, pages 86–91 (all from the original 1630s version), shows us that younger Browne in all his earliness, freely licensing himself to ignore the usual rules of consecutive, rational argument as he considers the credit of Scripture and other authoritative works. In sections 20–23 he has been discussing mere textual longevity and concludes that, although "[m]en's works have an age like themselves; and though they outlive their authors, yet have they a stint and period to their duration," whereas only the Bible "is a work too hard for the teeth of time" (91; pt. 1, sec. 23). In sections 25 and 26 he excoriates the sectarianism and fundamentalism that foment competing interpretations of sacred texts in the form of "ceremony, politic point, or indifferency" (95; pt. 1, sec. 26). From the immutability of Scripture itself, in other words, follows the vanity of beliefs in "several shapes" as ramified by the junior authorities of different sects. This is a reasonable and logical position.

But interposed between these two sets of remarks, section 24 disrupts the established logic by digressing into an unexpectedly cross-grained proposal:

> I have heard some with deep sighs lament the lost lines of Cicero; others with as many groans deplore the combustion of the Library of Alexandria: for my own part, I think there be too many in the world, and could with patience behold the urn and ashes of the Vatican, could I, with a few others, recover the perished leaves of Solomon. I would not omit a copy of Enoch's pillars, had they many nearer authors than Josephus, or did not relish somewhat of the fable.
>
> Some men have written more than others have spoken: Pineda quotes more authors in one work than are necessary in a whole world. Of those three great inventions in Germany, there are two which are not without their incommodities; and 'tis disputable whether they exceed not their use and commodities. 'Tis not a melancholy *utinam* of mine own, but the desire of better heads, that there were a general synod—not to unite the incompatible differences of religion, but for the benefit of learning: to reduce it as it lay at first, in a few and solid authors; and to condemn to the fire those swarms and millions of rhapsodies begotten only to distract and abuse the weaker judgements of scholars, and to maintain the trade and mystery of typographers. (91–92; pt. 1, sec. 24)

These sentiments are surprising, to say the least. It is not shocking that they dismiss most authority, for that is the general drift of the previous and subsequent sections: the Bible alone is reliable; all the wisdom of the ancients and the inflexible assertions of the histories, martyrologies, and rabbinical interpretations are but "the fallible discourses of man" (91; pt. 1, sec. 23). Its waspishness, however, is bizarre and very unlike the conciliatory outlook of much of the rest of the work; it is highly (and self-consciously, one feels) histrionic, opening with sighs and groans that are smartly dismissed with Browne's own pert conclusion: "for my own part, I think there be too many." The provocative claim that the Vatican Library might usefully be torched is breathtaking, not because it seems to play to anti-Roman sentiments, but because the Vatican collection is the nearest contemporary analogy of the Alexandrian Library. These sentiments, moreover, are not mitigated by Browne's next remarks in section 24, where Browne gratuitously insults Juan de Pineda (a perfectly reputable scholar he would cite approvingly a number of times in *Pseudo-doxia*) and regrets, of all things, the printing press, almost as if predicting the injury of the illegal appearance of *Religio Medici* in 1642. And even a first-time reader of Browne will detect that he is an unlikely supporter of book burning: it would be inimical to his irenic disposition, which disparages violent expressions of faith and fundamentalist habits of thought; neither does it sort with his voracious scholarly appetite (also apparent in *Religio*), an appetite hungry for information of all kinds and from whatever source.

In short, this section is startlingly out of character with the tone of the rest of the work. Has he succumbed to petulance? Is this a joke? Or is it a kind of adventitious and wayward thought experiment? If the last of these, we might read the whole of sections 20–26 as a set of ideas about the uses of authority, principally textual authority, during which a spontaneous remark about the "swarms and rhapsodies" of false authority leads to an unplanned and almost unsustainable "suppose." This, in turn, generates the unexpectedly severe conclusion that with so much detritus in the world of faith and of learning, to use it as kindling is at least a ready solution. As a compositional "accident"—a line of thought stumbled on and followed through to its unreasonable outcome—it shows us an eager mind ready to follow up ideas, even at the expense of sensible and orderly argument. If, however, section 24 is a joke, it is a reductio ad absurdum: having castigated the warring sects, scurrilous antagonists who rage over the "airy subtleties in religion" only to have their brains "unhinged" (69; pt. 1, sec. 9), Browne yields to one of their favorite strategies and imagines what it would be to destroy what he cannot approve. The punchline of such a telling joke would be: "be careful what you wish for, lest you become like your enemy." But section 24 may be neither thought experiment nor joke. It is possible that it shows us the captious mood of a young writer unable to sustain the hard compromises required of learning, a sensibility that, halfway through a grave deprecation of human authority, loses patience and recommends burning the lot. Or it is Browne's *impersonation* of such a sensibility, offered as an object lesson against intolerance of all kinds.

These problems of interpretation, centered on vocal nuances, cannot of course obviate the extreme difficulty presented to modern students by works like *Religio Medici*. Although my usual practice in teaching early modern literature is rather to insist on the *unlikeness* of the pre-Enlightenment, postmedieval sensibility, with the essay it is always more efficient to accede (in thinking about the dramatic monologue) to the literary expectations of our own time.

Note

1. I have modernized the spelling of quotations from Browne's *Major Works*.

Works Cited

Bacon, Francis. *The Essays.* Ed. John Pitcher. Harmondsworth: Penguin, 1985. Print.

Browne, Thomas. *The Major Works.* Ed. C. A. Patrides. Harmondsworth: Penguin, 1977. Print.

Coleridge, Samuel Taylor. *Marginalia.* Ed. George Whalley. London: Routledge; Princeton: Princeton UP, 1985. Print. Vol. 12 of *The Collected Works of Samuel Taylor Coleridge.* 16 vols. 1969– .

Dunn, Kevin. *Pretexts of Authority: The Rhetoric of Authorship in the Renaissance Preface.* Stanford: Stanford UP, 1994. Print.

Suggestions for Further Reading

Barnaby, Andrew, and Lisa J. Schnell. *Literate Experience: The Work of Knowing in Seventeenth-Century English Writing.* New York: Palgrave, 2002. Print.

Hall, Michael L. "The Emergence of the Essay and the Idea of Discovery." *Essays on the Essay: Redefining the Genre.* Ed. Alexander Butrym. Athens: U of Georgia P, 1989. 73–91. Print.

Langbaum, Robert. *The Poetry of Experience: The Dramatic Monologue in Modern Literary Tradition.* 1957. London: Chatto, 1972. Print.

Mulryne, J. R. "The Play of Mind: Self and Audience in *Religio Medici.*" *Approaches to Sir Thomas Browne: The Ann Arbor Tercentenary Essays.* Ed. C. A. Patrides. Columbia: U of Missouri P, 1982. 60–68. Print.

Post, Jonathan F. S. *Sir Thomas Browne.* Boston: Twayne, 1987. Print.

Preston, Claire. *Thomas Browne and the Writing of Early-Modern Science.* Cambridge: Cambridge UP, 2005. Print.

Webber, Joan. *The Eloquent "I": Style and Self in Seventeenth-Century Prose.* Madison: U of Wisconsin P, 1968. Print.

Robert E. Stillman

Mastering the Monster Text: Teaching Hobbes's *Leviathan*

When I teach William Shakespeare to undergraduates, who are often intimidated by that capital *S* superman of the literary canon, I promise accessibility—the eagerness of his texts to entertain, their readiness to accommodate competing interpretations, their openness to questions that matter here and now. Teaching Thomas Hobbes's *Leviathan* to a class of English majors is a radically different experience. The text sets out urgently to instruct, not to entertain; it sets out, too, to foreclose instead of to accommodate competing interpretations; and while it raises political questions of continuing importance—issues about authority and law, for example—it does so from the vantage of a world turned upside down, one beset by historical crises seemingly remote from the global politics of a late capitalist democracy. Once more, *Leviathan* is philosophical prose, not dramatic poetry. As such, it demands unfamiliar analytic skills. As philosophy, its argumentative rigor threatens unaccustomed intellectual labor, if not conceptual fatigue. As prose, it stands bare of almost every compensation that students regularly expect from the medium, stripped as it is of those narrative niceties—plot, character, and setting. For these reasons and others—the book's formidable size, its obsessive preoccupation with definition, its discomforting picture of innate human nastiness—

Hobbes's *Leviathan* emerges from the syllabus like some monster from the deep, a truly terrifying text for English majors. With Shakespeare, I work hard to dispel my students' fears in the interest of accessibility. With Hobbes, I work hard to focus their fears, since understanding the origin and design of those most important fears generated by the text affords one useful means to enable students to master its rhetorically brilliant design.

Focusing my students' fears requires, first, an introduction to that world turned upside down that Hobbes's *Leviathan* seeks so urgently to turn right again: "the greatest inconvenience that can happen to a commonwealth, is the aptitude to dissolve into civil war" (168).[1] Assigning a summary chapter from Christopher Hill can stimulate awareness about the cultural crises of England's civil-war era, those shockwaves resonating from the destruction of monarchy, the demolition of the church, and the triumph of the saints.[2] But *Leviathan* supplies its own more focused lens through which to view the catastrophe of the civil wars. When Hobbes assaults "the tongues and pens of unlearned divines," the instruments of those sectarian preachers whom he blames for the "seditious roaring of a troubled nation," he translates, characteristically, political problems into problems of knowledge and language (63). Like so many seventeenth-century thinkers, Hobbes is conscious of living in a world after Babel, and like several contemporaries who identified seditious language as cause and effect of sedition in the state, Hobbes attempts to intervene against "the diseases of a commonwealth" (310) with a new philosophy capable of remedying knowledge—that necessary medicine for the body politic—by remedying words. I approach the interpretive challenges and fears inspired by Hobbes's *Leviathan*, then, by situating the text in relation to those persistent debates about language that recent scholars, from James Bono and Robert Markley to Richard Kroll and Julie Solomon, have identified as essential to understanding the new philosophy of seventeenth-century England. As such scholars argue, questions of knowledge trade on questions about words, and such exchanges raise important issues about political authority.[3]

Pursuing Hobbes's translation of political problems into problems of language has special benefits for teaching *Leviathan* to undergraduates in an English class. In a broad sense, students profit by exposure to an important component of contemporary seventeenth-century cultural studies, those studies that highlight a crisis of representation as key to comprehending early modernism (Bono; Markley; Stillman). This is a century engaged in critical debates not only about the adequacy of words for representing knowledge but also about the value of a proliferating print culture, the legitimacy of rituals in religious expression, and political ceremonies in the state—a wide array of debates signaling disruptions broadly symbolic instead of purely linguistic in kind. Students often carry into class misleading assumptions about the Enlightenment's triumph of reason, and posing questions about the intersection between the quest for authority in the state and the quest for authority in the twin domains of knowledge and language can usefully unsettle such assumptions. Instrumental reason in the service of absolute sovereignty looks altogether less triumphant. In a more specific sense, pursuing Hobbes's translation of political problems into language problems benefits students in my English classes because doing so levels the playing field, so to speak. This approach opens attention to Hobbes's text as a verbal artifact whose claims about language can be analyzed by students who are trained to attend to language in action—to linguistic performance as an index of meaning. At the same time, it usefully disturbs their preconceptions about disciplinary boundaries, by asking them to take seriously the "literary" qualities of a philosophical text with the insistence that language use is a meaningful analytic category in all texts. Such attention has particular benefits in relation to Hobbes's treatment of metaphor—that most frequently instanced category of verbal corruption among new philosophers generally and in Hobbes particularly—and it is by examining metaphor that English students can best be taught how to focus their fears about *Leviathan*.

As an assignment, I divide my class into three groups and ask each group to compose a particular list as they read *Leviathan*. One group is asked to compile a list of Hobbes's comments about metaphor—metaphor construed in the broadest sense to include all forms of figurative speech; a second group is asked to compile a list of Hobbes's definitions of key terms in his argument—a list that I limit to ten or twelve, since the catalog would otherwise be endless; a third group is asked to compile a collection of Hobbes's own metaphors—a list again limited to ten or twelve items, since the catalog would be similarly endless. The work of making these catalogs encourages students to attend, as they read, both to the frequency of debates about language that punctuate Hobbes's argument and (as a fundamental aspect of that reading experience) to Hobbes's own language in action—to the meaning and power of *Leviathan*'s own logically and rhetorically complex prose. Making these catalogs jump-starts the process of turning English students, sometimes passively overawed by *Leviathan*'s political philosophy, into active readers capable of interrogating the text with skeptical advantage.

The design of my assignment is to pose a key interpretive question: How does one explain the contradiction between Hobbes's repeated and uncompromising exclusion of metaphoric language from "the rigorous search for truth" (*English Work* 3: 59) and *Leviathan*'s own recurrent inclusion of figurative language into its argument? (As is true of most questions posed for classroom discussion, this one succeeds better if students are asked to write a paragraph in response before class.) To explore that contradiction, I begin with questions inside the question, asking (for instance) why Hobbes objects to the use of metaphors, especially in philosophical literature. One advantage of having students ready in class with catalogs of those objections is the chance to examine the specific terms in which they are couched. For example, when Hobbes objects to metaphors in one early key passage as "senseless and ambiguous," as mere *ignes fatui* of the impassioned imagination, it can be useful to note his materialist's pun: words that fail to cohere with reason's reckonings about things are "sense-less," the products of always-dangerous desires, and are associated, in turn, with natural marvels and monsters (37). Concerns about monstrous desires quickly connect with other deeply important matters. Especially telling among Hobbes's complaints about metaphor are those that explicitly politicize its use: to reason on metaphors "is wandering amongst innumerable absurdities; and their end, contention and sedition" (37). Hobbes writes about language as if it were a state—a state in which the sovereignty of reason is perpetually challenged by the sedition of metaphor—just as Hobbes writes later about the state as if it were a linguistic entity, a text to be "authored." In both cases, studied attention to the prose highlights Hobbes's interest in provoking fear, as the expressed need to invest absolute authority in sovereignty trades on fears of monstrous desires and the monstrous anarchy of civil war.

As W. V. Quine once quipped, "The neatly worked inner stretches of science are an open space in the tropical jungle, created by clearing tropes away" (162). Quine's quotation makes good blackboard material and a good device for exploring Hobbes's persistent activity as a new philosopher in constructing definitions. How do you clear a space for a truly rigorous philosophy out of the fearsome jungle of tropical discourse? How do you rid philosophical prose of monstrous metaphors? If figurative language is the disease, then what is the remedy? With questions like these, I turn to my students who have cataloged Hobbes's definitions, asking them to consider initially not what the individual words defined might mean but what function the act of making definitions serves in the text. What the text does is as important as what it says. Almost any complex sentence from *Leviathan* speaks to the point well: "They also have *authority* to teach the people their *duty* to the *sovereign power*, and instruct them in the *knowledge* of what is *just*, and *unjust*" (228). Every word highlighted has its meaning regulated according to specific definitions supplied previously in the text, hence the need for the reader to proceed by translation, moving from definition to definition to reassemble the technical chain of the argument. As that argument advances, text is transformed into glossary—the completion of which provides a manual for civil philosophy in the university and sovereign power in the state. *Leviathan* is less a work of philosophy, from this vantage, than an illustration of philosophy in the making. Partly, philosophy gets made by the technological regulation of discourse, as Hobbes expels the monsters of metaphor by fashioning every definition on every page into plain and perspicuous prose.

Partly, too, philosophy gets made by the constant recourse inside these definitions to paraphrase. Paraphrase is a great purifier, and *Leviathan* works constantly to illustrate Hobbes's conviction that "for . . . all metaphors there is some real ground, that may be expressed in proper words" (448). All metaphors are capable—or so Hobbes says—of translation into ("proper") literal speech, of being made nonmetaphoric. When, for instance, Hobbes describes "reason" as "nothing but *reckoning*," he flattens what might seem a mathematical metaphor for mental operations by defining "*reckoning*" as the "adding and subtracting, of the consequences of general names agreed upon for the *marking* and *signifying* of our thoughts" (30). For Hobbes, there is nothing metaphoric about the mathematical operations of the brain; his terms constitute a literal account of the mind's operations on sensory data. Paraphrase purifies, as the familiar metaphors of everyday speech are translated into the geometrically precise definitions of science—and such purification is intended to allay fears about the distorting power of desire on "the rigorous search for truth." If the attack on metaphor excites fears, then the technological regulation of *Leviathan*'s own discourse *appears* designed to dispel them.

There are moments in every class where you need to ask students to pause, think, and reconsider—and this is an important one. I highlight "appears" for my students, since metaphor is replaced in Hobbes's text by logical discourse whose truth claims are merely nominal. The sovereignty of reason depends on a coherent (perspicuously defined) reckoning of names, and not on the correspondence of those names to things. Baseball helps here in making sense of an unfamiliar philosophical concept. A strike is a strike—the nominalist argues—not because the ball crosses the plate (as the realist believes), but rather a strike is a strike because the umpire says so. But who can possibly trust the umpire to make the right call? What guarantees that the "logical" authority established by the sovereign umpire's "reckoning upon words" is anything but arbitrary? Are Hobbes's "definitions" finally effective in dispelling fears about the legitimacy of authority?

Fear is not so easily dispelled as an analysis of Hobbes's definitions might lead students initially to assume, and this is a point worth highlighting as the class considers *Leviathan*'s frequent use of metaphors. My English majors have no trouble cataloging examples of Hobbes's figurative language. From the description of the commonwealth as a body to the account of the Roman Catholic Church as a kingdom of fairies, Hobbes relies heavily on tropes to advance his arguments. Identifying their presence is easy, but (once again) only searching questions are likely to inspire students to think carefully about their function in the text. Are Hobbes's metaphors designed to generate heat or to shed light—to carry emotional power or to clarify arguments? Because there is no single answer to such a question, the class can discuss a variety of purposes for *Leviathan*'s figures of speech—entertaining possible distinctions among its "spent metaphors," like the "body politic" (metaphors so familiar as to appear nearly literal); its "apt similitudes," like the comparison between the circulation of goods in the state and blood in the body (where likenesses between material processes achieve clarity); its conceptually useful metaphors taken from the language of covenants and authorization (arguably indispensable to his description of the institution of the sovereign); and its emotionally charged metaphors, like the characterization of "democratical writers" as mad dogs or the church as "the ghost of the deceased Roman empire" (tropes used, seemingly, to make an affective impact on the reader [315, 697]). Creating additional categories is easy enough, but the point of this exercise lies elsewhere. For as we consider the multiple purposes that individual uses of figurative language serve in *Leviathan*, it becomes necessary to reopen the question with which the class began: How do we explain the contradiction between Hobbes's unqualified exclusion of metaphor from the rigorous search for truth and his persistent use of it?

Writing is intended to focus the brain, and getting students to report about those paragraphs that they wrote before class produces a variety of answers. Some of those answers will be less immediately helpful, some more. Students have responded that Hobbes wants readers to focus on his logic, not the metaphors; that writing must include metaphors, so of course *Leviathan* features many of them; that perhaps *Leviathan* is not a search for truth but a rhetoric that shows readers how to execute such a search; that Hobbes is actually a closet novelist; that all writers contradict themselves; that Hobbes's key metaphors make his logic appear more logical than it is; that since philosophy is boring, Hobbes decided to give it some much-needed spice. My paraphrasing of real student responses, reported in no particular order, is a reminder about one real challenge of classroom discussion: you never know for sure what you will hear, or in what order you are likely to hear it. More predictably, however, experience tells me that students are likely to explain the contradiction either by dismissing its relevance ("all writers contradict themselves") and trivializing its importance (metaphor is spice for bland philosophy) or by imagining a rhetorically sophisticated Hobbes who uses rhetoric so skillfully as to disguise the reality of that contradiction. This last interpretation has found articulate and intelligent support in the critical work of Victoria Kahn, and my students inevitably hear me paraphrase her reading of Hobbes's deployment of rhetoric to disguise the use of rhetoric (Kahn 157–65).

On the theory that no response should go unheard, I spend some time teasing out the implications of "spicy" metaphors for thinking about Hobbes's understanding of language and desire, just as I attend to that quip about Hobbes as closet novelist to uncover some of the perverse and pleasurable implications of fiction making in *Leviathan*. Mainly, however, I invite discussion about that rhetorically cagey Hobbes who strategically battles rhetoric with rhetoric. Partly I invite that discussion because the characterization seems so plausible as one means of understanding its author. Hobbes was too accomplished and too self-conscious as a rhetorician to have been unaware of the contradiction between his principles and his practice. Partly, too, I invite that discussion to have the class question its underlying assumption: that Hobbes must have wanted to disguise whatever contradiction exists between what he preaches and what he practices. After all, what kind of philosopher—especially a philosopher in pursuit of rigorous truth—could actually advertise the contradictory nature of his philosophical precepts and his writing practice?

Inviting discussion and entertaining questions are teaching strategies that work only if students are persuaded that the text is open to multiple interpretations—or stated differently, with an eye to the sensitivities of a student audience, that their classroom is open to a range of answers to the questions that have been posed and that their freedom to answer differently will garner the best respect that good teaching can afford, considered attention. Especially when one teaches a text like *Leviathan*, even the appearance of an authoritarian pedagogy in pursuit of the "right" answer to the questions addressed is likely to elicit only that most frequent expression of student fear, silence. As the author of his own treatise about rhetoric, Hobbes's status as a self-conscious practitioner of the language arts is never at issue. Historical knowledge is part of what good teaching imparts—and students need such instruction. The consequences of such self-consciousness for evaluating a text as complex as *Leviathan*, however, are inevitably available to rival interpretations, and real acknowledgment of such multiplicity means that whatever answers we as teachers might suggest to those questions are best presented (to rescue a term from the sciences) as hypotheses—as possible frames for understanding, instead of as the settled conclusions of an authoritarian pedagogy.

Answering the question, then, about what kind of philosopher could choose to create a text whose every paragraph highlights the contradiction between his precepts and his practice means asking my students to entertain a hypothesis: that Hobbes deliberately creates an unsettling text to inspire fear in his readers and that such fear results in this instance from the extraordinarily high stakes set for evaluating metaphor. Making sense of my hypothesis means returning to the main question that organizes Hobbes's text. How are we to escape from lives that are nasty, short, mean, and brutish—from life in the state of nature, from life as it is endured (if at all) during civil wars? By the institution of sovereign power and, as a prior condition, by the knowledge (rigorous and truthful) of the necessity of instituting such power. After instructions to identify the logical certainty of a new philosophy crafted from perspicuous prose as the sole means of avoiding civil war, the failure of the text to supply the remedy essential for the health of the body politic disturbs and provokes. As metaphor multiplies on metaphor, the high stakes wagered against these vehicles of contentious and seditious equivocation appear actually to advertise the contradiction at the heart of our discussion—the gulf between Hobbes's own precepts and practice, thereby advertising *Leviathan*'s textual insufficiency, its apparent inability to remedy the disease whose cure has been its primary object from the start.

My hypothesis allows me to move in several directions. It points ahead to another class in which we examine how Hobbes attempts to authorize the institution of the sovereign, using fear against fear in one final, dramatic erasure of metaphor to turn his imaginary Leviathan from textual construct into historical being (Stillman 165–73). More to the point of this class discussion, the hypothesis helps explain Hobbes's fearsome reputation among his contemporaries as the monster of Malmesbury. Cataloging page after page of the *Leviathan*'s metaphors, John Eachard labels Hobbes a "formidable Monster of Wit" (29). Most important, however, my hypothesis enables a discussion of my students' own textual experiences, as it insists on recapturing *Leviathan* as the disturbing book that readers have always known it to be. Nothing is easier than getting students to discuss their fears of Hobbes. The object of my teaching, however, is to focus those fears. When class ends, I am not hoping that students have found *Leviathan* any kinder or gentler or more accessible—in the way that Shakespeare's plays become accessible. What I hope, instead, is that by submitting Hobbes's figurative language to the close analysis that English majors are accustomed to, those accidental fears that initially make *Leviathan* seem so monstrous—fears about its size, its preoccupation with definition, and its logical rigor—become comprehensible as complements to its philosophical and political aims. Students are scared of *Leviathan*, and properly so, because *Leviathan* is one scary monster of a book.

Notes

1. When I teach *Leviathan*, I prefer to use Macpherson's edition because it is both complete and inexpensive. For scholarly purposes, I use (as I do here) the text as edited in volume 3 of *The English Works*.

2. I assign three chapters from the dated, but still essential, Hill: "The Parchment and the Fire" (16–31), "Masterless Men" (32–45), and "A Nation of Prophets" (70–85). Achinstein's chapter "Royalist Reactions" (71–101) offers a more recent study relating social and political crisis in the civil wars to questions about language.

3. To prepare students for appreciating the cultural significance of those debates, I ask them to read Bacon's attacks against the idols of the marketplace in his *New Organon* and Wilkins's preface to his *Essay towards a Real Character and a Philosophical Language*.

Works Cited

Achinstein, Sharon. *Milton and the Revolutionary Reader*. Princeton: Princeton UP, 1994. Print.

Bacon, Francis. *The New Organon*. Ed. Fulton H. Anderson. Indianapolis: Bobbs-Merrill, 1960. Print.

Bono, James. *The Word of God and the Languages of Man: Interpreting Nature in Early Modern Science and Medicine*. Madison: U of Wisconsin P, 1995. Print.

Eachard, John. *Some Opinions of Mr. Hobbs Considered*. London, 1673. Print.

Hill, Christopher. *The World Turned Upside Down: Radical Ideas during the English Revolution*. New York: Viking, 1972. Print.

Hobbes, Thomas. *The English Works of Thomas Hobbes*. Ed. Thomas Molesworth. 11 vols. Darmstadt: Scientia Verlag Aalen, 1966. Print.

———. *Leviathan*. 1651. Ed. C. B. Macpherson. Baltimore: Penguin, 1968. Print.

Kahn, Victoria. *Rhetoric, Prudence, and Skepticism in the Renaissance*. Ithaca: Cornell UP, 1985. Print.

Kroll, Richard W. *The Material Word: Literate Culture in the Restoration and Early Eighteenth Century*. Baltimore: Johns Hopkins UP, 1991. Print.

Markley, Robert. *Fallen Languages: Crises of Representation in Newtonian England, 1660–1740*. Ithaca: Cornell UP, 1993. Print.

Quine, W. V. "A Postscript on Metaphor." *Critical Inquiry* 5.1 (1978): 161–62. Print.

Solomon, Julie Robin. *Objectivity in the Making: Francis Bacon and the Politics of Inquiry*. Baltimore: Johns Hopkins UP, 1998. Print.

Stillman, Robert E. *The New Philosophy and Universal Languages in Seventeenth-Century England: Bacon, Hobbes, and Wilkins*. Lewisburg: Bucknell UP; London: Associated, 1995. Print.

Wilkins, John. *An Essay towards a Real Character and a Philosophical Language*. London, 1668. Print.

Thomas Corns

"On Thursday Giant Despair Beats His Prisoners": Teaching Bunyan in an Unsympathetic Age

Superficially, the most popular elements within the Bunyan oeuvre have an accessibility rare among the most studied texts of the early modern English literary tradition. They are relatively unproblematic in linguistic and stylistic terms. Of course, like the prose of John Donne or Francis Bacon or John Milton, they are written in a language at some remove from our own; but syntactically, they pose fewer difficulties. A sentence by Milton may be two or three hundred words long yet have only one or two main clauses, supported by a wealth of subordinate clauses, which may in turn support further subordinate clauses. Donne, too, sometimes poses that kind of complexity, and Bacon is often wittily pointed, even elliptical. But Bunyan typically uses a familiar word order, and his longer sentences tend to be produced by coordination, instead of extensive subordination, though of course there is subordination of a simple kind. Again, at the lexical level, Bunyan uses a simpler vocabulary, with fewer words that require glossing. Moreover, the welter of Latinate loan words that characterize learned discourse in the seventeenth century is less prominent than in Donne or Bacon or Milton. These words are inherently less likely to be familiar to our students, and when they are familiar, there is the additional problem that their meaning has often shifted through the normal dynamics of semantic change. The student may well either understand such words in their modern, not seventeenth-century, senses or else assume the author is affectedly using them in their original Latin senses, attributing to the text a kind of mannered inkhornism viewed somewhat unsympathetically in an age when few undergraduates have even a smattering of classical languages. With Bunyan these problems rarely occur.

Rhetoric is as much a part of twenty-first-century political and forensic discourse as it was of seventeenth-century, but styles change, and now, emphatically, the art is to conceal the art. Yale-educated politicians affect the linguistic simplicities of a Texan cowpoke or a bluff naval officer. Oxford-educated, legally trained politicians favor a hesitating, monosyllabic exposition as a signifier of sincerity. In contrast, Donne in his pulpit and Milton on his soapbox are consciously heirs to great classical and neoclassical traditions that regard the developed tropes of rhetoric as the means by which eloquence communicates truth and virtue. They stand in a line that runs from Demosthenes's Athens through Cicero's Rome to their own day, and their formal education was central to preserving and advancing that tradition. Bunyan, on the other hand, need not affect simplicity to stand closer to our own current preferences: he writes with the simple clarity of an uneducated man because he is exactly that, a very limited autodidact who has not been exposed to classical and neoclassical high culture and its valorization of rhetorical elaboration.

Bunyan's most frequently read works (now as in his own age) are narrative in structure. They tell stories—of a life related in retrospect, as in *The Life and Death of Mister Badman*; or of his own experiences, as in *Grace Abounding to the Chief of Sinners*; or of the adventures on a single journey, as in *The Pilgrim's Progress*. Of course, the novel is the dominant form in our own print culture. Students feel comfortable with an account of causally connected events pertaining to one or two people and related in the order in which they occurred. Although allegory is the favored mode of much of Bunyan's most popular works, it is usually of a transparent kind: he tells his readers what things mean. The editors of the 2000 *Norton Anthology*, globally the default collection in the teaching of English literature at the undergraduate level, do include (to their immense credit) that most challenging of allegorical passages, the Garden of Adonis section of *The Faerie Queene* (book 3, canto 6). I wonder how much progress our students really make with this, in comparison with the straightforward and explicit correspondences of *The Pilgrim's Progress*.

Bunyan's lack of formal education also limits his range of reference. He makes little reference to seventeenth-century politics or political history. The classical learning recovered in the Renaissance does not figure. There is no engagement with philosophy. Even though he had cut his teeth in controversies with Quakers over such issues as the historical atonement of Christ, the role of the spirit within the believer, and the status of the Bible in Christian belief, sectarian infighting is absent from his major prose (though it abounds in plenty in the minor pieces to be found in the modern edition of his *Miscellaneous Works*). *The Pilgrim's Progress* offers an allegory of personal salvation; Bunyan himself subscribes to a hard-line Calvinist soteriology that regards salvation and damnation as doubly (that is, equally) predestined; and yet what is depicted is generalized ecumenically in a way that renders it acceptable across a wide range of Protestant faith communities.

So what's so hard about teaching Bunyan? While from the 1980s the notion of a literary canon has been, at the level of theory, picked over, dismantled, even (so the slogan once went) "exploded," in terms of practical pedagogy it is of course alive and well and living in the *Norton Anthology*, which, with a handful of useful and similar products, continues to serve our profession quite well. But Bunyan remains poorly provided for. In part, I suspect, this reflects the anthologists' evident and wholly reasonable enthusiasm for the richness of high-culture literature in the early modern period, a predilection no doubt shared by most university teachers of English. Yet the critique of canon formation has had its impact. We are looking to introduce our students to texts outside the cultural hegemony of metropolitan and propertied males. Bunyan, as a poor provincial, may seem a potential beneficiary. But there are plenty of alternatives that are, superficially at least, more challenging, oppositional and feisty. The Norton anthology has a section called "voices of the war," which includes John Lilburne, Gerrard Winstanley, Anna Trapnel, and Abiezer Coppe, variously more engaged, more confrontational, more visionary, more apocalyptic, more risqué, and stylistically more pyrotechnic. Plenty more could be added from the intellectual and cultural territory so effectively explored by Nigel Smith (*Collection*; *Literature*; *Perfection*) and Elaine Hobby. For example, among the Ranters Jacob Bauthumley is intellectually much more challenging than Bunyan, and there are numerous Quaker women prophets who write with a resonating defiance and an eloquent simplicity. Bunyan can seem bland and safe.

Probably no seventeenth-century English writer has been so widely appropriated as Bunyan. We can trace in the myriad translations of his work how waves of English evangelists, usually from the missionary wing of Anglicanism, have used particularly *The Pilgrim's Progress* in their operations in the British Empire and more widely. There are translations into many of the languages of North America, Africa, the Indian subcontinent, Oceania, and Australasia. There is an ever-present danger of unconsciously repeating that process. In a period of Christian revival in the United States and of renewed evangelical endeavor in much of the English-speaking world Bunyan can seem like a familiar friend who speaks the same language as such movements and missions, and the chasms that divide us from seventeenth-century dissent, from the viewpoint of a historically informed literary hermeneutic, may perilously be overlooked. In the process of such silent appropriation, Bunyan seems even more respectable.

How then would I teach Bunyan? Several interrelated themes may usefully be advanced. In his own age, Bunyan was perceived as deeply subversive, and his major works are prison writing. The issues that animate him are not transhistorical but reflect the religious sensibility of Calvinist dissent in its most alarming form. He challenges contemporary expectations about authors and authorship. He transforms established kinds of practical devotional writing into texts that negotiate a curious relation to high literary culture. Finally, he writes with a vivid intensity that is unique among the early modern authors our students are likely to encounter.

Bunyan was, in some ways, the purest manifestation of the world of the late 1640s and the 1650s, a world turned upside down, in which heterodox "sects" subscribing to a wide range of vaguely Protestant belief enjoyed an unprecedented (though not unlimited) religious toleration. In that world, Bunyan prospered, emerging as a significant apologist for a Calvinist and Baptist faith community, despite his lack of formal education. He was a proletarian writer wholly undeferential to his social superiors, because his theology was unceremonial and egalitarian, and it rested on his conviction of his own godliness. He was wholly unpatronizing to the poor, the unlearned, even to children, in ways that reflect his own awareness of social and political disempowerment. Christopher Hill, who among modern critics best appreciated Bunyan's subversiveness, observes, "The gentry knew their enemies" (107). Shortly after the Restoration he was arrested and imprisoned under anti-Dissenter legislation, an incarceration surely prolonged by his own intransigent refusal to give undertakings to leave off preaching. He was not released until 1672— "Only regicides and outstanding political figures . . . were treated with greater severity" (Hill 106)—and subsequently endured shorter periods in jail. Much of his finest work is prison writing.

Throughout *Grace Abounding* his social assumptions are clear. A vital stage in his spiritual development is triggered by conversation with "three or four poor women sitting at a door in the Sun, and talking about the things of God" (14). His persecutors are vaguely sketched, though allegedly duplicitous, "taking my plain dealing with them for a confession" (95); though prison brings a crisis of faith, they cannot really touch his mind and soul and the struggle within them. But Bunyan depicts himself brooding over the implications of incarceration for a propertyless man. Leaving his family is "as the pulling the flesh from my bones," not least because they are plunged into "hardship, miseries and wants," which are particularly threatening to his blind daughter, "who lay nearer to my heart than all I had besides" (98). We should point up the vividness and precision of such writing and link it to the urgent context of its composition.

Like *Grace Abounding*, the first part of *The Pilgrim's Progress* is explicitly a prison writing, though whether it was produced and held over from his early and long incarceration, which ended in 1672, or a second, shorter term later in the decade remains unclear. Though of course the allegorical level is important, crucial scenes throughout the book seem grounded in the actualities of impoverished, provincial life. Indeed, many of the finer moments of the text retain a mimetic quality, which once more students should be invited to consider. As the critical tradition has long recognized, the treatment of Christian and Faithful at Vanity Fair recalls the rough justice and flawed judicial processes meted out to nonconformists in provincial England. Their trial reflects the prejudice and hostility of the magistracy and packed juries, while the actual execution of Faithful, lanced and stoned and stabbed, seems closer to the spectacular punishment of some regicides (90–97).

Grace Abounding is in some ways the most rewarding of Bunyan's texts to teach, and the *Norton* gives a substantial selection from it, though it may need to be supplemented. It best points up the drama at the center of Calvinist soteriology. Students need to recognize the drama of the argument. The issues seem straightforward: either one is predestinately saved, through the grace of God instead of merit in oneself, and thus behaves, perhaps after a period of crises, morally like the saved; or one is predestinately damned, in which case no amount of good works or good behavior will effect salvation. But how may one know oneself to be saved? Again, if one believes oneself to be saved, is not that the sin of pride, which marks one for damnation? Or if one does not believe one is saved, then is not that a lack of faith, which again marks one for damnation? Questions like these bounce around the internal monologue of *Grace Abounding*, producing an extraordinary, terrified, and in its way terrifying description.

Such issues reach their climax in Bunyan's description of a prison experience, a leap of faith that is simultaneously an imagined leap to his death. The horror of the act itself can engage students' interest. Hanging was a primitive and public business in the early modern period. A rope was passed over the crossbar of the gallows and tied around the victim's neck. He or she was pushed, pulled, or prodded up a ladder placed against the gallows, and then obliged to jump or be kicked off, to throttle to death. It was surely a difficult death to contemplate, even if one felt confident about the fate of one's soul. For someone in turmoil there was an added anxiety that a public display of fear would be interpreted as evidence of a want of faith or of the conviction of one's own sinfulness. Bunyan was convinced that such an execution would be his fate. In as disturbing a passage of seventeenth-century prose that I know, he recounts vividly his obsessive, haunted meditation of his imagined end:

> [I]f I should make a scrabling shift to clamber up the Ladder, yet I should either with quaking or other symptoms of faintings, give occasion to the enemy to reproach the way of God and his People, for their timerousness: . . . I was ashamed to die with a pale face, and tottering knees.

As he muses, "that word dropped upon me, *Doth Job serve God for naught?*," and the sudden revelation completes the leap of faith, bringing comfort after despair (*Grace Abounding* 10–11). The reader feels deeply implicated in the thought process, as though we are sweating in the death cell with him and sharing his relief when spiritual confirmation arrives, albeit that confirmation may involve an acceptance of a grisly fate. Terror, too, defines the sensibility of at least the first part of *The Pilgrim's Progress*, as Christian flees the City of Destruction: "his Wife and Children perceiving it, began to cry after him to return: but the Man put his fingers in his Ears, and ran on crying, Life, Life, Eternal Life" (10). Of course, Christian imagines at this point eternal life only for himself.

Bunyan stands outside the social and cultural categories that define other major seventeenth-century authors. Indeed, even among radical writers he is unique. Some of those were university educated; mostly they came from a relatively prosperous background; and nearly all had some connections with London radical circles. Bunyan, socially, culturally, and geographically, was an outsider, and modern students may usefully be invited to reflect on the significance of that.

Yet Bunyan was a publishing phenomenon in his own day. *The Pilgrim's Progress* went into at least eleven editions in his lifetime. It enjoyed an immediate success, which continued through the century and beyond. The publisher of Bunyan's posthumous collected works, writing in 1692, observed that it "*hath been printed in* France, Holland, New-England, *and in* Welch, *and about a hundred thousand in England*" (*Miscellaneous Works* 456). If that figure were approximately accurate and if we posit a multiple readership for most copies, then we have an enormous proportion of the potential readership familiar with the work by the last decade of the century. Again, we may challenge our students to account for this success, while suggesting some explanations. Its appeal, no doubt, was in part genre related, for this is a work of improving, practical theology of a familiar kind. Yet, why such phenomenal success for *this* example of a common kind? The answers may rest in part on notions of an authorial voice, which is unpatronizing, direct, egalitarian, but also on the sheer brilliance of Bunyan's writing. Bunyan depicts holy terror and a psychomachia, yet his accounts, both in *The Pilgrim's Progress* and in *Grace Abounding*, are extraordinarily vivid and pervasively rooted in a sometimes oppositional representation of the world around him. But all of that is for our students to explore.

Works Cited

Bunyan, John. *Grace Abounding to the Chief of Sinners*. Ed. Roger Sharrock. Oxford: Clarendon, 1962. Print.

———. *The Life and Death of Mister Badman*. Ed. James F. Forrest and Roger Sharrock. Oxford: Clarendon, 1988. Print.

———. *The Miscellaneous Works of John Bunyan*. Ed. Roger Sharrock. 11 vols. Oxford: Clarendon, 1976–94. Print.

———. *The Pilgrim's Progress*. Ed. James Wharey. 2nd ed. Rev. Roger Sharrock. Oxford: Clarendon, 1960. Print.

Hill, Christopher. *A Turbulent, Seditious, and Factious People: John Bunyan and His Church, 1628–1688*. 1988. Oxford: Oxford UP, 1989. Print.

Hobby, Elaine. *Virtue of Necessity: English Women's Writing, 1649–1688.* London: Virago, 1988. Print.

The Norton Anthology of English Literature. M. H. Abrams and Stephen Greenblatt, gen. eds. 7th ed. 2 vols. New York: Norton, 2000. Print.

Smith, Nigel, ed. *A Collection of Ranter Writings from the Seventeenth Century.* London: Junction, 1983. Print.

———. *Literature and Revolution in England, 1640–1660.* New Haven: Yale UP, 1994. Print.

———. *Perfection Proclaimed: Language and Literature in English Radical Religion, 1640–1660.* Oxford: Clarendon, 1989. Print.

Part IV

Crossings and Pairings

Terry Reilly

Teaching Lyly's Euphuism through William Harrison's *The Description of England*: History, Parody, and Dialogic Form

This young gallant, of more wit than wealth, and yet of more wealth than wisdom, seeing himself inferior to none in pleasant conceits, thought himself superior to all in honest conditions, insomuch that he deemed himself so apt to all things that he gave himself almost to nothing, but practicing of those things commonly which are incident to these sharp wits: fine phrases, smooth quipping, merry taunting, using jesting without mean and abusing mirth without measure. As, therefore, the sweetest rose hath its prickle, the finest velvet its brack, the fairest flour its bran, so the sharpest wit hath his wanton will, and the holiest head his wicked way. And true it is that some men write and most men believe, that in all perfect shapes, a blemish bringeth rather a liking every way to the eyes, than a loathing any way to the mind. Venus had her mole in her cheek, which made her more amiable; Helen her scar on her chin, which Paris called *cos amoris*, the whetstone of love; Aristippus his wart; Lycurgus his wen: so likewise, in the disposition of the mind, either virtue is overshadowed with some vice, or vice overcast with some virtue. Alexander, valiant in war, yet given to wine. Tully eloquent in his glosses, yet vainglorious: Solomon wise, yet too, too wanton: David holy, but yet an homicide: none more witty than Euphues, yet at the first none more wicked.

—John Lyly, *Euphues: The Anatomy of Wit*

On the one hand, the lengthy quotation above, from the first page of the 1578 edition of John Lyly's *Euphues: The Anatomy of Wit*, provides a clear example of the highly elaborate and artificial style known as euphuism, which parodied classical forms of rhetoric through the extensive use of simile and illustration, balanced construction, alliteration, and antithesis. On the other hand, the length of the sentences, together with their dense grammatical constructs, esoteric allusions, confused and confusing reasoning, and antithetical logic, helps explain why Lyly's prose is so infrequently taught in colleges and universities today.[2] The following essay presents one approach to teaching euphuism at both the undergraduate and graduate levels, although the focus and expectations differ at each level. At the undergraduate level—especially while covering early modern English prose in the limited time afforded this topic in sophomore- or junior-level English-literature survey courses—students learn to highlight some of the basic features of euphuism and then try to write their own euphuistic parodies. The exercise provides students with examples of early modern English novelistic and historical discourse that can be taught between examples of poetry (Sidney and Spenser) and drama (Shakespeare). At the graduate level—especially in a course that includes selections of early modern English prose such as Lyly's works, Raphael Holinshed's *Chronicles*, Thomas Nashe's *The Unfortunate Traveller*, and Robert Greene's *Pandosto*—this exercise, as we shall see, can lead to a number of productive discussions and papers that focus on concepts of genre and style as ways to discuss relations between "history" and fiction.

For the most part, critics have been reluctant to analyze, in detail, Lyly's euphuistic style. Nancy Lindheim, for example, notes that "Lyly's euphuism has traditionally been defined in terms of patterns of sound rather than of meaning" (3), while Walter Nash laments that "trying to do a detailed rhetorical analysis on any passage from Lyly is rather like boning fish" (136). A number of scholars, including R. Warwick Bond, Peter Saccio, Jonas Barish, G. K. Hunter (*John Lyly*; *Lyly and Peele*), G. Wilson Knight, and David Bevington, have discussed Lyly's euphuistic style, but the main focus of criticism, by and large, has been to call attention to Lyly's influence on subsequent prose writers such as Thomas Lodge, Robert Greene, and Thomas Nashe and on playwrights such as George Peele, Thomas Dekker, and especially Shakespeare. Lyly's dialogic interaction with contemporary writers, however, has received relatively little critical attention.

Instead of focusing on classical rhetoric, classical allusions, or grammar in the teaching exercise that follows, I discuss euphuism through the writings of Lyly and William Harrison, a historian contemporary to Lyly who was able to imitate and parody Lyly's euphuistic style. As we shall see, a curious written dialogue developed between Lyly and Harrison as they imitated and satirized each other's style in a few passages concerning customs and customary law in Lyly's *Euphues and His England* and the first two editions of Harrison's *The Description of England*. My approach builds on and extends Georges Edelen's discussion of Harrison's relation to various contemporary writers. Edelen observes that Lyly included passages from Harrison's text in *Euphues and His England* and that, in the second edition of *The Description of England* (1587), Harrison "borrowed" rather extensively from texts that had appeared after the publication of the first edition in 1577. For example, in the 1587 edition, Harrison added an entire chapter on Parliament that is remarkably similar to Thomas Smith's *De Republica Anglorum*, published in 1583 (Edelen, Introduction xxi), and, according to Edelen, Harrison admired "Abraham Fleming's ornate style enough to appropriate swatches of it" in the 1587 edition of *The Description of England* (Introduction xxxiii).

My aim, then, is not only to help students recognize some of the basic features of euphuism and the dialogic interplay of Lyly's and Harrison's writing but also to call attention to ways that Harrison—purportedly writing "straight," "artless" social history—incorporates, at least in this selection, features of euphuism, a form that invokes and then often undermines the epistemological underpinnings of modes of traditional rhetorical inquiry. Moreover, the juxtaposition of exemplary passages from Lyly's and Harrison's texts demonstrates how both authors critique and question the logic, accuracy, and relevance of narrative "history" in determining "truth." Used as a teaching tool, this comparative approach can be productive in several ways. First, it helps students see *how* Harrison imitates Lyly's euphuistic style; once they are able to identify features of euphuism, they can then practice writing their own euphuistic arguments. Eventually, students begin to see that Harrison's use of a euphuistic style in his long description of "customary law" in his second edition raises questions about the accuracy of his "historical" account and foregrounds the interplay and instability of various literary styles and genres in early modern English prose.

The remainder of this article is divided into three parts. The first provides some relevant biographical information about Lyly and Harrison, and the second includes selections from *Euphues and His England* and from Harrison's entries on "customary law" in the first two editions of *The Description of England*. The third provides a close reading of the selections and suggests ways to expand these readings into broader classroom discussions.

John Lyly was born in 1554 in Canterbury, in Kent; graduated from Magdalen College, Oxford; and moved to London in 1576, where he served as a member of Parliament from 1589 to 1601. He was the grandson of William Lyly, a cleric and grammarian who wrote a book of rhetoric, grammar, and logic that was widely used in English grammar schools for almost one hundred and fifty years. John Lyly wrote two long prose pieces, *Euphues: The Anatomy of Wit* (1578) and *Euphues and His England* (1580) before turning playwright and writing eight classical comedies. Lyly, his two books about Euphues, and euphuism itself were all enormously popular during the 1580s and early 1590s, but both he and his style of writing fell out of favor and all but disappeared from the public eye by the end of the century, in part because of the inkhorn controversy of the late 1580s and early 1590s. During this heated debate about writing styles, purists—including William Harrison—who raged against elaborate conceits; wordy, copious phrases; and a flowery, affected style often cited Lyly's euphuism as an example of everything wrong with contemporary prose.

Harrison (1534–93) was a Londoner who took degrees at both Oxford and Cambridge before settling down to a rural clerical life as chaplain to Lord Cobham of Kent, then as rector of Radwinter in Essex, and finally as canon of Windsor. He was an avid traveler—although he never left England—and a prolific antiquarian who seemingly wrote down everything that occurred to him (Furnivall x–xii). He was also one of Raphael Holinshed's friends, and when Holinshed was tapped by Reginald Wolfe, the queen's printer, to write a "universal Cosmography of the whole world, and therewith also certain particular histories of every known nation," Harrison was one of the first people he enlisted to help him write the sections on Britain and England (Furnivall iv–v).

Harrison's *The Description of England*, which he described as "this foul frizzled treatise" (qtd. in Furnivall vii), appeared as the first part of Holinshed's *Chronicles* in the first edition, issued in 1577, and in the second edition, published in 1587. Both Holinshed and Harrison died before completing the "universal Cosmography of the whole world," and what remains are chronicle histories of England, Scotland, and Ireland. The two works are nonetheless valuable and extensive, and although a number of commentators, including Frederick J. Furnivall, have regarded them as relatively unvarnished and accurate accounts of daily life in

Elizabethan England, an important caveat must be noted. Since historical discourse typically appears in college and university curricula as "source material," it is often important to counter student assumptions that this material *is* unvarnished and completely accurate. Focusing on style is a convenient way to help students—who might otherwise be unfamiliar with the contexts and political nuances of the material that early modern historical writing represents—appreciate and perhaps understand the complex nature of early modern "historical" discourse.

Although many of Harrison's entries are rather straightforward, others contain complex allusions that call attention to and critique contemporary politics and policies. For example, on first reading, Harrison's "description" of "customary law" in the 1577 edition of *The Description of England* is short, terse, and to the point: "Customary law consisteth of certain laudable customs used in some private country, intended first to begin upon good and reasonable considerations, as gavelkind, which is all the male children to inherit, and continued to this day in Kent" (*Harrison's Description* 202).[3] It seems strange, perhaps even subversive, however, that Harrison would choose gavelkind for an example of a "laudable custom," since primogeniture—inheritance solely by the eldest son—was the customary form of inheritance for all of England except for the county of Kent. In the heated controversy over inheritance law during the Tudor-Stuart period, several monarchs and their parliaments tried unsuccessfully to eliminate Kentish gavelkind, while disinherited younger sons of the gentry saw Kent as a type of legal Forest of Arden.[4] As John Earle bluntly put it in his book *Microcosmography* in 1605, younger sons "would have long since revolted to the Spaniard but for Kent only which [they] hold in admiration" (69–70). Proponents of primogeniture, however—in other words, the ruling classes and courts of England—would certainly *not* have regarded gavelkind as a "laudable custom," founded on "good and reasonable considerations." While Harrison's choice to cast gavelkind in such a favorable light may be due to some heart-felt political convictions, it may also be due to more practical concerns: his patron, Lord Cobham, was a nobleman from Kent.

In "Euphues' Glass for Europe," the concluding chapter of *Euphues and His England*, published in 1580, Lyly parodies Harrison's laconic style and satirically redacts *The Description of England* down to eight pages. His one-paragraph discussion of English law—sandwiched humorously between categories titled "attire" and "savage beasts and vermin"—includes the following sentence fragment: "Then upon customable law,

which consisteth upon laudable customs used in some private country"
(Euphues [ed. Croll and Clemons] 422). By severely editing and digesting
The Description of England (in part by leaving out Harrison's cogent historical examples) and by having Euphues mouth Harrison's words, Lyly
confronts the reader with both plagiarism and parody, producing, paradoxically, both an exact copy and a harsh satiric miniature of the style and
content of *The Description of England*.

In the 1587 edition of *The Description of England*, Harrison answers
Lyly. Adding almost two hundred and fifty words to the end of the 1577
entry on "customary law," he imitates Lyly's euphuistic style and Euphues's
confused logic:

> Customary law consisteth of certain laudable customs used in some
> private country, intended first to begin upon good and reasonable
> considerations, as gavelkind, which is all the male children equally to
> inherit, and continued to this day in Kent: where it is only to my
> knowledge retained, and nowhere else in England. It was first devised
> by the Romans, as appeareth by Caesar in his commentaries, wherein
> I find, that to break and daunt the force of the rebellious Germans,
> they made a law that all the male children (or females for want of
> males, which holdeth still in England) should have their father's in-
> heritance equally divided amongst them. By this means also it came to
> pass, that whereas before time for the space of sixty years, they had
> put the Romans to great and manifold troubles, within the space of
> thirty years after this law made, their power did wax so feeble, and
> such discord fell out amongst themselves, that they were not able to
> maintain wars with the Romans, nor raise any just army against them.
> For as a river running with one stream is swift and more plentiful of
> water than when it is drained or drawn into many branches: so the
> lands and goods of the ancestors being dispersed amongst their is-
> sue males, of one strong, there were raised sundry weak, whereby the
> original or general strength to resist the adversary became enfeebled
> and brought almost to nothing. *Vis unita* (saith the philosopher) *for-
> tior est eadem dispersa*, and one good purse is better than many evil;
> and when every man is benefited alike, each one will seek to maintain
> his private estate, and few take care to provide for public welfare.
> (202–03)

Harrison's addition clearly echoes the "schoolmasterly" rhetorical formulations, antithetical logic, and confused three-part structure characteristic of Lyly's euphuistic style. After first describing gavelkind as a laudable
custom, he describes how the Romans forced it on the rebellious Germans

to "enfeeble" them, to produce discord, and to bring them "almost to nothing."[5] Also characteristic of euphuism are the proverbs, classical references, truisms, Latin epigrams, platitudes, and so forth traditionally used to support an argument but here, paradoxically, used to both support and undermine Harrison's points. Harrison tells us that a river is swifter and, strangely, more full when it is not drawn into many branches; further, shared inheritance produces "many evil" purses, the maintenance of private estates, and a neglect for "public welfare" (for the Germans, according to the logic of this passage, this meant "wars with the Romans"). In short, gavelkind, a laudable custom extant in Kent, was introduced by the Romans to the rebellious Germans to enfeeble them and bring about their annihilation. What Harrison does not explain in this passage, of course, is what the relation is between German and Kentish versions of gavelkind. What his readers certainly would also know without his explaining it is which side eventually won the war between the Romans and the Germans. Thus, it is not surprising that the concluding Latin epigram(s) are open to various interpretations: either that "power united is stronger than the same dispersed" (*Description* 172n23) or that unity is strength and, in the same way, dispersion is stronger.

In my upper-division undergraduate and graduate classrooms, students study the interplay of these passages in two main ways. First, they discuss possible alternatives as Harrison parodies the formal features of euphuism in this entry in the 1587 edition: Is Harrison endorsing gavelkind over primogeniture in this passage, or vice versa or neither or both? Is he using a euphuistic style to trivialize the contemporary argument about inheritance practices? Can we consider this an example of "straight" narrative history? Or is his imitation of Lyly's style a more personal voice, one whose end is simply to participate in a written war of words and styles? While these form interesting discussion questions in class that usually provoke lively debates, students eventually see that the inability to answer these questions with any degree of certainty may be due, in large part, to the nature of euphuism itself.

The second way students study this relation is by imitating the tropes, writing style, and logic of the entries. This seems to work best if students replicate the dialogic process by working in pairs. One actual example written by students perhaps explains the process better than I can narrate it. Student A wrote a brief description of a custom observed in certain places: Alternate-side-of-the-street parking is a custom practiced in many urban areas in the United States. Student B then used euphuistic features—proverbs, Latin phrases, esoteric allusions, skewed etymologies, antithetical logic, and so forth—to explain the genesis and perpetuation of the custom. In this case, student B began by noting that while the custom of alternate-side-of-the-street parking may appear to modern readers to have resulted from a desire to keep streets clean, it actually began during the early medieval period with the proverb "cleanliness is next to godliness" and the Christian tradition of pilgrimage. Student B then provided a long explanation of how pilgrims and palmers became so numerous at one point that they were assigned alternate sides of the road and traveled in opposite directions, although, student B notes, wars, disease, the Crusades, and other types of crises often led to one-way traffic.

Student A was then required to respond to student B's essay by parodying and amplifying on the topic and the style, much as Harrison does in his 1587 edition. In this case, student A compared alternate-side-of-the-street parking and the custom of pilgrimage to the life cycle of salmon as they move down one side of the river to the sea and then back up the other side to inland lakes. Extremely detailed and peppered with Latin phrases (the salmon are identified by their Latin names, and the essay included a wonderful euphuistic digression on differences between *anadromous* and O*ncorhynchus salmonids*), student A's essay replicated both Lyly's propensity for Latin digression and his frequent use of Pliny's questionable natural history. Ultimately, in classic euphuistic style, as student A's essay follows the salmon back up the river to spawn and die, the custom of alternate-side-of-the-street parking—if we recall that as the starting point of the essay—emerges not as a localized urban problem of space and cleanliness, but rather as a complicated natural, historical, and spiritual process that presages the apocalypse.

To conclude, while this exercise may not "explain" euphuism in terms of classical modes of rhetoric or in more conventional or orthodox forms of pedagogy, it provides students with practical ways to gain insight into the fluid nature of euphuism and into the culture in which it was produced. Moreover, it demonstrates ways that the euphuistic dialogic process can reshape "straight" secular and religious history, as well as scientific discourse, as parody.

Notes

1. I have modernized the spelling in this passage, but I have retained Lyly's idiosyncratic punctuation.

2. Walter Nash describes euphuism in terms of style, noting, "paragraphs begin and end with an antithetical counterpoise, [and] style is unrelated, by and

large, to the content and psychology of the text" (138). Or, as that would-be literary critic Philautus puts it when he tries to recapitulate one of Euphues's long tales of inheritance and prodigality in Lyly's *Euphues and His England*: "the beginning [of the story] I have forgotten, the middle I understand not, and the end hangeth not together" (Euphues [ed. Croll and Clemons] 228–29).

3. The publication history of Harrison's *The Description of England* is complicated. The first and a much longer second edition were published as the first three books of Holinshed's *Chronicles* in 1577 and 1587. Georges Edelen notes that the only subsequent complete version appears in the first volume of the 1807–08 reprinting of Holinshed's *Chronicles* (Preface vii). The New Shakespeare Society edition edited by Frederick Furnivall was published in four parts in London from 1877 to 1908. Edelen's 1968 Folger Shakespeare Library edition is based on three copies of the 1587 folio, as well as Furnivall's text, although Edelen describes the latter as "fitfully and quixotically annotated" (vii). Edelen edited or omitted several chapters of the original text and what he refers to as "readily detachable historical digressions" (vii). Since this essay discusses differences between the first and second editions of Harrison's text, the Furnivall edition is more appropriate than the Edelen edition, in that it is the only one to indicate clearly the changes, additions, and deletions Harrison made between the 1577 and 1587 editions. Thus this and all citations from Harrison's *The Description of England* are to the Furnivall edition and will be referred to by page number. I have modernized the spelling in cited passages from this text.

4. For more on the contemporary inheritance controversy, see Reilly 382–84.

5. McCulloch notes that legal writings as far back as Henri de Bracton's thirteenth-century *Tractatus de Legibus ed Consuetudinus Angliae* regarded Kentish gavelkind as a pre-Norman Anglo-Saxon custom (23). When the Romans conquered the "Germans," they presumably would have enforced Roman law; thus Harrison is likely inaccurately citing Caesar as a source for gavelkind.

Works Cited

Barish, Jonas A. "The Prose Style of John Lyly." *ELH* 23.1 (1956): 14–35. Print.
Bevington, David. "'Jack hath not Jill': Failed Courtship in Lyly and Shakespeare." *Shakesepare Survey: An Annual Survey of Shakespeare Studies and Production* 42 (1990): 1–13. Print.
Bond, R. Warwick, ed. *The Complete Works of John Lyly*. 3 vols. Oxford: Clarendon, 1973. Print.
Earle, John. *Microcosmography*. Ed. A. S. West. Cambridge: Cambridge UP, 1951. Print.
Edelen, Georges. Introduction. Harrison, *Description* xv–xxxv.
———. Preface. Harrison, *Description* vii–xiv.
Furnivall, Frederick J. Introduction. Harrison, *Harrison's Description* iv–xlv.
Harrison, William. *The Description of England: The Classic Contemporary Account of Tudor Social Life*. Ed. Georges Edelen. 1968. New York: Dover, 1994. Print. Folger Shakespeare Lib.

———. *Harrison's Description of England in Shakespeare's Youth.* Ed. Frederick J. Furnivall. 3 vols. in 2. Vaduz: Kraus Reprint, 1965. Print. New Shakespeare Society Publications.

Hunter, G. K. *John Lyly: The Humanist as Courtier.* Cambridge: Harvard UP, 1962. Print.

———. *Lyly and Peele.* London: Longmans, 1968. Print.

Knight, G. Wilson. "Lyly." *Review of English Studies* 15 (1939): 146–63. Print.

Lindheim, Nancy R. "Lyly's Golden Legacy: *Rosalynde* and *Pandosto.*" *Studies in English Literature* 15.1 (1975): 3–20. Print.

Lyly, John. *The Complete Works of John Lyly.* Ed. R. W. Bond. 3 vols. Oxford: Clarendon, 1967. Print.

———. Euphues: The Anatomy of Wit *and* Euphues and His England. Ed. Morris William Croll and Harry Clemons. 1916. New York: Russell, 1964. Print.

———. *Euphues: The Anatomy of Wit. Elizabethan Fiction.* Ed. Robert Ashley and Edwin M. Moseley. New York: Rinehart, 1953. 85–158. Print.

McCulloch, J. R. *A Treatise on the Succession to Property Vacant by Death.* London: Longmans, 1848. Print.

Nash, Walter. *Rhetoric: The Wit of Persuasion.* Oxford: Blackwell, 1989. Print.

Reilly, Terry. "*King Lear*: The Kentish Forest and the Problem of Thirds." *Oklahoma City University Law Review* 26.1 (2001): 379–401. Print.

Saccio, Peter. *The Court Comedies of John Lyly: A Study in Allegorical Dramaturgy.* Princeton: Princeton UP, 1969. Print.

Catherine R. Eskin

Literary Figures: Lodge's *Rosalynd* in the Undergraduate Classroom

I love the Elizabethan romance, and many undergraduate students love it, too. But Thomas Lodge's *Rosalynd* (1590) is more than just a good read: it is a text that engages students in generic, stylistic, and cultural questions pertinent to the study of early modern England. Teachers typically couple Lodge's text with William Shakespeare's *As You Like It*. While such a unit has obvious appeal, I suggest that teachers reconsider the prevailing belief (espoused by early-twentieth-century Shakespeare scholars like W. W. Greg) that Lodge cannot stand on his own. Especially in nonmajor, undergraduate survey courses, *Rosalynd* can initiate students' considerations of the stylistic and cultural impact of English literature. Further, Lodge's representation of female speech makes for an engaging unit on women in the early modern period. Even within the confines of a single lesson, the returns for teaching *Rosalynd*, or any of the other Elizabethan short fiction writers, are big enough to make the effort worthwhile.

That effort begins with finding an available text appropriate for students. Lodge's romance is accessible on a material, as well as a critical, level. *Rosalynd* appears in at least three edited versions: Donald Beecher's, Brian Nellist's, and Edward Chauncey Baldwin's. Beecher's edition is inexpensive; it includes an extensive introduction with glosses at the foot of the page, as well as endnotes and a brief biography; Nellist's offers a far shorter introduction, textual and gloss notes that are printed at the foot of each page, and a brief bibliography; Baldwin's is a rather awkwardly typeset printing of an e-book available free from Project Gutenberg. This last version reveals the ease with which students might access the whole text or just parts for free—and how faculty members might create a packet of excerpts relatively painlessly. Only if I plan to devote at least two class days to *Rosalynd* do I require students to purchase the text (the less expensive Beecher edition); generally, I create a packet and leave the text on reserve.

When teaching selections of *Rosalynd*, I focus less on re-creating the milieu of the pastoral romance and more on the representation of female speech in the text. The sheer volume of female voice in Lodge's romance makes the study of female speech—and literary dialogue in general—easy to accomplish. I may cut most of the rustic affair between Montanus and Phebe (along with much of the verse), but I retain the pivotal female speeches in their entirety.

Lodge's construction of women's words forms a basis on which to build a lesson about women's roles (real and imagined) in early modern England. Those words say something about the ways that speech as social interaction might have been enacted in an ideal setting, and they also introduce the students to some of the more popular conventions of Elizabethan contemporary literature. I often assign students to research various aspects of cultural history. They create annotated bibliographies of primary and secondary materials and give informal presentations of their findings. These activities help the class become more conversant with the issues. In most cases I think the prescriptive writers offer the most controversial (or at least startling) material for discussions of gender. I use Juan Luis Vives's *Instruction of a Christian Woman* (1529) and Thomas Salter's *Mirror of Modesty* (1579) to invite student observations and facilitate informed comments. By reading contemporary nonfiction or historical commentary after we have spent at least one class period on the romance, students first observe the female characters' behavior in the text and then see how prescriptive writers envision behavior. I prefer that students discover the literature first and then begin to glean the historical and social implications on their own: once they have made an investment in the narrative, students approach the period-related readings or assigned research with more at stake. Sarah Mendelson and Patricia Crawford's *Women in Early Modern England* is a great place to start for more information about women during the period.

Vives's and Salter's diatribes introduce the controversies regarding the romance genre and show the connections between literary form and the feminine. To illustrate Elizabethan attitudes, I often assign selections from Roger Ascham, an educator imagining a male audience, who advises against romance reading because of the romance's supposed potential to effeminize readers. Exposing students to such prohibitions helps them realize that *Rosalynd* may be equated with a modern dime-store romance. Once they do, their reactions are generally reflective of their own cultural and academic awareness or experiences (some titillated, some shocked, some intrigued). I will sometimes ask students to explore definitions of the romance as a genre and consider it vis-à-vis modern conceptions of the form. If time is limited, I explain how the popular romance, often considered a commercial instead of a literary form, is frequently identified with not just the feminine but also the lower class, the uneducated, and the young, so that it is sadly underrepresented in classrooms (Newcomb 6). Lori Humphrey Newcomb, Helen Hackett, and Caroline Lucas have written informative and readable critical texts on the implications of these associations. Further, an explanation of these stereotypes about genre may allow students either to empathize or sympathize with the text's cultural position based on their own conceptions of cultural worth and their own relationships to nonelite fictions.

The terms of engagement I encourage include character, use of language, sociopolitical positioning of gender, Elizabethan textuality, and the power of the canon. I initially ask each student to choose a favorite character and then to find at least one textual passage to explain that choice. If I assign a modernized edition of Lodge's romance (Nellist; Beecher), many undergraduates enjoy the prospect of a "story" in prose and are not intimidated by my request that they choose a passage to discuss. Given the pivotal roles played by women in the narrative (especially in the abbreviated text I create), the most popular character choices are Rosalynd and Alinda. Both characters reflect their culture through their behavior, speech, and attitudes toward situations and other characters, though each represents a particular role prescribed by Elizabethan society. Rosalynd's virtual silence when she is clothed as a lady is augmented by her extensive use of nonverbal communication and performative gestures such as blushing. Lodge's description of her changes dramatically when she takes on the clothing of a page, though it still conjures the more idealized image of the chaste, silent, and obedient female. Alinda's self-presentation is more radical, and her mastery of rhetoric begs the question of the appropriateness of formal female education. The subtle and not-so-subtle differences between these two female characters offer an opportunity to contrast the characters' methods of social interaction.

While undergraduates tend to identify Rosalynd's (Ganymede's) banter with Rosader as the finest example of her verbal prowess, Rosalynd's first meditation ("Rosalind's Passion") is a passage much better suited to introduce discussions of both women's speech and the stylized prose of the period. The meditation as a form for character revelation seems awkward and strange to students. Euphuism initially irks them because of its repetitious rhythms, arcane terminology, and obscure similes. One way to overcome a class's biases is to introduce the rhetorical practice of arguing both sides of a question (*in utramque partem*), a device Lodge uses to identify a character's priorities and to question them. A teacher need not include an entire unit on early modern education or rhetorical exercises; only a cursory look at how writers used such a practice may reveal the depths of a character. Readers can sympathize more with Rosalynd when we recognize the complex social obligations that make her attraction to Rosader so potentially volatile: "But consider, Rosalind, his fortunes and thy present estate. Thou art poor and without patrimony, and yet the daughter of a prince, he a younger brother and void of such possessions as either might maintain thy dignities or revenge thy father's injuries" (Lodge 116).[1] The heroine here shows her practical side, her ability to calculate the feasibility of marrying Rosader. Historically, such an accounting of the hero's "worth" could be expected; her subsequent consideration of her father separates her from other romance heroines as the picture of filial love and duty (she considers not just her own desires, but her duty to her father). The difference—for both contemporary readers and postmodern ones—is her conclusion to "harbor [no] such servile conceits as to prize gold more than honor, or to measure a gentleman by his wealth, not by his virtues" (117). Further, during the course of this meditation, Rosalynd mentions classical gods (Cupid) and authors (Horace) and uses Latin phrases to illustrate her points. I will use these seemingly pretentious inclusions to point out Rosalynd's native intelligence: such references (examples of *copia*, or literary plenty) are the stock and trade of euphuism. In order to get students to reconsider the diction of the passage, I suggest that the more examples she uses, the more Rosalynd demonstrates her own imaginative power—a feat that also demonstrates Lodge's skill.

The female speaker who demonstrates her power immediately to students is Alinda. Her commanding style appeals to postmodern readers. Alinda is conscious of the mores and customs that command her silence but is not always willing to stay within their limits. The heading "Alinda's Oration to Her Father in Defense of Fair Rosalind" introduces a speech that is a masterful demonstration of a legal-political oration. (If I have had time to assign Lodge's biography, students may remember that Lodge had law training and that the speech seems to belong in a courtroom.) I outline the structure of the speech, from exordium to peroration, explaining how rhetoric was an important part of education during the period. We look first at the way that Alinda employs the modesty topos in her opening: "If, mighty Torismond, I offend in pleading for my friend, let the law of amity crave pardon for my boldness" (119). She first ingratiates herself by referring to her adversary as "mighty," then attempts to mollify both her father and her society as she speaks out in public—the modesty topos was requisite for all rhetorical presentations, but particularly for female orators. Once she makes that initial concession, Alinda charges ahead with her narration (which lays out expectations of women's behavior during the period), division, proof, and refutation. Her final peroration, the students realize, is the most bold. And her bluff is called—her father *does* banish her along with Rosalynd. Rhetorical figures such as epagoge, a Ciceronian form of inductive reasoning in which the speaker leads his or her hearer to agree to certain facts and hence assent to the main proposition, offer opportunities for intense linguistic and structural analyses.

If students recognize the connection between speech and character identity, they will also understand that words matter not only in Elizabethan literature but in Elizabethan culture more generally. Sometimes using the paratextual to reinforce that point, I will ask them to consider the headings that introduce readers to the various speeches: "Rosalind's Passion" and "Alinda's Oration to Her Father in Defense of Fair Rosalind" may reveal contemporary attitudes toward the passages (the headings are reproduced in both Beecher's and Nellist's editions). I sometimes offer students a facsimile of the original text to show them how the book would have looked to early modern readers. Explaining the different formats in Elizabethan printing (folio, quarto, and octavo) enables a discussion of the relative esteem in which a text was held, allowing again for discussions of genre and even canon. Issues of genre and canon become even more pressing when the class moves on to later readings.

If I couple my reading of Lodge with Shakespeare, my students want to extend our discussions of *Rosalynd*, disappointed that the characters of Shakespeare's *As You Like It* are so different. They are particularly distressed by the downsized and shifting character of Celia (Alinda in Lodge). A preference for the new power they feel when reading prose also makes them hesitant to enter Shakespeare's verse. This skittishness is exacerbated by the canonical status of the bard; most students have never even heard of Lodge. The transition between Lodge and Shakespeare, then, offers challenges and rewards. Genre is certainly the most obvious, but generic status and the related question of an author's canonicity also allow for a variety of solid discussions.

As a fan of the popular Elizabethan romance, I know that my enthusiasm for the subject can play an important role in the level of enthusiasm expressed by my students. I also know that if I introduce prose early in the survey course, students start to identify the development of the language, the genre, and the concept of fiction more broadly. They recognize that prose is worthy of critical and close reading. Word choice, tone, style, and structure become just as important in the reading of prose as in the reading of poetry and Renaissance drama. Students are able to study the cultural positions of women, as well as the consonances and dissonances between expectations for and enactments of gender roles during the period. And of course, there is a happy ending.

Note

1. All quotations are from the Beecher edition of *Rosalynde*.

Works Cited

Ascham, Roger. *The Schoolmaster*. 1570. Ed. Lawrence V. Ryan. Ithaca: Cornell UP, 1967. Print.

Hackett, Helen. *Women and Romance Fiction in the English Renaissance*. Cambridge: Cambridge UP, 2000. Print.

Lodge, Thomas. *Rosalynde*. Ed. Donald Beecher. Ottawa: Dovehouse, 1997. Print.

———. *Rosalynde*. Ed. Brian Nellist. Staffordshire: Ryburn, 1995. Print.

———. *Rosalynde*. Ed. Edward Chauncey Baldwin. Boston: Ginn, 1910. *Project Gutenberg*. 29 Nov. 2005. Web. 2 May 2009.

Lucas, Caroline. *Writing for Women: The Example of Woman as Reader in Eliza-bethan Romance.* Milton Keynes: Open UP, 1989. Print.

Mendelson, Sara, and Patricia Crawford. *Women in Early Modern England, 1550–1720.* Oxford: Clarendon, 1998. Print.

Newcomb, Lori Humphrey. *Reading Popular Romance in Early Modern En-gland.* New York: Columbia UP, 2002. Print.

Erin Murphy

Infectious Knowledge: Teaching the Educational Tracts of John Milton and Mary Astell

In her 1694 *A Serious Proposal to the Ladies*, Mary Astell argued for the value of a women's educational retreat, proclaiming, "As Vice is, so Vertue may be catching" (95). Her description of learned ladies as infectious agents who purify the English kingdom provides a vivid image with which to introduce students to the political power of education. Pairing Astell's *Proposal* with John Milton's 1644 *Of Education* reveals the particular potency of this image in imagining the circulation of knowledge in seventeenth-century England. In *Of Education,* Milton's ideal "institute of breeding" (408) reproduces proper Englishmen through education, protecting them from the influence of foreign tutors. Astell's proposed educational retreat for English ladies propagates virtue while providing an escape from the tumult of the marriage market and the indignities of fashion. Considering these two tracts together allows students to see how both reach far beyond which grammar text to use or how much exercise children require and extends to claims about the shape of the emerging English nation. For Milton, education defines and extends England's power. For Astell, it provides a new way for women to become active members of the nation. As pamphlet warriors who debated the century's major political crises, both Milton and Astell recognize the power unleashed by the mid-century print explosion. Through their educational tracts, they attempt to define and harness the energy of the emerging public sphere.

When an instructor introduces the relation of education to broader agendas of nationalism and religion and highlights the role of gender in this relation, the pairing of these tracts can provide fruitful ground for undergraduates at many different levels of study. In a composition or gateway course, these texts open up discussions of the politics of literacy. In early modern literature surveys or seminars, these works focus attention on the issue of gender in the seventeenth-century literature of controversy. Finally, reading Milton and Astell together allows students of women's writing to consider female authors' active participation in England's exploding print culture.

Astell's direct print attacks on Milton demonstrate that, despite their unequal status in our canon, both writers were vociferous participants in the political conflicts of their time. Although publishing twenty years after Milton's death, Astell still assailed his antimonarchical politics and his belief in the potential of marriage. She accused him of hypocritically calling for the freeing of the people from the tyranny of kingship while failing to decry the enslavement of wives in marriage.[1] A comparison of their educational tracts reveals how the realm of knowledge was seen as yet another political battlefield. For these authors, both education and publication have the power to transform the nation through the spread of knowledge. Thus, an investigation of their works shows their efforts to reproduce virtue not only through exemplary Englishmen and infectious ladies but also through print.

The Ends of Learning

Through its clear articulation of a religious agenda, Milton's famous claim that "[t]he end then of learning is to repair the ruins of our first parents by regaining to know God aright" (366–67) can launch a productive discussion of the goals of these two tracts. If students have read carefully, however, they will quickly point out that Milton's plan has more earthly objectives as well. As Barbara Lewalski explains, the tract posits "both a religious and a civic humanist purpose for education" ("Milton" 209). Starting with Milton's claim for the reparative capacity of education, I ask students to identify the mix of religious and civic goals in his text, and then I call on them to repeat the same exercise with Astell's work. Ideally, this work should be conducted in small groups of four to five students. Through comparative close reading, students can begin to consider how gender issues drive the authors' seemingly parallel agendas apart.

Like Milton, Astell imagines education as a postlapsarian remedy, promising the ladies a "Happy Retreat! which will be the introducing you into such a Paradise as your Mother Eve forfeited" and arguing its benefits for all: "Having gain'd an entrance into Paradise themselves, they [the educated women] wou'd both shew the way, and invite all others to partake of their felicity" (74, 101). Though Milton's and Astell's different mobilizations of "our first parents" warrant discussion, their parallel descriptions of the redemptive force of education are easy to recognize.

Pointing to the civic commonalities of the two works, however, proves more complex and often leads to a much more varied set of responses from the student groups. Astell has no trouble finding a place for women in her deployment of Genesis, but the tradition of citizenship and leadership that Milton follows leaves little space for the ladies. Though both texts expand the role of education well beyond the salvation of the individual, their disparate methods reflect a gendered relation to the English nation. After having the small groups report back to the whole class, I ask the entire group why it is harder to compare the civic agendas than the religious ones. This leads the students to reexamine both their own assumptions and those of the authors about the meaning of *civic*.

Just a page after declaring the underlying religious objective of learning to "know God aright," Milton articulates his ends more concretely: "I call therefore a complete and generous education that which fits a man to perform justly, skillfully and magnanimously all the offices, both private and public, of peace and war" (377–79). If the religious agenda of education is to redress the Fall of mankind, what problems does this second version address? A close reading of the list of ill-prepared clergymen, lawyers, and statesmen (375–76) reveals that a lack of "true generous breeding" (375) has left them without virtue, vulnerable to the sway of money and flattery. Here, Milton fuses the Christian goal of redemption with the explicitly political goals articulated in the Greek tradition.[2] Young men become good Christians and good citizens in the same "spatious house" (379).

Despite her claims for women's education, Astell does not imagine learning as preparing women for the "public offices" of clergymen, lawyers, or statesmen, a point she later makes explicit in part two of her proposal:

"Women have no business with the Pulpit, the Bar or St. Stephen's Chapel" (196). Unlike Milton, who never mentions education's importance to the family, Astell asserts education's value for the performance of women's "private offices" as wives and mothers. She contends that "if a Mother be discreet and knowing as well as devout, she has many opportunities of giving such a Form and Season to the tender Mind of the Child, as will shew its good effects thro' all the stages of his Life" (106). Students often criticize Astell's emphasis on women's roles as wives and mothers. Such a response is invaluable because it prevents students from idealizing Astell's position, allowing them to see that contemporary gender roles constrain both writers.

Asking students to identify other kinds of breeding in both texts helps them consider whether Astell strands women in the family. Close analysis of Milton's passage on the benefits of travel reveals yet another level of his civic agenda. He argues that education will enable young Englishmen abroad "to enlarge experience, and make wise observation," while simultaneously protecting them from learning foreign "principles" that would undermine their virtue (414). No longer will they return as "mimics, apes, and Kicshoes," copying the French (414). Instead, he suggests that their presence will cause other nations "to visit us for their breeding, or else to imitate us in their own Country" (414). Proper education reverses the flow of influence. Instead of striving to become like others, the English become international breeders, reproducing their image within and beyond their own nation.[3] Thus, Milton's academy breeds both directly, by teaching students, and indirectly, through the example of those students.

If Milton imagines Englishmen abroad breeding through their example, does Astell imagine a similar exemplary role for her ladies? Is it only through their wombs that women create others like themselves? Though a realm of physical chastity, her retirement does have the potential for reproduction, as an institution that will both "stock the Kingdom with pious and prudent Ladies" (76) and "by that substantial Piety and solid Knowledge, fit us to propagate Religion when we return to the World" (100).[4] Through her language of infection and propagation, Astell creatively extends women's ability to reproduce, broadening the sphere of female influence beyond the family.

If one wishes to grapple fully with *A Serious Proposal*'s implications for women's influence, however, it is important to remind students that Astell does not seem to accept the same division between public and private offices that Milton does. She explains that the retirement "shall have a double aspect, being not only a Retreat from the World for those who desire that advantage, but likewise, an institution and previous discipline, to fit us to do good in it" (73). This "double aspect" seems to contest the very categories of the "private and public," categories Milton adopts and adapts from the ancient model of the *oikos* and the *polis*.[5] Milton's "spatious house" serves as a temporary stop for males, ages twelve to twenty-one. Astell's retreat serves a similar purpose for some, but for others it provides a permanent community.[6] As neither the private space of the family nor the public space of the *polis*, this society of women exists beyond the bounds of Milton's categories.

Still, Astell insists that her retreat does not exist in isolation: "It shall not so cut you off from the world as to hinder you from bettering and improving it, but rather qualify you to do it the greatest Good" (76). Though she excludes women from many "public offices," her own act of publication sanctions their ability to reach beyond the retreat, doing "good" in the world through the proliferation of texts.

The Text as Antidote

A close comparison of these texts' first paragraphs provides a wonderful opportunity to introduce the concept of an emerging public sphere and to discuss the ways that gender could determine one's access to it. The explosion of publication in the seventeenth century created a space in which those who held no "public office" could debate public concerns. As David Zaret argues, the Habermasian forum of public opinion played a vital role in English politics by the 1640s: "It was printing that brought Parliamentary debates on religion and politics into the streets, and printing also presented Parliament with popular views on these topics" (218). Milton, by contesting monarchic authority, and Astell, by supporting it, both participated in this contentious world of print. The openings of their educational tracts reveal their consciousness of the increasing power of this realm, as they strategically position their texts by addressing a particular reader or readers.

Of Education first appeared anonymously and without a title page, publisher's name, or date, but it did specify its intended recipient, through its address "to Master Samuel Hartlib." Born in Prussia, Samuel Hartlib studied at Cambridge and moved to England by 1628. By translating and publishing the works of John Amos Comenius, Hartlib promoted the discussion and reform of English educational practices. Thus, by naming

Hartlib, Milton responds not only to a particular individual but to the namesake of the "Hartlib circle," a group who read, wrote, and debated about education.

Students should consider the ambivalence of Milton's claim that "to search what many modern *Janua's* and *Didactics* more than ever I shall read, have projected, my inclination leads me not" (364–66), which suggests that he has neither read the works of Hartlib's mentor Comenius nor wishes to engage their philosophies.[7] Milton claims authority through his connection to Hartlib, but simultaneously insists on his own independence:

> Nor should the laws of any private friendship have prevailed with me to divide thus, or transpose former thoughts, but that I see those aims, those actions, which have won you with me the esteem of a person sent hither by some good providence from a far country to be the occasion and the incitement of great good to this island. (363)

Milton asserts that his personal relationship has become public, taking on both national and international dimensions. By emphasizing Hartlib's reputation beyond England, Milton places his comments on the world stage. His ability to move both within and without the Hartlib circle marks his position of power as a writer.

Astell, whose opinion has apparently been solicited by no one, declares that "I therefore persuade myself" that the *Proposal* will find an audience (51). In stark contrast to Milton's address to a definitive Master Hartlib, Astell's address to "the Ladies" suggests a far less distinct recipient of her text. Hartlib is a writer, translator, educational philosopher, and disciple of Comenius, but who are "the Ladies" and how does Astell characterize them? Astell's apology for the "rudeness" of her proposal, "which goes upon a supposition that there is something amiss" in her female readers, points to her peculiar relation to her explicit audience (56). Unlike Milton, who writes about the education of youth, Astell writes directly to those she intends to be educated. By engaging "the Ladies" in reflection on their own intellectual cultivation, Astell calls into being and proposes to nurture her audience.

It is beneficial to discussions of how Astell's text begins to create the community of women it describes if her circle of female associates is mentioned. Ruth Perry details how Astell's wealthy, female neighbors in Chelsea provided her financial support, stimulating conversation, access to books, and social standing, and she also traces Astell's influence on later women writers, such as Lady Mary Wortley Montagu, Lady Damaris Masham, and Lady Mary Lee Chudleigh (265–81). Astell experienced the fecundity of a community of learned ladies, and her text both performs this propagation and attempts to institutionalize it.

Even as both authors proclaim their distance from a community of experts, we can see how their language betrays their group identifications. Reconsider Milton's poke at Comenius—"To tell you therefore what I have benefited herein among old renowned authors, I shall spare; and to search what many modern *Janua's* and *Didactics* more than ever I shall read, have projected, my inclination leads me not" (364–66)—in relation to Astell's claim about her proposal: "The very offer is a sufficient inducement; nor does it need the set-off's of *Rhetorick* to recommend it, were I capable, which yet I am not, of applying them with the greatest force" (52). Though critics debate whether Milton's prose can be described properly as "Latinate," his placement of the main clauses "I shall spare" and "my inclination leads me not" after the subordinate clauses reflect his facility with Latin word order.[8] Milton's Latin writings demonstrate his particular mastery of the language, but familiarity with Latin syntax was common to male writers trained in grammar schools and universities. Despite Astell's self-effacement, students will also recognize the rhetorical skill of her sentence structure, as she piles on irony through an accretion of subordinate clauses. Though Astell depicts the unnecessary use of rhetoric and foreign languages as a means of keeping knowledge from women, it is crucial to remind students that the difference between the two writers' syntax also reflects a shift in English prose from the 1640s to the 1690s. Astell's embrace of plain language connects her to the power of royalist insiders, as much as it marks her as an "uneducated" woman who knows only English, French, and some Latin.

When Milton wrote his tract, he was running a small academy with a handful of students. Astell had never taught when she wrote her proposal but eventually ran a small charity school for girls, funded by her aristocratic female friends. The fact that Milton wrote as a schoolmaster, while Astell wrote to become a schoolmistress, exemplifies the different functions of their texts. Milton addresses the ready-made audience of the Hartlib circle, which solicited his participation in its conversation, while Astell not only advocates the creation of female intellectuals through education but also begins the process through her performative language of address.

Whether they use images of breeding, imitation, infection, or propagation, Milton and Astell both understand the power of education as a form of social reproduction. By bringing their arguments into print, they also acknowledge that the public sphere extends the circulation of knowledge beyond the classroom. Milton uses the space of the page to consolidate and export a national identity for England. Astell uses it to provide aristocratic women a way to propagate without having children. Through education and publication, both make knowledge infectious.

Notes

1. The seeming paradox of Astell's royalism and her advocacy for women has long been a central concern of Astell scholarship. For a summary of the criticism as well as crucial interventions, see Gallagher; Weil.

2. Dorian notes Plato's particular influence (Milton 377n55).

3. On Milton's educational imperialism, see Viswanathan.

4. On Astell and chastity, see Perry 120–48.

5. On Milton's revision of the ancient household, see Norbrook.

6. Astell initially describes her retreat as like a monastery but immediately changes terms to avoid charges of popery.

7. Though Hartlib solicited Milton's text, he did not write a preface to it, as he often did, raising questions about how favorably he and his fellow reformers received *Of Education*. Hartlib did, however, circulate the tract among his associates. Regarding Milton's relation to Hartlib's circle, see Sirluck; Raylor; and Lewalski (*Life*; "Milton").

8. See Corns; Hale.

Works Cited

Astell, Mary. *A Serious Proposal to the Ladies, Parts I and II.* 1694, 1697. Ed. Patricia Springborg. Peterborough: Broadview, 2002. Print.

Corns, Thomas N. *The Development of Milton's Prose Style.* Oxford: Oxford UP, 1982. Print.

Gallagher, Catherine. "Embracing the Absolute: Margaret Cavendish and the Politics of the Female Subject in Seventeenth-Century England." *Early Women Writers: 1600–1720.* Ed. Anita Pacheco. London: Longman, 1998. Print.

Hale, John. *Milton's Languages: The Impact of Multilingualism on Style.* Cambridge: Cambridge UP, 1997. Print.

Lewalski, Barbara. *The Life of John Milton.* Oxford: Blackwell, 2000. Print.

———. "Milton and the Hartlib Circle: Educational Projects and Epic *Paideia*." *Literary Milton: Text, Pretext, Context.* Ed. Diana Trevino Benet and Michael Lieb. Pittsburgh: Duquesne UP, 1994. 202–19. Print.

Milton, John. *Of Education.* Ed. Donald Dorian. *Complete Prose Works of John Milton.* Don M. Wolfe, gen. ed. Vol. 2. New Haven: Yale UP, 1959. 357–414. Print.

Norbrook, David. *Writing the English Republic: Poetry, Rhetoric and Politics, 1627–1660.* Cambridge: Cambridge UP, 2000. Print.

Perry, Ruth. *The Celebrated Mary Astell: An Early English Feminist.* Chicago: U of Chicago P, 1986. Print.

Raylor, Timothy. "New Light on Milton and Hartlib." *Milton Quarterly* 27 (1993): 19–31. Print.

Sirluck, Ernest. "*Of Education.*" Milton 184–216.

Viswanathan, Gauri. "Milton and Education." *Milton and the Imperial Vision.* Ed. Balachandra Rajan and Elizabeth Sauer. Pittsburgh: Duquesne UP, 1999. 273–93. Print.

Weil, Rachel. *Political Passions: Gender, the Family and Political Argument in England, 1680–1714.* Manchester: Manchester UP, 1999. Print.

Zaret, David. "Religion, Science, and Printing in the Public Spheres in Seventeenth-Century England." *Habermas and the Public Sphere.* Ed. Craig Calhoun. Cambridge: MIT P, 1992. 212–35. Print.

Deborah Uman

Translation, Nationalism, and Imperialism: Teaching Aphra Behn's "Essay on Translated Prose" and *A Discovery of New Worlds*

Translation in Early Modern England

When students see the topic of translation listed on a syllabus, they are often puzzled. For many undergraduates, translators are transparent. Even students who realize that the *Iliad* and *Candide* were not written in English rarely give the translators of these works a second thought. To introduce the topic of translation to students of early modern literature requires redefining their time-honored beliefs about originality and authorship, a redefinition that is, I would suggest, essential to an understanding of the English Renaissance. Because of the self-conscious project to revive classical culture, the practice of translation was crucial throughout early modern Europe. Seeing themselves as active participants in the Renaissance—in the rebirth of culture—writers were aware of the weighty task of carrying the glories of classical Greece and Rome into a modern, Christian setting. Similarly, the debate over translating the Bible into the vernacular was a crucial component of pre- and post-Reformation theology.[1] Translations of contemporary works were also common, and English writers admitted both a sense of inferiority to and competition with authors from the perceived cultural meccas of Italy and France.

Although translators of every century have questioned the validity of their tasks, these questions were particularly acute for writers who confronted at every turn their debt both to foreign innovators and to past masters. Before the late seventeenth century, this potential sense of inferiority was often compounded by a belief in the inadequacy of the English language compared with Latin and Greek or with other European vernaculars. In the prologue to his 1513 version of Vergil's *Aeneid*, written in "the language of Scottis natioun," Gavin Douglas comments that "Besyde our Latyn our language is imperfite," noting that Latin has more synonyms than Scots. With fewer exact correspondences at his disposal, Douglas relies on additional words to capture Vergil's sense, and his translation doubles the original's lines, replacing Vergil's hexameter with two lines of twenty syllables forming a rhymed couplet. For Thomas Hoby, the translator of Castiglione's *Book of the Courtier*, it is Englishmen themselves who are inferior to men of other nations because of their "barbarous tongue" and lack of classical learning, and he advocates the translation of Latin and Greek authors so that his countrymen may "perchaunce in time become as famous in Englande, as the learned men of other nations have been and presently are" (6–7).

Despite this apparent inferiority complex, early modern translations are also marked by a patriotic spirit. Both Douglas and Hoby couch their sentiments about the inadequacy of English (or Scots) within a discussion of how their projects will elevate both their languages and their nations, which language is seen as representing. Similarly, Richard Stanyhurst justifies his 1582 translation of the *Aeneid* by explaining that he is following Roger Ascham's suggestion that university students "applie theyre wittes in bewtifying oure English language with heroical verses" (137). He also claims that he is not "embeazling" the work of Vergil but rather that he is trying to honor English and "to advaunce thee riches of oure speeche" (138). Writing a century later, John Dryden displays a similar patriotism; his decision to translate not only the classics but also the works of Geoffrey Chaucer underscores his belief that English has finally achieved greatness.

Of particular interest during the sixteenth century is England's position on foreign countries and people. Writers of educational tracts point out the importance of regularizing English so foreigners will be able to learn English easily and so the language will set England apart from other nations. Similarly, many translators were eager to prove Englishmen comparable in terms of literary skill and linguistic ability to their Greek and

Roman predecessors and their continental counterparts while distinguishing themselves in terms of religion and character. Responding to Protestant opinions of Italians, John Harington uses the preface to his translation of Ludovico Ariosto's *Orlando Furioso* to defend the Italian romance both by comparing it to the *Aeneid* and pointing to its allegorical qualities. While reminding his reader that he is following in the tradition of great translators of Italian literature, Harington also explains that in the lascivious sections of the poem the author meant "to breed detestation and not delection" (11). In addition, Harington concludes each book of *Orlando* with his own commentary on the moral, historical, and allegorical meanings of the preceding episodes. Harington's "Briefe Apologie of Poetrie and of the Author and Translator of This Poem" reveals the predicament faced by translators who valued highly the cultural work of Italy but felt compelled to defend their work against fears such works were corrupted by the papist beliefs of their creators. On the one hand, Harington translates his Catholic predecessor into a generic Christian who writes "Christianly" and fills his romance with exhortation, doctrine, and example. Here Harington avoids distinguishing between Catholic and Protestant. On the other hand, Harington establishes his own Englishness by invoking an English literary tradition that goes back to Chaucer (whose writings are admired in England even though his words and sense "incurreth . . . the reprehension of flat scurrilitie" [12]) and culminates in the writings of a model Protestant—Philip Sidney, whom Harington frequently invokes as part of his defense of Ariosto. Harington's shifts throughout his preface suggest that even as translation "carries over" cultural commodities from one nation into another, it simultaneously establishes cultural, linguistic, and religious differences between countries.

While Harington takes great pains to defend his translation of poetic "Italian toyes" (15), translations of every sort proliferated during the early modern period. Although it is difficult to generalize about the differences between prose and verse translations, typically prose translations were more concerned with the often weighty subject matter of the original, whereas verse translations tended to be more interested in issues of style and artistry. Because prose translators did not need to worry about translating rhyme and meter, they were also more likely to produce what John Dryden called "metaphrase"—a close translation of the original (237); however, the most famous and respected prose translators, such as Thomas North, Philemon Holland, and John Florio, rejected what John

Denhem described as the "servile" practice of word-for-word translation (qtd. in Steiner 63). Critics frequently highlight the distinct Englishness of these translations, which is seen in everything from the use of colloquialisms to the transformation of a character from a Greek statesman into a perfect English gentleman.[2] Hoby, in his "Epistle of the Translator," points to the importance of translations such as his rendition of *The Book of the Courtier*, arguing that translation furthers learning for those unschooled in Latin and hoping that "we perchaunce in time become as famous in Englande, as the learned men of other nations have ben and presently are" (7). North suggests that English princes (and queens) have already achieved this level of greatness and—because of their religion— serve as even better exemplars than those presented in his translation of Plutarch. In his dedication to Elizabeth, he flatters the queen by presenting her as the logical conclusion of Plutarch's examples:

> Then well may the Readers thinke, if they have done this for heathen Kings, what should we doe for Christian Princes? If they have done this for glorye, what shoulde we doe for religion? If they have done this without hope of heaven, what should we doe that looke for immortalitie? And so adding the encouragement of these examples, to the forwardness of their owne dispositions: what serve is there in warre, what honor in peace, which they will not be ready to doe, for their worthy Queene? (iv)

Florio's half-hearted humility and North's language of comparison and competition underscore the nationalist goals often associated with translation. During an age of rapidly increasing exploration and "discovery," nationalist goals become almost indistinguishable from colonialist agendas. Over the last few decades, translation theorists have been exploring connections between translation and imperialism, and postcolonialist critics from various academic disciplines have argued for a view of translation as a tool of conquest and suppression.[3] This view exposes the parallels between the violent subjugation and linguistic domination that occur when nations meet as oppressor and oppressed, when native texts are translated into the language of the colonizer to facilitate the "education" of conquered people. In early modern translations of classical or vernacular texts, the exchange occurs between countries of relatively equal stature; thus there is no realistic threat of linguistic annihilation. Yet evidence of national difference and patriotic agenda remains. Because translations and translation prefaces frequently explore, either implicitly or explicitly, the differences among the source and target language, text, and country, the study of translation provides an excellent vehicle for discussing multicultural concerns and introducing postcolonial theory to students of early modern prose.

Aphra Behn's "Essay on Translated Prose" and *A Discovery of New Worlds*

Aphra Behn's translation of Bernard le Bovier de Fontenelle's *Entretiens sur la pluralité des mondes*, *A Discovery of New Worlds*, and the attached preface, "Essay on Translated Prose," provide excellent examples of how multicultural and nationalist concerns are reflected in translation and writings about translation. While Fontenelle's text is ostensibly concerned with the possibility of life on planets in outer space, its theme, highlighted by Behn's altered title, parallels Behn's own interest in the discoveries of earthly new worlds, and in her preface Behn also comments obliquely on the status of English as a language of imperialism in the early modern age of exploration and conquest. Like many of her predecessors, Aphra Behn discusses her theory of translation in concert with a discussion of linguistic, cultural, and national difference; thus, these two pieces work well in a unit or course on nationalism and colonialism.

For an upper-level course, secondary criticism is an invaluable tool for helping students understand the complex social relationships that characterize the expanding empires of the sixteenth and seventeenth centuries. In my experience, undergraduates have few opportunities to wade through critical material, and they find these assignments daunting and intimidating. It is useful initially to walk students through a piece that introduces important concepts and then to ask them to find concrete illustrations of these concepts within a literary text. Toward that end, I begin with Benedict Anderson's *Imagined Communities*. Despite Anderson's focus on the late eighteenth and early nineteenth centuries, his discussion of the impact of the Protestant Reformation and the accompanying validation of European vernaculars on the development of a national consciousness are clearly relevant to early modern studies. Moreover, his concept of imagined communities, linked by religion, language, dynasty, and finally by print culture, is foundational in the field of postcolonial studies and thus important for students to understand before reading more time-specific secondary material. To help students unpack Anderson's dense language, I start with a response paper or in-class assignment asking students to explain Anderson's ideas about national consciousness and how he links "the dawn of the age of nationalism but the dusk of religious modes of thought" (11). We also discuss Anderson's points about the vernacular and consider the relevance of his arguments for the period before the eighteenth-century commodification of print culture. In addition to chapters from *Imagined Communities*, I have assigned the introduction to Richard Helgerson's *Forms of Nationhood*. His argument that in the sixteenth century a sense of shared language was instrumental to the construction of an English national identity helps students understand Anderson's ideas about language and shows them the difficulties of fixing the origin of nationalism at a specific time or place. Students tend to find Helgerson's writing more accessible than Anderson's but generally are not yet ready to use the theory to develop their own ideas about the relevant literature.

Taking small steps, I then ask students to define nationalism as they see it working in Behn's "Essay on Translated Prose" and to base their definitions on specific textual examples of their choosing. The students find much to choose from in Behn's essay, and most of their examples focus on issues of language, such as Behn's claim that Italian is easier than French to translate into English because "the nearer the Genious and Humour of two Nations agree, the Idioms of their Speech are the nearer; and every Body knows that there is more Affinity between the English and Italian People, than the English and the French" (74). Students have noted that Behn's discussion of linguistic differences between the French and English languages reveals her preference for the English national character, which is so distinct from its neighbor and frequent enemy:

> But as the French do not value a plain Suit without a Garniture, they are not satisfied with the Advantages they have, but confound their own Language with needless Repetitions and Tautologies; and by a certain Rhetorical Figure, peculiar to themselves, imply twenty Lines, to express what an English Man would say, with more Ease and Sense in five; and this is the great Misfortune of translating French into English: If one endeavors to make it English Standard, it is no Translation. If one follows their Flourishes and Embroideries, it is worse than French Tinsel. (76)

In this example, Behn's definition of Englishness is apparent in its opposition to the frivolousness of the French, providing an illustration of Helgerson's point that "meaning arises not from central core identity but rather at a margin of differences. Self-definition comes from the not-self, from the alien other" (22).

Another passage, less obviously patriotic but still interested in national difference, is Behn's warning to Englishmen not to be too much like the French:

> It is Modish to Ape the French in every thing: Therefore, we not only naturalize their words, but words they steal from other Languages. I wish in this and several other things, we had a little more of the Italian and Spanish Humour, and did not chop and change our language, as we do our Cloths, at the Pleasure of every French Tailor. (75)

Behn's critique of the contamination of the English language, now littered with borrowings from the French, offers students an illustration of Helgerson's contrast between the rhetoric of nationhood, which he describes as "a rhetoric of uniformity and wholeness," and the denial of nationhood, which "is experienced as a denial of selfhood" (22). That Behn includes herself with the plural pronoun "we" suggests that she too has not succeeded in establishing either a unified English language or a unified England, whereas the French, she says, through money, weapons, and strategy, "have made their Language very universal of late." Behn sarcastically suggests that the French should be commended for this "[a]ccident, which they owe to the greatness of their King and their own Industry," even as she hints of a future shift in power, noting that "it may fall out hereafter to be otherwise" (75). I often include *Henry V* in my nationalism unit, and students quickly recognize the combative nature of Behn's comment and its reflection of the national enmity between two countries that is portrayed so vividly in the history plays. Also of interest for the study of early modern prose is Behn's belief in the universality of the French language and her equation of this development to national power. Philosophers of the seventeenth century, including John Wilkins and George Dalgarno, were toiling to invent a universal language that could express "the shape of reality" (Greenblatt 28). Behn's translation, with its focus on natural philosophy and concern to tell the story of the natural world in terms accessible to the general populace, fits squarely into the work of the Royal Society, which had commissioned Wilkins's *An Essay Towards a Real Character and a Philosophical Language*, and it reveals some of the pragmatic concerns underlying the more esoteric goals of seventeenth-century scientific inquiry.[4] A universal language would certainly facilitate colonialism. Moreover, as Behn seems to recognize, if

English replaced French as a "very universal" language, this would clearly demonstrate the increased national power of England.[5]

While students are typically unfamiliar with the notion of a created universal language, they have much to say about the near universality of English and the political power that this reflects. Their views may differ on an array of relevant issues, but students have all noticed that children in other countries learn other languages (typically English), that the president of the United States can only speak to other world leaders with the help of an interpreter, and, as one student pointed out, that the Miss Universe Pageant is hosted by an English-speaking celebrity no matter where the pageant actually takes place. At this point it is useful to discuss the early status of Latin as the language of the educated elite that facilitated communication throughout Europe. I have also mentioned the Esperanto movement, with which students are usually unfamiliar, if only to contrast a failed international effort, which had the lofty goal of uniting people and countries on "the basis of their common humanity," to the worldwide dominance of English, which is based on a history of social and economic imperialism (Kim 136). In a post-9/11 world, the topic of nationalism has become particularly pertinent, and students are often surprised to see such pressing issues raised in literature that initially seems foreign and strange. I find that reading critical theory on the topic of nationalism also gives students a more sophisticated understanding of the events they witness on a day-to-day basis.

After students feel comfortable with the vocabulary and concepts of postcolonial theory, I ask them to build on their knowledge in a more open-ended research project in which they read secondary material on imperialist practices of the late seventeenth and early eighteenth centuries and develop their own analyses of Behn's work. Although there is little published material on the *Discovery of New Worlds* and the "Essay on Translated Prose," works such as Laura Brown's chapter "The Romance of Empire: *Oroonoko* and the Trade in Slaves" in her *Ends of Empire* help students think about Behn's prose within the framework of the growing slave trade and the accompanying criticism of slavery, while Mary Louise Pratt's *Imperial Eyes: Travel Writing and Transculturation* provides additional ways to consider the role of science in Europe's move toward "planetary consciousness," characterized by "the descriptive apparatuses of natural history" (15).[6] Reading Behn's translation in these contexts illuminates connections between translation and imperialism, demonstrating how an "old world" view of national difference, in which one county establishes itself in contrast to another, relatively equal country, serves as a precursor for an "imperialist" view of national difference and dominance.

Although Behn uses much of her preface to describe the differences between the English and the French, students always notice an almost off-hand comment that Behn includes in her characterization of French as an overly ornate language: "I do not say this so much to condemn the French, as to praise our own Mother-Tongue, for what we think a Deformity, they may think a Perfection; as the Negroes of Guinney think us as ugly as we think them" (76). Despite its argument for cultural relativism, Behn's mention of the appearance of the "Negroes of Guinney" departs abruptly from her discussion of French language practices, even as it again serves as a reminder of the nationalist sentiment particularly apparent during this period of imperialist expansion. Behn qualifies her snub by reminding her readers that beauty is simply a question of standards and perspective; however, her shift from the subject of language to that of physical appearance seems somewhat insulting in that it implies that while the French are loquacious and excessive, the Africans of Guinea have no language that is even worth discussing let alone translating. Moreover, although "An Essay on Translated Prose" focuses primarily on France and England, countries on relatively equal political footing, Behn's somewhat chaotic linguistic history of Europe recognizes the trend of conquering nations imposing their languages on vanquished peoples. In defending her claim that Italian is nearer to English than French, Behn characterizes Italian as a mixture of Latin "and the Language of the Goths, Vandals, and other Northern Nations, who over-ran the Roman Empire, and conquer'd its Language with its Provinces" (74). Students finally recognize that the topic of Fontenelle's original work, the discovery of new worlds in space, mirrors the exploration of "new worlds" taking place throughout Africa and the Americas, exploration that Behn actively participated in and described.[7]

This same interest in other cultures appears throughout Behn's translation of *A Discovery of New Worlds*. Reproducing Fontenelle's first-person narration, Behn cross-dresses as Fontenelle's persona who recounts his conversation with the ever-so-curious and credulous marquiese. In their first exchange, they discuss the differences between night and day, comparing them to the differences between women with light and dark complexions:

> I confess, said she, the Day must yield to such a Night; the day which resembles a fair Beauty, which though more sparkling, is not so charming as one of a brown Complexion, who is a true Emblem of the Night. You are very generous, Madam, said I, to give the advantage to the brown, you who are so admirably fair your self: Yet without dispute,

> day is the most beautiful thing in Nature; and most of the Heroines in
> Romances, which are modeled after the most perfect *Idea* fancy can
> represent by the most ingenious of mankind, and are generally de-
> scribed to be fair. (94)

With long sentences that are choppy but certainly not repetitive, Behn
does seem to strive for a balance between her understanding of the English plain style and the French ornate style. Here she translates an early
conversation in which the male speaker uses literary allusions to prove the
universally superior beauty of pale women. That the female speaker should
champion women of a brown or dark complexion recalls Behn's earlier
statement about the "Negroes of Guinney" and may even suggest that
women are capable of a more sympathetic view of racial difference.

In a subsequent conversation the marquiese asks about the possibility
that there are men in the moon, to which her companion and teacher
replies:

> I do not believe there are Men there, Madam, but some other odd
> sort of Creatures: Pray, Madam, consider but how much the Face of
> Nature is chang'd betwixt this and *China*. . . . When one travels to-
> wards the new discovered World of *America*, &c. and finds the Inhab-
> itants there to be hardly Men, but rather a kind of Brutes in Humane
> shape, and that not perfect neither, so that could we travel to the Orb
> of the Moon, I do not think we should find Men and Women there.
> (120–21)

The narrator goes on for almost twenty more lines, repeating and elabo-
rating his point that the inhabitants of the moon, like those of other
earthly worlds, could not possibly be as rational and wise as European
mankind. His repetitions and use of multiple analogies and extended descriptions recall Behn's earlier criticism of French verbosity. Meanwhile,
the marquiese barely gets a word in edgewise; when she finally does, her
comment seems, in comparison, not only more concise but more compas-
sionate than her instructor's:

> We are then secure enough . . . that the Inhabitants of the Moon will
> never guess what we are; but I wish we could attain to the knowledge
> of them; for I must confess it makes me uneasie to think there are
> Inhabitants in the Moon, and yet I cannot so much as fansie what
> kind of Creatures they are. (121)

With a reference to her inadequate imagination, the marquiese shows the
inadequacy of Fontenelle's excessive comparisons, subtly criticizing her

teacher as Behn does more directly in her preface. Explaining that among the speakers it is the woman "whom he feigns never to have heard of any such thing as Philosophy before," Behn suggests that Fontenelle must create a complete fabrication in order to depict a woman of such limited learning and intellect, and she follows this observation with a litany of reasons why he failed in his design:

> for endeavouring to render this part of Natural Philosophy familiar, he hath turned it into Ridicule; he hath pushed his wild Notion of the Plurality of Worlds to that height of Extravagancy, that he most certainly will confound those Readers, who have not Judgment and Wit to distinguish between what is truly solid (or, at least, probably) and what is trifling and airy; and there is no less Skill and Understanding required in this, than in comprehending the whole Subjects he treats of. And for his Lady Marquiese, he makes her say a great many very silly things, tho' sometimes she makes Observations so learned, that the greatest Philosophers in Europe could make no better. (77)

While I would hesitate to equate the Marquiese with Behn, just as I remind my students that the text's first-person narrator is not Fontenelle, the difference between teacher and student highlights some of the differences of nationality, gender, and position between the author and translator of this work. Moreover, their perspectives show a sophisticated understanding of the complex issues surrounding the exploration and colonization of new worlds. Behn's preface read in concert with her translation seems to critique imperialist attitudes toward native people while upholding an attitude of nationalist superiority.

Looking at these two texts in combination with other translations and translation prefaces also reveals the widespread fascination with European exploration as well as the subtle connections between translation and nationalism. Florio's 1603 translation of Montaigne's *Essays,* with its famous sections "Of Cannibals" and "Of Coaches," offers students a more fully developed argument for cultural relativism. Notably, in his dedicatory epistle to the translation, Florio describes his challenging task by comparing himself both to an unfortunate explorer, who is "sea-tosst, wether-beaten, shippe-wrackt, almost drowned" and to "a captived Canniball fattend against my death" (3, 4). These metaphors reflect the complex subject position of a translator vis-à-vis the original author and the hoped-for patrons, and they suggest that Florio himself thought of the translation process as a type of dangerous but illuminating multicultural encounter. More explicitly, Richard Eden translated several travel narratives, including Pietro Martire d'Anghiera's *Decades of the Newe Worlde* (1555), to which he affixed a patriotic preface urging the English to explore the Americas and establish their own empire in imitation of the noble efforts of the Spanish (Eden 16–19). Eden's view of the Indians, whose bondage to the Spanish "is much rather to be desired then theyr former libertie which was to the cruell Canibales rather a horrible licenciousnesse than a libertie" (18), offers a stark contrast to Montaigne's more critical view of colonialist practices as well as a clear example of using translation to further a nationalist agenda.

In *The Cambridge History of English Literature*, Charles Whibley characterizes the Renaissance translators as

> [pursuing] their craft in the spirit of bold adventure which animated Drake and Hawkins. It was their ambition to discover new worlds of thought and beauty. They sailed the wide ocean of knowledge to plant their colonies of the intellect where they might, or to bring back to our English shores some eloquent stranger, whom their industry had taught to speak with our English tongue. (1)[8]

Despite his uncritical optimism, Whibley's choice of metaphor is apt. Early modern translators viewed themselves as ambassadors who brought to England cultural artifacts from other nations. While they may have hoped to discover "new worlds of thought and beauty," translators also hoped to improve England's intellectual and political status among its European counterparts. While they may have endeavored "to plant their colonies of the intellect," translators were also complicit in the imperialist project of colonizing conquered peoples. Because early modern translators were aware of their roles as ambassadors and colonizers, their works offer students an excellent opportunity to learn about theories of nation and nation building. Teaching Behn's "Essay on Translated Prose" and *A Discovery of New Worlds* in concert with such theories helps students understand the literary and cultural significance of early modern prose translations, which offer provocative comparisons between the English self and foreign others at a time when knowledge of different cultures was rapidly increasing.

Notes

1. Greg Kneidel considers the prose aesthetics of vernacular Bibles in his essay on teaching the early modern Bible in this collection. For a comprehensive analysis of the role of vernacular translations of the Bible within the Reformation, see Cummings.

2. For discussions of early modern prose translations, see Bush; Matthiessen; and Sampson.

3. For examples, see Asad and Dixon; Ngũgĩ wa Thiong'o; Viswanathan; Niranjana; Cheyfitz; and Venuti.

4. Bratach argues that Behn imitates "the detailed and circumstantial language of the Royal Society" when describing the Surinam locale of *Oroonoko* (210). In addition, Behn was probably familiar with Wilkins's work. Todd points out that Behn's historical chronicle of language development may paraphrase Wilkins's ideas in his essay on the development of a universal language. Finally, *A Discourse Concerning a New World and Another Planet* (1640) may have set a precedent for Fontenelle's *Entretiens sur la pluralité des mondes* (Behn 73, note d).

5. McEachern discusses the problems that the desire for a common language causes in Restoration England. She looks at the availability of vernacular Bibles as both a symptom of Babel's curse and its remedy (118).

6. For explicit discussions of Behn's translation and preface, see Cottegnies; Kitagaki. Other scholars who offer useful contexts for Behn's prose include Ferguson; Carey, Ellis, and Salih.

7. For a discussion of the likelihood that Behn, like her counterpart in *Oroonoko*, lived in Surinam, see Todd 35–45.

8. Interestingly, Matthiessen relies on a similar metaphor: "The translator's work was an act of patriotism. He, too, as well as the voyager and merchant, could do some good for his country: he believed that foreign books were just as important for England's destiny as the discoveries of her seamen, and he brought them into his native speech with all the enthusiasm of a conquest" (1).

Works Cited

Anderson, Benedict. *Imagined Communities: Reflections on the Origin and Spread of Nationalism*. Rev. ed. London: Verso, 1991. Print.

Asad, Talal, and John Dixon. "Translating Europe's Others." *Europe and Its Others: Proceedings of the Essex Conference on the Sociology of Literature, July 1984*. 2 vols. Ed. Francis Barker et al. Colchester: U of Essex, 1985. 170–77. Print.

Behn, Aphra, trans. *A Discovery of New Worlds*. Trans. of *Entretiens sur la pluralité des mondes*. By Bernard le Bovier de Fontenelle. *The Works of Aphra Behn*. Ed. Janet Todd. Vol. 4. London: Pickering, 1993. 71–165. Print.

Bratach, Anne. "Following the Intrigue: Aphra Behn, Genre, and Restoration Science." *Journal of Narrative Technique* 26 (1996): 209–27. Print.

Brown, Laura. *Ends of Empire: Women and Ideology in Early Eighteenth-Century English Literature*. Ithaca: Cornell UP, 1993. Print.

Bush, Douglas. *English Literature in the Earlier Seventeenth Century, 1600–1660*. 2nd ed. Oxford: Clarendon, 1966. Print.

Carey, Brycchan, Markman Ellis, and Sara Salih, eds. *Discourses of Slavery and Abolition: Britain and Its Colonies, 1760–1838*. New York: Palgrave, 2004. Print.

Cheyfitz, Eric. *The Poetics of Imperialism: Translation and Colonization from The Tempest to Tarzan*. Exp. ed. Philadelphia: U of Pennsylvania P, 1997. Print.

Cottegnies, Line. "The Translator as Critic: Aphra Behn's Translation of Fontenelle's *Discovery of New Worlds* (1688)." *Restoration* 27.1 (2003): 23–38. Print.

342   Translation, Nationalism, and Imperialism

Cummings, Brian. *The Literary Culture of the Reformation: Grammar and Grace.* Oxford: Oxford UP, 2003. Print.

Douglas, Gavin. *Selections from Gavin Douglas.* Ed. David F. C. Coldwell. Oxford: Clarendon, 1964. Print.

Dryden, John. "Preface to Ovid's Epistles." *Essays of John Dryden.* Ed. W. P. Ker. Vol. 1. Oxford: Clarendon, 1926. 230–43. Print.

Eden, Richard. "*The Decades of the Newe Worlde; or, West India* (1555), 'The Preface to the Reader.'" *Amazons, Savages, and Machiavels: Travel and Colonial Writing in English, 1550–1630: An Anthology.* Ed. Andrew Hadfield. Oxford: Oxford UP, 2001. 16–19. Print. Excerpt from *Decades of the Newe Worlde; or, West India.* By Pietro Martire d'Anghiera. Trans. Eden.

Ferguson, Moira. *Subject to Others: British Women Writers and Colonial Slavery, 1670–1834.* New York: Routledge, 1992. Print.

Florio, John. "The Epistle Dedicatorie." *The Essayes of Michael Lord of Montaigne.* 1603. Trans. Florio. Ed. A. R. Waller. Vol. 1. London: Dent, 1910. Print.

Greenblatt, Stephen J. *Learning to Curse: Essays in Early Modern Culture.* New York: Routledge, 1990. Print.

Harington, John. "A Preface or Rather, A Briefe Apologie of Poetrie and of the Author and Translator of This Poem." *Lodovico Ariosto's* Orlando Furioso. Trans. Harington. 1591. Ed. Robert McNulty. Oxford: Clarendon, 1972. 1–15. Print.

Helgerson, Richard. *Forms of Nationhood: The Elizabethan Writing of England.* Chicago: U of Chicago P, 1992. Print.

Hoby, Thomas. "The Epistle of the Translator." *Book of the Courtier.* By Baldassare Castiglione. Trans. Hoby. Ed. Virginia Cox. London: Everyman, 1994. 3–9. Print.

Kim, Young S. "Constructing a Global Identity: The Role of Esperanto." *Constructing World Culture: International Nongovernmental Organizations since 1875.* Ed. John Boli and George M. Thomas. Stanford: Stanford UP, 1999. 127–48. Print.

Kitagaki, Muneharu. *Principles and Problems of Translation in Seventeenth-Century England.* Kyoto: Shoten, 1981. Print.

Matthiessen, F. O. *Translation: An Elizabethan Art.* New York: Octagon, 1965. Print.

McEachern, Claire. *The Poetics of Nationhood, 1590–1612.* Cambridge: Cambridge UP, 1996. Print.

Ngũgĩ wa Thiong'o. *Moving the Centre: The Struggle for Cultural Freedoms.* Portsmouth: Heinemann, 1993. Print.

Niranjana, Tejaswini. *Siting Translation: History, Post-structuralism, and the Colonial Context.* Berkeley: U of California P, 1992. Print.

North, Thomas. "To the Most High and Mighty Princesse Elizabeth." *The Lives of the Noble Grecians and Romanes.* Trans. North. London: Nonesuch, 1929. iii–iv. Print.

Pratt, Mary Louise. *Imperial Eyes: Travel Writing and Transculturation.* London: Routledge, 1992. Print.

Sampson, George. *The Concise Cambridge History of English Literature.* New York: Macmillan, 1941. Print.

Stanyhurst, Richard. "From the Translation of the *Aeneid.*" *Elizabethan Critical Essays.* Ed. Gregory G. Smith. Vol. 1. Oxford: Oxford UP, 1904. 135–47. Print. 2 vols. Excerpt from *The Aeneid.* By Vergil. Trans. Stanyhurst. Leiden: Pates, 1582.

Steiner, T. R. *English Translation Theory, 1650–1800.* Assen: Gorcum, 1975. Print.

Todd, Janet. *The Secret Life of Aphra Behn.* Rutgers: Rutgers UP, 1997. Print.

Venuti, Lawrence. *The Scandals of Translation: Towards an Ethics of Difference.* New York: Routledge, 1998. Print.

Viswanathan, Gauri. *Masks of Conquest: Literary Study and British Rule in India.* New York: Columbia UP, 1989. Print.

Whibley, Charles. "Translators." *The Cambridge History of English Literature: An Encyclopedia in Eighteen Volumes.* Ed. A. W. Ward and A. R. Waller. Vol. 4. New York: Macmillan, 1933. 1–28. Print.

Gregory Kneidel

Teaching the Early Modern Bible, Fully and Perfectly

I teach the Bible as a cornucopian text. This is an avowedly humanistic approach to a sacred text that inspired much controversy and violence in early modern England, but it would not have been an anachronism. The preface "To the Reader" in the 1611 King James Bible inquires:

> The Scriptures then being acknowledged to be so full and perfect, how can we excuse ourselves of negligence, if we do not study them, of curiosity, if we be not content with them? Men talk much . . . of Cornucopia, that it had all things necessary for food in it, . . . [and] of Vulcan's armor, that it was an armor of proof against all thrusts, and all blows, etc. Well, that which they falsely or vainly attributed to these things for bodily good, we may justly and with full measure ascribe unto the Scripture, for spiritual. (A4v)

This passage both describes and illustrates what Mary Thomas Crane has called the humanist dialectic between "plenitude and control," copia and decorum, having a lot to say and saying the right thing (53–76). The Bible is "full and perfect," a commonplace claim within the period's dominant Protestant culture. As if to reveal the tension between fullness and perfection, the translators' praise of its fullness (which I've abbreviated) ends without ending ("etc.") but is then peremptorily corrected ("Well . . .") with an assertion that this praise is imperfect. The Bible is better than an imaginary or literary cornucopia because it is true and spiritual, but it is still a cornucopia.

There are several advantages to introducing the early modern Bible using the humanist dialectic of plenitude and control as a framework. First, I can establish ideals for prose composition that are alien to most of my students. They have been made to worship at the altars of clarity, brevity, and simplicity. Any introduction to early modern prose, secular or religious, should at least tempt them with copia and wit. Second, I can wait to introduce post-Reformation theological distinctions (Protestant versus Catholic, Puritan versus Anglican) that, in the context of biblical translation at least, seem to me less decisive than we are often told and that, in my experience, can quickly make students overly self-conscious or defensive. I try to let Reformation controversies emerge from, instead of frame, the discussion. Third, I can better avoid the charge of blasphemy or, worse, the heart-hardening glares of students who won't even deign to level the charge. By teaching the Bible as a Renaissance book, religious, irreligious, and antireligious students can usually get enough critical distance to participate without fear of punitive lightning strikes. And lastly, I can have my students contemplate the wholeness of the Bible instead of its partiality. Instead of talking about which quotations in which translations were used to club which beliefs, I ask them to consider how such a hugely heterogeneous text was thought to be full and perfect, what kind of problems this thinking might create, and what kinds of solutions literary terminology might offer.

I start with the novelty of the vernacular Bible as printed book to give a cultural instance of the dialectic between plenitude and control. Since images are the lay person's text, I show my students the famous frontispiece of the 1539 Great Bible (available on the Web or, with much else, from David Daniell's *The Bible in English*). In the top inch of the page, we see God speaking and pointing to Henry VIII, who is kneeling, with crown deferentially doffed, to receive God's word. It is easy to miss this small image of Henry because, immediately below the severely foreshortened God, he appears again, much larger, crowned, enthroned, and positively pontifical. He is speaking to Archbishop Thomas Cranmer on the left and Secretary of State Thomas Cromwell on the right (both bareheaded) and distributing to each a book bearing the words "Verbum Dei." As Henry did, Cranmer and Cromwell appear again below themselves,

346 Early Modern Bible

wearing hats that betoken their respective offices and distributing smaller copies of the "Verbum Dei" to members of the clergy and nobility. In the bottom third of the page, the recipient of Cranmer's Bible appears again, this time in an outdoor pulpit preaching (not reading) to a jumble of some twenty men and a few women and children. A handful are listening to the sermon. Several say "Vivat Rex"; two speak its rough English equivalent, "God save the Kinge." Opposite the preacher is a prison containing two glum souls who are attracting at least as much attention as the preacher. They are being told but they are not saying "vivat rex."

This frontispiece nicely introduces the early history of the printed Bible and is replete with ironies. Only three years earlier, in 1536, Henry's agents had captured and executed William Tyndale, the exiled Lutheran scholar who had been in hiding in Antwerp. It was Tyndale who translated and printed the first complete English New Testament in 1526 and who was most responsible for the stylistic brilliance of all subsequent translations leading up to and including the King James Version. Virtually everyone in the frontispiece speaks Latin, which is neither vernacular nor scriptural (lest Mel Gibson give the wrong impression, it is worth reminding students that the New Testament was written in Greek). And the biblical verses spoken by God, Henry, Cranmer, and Cromwell do not mention any theological concepts—faith, works, sin, grace, salvation, damnation, and so forth—but stress obedience, authority, and order. The take-home message is baldly political. Here the plenitude of the vernacular Bible, made possible by the advent of the printing press, is deeply feared, and the social mechanisms for controlling its meaning are everywhere evident.

It is worth asking students to consider the arguments against vernacular scriptures. Is Scripture too important to be entrusted to every (literate) believer or too important not to be? I ask students to think of analogies about the dangers of disseminating knowledge—"secrets of state" is a clear and current one—but the force of the early Reformation at least was to insist that such analogies categorically did not hold. The Bible is a unique case. One reason is that for Protestants, the Bible's words had to be felt, not just known. Tyndale distinguished between "historical faith" and "feeling faith," between knowing biblical facts in one's head and experiencing affectively the word in one's heart. So what kind of prose style can best do this moving? In classical rhetoric, it was often polish, grace, and elevated diction that were said to move, but, as Debora Shuger and David Norton have shown, sixteenth- and seventeenth-century rhetoricians formulated an alternative: brevity and roughness (often coded as Hebraicisms) could move one forcefully as well. Here one can list the confessional agendas of the period's major translations—the Lutheran Tyndale-Coverdale, the Calvinist Geneva, the Roman Catholic Douay-Rheims, and the less polemically Protestant King James—and sketch out corresponding prose aesthetics (architectural analogies help: I ask the class to compare the style of a medieval cathedral with a New England meeting house). With Samuel Bagster's *Hexapla* or Luther Weigle's *Octapla* or the Web, it is easy enough to demonstrate that each translation renders certain words to its theological liking (early flashpoints were "congregation" for "church," "seniors" or "elders" for "priests," and "love" for "charity"). As far as word choice goes, Tyndale favors the Anglo-Saxon, the Douay-Rheims the Latinate, the others a mixture of both.[1] There are howlers on both extremes (in the Douay-Rheims "Our Father," Jesus prays, "Give us to day our supersubstantial bread" [Matt. 6.9]), but it is important to note that none of the major translations is blindly programmatic. For example, it is Tyndale who, for polemical reasons, translates the Greek *ekklesia* as "congregation," not "church," surely the shorter, simpler, more Anglo-Saxon choice.

With important exceptions such as Paul's more densely theological passages, the translations read more alike than their own, voluminous, and often bitterly divisive marginalia would have you believe. Other, largely forgotten translations offered more choices but lacked institutional backing (and hence buyers) and failed to make an impact. The French Protestant heretic Sebastian Castellio, for example, translated the Bible into polished humanist Latin, so *ekklesia*, for example, became *respublica*. This Bible was published in 1551 with a dedication to Edward VI but quickly condemned in both Geneva and Rome. At almost exactly the same time, John Cheke, Edward's tutor, started to translate the Bible with as few sacrosanct-sounding Latinate words as possible, so Jesus is "crossed" instead of crucified, and his resurrection is an "uprising." Cheke only finished the Gospel of Matthew, and it was left unpublished until 1843. Similarly, it is difficult to peg broader matters of style and scholarship to specific confessions. Janel Mueller has shown that Tyndale and other Protestant practitioners of what we sometimes pigeonhole as the plain style—short sentences, early noun-verb-object phrases, and little syntactic subordination—could turn a phrase with zeal, especially the lists, antitheses, and parallelisms of Paul's rousing exhortations and prayers. The Douay-Rheims translators wrote their prefatory material in aureate prose, but for whatever reason they rarely force this style on their translations.

Nevertheless, the result of all this competition among vernacular Bibles was to increase and display the copious resources of the English language.

The Bible is obviously also full in other ways—for example, of genres, theologies, histories. What does it mean to call this amalgamation "perfect"? Here it is possible to discuss two related topics: scriptural allegory as a strategy for making everything in the Bible, no matter how inconsequential or objectionable (e.g., Noah's drunkenness, Lot's betrayal of his daughters, and David's and Samson's sexual escapades), seem important and edifying, and typology, since perfection means not just self-sufficient or morally upstanding but also completed or finished. Typology, it seems to me, is the most fundamental for appreciating the religious prose of early modern England and America. If Christ's death instituted a new dispensation of spiritual instead of carnal worship, what is the value of retaining the detailed regulations about cultic worship (e.g., the scapegoat ritual in Leviticus 16)? I explain that this problem—essentially, why put what Christians call the Old Testament in the same book as the New?—can stand as a metonymy for any number of theological conflicts in post-Reformation England (works vs. grace, law vs. liberty, institutional church vs. individual conscience). Typology provided an answer by identifying Old Testament types or promises that are fulfilled by New Testament antitypes.[2] Jesus himself licenses this kind of thinking (see Matt. 12.40). Whereas allegory has one foot in the Bible and the other out of it (in faculty psychology, in papal politics, etc.), typology has one foot in the Old Testament and the other in the New.

So typological patterning binds the two testaments together, and, again, title pages help explain what kinds of problems this can raise. The 1560 Geneva Bible title page, for example, presents an emblem of the Israelites fleeing across the Red Sea, following a divine "pillar of cloud" and being chased by their Egyptian rulers. The Geneva translators, many of whom were exiles under Mary, want readers to imagine themselves as Israelites, a persecuted nation for whom, according to the accompanying text, "the Lord shal fight" (Exod. 14.14).[3] This sounds great, but this type-antitype construct (Israelites equal English Bible readers) gets trickier if you look at 1 Corinthians 10. There, Paul describes the crossing of the Red Sea as a type of Christian baptism and the Israelites' meals of manna as a type of the sacrament of communion. Again, so far, so good. But then Paul recalls that the divinely favored Israelites lapsed into idol worship: "Now these are ensamples to us, to the intent that we shulde not lust after evil things as they also lusted" (1 Cor. 10.6). So if the English church is a third type of the elect nation, after the Israelites and Corinthians, then it would seem to have been divinely ordained to relapse into idolatry and fornication. But, if the Israelites are negative "ensamples," then the Corinthians and English alike must reject their sins and be not merely old perfected but altogether new. If this is true, why insist on identifying with them at all? We know that the King James translators argued bitterly over how to render Paul's word *typoi* in 1 Corinthians 10.6. Are the Israelites "ensamples" (implying bad behavior to avoid) or "types" (implying godly favor to be claimed)? In the end, the King James translators put "ensamples" in the text, and "types" as a gloss in the margins. The King James Bible's frontispiece removes all ambiguity by treating the Old Testament, in the figures of Moses and Aaron, as a monumental institution literally upholding the New Testament.

Allegory and typology are examples of what Terence Cave describes as using "a thief to catch a thief" (91)—in other words, using literary concepts that introduce ambiguity or polysemy to circumscribe the Bible's ambiguity or polysemy. Moreover, modern biblical critics such as Elaine Scarry, Regina Schwartz, and Gabriel Josipovici have shown that the problem of cornucopia and the dialectic of plenitude and control are fundamental to biblical literature in other ways: they inform the rhythm of individual biblical narratives (lists vs. action); the basic cultural problems of endogamy, monotheism, and exceptionalism (King Lear's "who loses and who wins; who's in, who's out" [5.3.15]); and the vagaries of textual recension (e.g., the J and the P creation stories). Many of my students still retain romantic notions of artistic originality and emotional intensity. But I stress that a good deal of formal literary analysis can be done simply by detecting where patterns start and where they stop (which is good news for unemotional lovers of literature). And this method of literary analysis was developed, in part at least, to prove that the Bible is indeed "full and perfect."

Notes

1. The best study of the comparative styles of the major translations is Hammond. For more comprehensive treatments, see Greenslade; Daniell.

2. The logic of typology can be glimpsed in the titles of two seventeenth-century compendiums of typological correspondences, William Guild's *Moses Unveiled* (1620) and Thomas Tyler's *Christ Revealed* (1635). The most important modern study of the history of typological interpretation is Auerbach's 1944 essay "Figura."

3. Citations to the Geneva Bible are to Berry's edition.

Works Cited

Auerbach, Erich. "Figura." 1944. *Scenes from the Drama of European Literature.* New York: Meridian, 1959. 11–76. Print.

Berry, Lloyd E., ed. *The Geneva Bible, a Facsimile of the 1560 Edition.* Madison: U of Wisconsin P, 1969. Print.

The Bible. London, 1611. *Early English Books Online.* PDF. King James Vers.

Cave, Terence. *The Cornucopian Text: Problems of Writing in the French Renaissance.* Oxford: Oxford UP, 1979. Print.

Cohen, Charles Lloyd. *God's Caress: The Psychology of Puritan Religious Experience.* Oxford: Oxford UP, 1986. Print.

Crane, Mary Thomas. *Framing Authority: Sayings, Self, and Society in Sixteenth-Century England.* Princeton: Princeton UP, 1993. Print.

Daniell, David. *The Bible in English.* New Haven: Yale UP, 2003. Print.

The Great Bible 1539. St. John's Coll., U of Cambridge. 2008. Web. 4 May 2009.

Greenslade, S. L., ed. *The Cambridge History of the Bible.* Vol. 3. Cambridge: Cambridge UP, 1963. Print.

Hammond, Gerald. *The Making of the English Bible.* 1982. New York: Philosophical Lib., 1983. Print.

Josipovici, Gabriel. *The Book of God: A Response to the Bible.* New Haven: Yale UP, 1988. Print.

Mueller, Janel. *The Native Tongue and the Word: Developments in English Prose Style, 1380–1580.* Chicago: U of Chicago P, 1984. Print.

Norton, David. *A History of the English Bible as Literature.* Rev. ed. Cambridge: Cambridge UP, 2000. Print.

Scarry, Elaine. *The Body in Pain: The Making and Unmaking of the World.* Oxford: Oxford UP, 1985. Print.

Schwartz, Regina M. *The Curse of Cain: The Violence of Monotheism.* Chicago: U of Chicago P, 1997. Print.

Shakespeare, William. *King Lear. The Riverside Shakespeare.* Ed. G. Blakemore Evans et al. Vol. 2. Boston: Houghton, 1972. 1249–1305. Print.

Shuger, Debora K. *Sacred Rhetoric: The Christian Grand Style in the English Renaissance.* Princeton: Princeton UP, 1988. Print.

Tyndale, William. *Tyndale's New Testament.* Ed. David Daniell. 2nd ed. New Haven: Yale UP, 1995. Print.

Part V

Selected Resources
for Teachers

Margaret W. Ferguson, Susannah Brietz Monta,
Magdalena Nerio, Genevieve Pearson, and
Vanessa Rapatz

Selected Resources for Teachers

We have divided these resources into two categories: multiauthor print
anthologies containing significant selections of early modern English prose
and electronic resources useful for teaching prose. For major scholarship
on particular authors or genres, or for suggestions about single-author
editions, please see the works-cited and "Suggestions for Further Reading" lists at the end of individual essays. For an overview of selected major
scholarship on prose in the field, please see the introduction to this volume and its works-cited list.

Print Resources: Anthologies including Substantial Selections of Prose Writings

*Amazons, Savages, and Machiavels: Travel and Colonial Writing in English, 1550–
1630: An Anthology.* Ed. Andrew Hadfield. Oxford: Oxford UP, 2001.
  As the title suggests, this anthology contains a collection of travel writings
  by male explorers, essayists, and travelers composed between the reigns of
  Mary I and James I. The writings are printed materials widely available during the period and include a number of translations. The book's sections
  group materials according to geographic region ("Europe," "Africa and the
  Near East," "The Far East and the South Sea Islands," and "The Americas"),

with the exception of the first, more general chapter, titled "Motives for Travel and Instructions to Travelers." The anthology includes an introduction that briefly surveys emergent discourses and debates surrounding postcolonial studies, as well as a chronology and full bibliography; the texts are lightly annotated and in early modern spelling.

American Women Writers to 1800. Ed. Sharon M. Harris. New York: Oxford UP, 1996.

This anthology provides what the editor suggests is a sampling of writings by early modern American women from diverse backgrounds; it includes but also looks beyond the canonical offerings of Anne Bradstreet, Mary Rowlandson, and Sarah Kemble Knight. This collection includes letters, diaries and journals, memoirs, spiritual autobiographies, captivity and conversion narratives, scientific tracts, petitions, histories, and more. Selections of drama and poetry are included, and prose texts are divided thematically into three sections: "The Ages of Women," "Emerging Feminist Voices," and "Origins, Revolutions, and Women in the Nations." The anthology includes a general introduction as well as section and biographical introductions; it is lightly annotated and retains original spelling.

An Anthology of Elizabethan Prose Fiction. Ed. Paul Salzman. Oxford: Oxford UP, 1998.

This useful anthology includes (in full) George Gascoigne's *The Adventures of Master F. J.*, John Lyly's *Euphues: The Anatomy of Wit*, Robert Greene's *Pandosto*, Thomas Nashe's *The Unfortunate Traveller*, and Thomas Deloney's *Jack of Newbury*; spelling has been modernized. Each text is lightly annotated, and the brief introduction is student friendly.

An Anthology of Seventeenth-Century Fiction. Ed. Paul Salzman. Oxford: Oxford UP, 2001.

This anthology contains book 1 of Mary Wroth's *Urania*, selections from Percy Herbert's *The Princess Cloria*, Margaret Cavendish's *The Blazing World*, Thomas Dangerfield's *Don Tomazo*, selections from John Bunyan's *The Life and Death of Mr. Badman*, William Congreve's *Incognita*, and Aphra Behn's *The Unfortunate Happy Lady*. As with Salzman's anthology of sixteenth-century prose fiction, the editions here feature modernized spelling and light annotation.

Chaucer to Spenser: An Anthology of Writings in English, 1375–1575. Ed. Derek Albert Pearsall. Malden: Blackwell, 1998.

In addition to selections from *The Travels of Sir John Mandeville*, Julian of Norwich's *Revelations*, *The Book of Margery Kempe*, and other early prose texts, this anthology contains a small collection of early modern prose writings. These texts include selections from *The First English Life of Henry V*, *A Mirror for Magistrates*, Thomas More's *The History of King Richard III* and *Utopia*, Hugh Latimer's "Sermon on the Plougher," Roger Ascham's *The Schoolmaster*, John Foxe's *Acts and Monuments*, and George Gascoigne's *The Steel Glass* and *The Spoil of Antwerp*. The texts are lightly annotated and the volume offers brief biographical introductions to each author.

Early Modern Catholicism: An Anthology of Primary Sources. Ed. Robert S. Miola. Oxford: Oxford UP, 2007.

This anthology is the first on its subject. It contains a number of selections from important prose works in a range of genres, including polemic, biography and hagiography, devotional prose, and histories. Most selections were originally published in English, though Miola also provides translated selections from a number of important Latin texts. There are brief, informative introductions to each selection as well as a lengthier introduction to the anthology as a whole and suggestions for further reading.

The Early Modern Englishwoman: A Facsimile Library of Essential Works. Betty Travitsky, and Anne Lake Prescott, series eds. Patrick Cullen, senior ed. emeritus. Aldershot: Ashgate, 1996– . www.ashgate.com.

This is an ambitious, ongoing publication project that aims to provide a "comprehensive and focused collection of writings in English from 1500 to 1750, both by women and for and about them." This project has thus far published numerous volumes in two series of facsimiles: Printed Writings and Essential Works for the Study of Early Modern Women and of Manuscript Writing. Printed Writings is divided into three multivolume parts: 1500–1640, 1641–1700, and 1700–50. Many of the volumes contain prose works, including recipes, medical treatises, defenses of women, romances, and political and theological documents. Various scholars have edited individual volumes. There is, in addition, a complementary series of editions, The Early Modern Englishwoman, 1500–1750: Contemporary Editions; this includes both old-spelling and modernized editions of printed and manuscript works by and about women and gender in early modern England.

The Early Modern Period. Ed. Constance Jordan and Clare Carroll. *The Longman Anthology of British Literature.* Vol. 1B. New York: Longman, 1999.

This extensive anthology includes Thomas More's *Utopia*, Philip Sidney's *The Apology for Poetry*, and substantial prose selections from Elizabeth 1, Aemilia Lanyer, and Walter Raleigh. These selections are accompanied by thematic sections titled "Perspectives" that feature short excerpts of prose writings ranging from the political offerings of Juan Luis Vives, John Foxe, Baldassare Castiglione, James I, Roger Ascham, and Richard Mulcaster to tracts on gender by Erasmus, Joseph Swetnam, and Rachel Speght. The last part of the anthology, titled "The Development of English Prose," includes selections by Francis Bacon, Mary Wroth, Thomas Hobbes, Thomas Browne, Robert Burton, John Milton, Anna Trapnel, Daniel Defoe, and John Bunyan. The anthology includes a general introduction as well as introductions to specific sections and authors; there are also various appendixes. Texts are lightly annotated and spelling and punctuation are modernized.

Early Modern Women's Writing: An Anthology, 1560–1700. 2000. Ed. Paul Salzman. Oxford: Oxford World's Classics, 2008.

In addition to poetry and dramatic writings, this anthology includes the full texts of Aphra Behn's *The Wandering Beauty: A Novel;* Hester Biddle's prophetic tract "The Trumpet of the Lord Sounded Forth"; Margaret Cavendish's preface to *Observations upon Experimental Philosophy* and "The Matrimonial Agreement" from *Nature's Pictures;* and Priscilla Cotton and Mary Cole's 1655 defense (of a woman's right to preach), "To the Priests and People of England." The anthology also contains sections from Aemilia

Lanyer's *Salve Deus Rex Judaeorum*; Anne Clifford's diary; Eleanor Davies's *Revelations: The Everlasting Gospel*; and Dorothy Osborne's letters. This volume also includes a general introduction with biographical sketches of the writers. The texts are lightly annotated and the spelling has been modernized.

Elizabethan Backgrounds: Historical Documents of the Age of Elizabeth I. Ed. Arthur F. Kinney. Hamden: Archon, 1975.

This collection includes eyewitness accounts, journal records, proclamations, and pamphlets that represent national accounts of historical events, political declarations, and achievements during Elizabeth I's reign. The volume begins with the *Proclamation of Accession* (1558) and ends with *A Letter from a Soldier of Good Place in Ireland* (1602). Textual notes follow each of the nineteen selections, which are then succeeded by explanatory notes. The editor retains the texts' original spelling.

Elizabethan Fiction. Ed. R. Ashley and E. M. Moseley. New York: Rinehart, 1953.

Aiming at a "readable text for the average college student," the editors have partially modernized the entire texts of George Gascoigne's *The Adventures of Master F. J.*, John Lyly's *Euphues: The Anatomy of Wit*, Thomas Nashe's *The Unfortunate Traveller*, and Thomas Deloney's *Jack of Newbury*; also included is a thirty-three-page selection from books 1 and 2 of *The Countess of Pembroke's Arcadia*, by Philip Sidney. This is the text compiled by Sidney's sister Mary and first printed in 1593; it is a hybrid version of great literary-historical interest, although teachers may prefer to introduce students to Sidney's romance through excerpts taken from the modern scholarly editions of the five-book version known as the old *Arcadia* or the two-book revision thereof left unfinished at Sidney's death. See *The Countess of Pembroke's Arcadia (The Old Arcadia)*, ed. Jean Robertson (Oxford: Clarendon, 1973); and *The New Arcadia*, ed. Victor Stretkowicz (Oxford: Clarendon, 1987).

Elizabethan Prose Fiction. Ed. Merritt E. Lawlis. New York: Odyssey, 1967.

This anthology includes George Gascoigne's *The Adventures of Master F. J.*, John Lyly's *Euphues: The Anatomy of Wit*, Barnaby Rich's *Of Apolonius and Silla* from *Farewell to the Military Profession*, Robert Greene's *Pandosto* and *A Notable Discovery of Cozenage*, Thomas Lodge's *Rosalind*, Thomas Nashe's *The Unfortunate Traveller*, and Thomas Deloney's *Thomas Reading*. The volume is lightly annotated and features a brief general introduction, introductions for each text, and biographical sketches.

English Women's Voices, 1540–1700. Ed. Charlotte F. Otten. Miami: Florida Intl. UP, 1992.

With the exception of two poems, this anthology is a collection of nonfiction prose writings divided into eight thematic sections related to the lives of early modern Englishwomen. The themes include writings on abuse, life in prison, politics, love and marriage, health care, childbirth, sickness and death, meditation, prayer, and the right to preach. Within this range of topics, the texts represent a wide spectrum of prose genres such as diaries, letters, autobiographies, trial records, petitions, mothers' legacies, and spiritual narratives. While a few of the writers included in this volume have been anthologized elsewhere (e.g., Lady Jane Grey, Anna Trapnel, Mary Carey, Jane

Sharp, and Elizabeth Cellier), most have not. The book includes brief introductions to sections and is lightly annotated; spellings have been modernized and Americanized.

Everyday English, 1500–1700: A Reader. Ed. Bridget Cusack. Ann Arbor: U of
Michigan P, 1998.

This reader contains samples of what the editor calls "non-literary prose"
from the early modern period. Each selection is brief, in original spelling,
and heavily annotated. Various kinds of prose are included: accounts, letters, wills, memoirs, journals, presentments, and a category the editor terms
"abuse." Male and female writers are both well represented.

Female and Male Voices in Early Modern England. Ed. Betty Travitsky and Anne
Lake Prescott. New York: Columbia UP, 2000.

This anthology reviews the cultural background of early modern England
through a gendered lens by juxtaposing women's writings with men's. The
book surveys various genres and is divided into thematic topics including
domestic affairs, religion, politics and society, and love and sexuality. Each
section is then subdivided into pairs or groups where one can read excerpts
from Jane Sharp's *The Midwives Book* next to John Sadler's *Advice on the
Uterus* or an excerpt from *A True Relation of the Confession of Elizabeth Saw-
yer* next to a scene from *The Witch of Edmonton* by Thomas Dekker, John
Ford, and William Rowley. The anthology includes brief, student-friendly
introductions for each group of writers; it is lightly annotated and spellings
have been modernized.

The Golden Hind: An Anthology of Elizabethan Prose and Poetry. Ed. Roy Lamson
and Hallett Darius Smith. New York: Norton, 1942.

This volume contains sections divided chronologically by author and includes
brief biographical introductions along with light annotations. The fiction
and nonfiction prose selections are generally presented as excerpts and range
from historical narratives and courtesy books to travel writings and pamphlets. Selections are taken from authors such as Thomas Hoby, John Foxe,
Roger Ascham, Elizabeth I, Raphael Holinshed, John Lyly, Stephen Gos-
son, Philip Sidney, Thomas Lodge, Thomas Nashe, Richard Hakluyt, Walter Raleigh, and Thomas Dekker.

*Half Humankind: Contexts and Texts of the Controversy about Women in En-
gland, 1540–1640.* Ed. Katherine Usher Henderson and Barbara F. McManus.
Urbana: U of Illinois P, 1985.

This anthology contains extensive selections from pamphlets contributing
to the debate about women (*la querelle des femmes*) in early modern England, including the infamous Joseph Swetnam and some of the more famous responses to him (from Esther Sowernam and the pseudonymous
Constantia Munda) as well as the *Hic Mulier / Haec Vir* pamphlets on cross-
dressing. The editors provide a substantive introduction.

Her Own Life: Autobiographical Writings by Seventeenth-Century Englishwomen.
Ed. Elspeth Graham, Hilary Hinds, and Elaine Hobby. New York: Routledge, 1989.

This anthology contains selections from autobiographical work by female
writers from various socioeconomic and religious backgrounds: Anne Clifford,

An Collins, Anna Trapnel, Margaret Cavendish, Susanna Parr, Katharine Evans and Sarah Cheevers, Mary Carleton, Alice Thornton, Sarah Davy, Anne Wentworth, Hannah Allen, and Joan Vokins. Each selection is prefaced by a brief but useful introduction.

Lay by Your Needles Ladies, Take the Pen: Writing Women in England, 1500–1700. Ed. Suzanne Trill, Kate Chedgzoy, and Melanie Osborne. London: Arnold, 1997.

As with the anthology *Female and Male Voices,* this collection places women's prose writings alongside texts by male contemporaries. The excerpts are ordered according to publication dates and include a mixture of generic forms, since many of the texts challenge expected generic categorizations. The texts also feature male and female writers on gender roles and women's writing during the early modern period. Some writers included in this volume are John Knox, Thomas Salter, Mary Sidney, Margaret Hoby, Joseph Swetnam, Rachel Speght, Esther Sowernam, Mary Wroth, William Gouge, Anna Trapnel, Margaret Cavendish, Jane Sharp, Robert Whitehall, Mary Rowlandson, and Aphra Behn. The collection features a student-accessible introduction; each text is lightly annotated and generally retains original spelling.

Letterwriting in Renaissance England. Ed. Alan Stewart and Heather Wolfe. Seattle: U of Washington P, 2004.

This catalog was published in conjunction with the exhibition *Letterwriting in Renaissance England,* presented at the Folger Shakespeare Library from November 2004 through April 2005. The volume includes manuscript facsimiles and transcriptions of manuscript letters and handwritten documents. Because this project is based on an exhibition on letter writing, it includes information about the processes involved in this textual production—penning, sending, receiving, reading, circulating, copying and saving letters—along with letters themselves.

Life-Writings by British Women, 1660–1815: An Anthology. Ed. Carolyn A. Barros and Johanna M. Smith. Boston: Northeastern UP, 2000.

This anthology contains "life-writings" of British women from the long eighteenth century. These writings include a variety of genres such as autobiographies, journals, travel narratives, apologies, and testimonials. Some of the more famous women represented among the many in this collection are Ann Fanshawe, Mary Wortley Montagu, Ann Radcliffe, and Mary Wollstonecraft. The texts are ordered chronologically and are lightly annotated; the editors have retained original spelling.

Major Women Writers of Seventeenth-Century England. Ed. James Fitzmaurice et al. Ann Arbor: U of Michigan P, 1997.

In addition to significant selections of poetry by women writers, this anthology includes some prose selections (from Mary Wroth's *Urania,* Margaret Cavendish's letters, and Rachel Speght's and Esther Sowernam's polemical defenses of women). Brief introductions situate each writer in historical and literary contexts. The spelling, capitalization, punctuation, and word divisions have been modernized; the texts contain extensive footnotes on context, editorial decisions, and manuscript variations.

The Meridian Anthology of Early Women Writers: British Literary Women from Aphra Behn to Maria Edgeworth, 1660–1800. Ed. Katharine M. Rogers and William McCarthy, New York: Meridian, 1987.

In addition to a poetical miscellany, this anthology features prose letters, essays, journals, and narrative fiction. The prose texts include Aphra Behn's "An Epistle to the Reader" and *Oroonoko*, selections from Mary Astell's *A Serious Proposal* (parts 1 and 2) and *Some Reflections on Marriage*, selected letters of Mary Wortley Montagu, selections from Hester Thrale Piozzi's *Thraliana*, Anna Laetitia Barbauld's *Address to the Opposers of the Repeal* . . . , selections from Frances Burney d'Arblay's *Journals*, excerpts from Mary Hays's *Letters and Essays* and *An Appeal to the Men* . . . , and Maria Edgeworth's "An Essay on . . . Self Justification." The volume is lightly annotated with a brief introduction on women writers who predate Jane Austen; spelling and punctuation have been modernized and Americanized.

The Paradise of Women: Writings by Englishwomen of the Renaissance. Ed. Betty Travitsky. Westport: Greenwood, 1981. Contributions in Women's Studies 23.

While some of the section divisions are idiosyncratic and most of its selections are very brief, this anthology has the decided advantage of range: a number of lesser-known figures are made accessible for classroom use. The prose genres represented also range widely, including prose prayers, mothers' legacies, letters, diaries, prefaces, histories, and autobiography.

Popular Fiction by Women, 1660–1730: An Anthology. Ed. Paula R. Backscheider and John J. Richetti. Oxford: Oxford UP, 1997.

This anthology includes Aphra Behn's *The History of the Nun* (1689), Mary de la Rivière Manley's *The Secret History of Queen Zarah and the Zarazians* (1705), Jane Barker's *Love Intrigues* (1713), Penelope Aubin's *The Strange Adventures of the Count de Vinevil and His Family* (1721), Eliza Haywood's *The British Recluse* (1722) and *Fantomina* (1725), Mary Davys's *The Reformed Coquet* (1724), and selections from Elizabeth Singer Rowe's *Friendship in Death* (1728). The collection is lightly annotated.

Reading Early Modern Women: An Anthology of Texts in Manuscript and Print, 1550–1700. Ed. Helen Ostovich and Elizabeth Sauer. New York: Routledge, 2004.

This substantial anthology, the product of collaboration among eighty scholars, makes available a variety of manuscripts and printed texts by early modern women. There are some examples of poetry and drama, but most of the selections are prose works. Divided according to genre, the chapters include legal documents, apologies and defenses, medical manuals, letters, life writing (both fiction and nonfiction), as well as translations. The book contains works of prose by women such as Elizabeth I, Rachel Speght, Ester Sowernam, Margaret Cavendish, Mary Astell, Aphra Behn, Isabella Whitney, Jane Sharp, Elizabeth Cellier, Anne Askew, and Anna Trapnel, as well as several other lesser known female writers. The texts are framed by chapter introductions that synthesize and contextualize the materials and extensive commentary. Manuscript facsimiles are accompanied by transcriptions; original spelling, punctuation, and capitalization have been preserved.

Religious Prose of Seventeenth-Century England. Ed. Anne Ferry. New York: Knopf, 1967.

This anthology contains religious prose written by John Donne, John Milton, John Bunyan, George Herbert, Thomas Sprat, and George Fox. The prose works include sermons, devotions, confessions of faith, piety manuals, polemical tracts, meditations, and spiritual autobiographies. The collection is lightly annotated and is prefaced by a substantial general introduction.

The Renaissance and the Early Seventeenth Century. Vol. 2 of *The Broadview Anthology of British Literature*. Ed. Joseph Laurence Black. Peterborough: Broadview, 2005.

This substantial anthology of writings from John Skelton to John Milton includes prose selections covering a wide spectrum of genres. Prose writers represented include Anne Askew; John Foxe; Thomas Wyatt; Lady Jane Grey; Elizabeth I; Mary, Queen of Scots; Aemilia Lanyer; Walter Raleigh; Rachel Speght; Ester Sowernam; Thomas Hobbes; and Izaak Walton. The volume contains useful appendixes, complete with maps, glossaries, and indexes; its introductions and other critical materials provide valuable contexts for students. The table of contents also includes supplemental texts and materials that can be accessed on *The Broadview Anthology of British Literature* Web site: www.broadviewpress.com/babl/.

The Renaissance in England: Non-dramatic Prose and Verse of the Sixteenth Century. Ed. Hyder E. Rollins and Herschel Baker. Boston: Heath, 1954.

Like *The Golden Hind*, this anthology contains a wide sampling of canonical authors. The texts are divided into sections that are generally based on either period (early Tudor, early Elizabethan) or genre (prose fiction, translations, critical theory). Spelling is often modernized, with certain exceptions, while punctuation has been modernized throughout.

The Renaissance in Europe: An Anthology. Ed. Peter Elmer, Nicholas Webb, and Roberta Wood. New Haven: Yale UP, 2000.

This anthology was commissioned for an Open University course titled The Renaissance in Europe: A Cultural Enquiry. Among the various selections divided into topics ranging from humanism and politics to Renaissance science and Michel de Montaigne, the volume contains a chapter devoted to Renaissance England. This section contains prose writings such as Fulke Greville's *The Life of the Renowned Sir Philip Sidney*, John Bale's *The Examinations of Anne Askew*, Philip Sidney's *An Apology for Poetry*, George Puttenham's *The Arte of Poesie*, Johannes de Witt's *Remarkes on the London Theatres*, and Thomas Platter's *Visits to London Theatres*. The volume is lightly annotated and the textual selections retain original spelling.

Restoration Literature: An Anthology. Ed. Paul Hammond. Oxford: Oxford UP, 2002.

While the editor admittedly favors the poems and prose of John Dryden and John Wilmot, Second Earl of Rochester, this anthology also contains significant prose writings in a variety of generic forms. The volume is ordered thematically into five sections: "Politics and Nations," "Town and Country," "Literature and Theatre," "Love and Friendship," and "Religion and Philosophy." It includes prose texts by Samuel Pepys, John Evelyn, Margaret

Cavendish, Aphra Behn, John Milton, John Bunyan, and Lucy Hutchinson; selections range from diary entries and letters to prologues, epilogues, and fictional narratives. The anthology has brief explanatory and bibliographical notes; the texts have been modernized throughout.

Restoration Prose Fiction, 1666–1700: An Anthology of Representative Pieces. Ed. Charles C. Mish. Lincoln: U of Nebraska P, 1970.

This anthology contains a collection of prose fictions by French and British writers both male and female that Mish sees as representing the "seedbed of the modern novel." The volume includes *Five Love-Letters from a Nun to a Cavalier* (1678), *The Art of Cuckoldom* (1697), Mademoiselle de La Roche's *Almanzor and Almanzaida* (1678), Aphra Behn's *The History of the Nun* (1689), John Shirley's *London's Glory* (1686), and others. The anthology is lightly annotated and retains original spelling.

Seventeenth-Century English Prose. Ed. David Novarr. New York: Knopf, 1967.

This anthology includes substantial selections of prose from Francis Bacon, Robert Burton, Izaak Walton, Thomas Browne, John Bunyan, and Samuel Pepys, as well as smaller offerings from authors such as John Donne and Walter Raleigh. The major prose genres, as Novarr labels them, include essays, short lives, epistles, and characters. The volume is lightly annotated and texts are in the original spellings.

The Seventeenth-Century Resolve: A Historical Anthology of a Literary Form. Ed. John Leon Lievsay. Lexington: UP of Kentucky, 1980.

The editor sets out in this anthology to pull together a collection of "resolves," a genre he describes as "preponderantly of religious inspiration, an instrument for the perfecting or reforming of private and public morals"(1), or the theological counterpart to utopian writings. The collection includes resolves in the form of meditations and essays composed by male writers. The texts are lightly annotated and the original spellings have been preserved.

Sixteenth-Century English Poetry and Prose: A Selective Anthology. Ed. Paul Delany, Philip J. Ford, and Robert W. Hanning. New York: Holt, 1976.

This anthology includes prose selections, often excerpted from longer works, by authors such as Thomas More, Thomas Elyot, George Gascoigne, Thomas Sackville, Walter Raleigh, Philip Sidney, Fulke Greville, Richard Hooker, John Harington, Thomas Nashe, and John Marston. The volume includes a brief contextual introduction, introductory notes for each author, and light annotation; texts have been modernized throughout.

The Thought and Culture of the English Renaissance. Ed. Elizabeth M. Nugent. Cambridge: Cambridge UP, 1956.

This anthology of Tudor prose is divided into five parts: Tudor humanists and "grammars," political and social order and medicine, sermons and religious treatises, chronicles and histories, and romances and tales. The anthology includes Margaret Beaufort's preface to *Statutes of Christ's College, Cambridge*, a few anonymous sources, and the works of canonical authors.

Three Early Modern Utopias: Utopia *by Sir Thomas More*, New Atlantis *by Francis Bacon, and* The Isle of Pines *by Henry Neville.* Ed. Susan Bruce. Oxford: Oxford UP, 1999.

This collection of three utopian texts includes a brief, student-accessible introduction as well as a selected bibliography, chronologies of the authors, explanatory notes, and a glossary of terms. The works are reproduced in full and are usefully based on specified editions; More's *Utopia* includes an appendix with ancillary materials. Spelling and some punctuation have been silently modernized.

Unsuitable for Ladies: An Anthology of Women Travellers. Ed. Jane Robinson. New York: Oxford UP, 1994.

This anthology contains a wide collection of women's letters and excerpts from a variety of other travel writings ranging from the fifteenth to the twentieth century. These texts are printed in sections generally based on the geographic locations they describe. Each section is briefly prefaced and introduces the "characters," or travelers, whose writings have been brought together in this book.

When Flesh Becomes Word : An Anthology of Early Eighteenth-Century Libertine Literature. Ed. Bradford K. Mudge. New York: Oxford UP, 2004.

This anthology brings together a collection of erotic poems and prose works such as *The School of Venus* (1680), the earliest English translation of *L'ecole des filles* (1655); the second half of John Marten's medical treatise *Gonosologium Novum* (1709); *Venus in the Cloister* (1725), a translation of Jean Barrin's *Venus dans le cloître, ou la religieuse en chemise* (1683); Thomas Stretzer's *A New Description of Merryland* (1741); and Henry Fielding's *The Female Husband* (1746). The anthology is lightly annotated and retains original spelling and editing practices.

Women Critics, 1660–1820: An Anthology. Bloomington: Indiana UP, 1995. Folger Collective on Early Women Critics.

This anthology contains critical writings of women from Margaret Cavendish to Jane Austen, and although it primarily represents texts by Englishwomen, it also includes some works by writers from France, Germany, and the United States. The women featured in this collection entered into debates about literature, art, and culture, and their writings cover a large range of genres, as one finds criticism embedded in plays, novels, and poems and presented in more conventional critical forms such as prefaces, essays, and treatises. Aphra Behn, Anne Finch, Eliza Haywood, Mary Alcock, Hannah More, Frances Burney d'Arblay, Mary Wollstonecraft, Ann Radcliffe, and Maria Edgeworth are just a few of the women critics brought together in this volume. The texts are divided chronologically by the authors' dates of birth, each with a brief biographical introduction and lightly annotated; the editors have retained original spelling and punctuation practices.

Women Writers in English, 1350–1850. Susanne Woods, series ed. New York: Oxford UP, 1993– .

This series of books is a publication project that stems from the Brown University Women Writers Project (see Electronic Resources, below). The books in this series are all lightly annotated and generally retain original spellings. They include substantive introductions. The series currently includes individually bound editions of prose works by Anne Askew, Jane Barker, Mary Chudleigh, Eleanor Davies, Eliza Haywood, Judith Sargent Murray, Jane

Sharp, Mary Shelley, Charlotte Smith, and Rachel Speght, as well as anonymously authored texts.

Women's Writing in Stuart England: The Mother's Legacies of Dorothy Leigh, Elizabeth Joscelin, and Elizabeth Richardson. Ed. Sylvia Brown. New ed. Stroud: Sutton Pub Ltd, 1999.

As the title suggests, this volume contains the writings of three women who are part of a genre known as the "mother's legacy," which usually entails advice passed on from a mother to her children, often quite literally from the mother's deathbed, in forms such as letters, prayers, and blessings. The book includes a general introduction to this generic form, and individual introductions and textual notes for each writer. The texts retain original spelling.

Women Writers in Renaissance England. Ed. Randall Martin. London: Longman, 1997.

This anthology is divided into three general textual categories—prose, prose autobiography, and verse—and is prefaced by a chapter of collected epistles that preceded main texts. The volume includes a selection of women writers from various socioeconomic backgrounds; among the writers of prose are Rachel Speght, Katherine Parr, Anne Askew, Jane Anger, and Mary Ward. The sections contain substantial annotation; spelling and punctuation have been modernized.

Electronic Resources

The Aphra Behn Society: Celebrating Women and the Arts, 1660–1830. The Aphra Behn Society. 2 Feb. 2009. Web. 2 Feb. 2009.

"The Aphra Behn Society is dedicated to encouraging and advancing research that focuses on issues of gender and/or women's role in the arts of early modern culture, circa 1660–1800. Through its newsletter, website, and biannual meeting, the Aphra Behn Society seeks to promote an exchange of information and ideas among members of the various disciplines engaged in related research." This site contains many links and references to Behn as well as links to other literary societies and eighteenth-century resources.

Archive of Americana. Readex, A Division of News Bank. N.d. Web. 2 Feb. 2009.

Full-text access to selected historical American books, imprints, newspapers, and government publications. Database comprises the following collections: Early American Imprints, including coverage from 1639 to 1819 (books, pamphlets, broadsides, and other imprints); Early American Newspapers: Series 1, 1690–1876; American State Papers, 1789–1838 (legislative and executive documents); and the United States Congressional Serial Set, 1817–1980 (reports, documents, and journals of the United States Senate and House of Representatives). The collections include digital reproductions with searchable full text.

Digital Scriptorium. Columbia Univ. Libs. N.d. Web. 2 Feb. 2009.

"The Digital Scriptorium is an image database of medieval and renaissance manuscripts that unites scattered resources from many institutions into an international tool for teaching and scholarly research. It bridges the gap between a diverse user community and the limited resources of libraries by means of sample imaging and extensive rather than intensive cataloguing."

The Early Modern Center. Department of English, University of California, Santa Barbara. N.d. Web. 2 Feb. 2009.

"The Early Modern Center Gallery is a featured resource of the center, containing reproductions of many important period images in thumbnail, browser, and large high-quality sizes" (home page). Also available on this site: the EMC English Broadside Ballad Archive and links to other helpful Web sites.

Early Stuart Libels. Arts and Humanities Research Council. 23 July 2005. Web. 2 Feb. 2009.

" 'Early Stuart Libels' is a web-based edition of early seventeenth-century political poetry from manuscript sources. It brings into the public domain over 350 poems, many of which have never before been published." The site provides useful contextual material for early modern political prose.

EEBO: Early English Books Online. ProQuest. 2003–09. Web. 2 Feb. 2009.

"From the first book published in English, through the age of Spenser and Shakespeare, and the tumult of the English Civil War, Early English Books Online (EEBO) will contain over 125,000 titles listed in Pollard and Redgrave's Short-Title Catalogue (1475–1640), Wing's Short-Title Catalogue (1641–1700), the Thomason Tracts (1640–1661), and the Early English Tract Supplement."

Eighteenth Century Collections Online. Gale Digital Collections. N.d. Web 2 Feb. 2009.

This database provides digital editions of every significant English-language and foreign language title printed in Great Britain during the eighteenth century, along with thousands of important works from the Americas. It is the later companion to *EEBO: Early English Books Online*, and has the important added feature of full-text-search capabilities.

Emory Women Writers Resource Project. Dir. Sheila Cavanagh. Women Writers Resource Project at the Lewis H. Beck Center. Emory Univ. 14 Feb. 2000. Web. 2 Feb. 2009.

"The Emory Women Writers Resource Project is a collection of edited and unedited texts by women writing in English from the seventeenth century through the nineteenth century. The Project is a pedagogical tool, designed to offer graduate and undergraduate students in various disciplines the opportunity to edit their own texts." The site also contains bibliographies, pedagogical suggestions, and links to a number of related Web sites.

English Broadside Ballad Archive. Univ. of California, Santa Barbara. N.d. Web. 2 Feb. 2009.

Dedicated to mounting online extant early modern ballads printed in English (with priority given to black-letter broadside ballads of the late sixteenth- and seventeenth-centuries), the English department's Early Modern Center at the University of California, Santa Barbara, has launched the English Broadside Ballad Archive (EBBA). The project began with the research team archiving the over 1,800 ballads in the Samuel Pepys Collection.

English Short Title Catalogue. British Lib. N.d. Web. 2 Feb. 2009.
This database "lists over 460,000 items published between 1473 and 1800, published mainly in Britain and North America, mainly, but not exclusively, in English, from the collections of the British Library and over 2,000 other libraries."

The Folger Shakespeare Library. Web. 10 August 2009.
Among the Folger's many publicly available materials are extensive resources for K–12 teachers, including short selected passages from a range of Renaissance prose texts.

Humanities Research Institute Online. Univ. of Sheffield. Web. 2 Apr. 2009.
"HRI Online Publications is the publishing arm of the Humanities Institute at the University of Sheffield." All publications are peer reviewed. Among the resources available are *The Old Bailey Proceedings Online,* a searchable collection of approximately 200,000 criminal trials held between 1674 and 1913; John Strype's *Survey of London,* including text, street images, and illustrations; *John Foxe's Book of Martyrs Variorum Edition Online,* a digital edition with full textual apparatus; and The Hartlib Papers, second edition, with over 25,000 folios from the correspondence of Samuel Hartlib (c. 1600–62).

The International Margaret Cavendish Society. N.d. Web. 2 Feb. 2009.
"[T]he Margaret Cavendish Society was established to provide a means of communication between scholars worldwide and to increase awareness of Cavendish and her writings. . . . This site contains current and past newsletters, contacts, information on joining the Society, images, conference details and links to bibliographies, books, e-text and related sites." This site also contains links to research libraries, articles, audio recordings, and other resources relating to early modern women and sixteenth- and seventeenth-century studies.

Internet History Sourcebooks Project. Ed. Paul Halsall. Fordham Center for Medieval Studies. 10 Dec. 2006. Web. 2 Feb. 2009.
This Web page contains links to "public domain, copy-permitted historical texts presented cleanly (without advertising or extensive layout) for educational use." This site is an excellent gateway to nonfiction prose available on the Web. In addition to extensive sets of links for ancient, medieval, and modern materials, there are sets of links for the Reformation, the scientific revolution, the "early modern world," "everyday life," and colonial North and Latin America.

Internet Shakespeare Editions. Univ. of Victoria and the Social Sciences and Humanities Research Council of Canada. N.d. Web. 2 Feb. 2009.
"The aim of the Internet Shakespeare Editions is to inspire a love of Shakespeare's works in a world-wide audience. To do so, we create and publish works for the student, scholar, actor, and general reader in a form native to the medium of the Internet: scholarly, fully annotated texts of Shakespeare's plays, multimedia explorations of the context of Shakespeare's life and works, and records of his plays in performance."

LEME: Lexicons of Early Modern English. Ed. Ian Lancashire. Univ. of Toronto P. 2009. Web. 2 Feb. 2009.
"*Lexicons of Early Modern English* (*LEME*) is a historical database of monolingual, bilingual, and polyglot dictionaries, lexical encyclopedias, hard-word

glossaries, spelling lists, and lexically-valuable treatises surviving in print or manuscript from the Tudor, Stuart, Caroline, Commonwealth, and Restoration periods." Some public-search capabilities are available; the full database is available through licensing only.

Literary Resources-Renaissance. Maintained by Jack Lynch. Rutgers Univ. N.d. Web. 2 Feb 2009.

This list of resources includes sites in the following categories: Renaissance literature, drama, poetry and ballads, centers and institutes, journals, and authors. Each entry heading is a hyperlink to the listed resource, which allows for easy browsing and connection to many other early modern resources.

The Literature Network. Jalic Inc. 2000–09. Web. 2 Feb. 2009.

This is a searchable online literature database. One notable feature is the site's ability to cross-link literary works so that students can easily search for the use of a word across multiple works to see where similar diction occurs. For access to Shakespeare's works through *The Literature Network*, click on the Shakespeare link.

Luminarium: Anthology of English Literature. Ed. Anniina Jokinen 1996–2007. Web. 2 Feb. 2009.

This site is a searchable, online anthology of primary works, quotations, and secondary materials, including historical notes on the authors, study resources, scholarly articles, discussion forums, and more. *Luminarium* covers medieval through eighteenth-century materials.

The Map of Early Modern London. Ed. Janelle Jenstad. 20 Feb 2008. Web. 2 Feb. 2009.

"This site maps the streets, sites, and significant boundaries of late sixteenth-century and early seventeenth-century London. . . . The *Library* contains editions of royal entries and mayoral pageants. The *Topics* section contains articles on institutions and various aspects of London life. The *Sources* page provides a regularly updated bibliography of all works cited in the project."

Open Source Shakespeare. Bernini Communications. 2003–09. Web. 2 Feb. 2009.

Open Source Shakespeare includes a concordance, plays, sonnets, search by character, and links to other resources.

Oxford English Dictionary.

This is a subscription-only Web site. "*The Oxford English Dictionary* . . . traces the usage of words through 2.5 million quotations from a wide range of international English language sources, from classic literature and specialist periodicals to film scripts and cookery books."

The Perdita Project: Early Modern Women's Manuscript Catalogue. AHRB, Trent Univ., Warwick Univ. N.d. Web. 2 Feb. 2009.

"The Perdita Project, established in January 1997 by Nottingham Trent University, purchased a microfilm collection of about 400 manuscripts compiled by women in the British Isles. These manuscripts, now lodged at Warwick University, were compiled during the sixteenth and seventeenth centuries, and consist of poetry, religious writing, autobiographical material, cookery and medical recipes, and accounts. . . . The catalogue offers bibliographical information and detailed descriptions of contents for the information of historians and literary scholars. The catalogue will also include the team's research on the manuscripts and their compilers."

Perseus Project. Ed. Gregory R. Crane. Tufts Univ. N.d. Web. 2 Feb. 2009.

Perseus aims "to make the full record of humanity—linguistic sources, physical artifacts, historical spaces—as intellectually accessible as possible." Its current focus is on classical Greek and Latin and on connections between classics and other humanities fields. This site includes the Lewis and Short Latin dictionary, the Liddell and Scott Greek dictionary, Latin and Greek grammar tools, and a growing selection of Renaissance materials, including, e.g. the Faust book, Hakluyt's *Principal Navigations*, and Wilson's *Arte of Rhetorique*. In addition, many Renaissance translations of classical texts are publicly available.

Renaissance: The Elizabethan World. 27 Nov. 2008. Web. 2 Feb. 2009.

This site compiles over a hundred links and short descriptions for online Renaissance resources. Links are organized by topics, which include research, people, costume, literature, food, gardens, music, games, swordplay, exploration, wordplay, guilds, fairs, fonts, and scripts.

Renascence Editions. 23 Oct. 2008. Web. 10 August 2009.

This publicly available site is "an online repository of works printed in English between the years 1477 and 1799." Texts are taken from editions in the public domain; numerous important prose texts are included in the archive.

Schoenberg Center for Electronic Text and Image. Web. 10 August 2009.

Hosted by the University of Pennsylvania, SCETI seeks to "create archive-quality digital facsimiles and make them available online." Featured in SCETI are the Horace Howard Furness Shakespeare Collection, which includes numerous early modern prose texts, and English Renaissance in Context, a series of student-friendly tutorials on major textual issues.

Tyburn Tree: Public Execution in Early Modern England. Created by Zachary Lesser. Maintained by Charlie Mitchell. 1995. Web. 2 Feb. 2009.

"Tyburn Tree is designed to provide information on the Web about public execution in Early Modern England, specifically London."

Women Writers Online. The Brown University Women Writers Project. Brown Univ. N.d. Web. 2 Feb. 2009.

"The Brown University Women Writers Project is a long-term research project devoted to early modern women's writing and electronic text encoding. Our goal is to bring texts by pre-Victorian women writers out of the archive and make them accessible to a wide audience of teachers, students, scholars, and the general reader. We support research on women's writing, text encoding, and the role of electronic texts in teaching and scholarship."

The authors would like to thank Frances E. Dolan for her input and suggestions.

Notes on Contributors

Sheila T. Cavanagh is Masse-Martin / NEH Distinguished Teaching Professor at Emory University and editor of the *Spenser Review*. She is the author of *Cherished Torment: The Emotional Geography of Lady Mary Wroth's* Urania; *Wanton Eyes and Chaste Desires: Female Sexuality in* The Faerie Queene; and articles on Renaissance literature and on pedagogy. She is director of the Emory Women Writers Resource Project.

Thomas Corns is professor of English literature at the University of Wales, Bangor. His publications include *Milton's Language*; *Uncloistered Virtue: English Political Literature, 1640–1660*; and *Regaining* Paradise Lost. He edited *A Companion to Milton* and serves as general editor, with Gordon Campbell, of the *Complete Works of John Milton*, the first volume of which was published in 2008. With Campbell he is the author of *John Milton: Life, Work, and Thought*.

Ronald Corthell is professor and chair of the Department of English at Kent State University. He is the author of *Ideology and Desire in Renaissance Poetry: The Subject of Donne* and essays on seventeenth-century poetry and prose. He coedited the anthology *Catholic Culture in Early Modern England*, and he is the editor of *Prose Studies: History, Theory, Criticism*.

Catherine R. Eskin teaches sixteenth- and seventeenth-century English literature at Florida Southern College. She has published essays on the rhetorical strategies employed in early modern prose and on femininity in conduct literature. Her current research examines the ways women's voices are figured in late-sixteenth-century prose romances and rhetorics. She is writing an article on Robert Greene's *Ciceronis Amor* (1589).

Stephen M. Fallon is Cavanaugh Professor of the Humanities at the University of Notre Dame. He is the author of *Milton's Peculiar Grace: Self-Representation and Authority* and *Milton among the Philosophers*; he is coeditor of the Modern Library *Complete Poetry and Essential Prose of John Milton*. He teaches seminars on literary and philosophical classics at the South Bend Center for the Homeless.

Margaret W. Ferguson is Distinguished Professor of English at the University of California, Davis. She was chair of English from 2006 to 2009. The author of *Trials of Desire: Renaissance Defenses of Poetry* and *Dido's Daughters: Literacy, Gender, and Empire in Early Modern England and France*, she has coedited eleven volumes, among them *Re-membering Milton: The Texts and the Traditions* and *Rewriting the Renaissance: The Discourses* *of Sexual Difference in Early Modern Europe.* Her current project is a study of Aphra Behn's theory and practice of translation.

Lori Anne Ferrell holds a joint appointment in the departments of history and English at the Center for the Humanities, Claremont Graduate University. She is the author of *Government by Polemic: James I and the King's Preachers* and coeditor of *Religion and Society in Early Modern England* and *The English Sermon Revised.* Her most recent book, *The Bible and the People,* was published by Yale University Press in 2008.

Deborah E. Harkness is professor of history at the University of Southern California. She specializes in the history of science and medicine from antiquity to the present. Her books include *John Dee's Conversations with Angels* and *The Jewel House: Elizabethan London and the Scientific Revolution.* Her current project is "Living the Experimental Life in Early Modern Britain," on the intersection of scientific and domestic cultures in the seventeenth century.

Peter C. Herman is professor of literature at San Diego State University. He is the author of *Destabilizing Milton:* Paradise Lost *and the Poetics of Incertitude* and the editor of *Approaches to Teaching Milton's Shorter Poetry and Prose.* His essays have appeared in *Renaissance Quarterly, Studies in English Literature,* and *Journal of Medieval and Early Modern Studies.* His *"Royal Poetrie": Monarchic Verse and the Political Imaginary of Early Modern England* is forthcoming.

Elizabeth Hodgson is associate professor of English at the University of British Columbia. She is the author of *Gender and the Sacred Self in John Donne* and articles on Milton, Philips, Lanyer, Donne, Shakespeare, and Renaissance homiletic literature in *Studies in English Literature, Milton Studies, Prose Studies, Early Modern Literary Studies, Medieval and Early Modern Drama,* and *Women's Writing.* Her current book project is entitled "The Weapon of Grief for Women Writers of Renaissance England."

Christopher Ivic is senior lecturer at Bath Spa University. He is coeditor of *Forgetting in Early Modern English Literature and Culture: Lethe's Legacies.* His articles have appeared in *Archipelagic Identities* and *British Identities and English Renaissance Literature,* as well as in the journals *Ariel, Genre,* and the *Journal of Medieval and Early Modern Studies.* He is at work on a book-length project entitled "The Subject of Britain."

Gregory Kneidel teaches English at the University of Connecticut, Hartford. His research interests center on the reception of classical rhetoric in Protestant theology and English poetry. He is the author of *Rethinking the Turn to Religion in Early Modern English Literature.* His current research project focuses on legal fictions in Donne and Spenser.

Mary Ellen Lamb is professor of English at Southern Illinois University. She is the author of *Popular Culture of Shakespeare, Spenser, Jonson*; *Gender and Authorship in the Sidney Circle*; and articles on early modern women's writing and the politics of reading. She is at work on a book-length manuscript entitled "Early Modern Women Readers and Discourses of Consumption."

Kate Lilley teaches feminist literary history and theory at the University of Sydney. A published poet, she is the author of *Versary*. She is the editor of Margaret Cavendish's The Blazing World *and Other Writings*. She has published essays on Cavendish, Philips, and Wroth. Her work has focused on utopian visions and elegy in seventeenth-century English women's writing, as well as on a homosocial community of eighteenth-century women poets.

Leah S. Marcus is Edwin Minns Professor of English and director of the program in Jewish studies at Vanderbilt University. She is the author of *Childhood and Cultural Despair*; *The Politics of Mirth*; *Puzzling Shakespeare: Local Reading and Its Discontents*; and *Unediting the Renaissance: Shakespeare, Marlowe, Milton* and coeditor of *The Collected Works of Queen Elizabeth I*. She has also published an Arden edition of Webster's *The Duchess of Malfi*.

Lauryn S. Mayer is associate professor of medieval literature at Washington and Jefferson College. She is the author of *Words Made Flesh: Reading Medieval Manuscript Culture*. She is at work on a second book on the manuscripts of John Trevisa's translation of Ranulf Higden's *Polychronicon*.

Susannah Brietz Monta is John Cardinal O'Hara, C.S.C., and Glynn Family Honors Associate Professor of English at the University of Notre Dame. Her book *Martyrdom and Literature in Early Modern England* won the Book of the Year award from the Conference on Christianity and Literature. She has published articles on history plays, saints and martyrs, early modern women, and pedagogy and is the editor of *Religion and Literature*. Her current projects include work on Catholicism and time and research on miracles in early modern writing.

Mary Moore is professor of English at Marshall University, where she teaches Renaissance literature, modernist poetry, poetry, and writing. She has published articles on Lady Mary Wroth's sonnets, Shakespeare's *The Tempest*, and Mary Herbert Sidney's elegy to her brother as well as two books: *Desiring Voices, Women Sonneteers and Petrarchism* and *The Book of Snow*, a collection of poetry. She currently has work in hand on monstrosity and women in Renaissance philosophical, medical, and literary texts.

Roger E. Moore is senior lecturer in English and director of undergraduate writing at Vanderbilt University. He has published articles on Philip Sidney, Jane Austen, and Christopher Marlowe. Current projects include research on the cloister in the English literary imagination and on prophecy and inspiration in early modern writing.

Erin Murphy is assistant professor of English at Boston University. She has published on the work of John Milton, and her book, *Familial Forms: Politics and Genealogy in Seventeenth-Century English Literature*, is forthcoming from the University of Delaware Press. She has begun a new book project entitled "Wartimes: Seventeenth-Century Women's Writing and Its Afterlives."

Magdalena Nerio is a graduate student in the English department at the University of Notre Dame. Her research interests include Shakespeare, Spenser, and early modern women's writing. She is writing about representations of Mary, Queen of Scots, and Elizabeth I in sixteenth-century polemic.

Genevieve Pearson is a PhD candidate in English at the University of California, Davis. Her research and teaching interests focus on early modern drama, prose, and popular works in various media. Her dissertation explores textual representations of the burgeoning protocapitalistic market in early modern English literature.

Claire Preston is a lecturer in English literature at Sidney Sussex College, Cambridge University. She specializes in early modern English literature and American literature of the Gilded Age to 1940. Her publications include *Thomas Browne and the Writing of Early Modern Science,* the cultural history *Bee,* and *Edith Wharton's Social Register.* She is working on a book about scientific pastoral in the long seventeenth century.

Vanessa Rapatz is a PhD candidate at the University of California, Davis, where she teaches expository writing as well as introductory literature courses. Her research is focused on early modern drama, specifically novices and convents in early modern problem plays.

Terry Reilly is professor of English at the University of Alaska, Fairbanks. He has published on William Shakespeare, James Joyce, Thomas Pynchon, Doris Lessing, and Geoffrey Chaucer. He teaches courses in British literature, academic writing, and early modern literature and has won awards for his work as a teacher and mentor.

Mary Beth Rose is director of the Institute for the Humanities and professor of English at the University of Illinois, Chicago. She is the author of *The Expense of Spirit: Love and Sexuality in English Renaissance Drama* and *Gender and Heroism in Early Modern English Literature.* She was the editor of *Renaissance Drama* and the director of the Newberry Library Center for Renaissance Studies and is the coeditor of *Elizabeth I: Collected Works.* She is working on a study tentatively entitled "The Dead Mother Plot: Family and Authority in Early Modern Literature."

Gary Schneider is associate professor of English at the University of Texas, Pan American. He is the author of *The Culture of Epistolarity: Vernacular Letters and Letter Writing in Early Modern England* and of articles on Shakespeare and early modern manuscript culture. His current scholarship concerns printed letters in seventeenth-century England.

P. G. Stanwood, professor emeritus of English at the University of British Columbia, is a scholar of Renaissance and seventeenth-century nondramatic literature. He has edited numerous early modern texts, including Richard Hooker's *Lawes of Ecclesiastical Polity*, books 6, 7, and 8, and Jeremy Taylor's *Holy Living* and *Holy Dying*. He is researching operatic versions of Milton's *Paradise Lost* from Dryden to Penderecki.

Eric Sterling is Distinguished Teaching Professor of English at Auburn University Montgomery, in Montgomery, Alabama. His publications include *The Movement towards Subversion: The English History Play from Skelton to Shakespeare* and articles on Shakespeare, Spenser, Jonson, and the Renaissance country-house poem. His book (with Robert C. Evans), *Seventeenth-Century Literature Handbook*, will be published in 2009.

Robert E. Stillman is Lindsay Young Professor in the English department at the University of Tennessee, Knoxville. He is the editor of *Spectacle and Public Performance in the Late Middle Ages and the Renaissance* and the author of *Sidney's Poetic Justice: The Old Arcadia, Its Eclogues and Renaissance Pastoral Traditions*; *The New Philosophy and Universal Languages in Seventeenth-Century England*; and *Philip Sidney and the Poetics of Renaissance Cosmopolitanism*. He is writing a book about Shakespeare and missed connections.

Donald Stump is professor of English at Saint Louis University and author of articles on Sidney, Spenser, and Renaissance drama. His research has concentrated on the court literature of Elizabeth I and on the reception of biblical and classical texts in her reign. He was lead editor for *Elizabeth I and Her Age: A Norton Critical Edition*; *'Hamartia': The Concept of Error in the Western Tradition*; and *Sir Philip Sidney: An Annotated Bibliography of Texts and Criticism (1554–1984)*. He also edits two Web sites—the *Sidney World Biography* and the *Spenser World Biography*—and is cofounder of the Queen Elizabeth I Society.

Deborah Uman is associate professor of English and director of the women and gender studies program at Saint John Fisher College. She is completing a book project on women translators in early modern England. She has published essays on Shakespeare, translations by Margaret Tyler and Jane Lumley, and teaching close reading.

Index of Names

Achinstein, Sharon, 290n2
Addison, Joseph, 2
An Admonition to Parliament, 217
Alcock, Mary, 362
Alençon, François, duc d', 196
Alexander (the Great), 129, 130, 303
Alfield, Thomas, 88–90
Allen, Hannah, 358
Anderson, Benedict, 202, 333–34
Andrewes, Lancelot, 32, 65
Anger, Jane, 363
Aquinas, Thomas, 214
Aretino, Pietro, 201, 211n9
Ariosto, Ludovico, 331
Aristippus, 303
Aristotle, 35, 37, 53n2, 54n16, 145, 181, 183
Arnobius, 221n2
Asad, Talal, 341n3
Ascham, Roger, 206, 315, 330, 355, 357, 358
Ashley, Robert, 356
Askew, Anne, 5, 27, 84–86, 88, 354, 360, 363
Astell, Mary, 12, 108, 320–27, 359, 360
Atherton, John (bishop of Waterford and Lismore), 40
Aubin, Penelope, 359
Auerbach, Erich, 349n2
Augustine (of Hippo), 45, 54n16, 115, 214, 268
Austen, Jane, 174, 359, 362

Backscheider, Paula R., 359
Bacon, Francis, 2, 3, 4, 13, 14n3, 22, 23, 58, 74–76, 77, 78, 95, 96, 99–101, 102–07, 109, 110nn3–4, 110n6, 143, 145, 164, 221, 246–58, 272, 274, 277, 290, 292, 359, 361, 362
Bacon, Nicholas, 248
Bagster, Samuel, 347
Bahktin, Mikhail, 180, 210n1
Baker, Herschel, 360
Baldwin, Edward Chauncey, 313–14
Bale, John, 27, 36, 84, 85, 88, 360
Barbauld, Anna Laetitia, 359

Barish, Jonas, 304
Barker, Jane, 359, 363
Barrin, Jean, 362
Barrington, Joan, 160
Barros, Carolyn A., 358
Barrow, Henry, 92
Barthes, Roland, 44, 53n4
Bauthumley, Jacob, 294
Bayly, William, 133, 134, 135
Beaufort, Margaret (Countess of Richmond and Derby), 361
Beaumont, Francis, 177
Bedford, Countess of (Lucy Harington Russell), 107
Beecher, Donald, 313–14, 315, 317, 318n1
Behn, Aphra, 12, 79, 329, 333–40, 341(nn4, 6–7), 354, 355, 358, 359, 360, 361, 362, 363
Beilin, Elaine, 84
Belsey, Catherine, 117
Bensmaïa, Réda, 97
Beowulf, 164, 165, 168
Berry, Lloyd E., 349n3
Berryman, John, 202
Betteridge, Thomas, 86
Bevington, David, 304
Bible, 5, 14n4, 23, 54n17, 62, 135, 136, 185, 206, 270, 278, 279, 294, 329, 340n1, 341n8, 344–49
Bible, Douay-Rheims (Roman Catholic), 347–48
Bible, Geneva (Calvinist), 347–48, 349n3
Bible, Great (1539 edition), 345
Bible, King James, 23, 133, 138, 144, 344, 346–48, 349
Bible, Tyndale-Coverdale (Lutheran), 347–48
Biddle, Hester, 355
Bizzell, Patricia, 32, 54n16
Black, Joseph Laurence, 354
Black, Scott, 111
Blackwood, Adam, 90
Blank, Paula, 9, 10
Boccaccio, Giovanni, 168
Bodley, Thomas, 254–55
Bond, R. Warwick, 304

Index of Selected Resources

Modern Language Association of America
Options for Teaching

Teaching Early Modern English Prose. Ed. Susannah Brietz Monta and Margaret W. Ferguson. 2010.

Teaching Italian American Literature, Film, and Popular Culture. Ed. Edvige Giunta and Kathleen Zamboni McCormick. 2010.

Teaching the Graphic Novel. Ed. Stephen E. Tabachnick. 2009.

Teaching Literature and Language Online. Ed. Ian Lancashire. 2009.

Teaching the African Novel. Ed. Gaurav Desai. 2009.

Teaching World Literature. Ed. David Damrosch. 2009.

Teaching North American Environmental Literature. Ed. Laird Christensen, Mark C. Long, and Fred Waage. 2008.

Teaching Life Writing Texts. Ed. Miriam Fuchs and Craig Howes. 2007.

Teaching Nineteenth-Century American Poetry. Ed. Paula Bernat Bennett, Karen L. Kilcup, and Philipp Schweighauser. 2007.

Teaching Representations of the Spanish Civil War. Ed. Noël Valis. 2006.

Teaching the Representation of the Holocaust. Ed. Marianne Hirsch and Irene Kacandes. 2004.

Teaching Tudor and Stuart Women Writers. Ed. Susanne Woods and Margaret P. Hannay. 2000.

Teaching Literature and Medicine. Ed. Anne Hunsaker Hawkins and Marilyn Chandler McEntyre. 1999.

Teaching the Literatures of Early America. Ed. Carla Mulford. 1999.

Teaching Shakespeare through Performance. Ed. Milla C. Riggio. 1999.

Teaching Oral Traditions. Ed. John Miles Foley. 1998.

Teaching Contemporary Theory to Undergraduates. Ed. Dianne F. Sadoff and William E. Cain. 1994.

Teaching Children's Literature: Issues, Pedagogy, Resources. Ed. Glenn Edward Sadler. 1992.

Teaching Literature and Other Arts. Ed. Jean-Pierre Barricelli, Joseph Gibaldi, and Estella Lauter. 1990.

New Methods in College Writing Programs: Theories in Practice. Ed. Paul Connolly and Teresa Vilardi. 1986.

School-College Collaborative Programs in English. Ed. Ron Fortune. 1986.

Teaching Environmental Literature: Materials, Methods, Resources. Ed. Frederick O. Waage. 1985.

Part-Time Academic Employment in the Humanities: A Sourcebook for Just Policy. Ed. Elizabeth M. Wallace. 1984.

Film Study in the Undergraduate Curriculum. Ed. Barry K. Grant. 1983.

The Teaching Apprentice Program in Language and Literature. Ed. Joseph Gibaldi and James V. Mirollo. 1981.

Options for Undergraduate Foreign Language Programs: Four-Year and Two-Year Colleges. Ed. Renate A. Schulz. 1979.

Options for the Teaching of English: Freshman Composition. Ed. Jasper P. Neel. 1978.

Options for the Teaching of English: The Undergraduate Curriculum. Ed. Elizabeth Wooten Cowan. 1975.